AF772504

Security, Conflict and Cooperation in the Contemporary World

Series Editors
Effie G. H. Pedaliu
LSE Ideas
London, United Kingdom

John W. Young
University of Nottingham
Nottingham, United Kingdom

The Palgrave Macmillan series, Security, Conflict and Cooperation in the Contemporary World aims to make a significant contribution to academic and policy debates on cooperation, conflict and security since 1900. It evolved from the series Global Conflict and Security edited by Professor Saki Ruth Dockrill. The current series welcomes proposals that offer innovative historical perspectives, based on archival evidence and promoting an empirical understanding of economic and political cooperation, conflict and security, peace-making, diplomacy, humanitarian intervention, nation-building, intelligence, terrorism, the influence of ideology and religion on international relations, as well as the work of international organisations and non-governmental organisations.

More information about this series at
http://www.springer.com/series/14489

Luc-André Brunet

Forging Europe: Industrial Organisation in France, 1940–1952

palgrave
macmillan

Luc-André Brunet
The Open University
Milton Keynes, United Kingdom

Security, Conflict and Cooperation in the Contemporary World
ISBN 978-1-349-95197-0 ISBN 978-1-349-95198-7 (eBook)
DOI 10.1057/978-1-349-95198-7

Library of Congress Control Number: 2017940278

© The Editor(s) (if applicable) and The Author(s) 2017
The author(s) has/have asserted their right(s) to be identified as the author(s) of this work in accordance with the Copyright, Designs and Patents Act 1988.
This work is subject to copyright. All rights are solely and exclusively licensed by the Publisher, whether the whole or part of the material is concerned, specifically the rights of translation, reprinting, reuse of illustrations, recitation, broadcasting, reproduction on microfilms or in any other physical way, and transmission or information storage and retrieval, electronic adaptation, computer software, or by similar or dissimilar methodology now known or hereafter developed.
The use of general descriptive names, registered names, trademarks, service marks, etc. in this publication does not imply, even in the absence of a specific statement, that such names are exempt from the relevant protective laws and regulations and therefore free for general use.
The publisher, the authors and the editors are safe to assume that the advice and information in this book are believed to be true and accurate at the date of publication. Neither the publisher nor the authors or the editors give a warranty, express or implied, with respect to the material contained herein or for any errors or omissions that may have been made. The publisher remains neutral with regard to jurisdictional claims in published maps and institutional affiliations.

Cover Image: 1st pic Flag: © RubberBall / Alamy Stock Photo 2nd pic / the man (Maréchal Henri Philippe Pétain portrait. Ruler of Vichy France. 24 April 1856-23 July 1951. Uniform. Caption reads) © Lebrecht Music and Arts Photo Library / Alamy Stock Photo

Printed on acid-free paper

This Palgrave Macmillan imprint is published by Springer Nature
The registered company is Macmillan Publishers Ltd.
The registered company address is: The Campus, 4 Crinan Street, London, N1 9XW, United Kingdom

To My parents

Acknowledgements

This book originated as a doctoral dissertation, submitted to the London School of Economics in 2014. Research for this project has been facilitated by the support of a number of funding bodies. The Social Sciences and Humanities Research Council of Canada generously awarded me a Doctoral Fellowship which provided the resources for me to complete this project. Academic Partnerships at LSE also provided me with a scholarship to spend several months at Sciences Po, which enabled me to complete a significant amount of archival research in Paris. Additional grants from the Economic History Society, the Association Jean Monnet, the International History Department at LSE, and the Max Weber Programme at EUI supported further archival trips which greatly enriched this study.

First and foremost, I would like to thank my doctoral supervisor, Piers Ludlow. His insightful feedback and steadfast encouragement during my PhD and ever since have made this a stronger work than it otherwise could have been. I am also grateful to Alan Sked, who very kindly took me on as a PhD student and acted as supervisor for the first stages of my doctorate. I would also like to thank Julian Jackson and Richard Vinen, my PhD examiners, for providing invaluable advice on revising the thesis for publication and for their continued support.

I have also benefitted from friends and colleagues who have read and commented on drafts of my chapters. Thanks go to Claire Andrieu, Antony Best, Laura Lee Downs, Annika Mombauer, and Antonio Varsori. Federico Romero also provided precious advice at several important junctures. A special thank you goes to Eirini Karamouzi for her unflagging support and invaluable feedback.

Over the course of this project, I have been lucky to have had rich discussions with Robert Boyce, James Casteel, Mario Del Pero, James Ellison, Kiran Klaus Patel, Arne Westad, and Vladislav Zubok. Conversations with Eric Bussière, Matthew Connelly, Fernando Guirao, Talbot Imlay, Frances Lynch, Georges-Henri Soutou, Maurice Vaïsse and Laurent Warlouzet have also been influential.

At LSE IDEAS, where I held the Pinto Post-doctoral Fellowship, I am grateful to Arne Westad, Mick Cox, Svetozar Rajak, and Nigel Ashton. This fellowship afforded me a valuable opportunity immediately following the completion of my PhD to revise my dissertation for publication while taking part in the vibrant activities of the centre. I am also thankful to Emilia Knight and the whole team at LSE IDEAS.

As a Max Weber Post-doctoral Fellow, the European University Institute provided the ideal setting to prepare this manuscript for publication. At EUI, thanks go to Emily Baughan, Emmanuel Comte, Guillemette Crouzet, Muriam Haleh Davis, Simon Macdonald, Molly Pucci, and Simon Stevens.

It has been a privilege to complete this study while teaching at the Open University. I am particularly grateful to Karl Hack and Paul Lawrence for accommodating me in the final months before submitting my manuscript. At Palgrave Macmillan, I would like to thank Effie Pedaliu and John Young, the editors of this series, and Oliver Dyer.

Research for this project has taken me to archives in seven countries, and I have benefitted greatly from the help of archivists. I would particularly like to thank Régis Clavé and Philippe Klein at the Fondation Jean Monnet pour l'Europe in Lausanne, Dieter Schlenker at the Historical Archives of the European Union in Florence, Gersande Piernas at the Centre d'Archives du Monde du Travail in Roubaix, Andrea Maier at the Bundesarchiv-Militärarchiv in Freiburg, and Virginie Hébrard at the Institut d'Histoire Sociale in Nanterre.

Finally, I must thank four people. First, my wife Rebecca, to whom I'm grateful for so many reasons, not least her boundless encouragement throughout the writing of this book. Second, our daughter Charlotte, who arrived in the final months before I submitted this manuscript. Her decision to begin sleeping through the night from a very young age has undoubtedly meant that this study is more coherent than it might otherwise have been. Finally, I would like to thank my parents for their unwavering support and for tirelessly reading drafts of my work. To them this book is dedicated.

Contents

1 Introduction 1

2 France's New Industrial Order: Reorganising Industrial Production After the Fall of France 19

3 Twixt the Cup and the Lip: Building the New Industrial Order, 1940–1941 53

4 The Organisation Committees Between Collaboration and Resistance, 1941–1944 79

5 *Nous serons les successeurs, sinon les héritiers de Vichy*: Maintaining the New Industrial Order in Post-Vichy France 115

6 *Conserver la forme en réformant l'esprit*: Reforming Vichy's Industrial Order, 1944–1946 147

7 From Organisation Committees to Monnet's Modernisation Commissions 177

8 *L'Unité de l'Europe est à ce prix:* The Struggle Between CORSID's Successors and the Creation of the ECSC 213

9 Conclusions 253

Bibliography 267

Index 287

List of Abbreviations

AN	Archives nationales, Paris/Pierrefitte-sur-Seine (France)
ANMT	Archives nationales du monde du travail, Roubaix (France)
BA-MA	Bundesarchiv-Militärarchiv, Freiburg im Breisgau (Germany)
BNS	Bureau de normalisation de la sidérurgie
CAEF	Centre des archives économiques et financières, Savigny-le-Temple (France)
CFLN	Comité français de Libération nationale
CFTC	Confédération française des travailleurs chrétiens
CGP	Commissariat général du Plan
CGPF	Confédération générale du patronat français
CGT	Confédération générale du travail
CGTU	Confédération générale du travail unitaire
CMSID	Commission de modernisation de la sidérurgie
CNPF	Conseil national du patronat français
CO	Comité d'organisation
COA	Comité d'organisation de l'automobile et du cycle
COH	Comité d'organisation de l'industrie des combustibles minéraux solides (houillères)
CORSID	Comité d'organisation de la sidérurgie
CPS	Comptoir des produits sidérurgiques
CSSF	Chambre syndicale de la sidérurgie française
DGEN	Délégation générale de l'équipement national
EDC	European Defence Community
EDF	Electricité de France
ECSC	European Coal and Steel Community
EMU	Economic and Monetary Union
EURATOM	European Atomic Energy Community (also EAEC)

FJME	Fondation Jean Monnet pour l'Europe, Lausanne (Switzerland)
GDF	Gaz de France
GPRF	Gouvernement provisionnel de la République française
HAEU	Historical Archives of the European Union, Florence (Italy)
IHS	Institut d'histoire sociale, Nanterre (France)
IHTP	Institut d'histoire du temps présent, Paris (France)
LAC	Library and Archives Canada, Ottawa (Canada)
MAE	Ministère d'affaires étrangères, La Courneuve (France)
MAEB	Ministère d'affaires étrangères, Bruxelles (Belgium)
MBF	Militärbefehlshaber in Frankreich
MRP	Mouvement républicain populaire
TNA	The National Archives, Kew Gardens, London (United Kingdom)
OCM	Organisation civile et militaire
OCRPI	Office central de répartition des produits industriels
OP	Office professionnel
OPSID	Office professionnel de la sidérurgie
PCF	Parti communiste français
PRL	Parti républicain de la liberté
RPF	Rassemblement du peuple français
SFIO	Section française de l'internationale ouvrière
SIDENOR	Groupement des industries sidérurgiques du Nord et du Pas-de-Calais
SME	Small- and medium-sized enterprises
SOLLAC	Société lorraine de laminage continu
STO	Service du travail obligatoire
USINOR	Union sidérurgique du Nord de la France

CHAPTER 1

Introduction

During the campaign preceding the British referendum on EU membership in June 2016, one of the more sensational claims made by former London Mayor and prominent Brexit campaigner Boris Johnson was that the European Union was essentially the realisation of Adolf Hitler's ambitions. 'Hitler tried' to unify Europe, Johnson asserted, 'and it end[ed] tragically. The EU is an attempt to do this by different methods.'[1] While Johnson's assertions were widely dismissed as inappropriate and ill-founded,[2] they nevertheless reflected a long-standing tendency amongst Eurosceptics in Britain to associate the European Union and its attempts at peaceful European unity with the Nazis' military domination of continental Europe.[3] Despite the controversy generated by Johnson's

[1]'Boris Johnson: The EU wants a superstate, just as Hitler did', *Sunday Telegraph*, 15 May 2016. Johnson, a Conservative MP, was the de facto leader of the campaign for Britain to leave the EU, which won the referendum.

[2]'Tories Divided by Boris Johnson's EU–Hitler Comparison', *The Guardian*, 16 May 2016.

[3]In 1990, Nicholas Ridley was compelled to resign as Secretary for Trade and Industry in Margaret Thatcher's government after comparing Britain's joining the nascent European Union (EU) to surrendering to Hitler, claiming 'you might just as well give [British sovereignty] to Adolf Hitler, frankly'. See 'Saying the Unsayable about the Germans', *The Spectator*, 14 July 1990. A more erudite if at times muddled and politically motivated study of the supposed Nazi origins of the EU is provided by John Laughland in *The Tainted Source: The Undemocratic Origins of the European Idea* (London: Little, Brown and Company, 1997).

© The Author(s) 2017

L.-A. Brunet, *Forging Europe: Industrial Organisation in France, 1940–1952*, Security, Conflict and Cooperation in the Contemporary World, DOI 10.1057/978-1-349-95198-7_1

comments, they were by no means unprecedented and tapped into long-held associations between the European Union and Hitler's 'New European Order'. Indeed, the early initiatives aimed at uniting European democracies in the decade following the end of the Second World War were criticised at the time because of the apparent similarities with Nazi propaganda concerning 'Europe'. As the French Communist François Billoux put it in response to the Pleven Plan to create a European Army in 1950: 'Europe is an idea of Hitler's'.[4] Despite the chronic evocations of Hitler by opponents of the European Union and its forerunners, remarkably few scholarly studies exist that analyse the legacies of the New European Order on post-war European integration. This book helps close this gap by considering France's place within this New European Order and the country's efforts after the war to bring about some form of European cooperation. Vichy France provides a unique lens through which to view Hitler's Europe, given the country's economic and political importance – it was the only 'great power' to have capitulated to the Reich – and since the Vichy government had a degree of sovereignty uncharacteristic among the countries conquered by the Wehrmacht in 1939–1940.[5] As such, the Vichy regime was in a position to freely choose to embark upon the path of collaboration with the Reich and to take part in any 'European' initiatives. Given that economic and, in particular, industrial cooperation was at the heart of both Nazi schemes to harness the productive potential of the continent and post-war projects for European integration, this book focuses on the organisation of French industry from the Fall of France in 1940 to the creation in 1952 of the European Coal and Steel Community (ECSC), Europe's first supranational institution and the forerunner to today's EU.

This book examines the organisation of French industry during this period chiefly via a study of its institutions. As such, it focuses on the

[4]Qtd in Eric Roussel, *Jean Monnet* (Paris: Fayard, 1996), 588.

[5]Myriad factors nevertheless constrained Vichy's ability to act freely, particularly regarding defence and foreign policy. See Peter Jackson and Simon Kitson, 'The Paradoxes of Foreign Policy in Vichy France, 1940–1942' in Jonathan Adelman, ed., *Hitler and His Allies in World War II* (London: Routledge, 2007). Despite the title of the edited volume, Vichy France was never formally an ally of the Reich.

central pillars of Vichy's 'New Industrial Order'[6] erected in the aftermath of France's capitulation to Nazi Germany, namely the Organisation Committees (*comités d'organisation*). Created with the Vichy law of 16 August 1940, an Organisation Committee was established for each vital branch of industry and was given sweeping powers to coordinate production across the country. These institutions remained in place after the Liberation of France in 1944 and were eventually dissolved in 1946. There are a number of reasons for focusing on these Organisation Committees. As institutions created by the State and placed under the Ministry of Industrial Production, yet run by industrialists acting in the interests of their profession, the Committees are uniquely situated at the intersection of government and industry. Unlike employers' associations such as the pre-war *Comité des forges* or ministerial offices staffed with civil servants, the Organisation Committees may be seen as a hybrid of private and public interests. As such, the Committees provide an original lens through which to examine the actions and motivations of state and business actors, as well as the interactions between these two groups during a crucial period in French and European history. Furthermore, the Committees represented an unprecedented innovation in French industrial organisation and were created as a direct result of the Fall of France, remaining the foundation of French industrial organisation throughout the war. They were then maintained after the Liberation of France and went on to influence post-war structures, notably the Monnet Plan. Interestingly, the formal existence of the Committees, from the summer of 1940 until October 1946, corresponds almost exactly with the period between the end of the Third Republic on 10 July 1940 and the establishment of the Fourth Republic on 27 October 1946, a period that may be referred to as *l'entre-deux-républiques*. A rigorous study of the economic and political dimensions of the Organisation Committees thus provides an invaluable perspective into this tumultuous period. Similarly, looking at how these Committees and their successor institutions shaped such crucial post-war projects as the

[6]The term 'New Industrial Order' used in this study is derived from the similar phrases '*nouvel ordre européen*' and '*nouvel ordre économique*'; the French term would therefore be '*nouvel ordre industriel*'. A similar phrase was used by Richard Vinen as a chapter title, 'An Industrial New Order?' in *The Politics of French Business, 1936–1945* (Cambridge: Cambridge University Press, 1991), 151–162.

Monnet Plan and the ECSC offers a new perspective on the origins of these French and ultimately European innovations and allows us to investigate the legacy of Vichy on these post-war developments. This book thus offers the most in-depth study yet published of Vichy's Organisation Committees and re-evaluates their creation in 1940, their actions throughout the war, their reform in liberated France, and their abolition in 1946, followed by a discussion of the role of their successors in the creation of the ECSC.

In analysing the organisation of French industry between 1940 and 1952, this study focuses on the steel and, to a much lesser extent, coal industries. There are four chief reasons for concentrating on these industries in particular. First, the importance of steel and coal in the history of post-war Europe is most clearly exemplified by the creation of the ECSC. A critical analysis of how these two industries were organised in the decade preceding the Schuman Declaration of May 1950 thus deepens our understanding of the history of European integration. Second, Vichy's earliest industrial reforms focused exceptionally on these two industries, singling out their employers' organisations for dissolution in November 1940. From the very beginning, these two industries were at the centre of Vichy's reforms, and examining the organisation of these industries thereby furthers our understanding of the regime's broader policies. Third, steel assumed an exceptional importance in France's post-war plans for economic recovery. Jean Monnet identified steel as the central industry on which France's post-war fortunes depended, describing the industry's production programme as 'unconditional, which will be executed regardless of the overall state of the economy. It is ultimately steel that determines all other French production [and] it is therefore indispensable that the steel industry enjoy all the resources it needs with an absolute priority.'[7] Not only was steel central to France's economic renewal, but Monnet framed this recovery as a prerequisite for France to regain its rightful *grandeur* on the international stage, lest it be 'reduced to the rank of a second-rate power'.[8] Finally, following the imposition of

[7] 'Présentation des programmes de base', note written by Jean Monnet, 5 September 1946, AMF 5 9, FJME.

[8] 'Memorandum sur le Plan de Modernisation et d'Equipement', 13 December 1945, 80 AJ 1, AN.

the British blockade in 1940, the French steel industry became utterly dependent for coal on Germany, and on the Ruhr in particular.[9] This dependence encouraged French heavy industry under Vichy to produce extensively for the German war economy, as this was the only way to ensure relatively regular shipments of coking coal from Germany. After the Liberation, Monnet insisted that the revival of France's economy, and indeed its place in the world, depended on the French steel industry receiving sufficient quantities of coal from Germany. This consideration guided French foreign policy in the post-war period, and ultimately motivated the French proposal to pool French and German coal and steel industries through the Schuman Plan. By focusing on the French steel industry and its dependence on German coal between 1940 and 1952, this study adds significantly to historiographies ranging from business history under Vichy to the history of European integration.

Much of the existing literature on the history of European integration continues to treat this undertaking as an exclusively post-1945 one, with the end of the Second World War marking a 'Year Zero' for Europe.[10] In this respect the history of European integration lags behind related fields such as the history of the Cold War, which has more readily incorporated the period preceding 1945, despite generally being considered a post-war phenomenon.[11] Works of European integration history that do reach back

[9]Until the summer of 1940 France imported a full third of its coal from Great Britain.

[10]See, for example, Sylvain Kahn, *Histoire de la construction de l'Europe depuis 1945* (Paris: Presses universitaires de France, 2011); the first chapter, covering the years 1945–1950, is entitled 'Europe année zéro'. For a discussion of the ambiguity of 1945 as a *Stunde Null*, see Richard Overy, 'Interwar, War, Postwar: Was There a Zero Hour in 1945?' in Dan Stone, *The Oxford Handbook of Postwar European History* (Oxford: Oxford University Press, 2012). A number of recent, innovative studies tracing the origins of European integration have similarly maintained 1945 as their starting point; see, for example, Wolfram Kaiser, Brigitte Leucht and Michael Gehler (eds), *Transnational Networks in Regional Integration: Governing Europe 1945–1983* (Basingstoke: Palgrave Macmillan, 2010).

[11]Among the classic works that treat the Cold War as a phenomenon dating from the October Revolution are André Fontaine, *Histoire de la Guerre froide, vol. I, De la révolution d'octobre à la guerre de Corée* (Paris: Fayard, 1967) and D.F. Fleming, *The Cold War and Its Origins, 1917–1960* (London: Allen and Unwin, 1961). For more recent studies using this approach, see Melvyn P. Leffler, *The Specter of Communism: The United States and the Origins of the Cold War, 1917–1953* (New York: Hill and Wang, 1994) and Jonathan Haslam, *Russia's Cold War: From the October Revolution to the Fall of the Wall* (New Haven: Yale University Press, 2011).

beyond 1945 for the origins of post-war European integration tend to concentrate on projects discussed within Resistance movements during the war; the classic works of Walter Lipgens maintain that it was these shared ideas about Europe that developed in the transnational Resistance against Nazism which created the foundation for European integration after the war.[12] Similarly, studies that touch on European integration, and especially Franco-German cooperation, in the interwar period generally focus on the diplomatic efforts of Aristide Briand and Gustav Stresemann, but lament that no meaningful developments towards European unity were made between the rise of Hitler in 1933 and the end of the Second World War.[13] Accordingly, the influence of the 'New European Order' on post-war integration is seldom evoked, aside from occasionally regretting that the Reich's use of the term 'Europe' added an obstacle to post-war projects. In the case of France, this emphasis on the Resistance and the concomitant discounting of developments under the Vichy regime has meant that the *années noires* under Pétain continue to be treated as a parenthesis in the history of European integration. While the Vichy period was initially seen as 'four years to cross out from our history', and the orthodox literature on the Second World War in France tended to consider Vichy as a self-contained aberration in the nation's history,[14] since the 1970s it has been one of the most heavily mined seams among historians

[12]Walter Lipgens, *Documents on the History of European Integration* (Berlin: Walter de Gruyter, 1984); see also Gérard Bossuat (ed.), *D'Alger à Rome, 1943–1957* (Louvain: Ciaco, 1989) and Michel Dumoulin (ed.), *Plans de temps de guerre pour l'Europe d'après-guerre, 1940–1947* (Bruxelles: Bruylant, 1995). There is also a vast literature on the history of the idea of Europe, often going back to the Enlightenment, Charlemagne, and even the Roman Empire. Indicatively, Eric Bussière, Michel Dumoulin and Gilbert Trausch (eds), *Europa: L'idée et l'identité européenne, de l'antiquité au XXIe siècle* (Brussels: Mercator, 2001), Mario Telò, *Dallo Stato all'Europa. Idee politiche e istituzioni* (Rome: Carocci, 2004) and Patrick Pasture, *Imagining European Unity since 1000 AD* (Basingstoke: Palgrave Macmillan, 2015).

[13]With the aforementioned exception of the allegedly European ideals of the anti-Nazi Resistance. See, for example, Elisabeth Du Réau, *L'idée européenne au XXe siècle* (Bruxelles: Complexe, 1996) and Gérard Bossuat, *Histoire de l'Union européenne. Fondations, élargissements, avenir* (Paris: Belin, 2009).

[14]The quotation is from André Mornet, *Quatre ans à rayer de notre histoire* (Paris: SELF, 1949). Among the best early 'orthodox' works on Vichy are Raymond Aron, *Histoire de Vichy* (Paris: Fayard, 1954) and Henry Michel, *Vichy Année 40* (Paris: Robert Laffont, 1966).

of France. As such, there is now a significant literature on the legacies of Vichy's legislation in the post-war Fourth Republic (1946–1958).[15] On the other hand, the literature on post-war France and the history of European integration has tended to emphasise the decisive role played by France under the Fourth Republic on the establishment of Europe's first supranational insititutions.[16] Given the influence of Vichy on the Fourth Republic, and the critical role played by the Fourth Republic in bringing about the first European institutions, this book brings together these two important yet largely distinct bodies of literature by reassessing the influence of Vichy's institutions on the ECSC. Furthermore, this approach challenges the notion of 1945 as a 'Year Zero' in European history from an original angle.

In recent scholarship on European integration, there has additionally been a move to better historicise the emergence of the ECSC. A growing body of literature on transnational networks and their influence on European integration, for example, has sought to explain how cross-border networks of politicians, interest groups, and policy experts helped shape the treaty creating the ECSC and subsequent developments in the European Communities.[17] Kiran Patel has argued for the need to contextualise the emergence of the ECSC among the proliferation of international institutions that emerged in the early post-war years in order to

[15]The classic work remains Robert Paxton, *Vichy France. Old Guard and New Order, 1940–1944* (New York: Knopf, 1972). See also Andrew Shennan, *Rethinking France: Plans for Renewal 1940–1946* (Oxford: Clarendon, 1989); Richard Golsan, *Vichy's Afterlife: History and Counterhistory in Postwar France* (Lincoln: University of Nebraska Press, 2000); and Andrew Knapp (ed.), *The Uncertain Foundation: France at the Liberation, 1944–1947* (Basingstoke: Palgrave Macmillan, 2007).

[16]Gérard Bossuat, *L'Europe des Français, 1943–1959: La IVe République aux sources de l'Europe communautaire* (Paris: Publications de la Sorbonne, 1996); Matthias Kipping, *La France et les origines de l'Union européenne. Intégration économique et compétitivité internationale* (Paris: CHEF, 2002); Michael Sutton, *France and the Construction of Europe, 1944–2007* (Oxford: Barghahn, 2007).

[17]Wolfram Kaiser, *Christian Democracy and the Origins of European Union* (Cambridge: Cambridge University Press, 2007) and Brigitte Leucht, *The Transatlantic Origins of European Competition Policy*, forthcoming. On the influence of transnational networks of economic elites on European integration, see Eric Bussière, Michel Dumoulin and Silvain Schirmann (eds), *Milieux économiques et intégration européenne au 20e siècle. La crise des années 1970* (Brussels: Peter Lang, 2006).

'historicise allegedly new traits of the European integration process'.[18] While this book similarly situates the creation of the ECSC in its full historical context, it does so by adopting a different, original approach. By tracing the organisation of French industry in the decade preceding the Schuman Declaration, including the crucial but generally overlooked Vichy period, this study allows us to understand the French proposal to pool coal and steel industries in the context of institutions, debates, and individuals that emerged as a result of the Fall of France in 1940.

Recently, a small number of fascinating and provocative studies have begun to challenge the long-held notion of discontinuity from Vichy to the ECSC, yet these remain focused on intellectual history, exploring how the idea of 'Europe' was used by intellectuals under Vichy and later in post-war Europe. These works thus use a similar approach to other studies of the supposedly illiberal intellectual origins of liberal post-war institutions and concepts,[19] and to recent works tracing the history of ideas from the Third Republic to Vichy which explore whether Vichy's origins were indeed 'republican'.[20] Bernard Bruneteau has shown that many intellectuals who advocated European federalism in the interwar years supported Nazi-led efforts to unify Europe during the Second World War, and went on to champion post-war efforts at European integration. For these hard-line Europeanists, the unity of Europe was the ultimate end, regardless of how unsavoury the means of achieving it might be.[21] Antonin Cohen, meanwhile, has traced the ideas of 'community' and

[18]Kiran Klaus Patel, 'Provincialising European union: Co-operation and Integration in Europe in a Historical Perspective', *Contemporary European History* 22:4, 2013, 649–673, 671.

[19]Mark Mazower, *No Enchanted Palace: The End of Empire and the Ideological Origins of the United Nations* (Princeton: Princeton University Press, 2009) and Samuel Moyn, *The Last Utopia: Human Rights in History* (Cambridge, MA: Harvard University Press, 2012).

[20]Gérard Noiriel, *Les origines républicaines de Vichy* (Paris: Fayard, 1999); Jackie Clarke, *France in the Age of Organization: Factory, Home and Nation from the 1920s to Vichy* (Oxford: Berghahn, 2011); Philip Nord, *France's New Deal. From the Thirties to the Postwar Era* (Princeton: Princeton University Press, 2010). There is also an important literature on the 'non-conformist' thinkers of the 1930s, some of whom later held influential positions in Vichy. The classic work remains Jean-Louis del Bayle, *Les non-conformistes des années 1930* (Paris: Seuil, 1969), while the most thorough evaluation of the non-conformists is Oliver Dard, *Le rendez-vous manqué des relèves des années trente* (Paris: Presses universitaires de France, 2002).

[21]Bernard Bruneteau, *«L'Europe nouvelle de Hitler»: une illusion des intellectuels de Vichy* (Monaco: Rocher, 2003) and *Les «collabos» de l'Europe nouvelle* (Paris: CNRS, 2016).

'authority' integral to the ECSC and its High Authority to Vichy's National Revolution, arguing that the Schuman Plan of 1950 may be seen as the culmination of ideas held by Vichy intellectuals rather than simply as the starting point for the process of European integration that followed.[22] Given their approach and the scope of their books, however, neither Bruneteau nor Cohen has provided a study of institutional continuities from Vichy to the ECSC; by considering industrial policies and institutions from 1940 until 1952, this book complements these existing studies of intellectual history and makes an original contribution to this emerging field.

For its part, the historiography on industrial organisation under Vichy, and particularly the Organisation Committees, is somewhat limited. For many years the key text on the Organisation Committees to which historians of Vichy referred was a 1976 Master's thesis, albeit one by an exceptionally gifted historian, Henry Rousso; this was reworked into an article that appeared in 1979 and remains one of the standard references in the literature on Vichy's economy.[23] While both pieces remain useful for providing an overview of the institutions created by Vichy, they are hindered by the uneven availability of archival documents available to researchers in the 1970s. Thanks to extensive work on business history under Vichy over the past 25 years, there are now many useful studies on French industry during the war, with the emphasis often being on how much freedom of action businesses actually had under Vichy.[24] Related issues such as the role of businesses in 'Aryanisation'[25] and broader studies

[22]Antonin Cohen, *De Vichy à la Communauté européenne* (Paris: Presses universitaires de France, 2012).

[23]Henry Rousso, 'Les Comités d'organisation, aspects structurels et économiques (1940–1944)', Master's thesis, Université de Paris I, 1976; Rousso, 'L'organisation industrielle de Vichy: perspectives de recherche' reprinted in Rousso, *Vichy. L'événement, la mémoire, l'histoire* (Paris: Gallimard, 1992).

[24]Indicatively, Vinen, *The Politics of French Business*; Alain Beltran et al. (eds), *La vie des entreprises sous l'Occupation* (Paris: Belin, 1994); Renaud de Rochebrune and Jean-Claude Hazéra, *Les patrons sous l'Occupation* (Paris: Odile Jacob, 1995); Annie Lacroix-Riz, *Industriels et banquiers sous l'Occupation* (Paris: Armand Colin, 1999); Olivier Dard et al., *L'Occupation, l'Etat français et les entreprises* (Paris: ADHE, 2000); Talbot Imlay and Martin Horn, *The Politics of Industrial Collaboration During World War II* (Cambridge: Cambridge University Press, 2014).

[25]'Aryanisation' was the term used for the confiscation of Jewish-owned goods and businesses. See Philippe Verheyde, *Les mauvais comptes de Vichy. L'aryanisation des entreprises juives* (Paris: Perrin, 1999); Claire Andrieu (ed.), *La spoliation financière. Mission d'étude sur*

of Nazi Germany's economic policies in occupied Europe have also been the focus of recent scholarship.[26] In general, however, the key institutions involved in industrial organisation, such as the Organisation Committees, are treated only in a peripheral way. The sole book-length study of the Organisation Committees produced since their dissolution is an edited volume by Hervé Joly. Despite the value of a number of its chapters, this collection displays one of the most widespread tendencies in studies of the Organisation Committees: it focuses exclusively on the Vichy period, even though the bodies outlived the regime and continued to exist until 1946.[27] This shortcoming in the historiography was highlighted by Claire Andrieu in 1990,[28] yet it has persisted in the literature. By providing a thorough examination of the Committees not only under Vichy but also beyond the end of the regime that created them, this study closes an enduring gap in the literature on industry and business under Vichy and the early post-war period by demonstrating how Vichy's policy

la spoliation des Juifs en France (Paris: Documentation française, 2000); Jean-Marc Dreyfus, *Pillages sur ordonnances: aryanisation et restitution en banques en France, 1940–1953* (Paris: Fayard, 2003); Tal Bruttman (ed.), *Persécutions et spoliations des Juifs pendant la seconde guerre mondiale* (Grenoble: Presses universitaires de Grenoble, 2004).

[26]For an overview of Nazi policies in Europe, see Yves Durand, *Le nouvel ordre nazi, 1938–1945* (Paris: Editions Complexe, 1990) and Mark Mazower, *Hitler's Empire: How the Nazis Ruled Europe* (New York: Penguin, 2008). Two recent economic histories of Europe during the war are Christophe Buchheim and Marcel Boldorf, *Europäische Volkwirtschaften unter deutscher Hegemonie, 1938–1945* (Munich: Oldenbourg Akademie Verlag, 2012) and Hein Klemann and Sergei Kudryashov, *Occupied Economies: An Economic History of Nazi-Occupied Europe, 1939–1945* (London: Berg, 2012). For Nazi Germany's domestic economic policies, with some discussion of economic policies pursued by the Nazis in France, see Götz Aly, *Hitlers Volksstaat: Raub, Rassenkrieg und nationaler Sozialismus* (Frankfurt: S. Fischer Verlag, 2005) and Adam Tooze, *Wages of Destruction: The Making and Breaking of the Nazi Economy* (London: Penguin, 2007).

[27]Hervé Joly (ed.), *Les Comités d'organisation et l'économie dirigée du régime de Vichy* (Caen: CRHQ, 2004). This was part of a CNRS-funded research project on 'Les entreprises françaises sous l'Occupation', which ran from 2002 to 2009 and yielded a number of other edited volumes on Vichy's business history. The only other book-length study of the Organisation Committees is a thesis in law published in occupied France: Jean-Guy Mérigot, *Les comités d'organisation* (Bordeaux: Université de Bordeaux, 1943).

[28]Claire Andrieu, *La Banque sous l'Occupation: Paradoxes de l'histoire d'une profession* (Paris: FNSP, 1990), 128.

innovations from 1940 outlived the regime and helped shape some of France's key post-war institutions.[29]

In examining industrial organisation in France between 1940 and 1952, this study engages with the establishment of the Monnet Plan between 1945 and 1947 as well as the ECSC. As with the literature on European integration history, most works on the French economy of the early post-war years begin at the earliest with 1944, typically limiting the discussion of Vichy to a short explanation of how the Occupation was devastating for France's financial, economic, and industrial situation.[30] Similarly, the historiography on the Monnet Plan tends to emphasise its 'republican' origins by focusing on Monnet's wartime involvement in the *Comité français de Libération nationale* (CFLN)[31] and his actions under the Provisional Government of the French Republic (1944–1946).[32]

[29]Two indispensable studies that attempt to trace the emergence of a distinct, French variety of capitalism in the twentieth century that include the period between 1940 and 1952 are Richard Kuisel, *Capitalism and the State in Modern France: Renovation and Economic Management in the Twentieth Century* (Cambridge: Cambridge University Press, 1981) and Michel Margairaz, *L'Etat, les finances et l'économie. Histoire d'une conversion, 1932–1952* (Paris: CHEFF, 1991). For a more recent assessment of Vichy's influence on the economy of post-war France, see Margairaz, 'Les politiques économiques sous et de Vichy', *Histoire@Politique. Politique, culture, société*, no. 9, septembre–décembre 2009. The literature on the French steel industry in this period has been dominated by Philippe Mioche; see Mioche, *La sidérurgie et l'Etat en France des années quarante aux années soixante*, Doctorat d'Etat, Université de Paris IV, 1992 and, for a study of relations between French and German steel industrialists, Françoise Berger, *La France, l'Allemagne et l'acier (1932–1952): de la stratégie des cartels à l'élaboration de la CECA*, Thèse de doctorat, Université de Paris I, 2000. For the coal industry, see Régine Perrin, *Le marché du charbon, un enjeu entre l'Europe et les Etats-Unis de 1945 à 1958* (Paris: Publications de la Sorbonne, 1996) and Richard Vinen, 'The French Coal Industry during the Occupation', *The Historical Journal*, 33:1, 1990, 105–130.

[30]See, for example, Jean-François Eck, *Histoire de l'économie française depuis 1945* (Paris: Armand Colin, 2004) and Frances Lynch's excellent *France and the International Economy: From Vichy to the Treaty of Rome* (London: Routledge, 1997).

[31]The CFLN, based in Algiers, was the main overseas Resistance organisation that acted as a government-in-waiting. Created in 1943, Charles de Gaulle soon emerged as its leader.

[32]Philippe Mioche, *Le Plan Monnet. Genèse et élaboration, 1941–1947* (Paris: Publications de la Sorbonne, 1987); Roussel, *Jean Monnet*. The influence of the United States, both as a model for Monnet's innovations and as a source of political influence thanks to Monnet's transatlantic network, is also emphasised in the literature. See Kuisel, *Capitalism and the State in Modern France* and Sherrill Brown Wells, *Jean Monnet: Unconventional Statesman* (London: Lynne Rienner, 2011).

Richard Kuisel and Philippe Mioche have discussed abortive plans drawn up under Vichy for economic planning as possible antecedents for the Monnet Plan, although they both reject the notion of any institutional continuities from Vichy to the Monnet Plan.[33] By examining industrial organisation on French territory – that is, under Vichy – in the years preceding the creation of the Monnet Plan, this book challenges the generally accepted narrative of the origins of the Monnet Plan's institutions, revealing significant continuities from the Organisation Committees to the offices of the Monnet Plan.

One vital characteristic of the organisation of French industry throughout the period in question is the centrality of state policy. The law creating the Organisation Committees was drafted by the Minister for Industrial Production and a handful of associates, and subsequent legislation concerning industrial organisation was likewise directed by the French government. Given the importance of government policy in the organisation of French industry, this study focuses on the role of the State, ranging from broad governmental policies to the projects of the Ministry of Industrial Production to the workings of individual Organisation Committees. Accordingly, the individuals studied range from industrialists to high-level civil servants to members of government and heads of state. While this approach does not extend to transnational networks of industrialists or supporters of economic planning, the degree of influence exerted by industrialists on policy-making, the role of individuals, and the functioning of the relevant institutions at the national level, where the key decisions were made, are considered throughout.[34]

[33]Kuisel, 'Vichy et les origines de la planification économique, 1940–1946'; Mioche, *Le Plan Monnet*. Philip Nord makes a similar claim in *France's New Deal*. Adrian Jones, meanwhile, rejects any continuity in the idea of economic planning from Vichy to Monnet; see Jones, 'Illusions of Sovereignty: Business and the Organization of Committee of Vichy France', *Social History*, January 1986.

[34]Eric Bussière argues that transnational networks of industrialists in the first half of the twentieth century helped create a European identity among business elites; Morten Rasmussen criticises this assessment on the grounds that these elites did not have any clear influence on the process of European integration in the early post-war period. See Bussière, 'Les milieux économiques face à l'Europe au XXe siècle', *Journal of European Integration History*, 3:2, 1997, 5–21 and Rasmussen, 'European Rescue of the Nation-State? Tracing the Role of Economics and Business' in Wolfram Kaiser and Antonio Varsori (eds), *European Union History: Themes and Debates* (Basingstoke: Palgrave Macmillan, 2010).

This approach is reflected in the selection of archival sources. One major challenge facing any historian interested in the Organisation Committees is the myriad gaps in the existing archives. The archives of the Committees themselves have been destroyed, denying historians their most obvious source base.[35] Complicating matters further is the fact that many of the archives of the first Monnet Plan, covering the years until 1952, have similarly not been preserved.[36] Given the scope of this study, these archival gaps have presented a significant but by no means insurmountable challenge. Indeed, during the research for this book, I was fortunate enough to discover a complete set of the minutes from the monthly meetings of the Organisation Committee for Steel from 1940 until 1944. This book is based in part on this previously unexploited source which provides unprecedented insight into the workings of the Organisation Committee during the war. The discussion of the Monnet Plan, meanwhile, is largely based on the Jean Monnet papers housed at the *Fondation Jean Monnet pour l'Europe* in Lausanne, along with the existing documentation from the General Commissariat for the Plan in the French *Archives nationales.*

Much of the research for this study was completed at the *Archives nationales* in Paris, which relocated to Pierrefitte-sur-Seine during this project. This study draws on the documentation of various ministries and government offices, with the archives of the Ministry for Industrial Production, the General Delegation for Franco-German Economic Relations, and the General Commissariat for the Plan (CGP) being amongst the most important. The private papers of individuals such as Charles de Gaulle and Jean Bichelonne were indispensable, as were those of René Belin, housed at the *Institut d'Histoire Sociale* in Nanterre, and Pierre Uri, at the Historical Archives of the European Union in Florence. The collections of the *Centre des archives économiques et financières* in Savigny-le-Temple and the *Institut d'histoire du temps présent* in Paris were

[35]According to Rousso, the archives of the Organisation Committees were preserved until the 1970s in the fort of Montlignon, near Paris, but inexplicably 'disappeared or became unusable'. It remains unclear what happened to these archives. See Rousso, 'L'organisation industrielle de Vichy'.

[36]Most importantly, the archives of the Modernisation Commissions (*commissions de modernisation*), described by Monnet as the 'keystones' of the Monnet Plan, have not been preserved.

also helpful. The archives of the German Military Administration in France, kept at the *Bundesarchiv-Militärarchiv* in Freiburg im Breisgau, were invaluable. The National Archives in London yielded some useful documentation, particularly regarding the situation of French industry in 1940 and the international reaction to the Schuman Declaration in 1950. On the latter, the archives of the Belgian Foreign Ministry in Brussels and the Library and Archives of Canada in Ottawa were similarly beneficial. Finally, the archives of individual steel firms and of employers' associations were consulted at the *Archives nationales du Monde du travail* in Roubaix. These sources were supplemented by published primary sources, from the memoirs of relevant individuals to a range of newspapers.

Historians working on Vichy face the difficult question of how much weight to give to German archives. While the wave of revisionist scholarship on Vichy from the late 1960s and 1970s relied heavily on German archives,[37] largely because many of the key French archives from the Second World War were not yet open, studies published in the 1980s and 1990s tended to rely extensively, if not always exclusively on newly declassified French archival sources.[38] More recently, there has been a tendency in the historiography to draw more heavily on German sources in reaction to what some have called an overly 'Franco-French' frame of analysis.[39] Given the scope of this project, and the centrality of the French State to the organisation of the nation's industry throughout the period of study, this book is based predominantly on the archives of different French actors, from the Head of State to various ministries to steel firms, including heretofore unused documentation. These French sources have been supplemented by archival collections from six further countries, and the German archives in particular have been especially useful when discussing the establishment of the Organisation Committees in 1940, as there is an

[37]Eberhard Jäckel, *Frankreich in Hitlers Europa* (Stuttgart: Deutsche Verlags-Anstalt, 1966); Hans Umbreit, *Der Militärbefehlshaber in Frankreich 1940–1944* (Boppard am Rhein: Harald Boldt Verlag, 1968); Alan Milward, *The New Order and the French Economy* (Oxford: Oxford University Press, 1970); Paxton, *Vichy France*.

[38]Kuisel, *Capitalism and the State in Modern France*; Andrieu, *La Banque sous l'Occupation*; Margairaz, *L'Etat, les finances et l'économie*; Vinen, *The Politics of French Business*.

[39]Arne Radtke-Delacor, 'Produire pour le Reich: les commandes allemandes à l'industrie française', *Vingtième siècle*, no. 70 (April–June 2001); Hervé Joly (ed.), *L'Economie de la zone non occupée 1940–1942* (Paris: CTHS, 2007); Imlay and Horn, *The Politics of Industrial Collaboration during World War II*.

important debate in the literature over the role of the German authorities in bringing about their creation.[40] Given that the narrative of this book is largely a French one, albeit with an important international dimension, this approach provides the most thorough account of how French industry was organised between 1940 and 1952.

This book is structured chronologically, from the creation of the Organisation Committees to the establishment of the ECSC. This approach has the advantage of focusing on the evolution of the Committees and highlighting continuities throughout the period. This structure nevertheless allows for a thematic organisation of the chapters, in that contemporary developments in Vichy and the Resistance are treated in separate chapters. Given that this study focuses on institutional change within the organisation of the French steel industry, periods of significant change are accorded more weight. Consequently, the timeframe considered in each chapter varies, ranging from a few months, as in Chapters 2 and 7, to several years, as in Chapters 4 and 8. While this necessarily means that some issues related to the French economy under Vichy or in the late 1940s may be dealt with in a more cursory way, this is done in order to provide as comprehensive a study as possible of the organisation of France's heavy industry over an exceptionally eventful 12-year period.

The next chapter considers the context of French industry immediately following the Fall of France and the initial reforms undertaken by the newly established Vichy regime. It reveals that, despite the pride of place given to the law of 16 August 1940 in the literature on the topic, virtually all of the elements of the legislation had in fact been agreed upon with the German authorities in the month preceding the law. By demonstrating German support for these measures, the chapter calls into question the standard narrative that the creation of the Organisation Committees surprised and angered the Nazi authorities. The broader context in which these measures were taken, particularly the backdrop of the German Minister for the Economy's much-publicised plans to create a 'new European economic order', is also discussed.

Chapter 3 looks at the implementation of the law of 16 August 1940, particularly the creation of the Organisation Committees for Steel and for

[40] See Arne Radtke-Delacor, 'La position des comités d'organisation face aux autorités d'occupation' in Joly, *Les Comités d'organisation*.

Coal in November 1940. It shows how, despite the law foreseeing the representation of workers as well as employers and the State within the Committees, this tripartism was never put into practice. While the fact that the Committees were dominated by employers has led some historians to argue that the Committees were simply the continuation of pre-war employers' associations such as the *Comité des forges*, this argument is challenged through an analysis of the individuals appointed to the Committees.

Having assessed the creation of the Committees, Chapter 4 deals with how the Committees responded to the industrial policies of the Vichy regime. Based on previously unused archives, including detailed minutes of the meetings of the Organisation Committee for Steel from 1940 until 1944, this chapter discusses the Committee's responses to Vichy's National Revolution, the deportation of French workers to Germany through the *Service du travail obligatoire* (STO), and schemes for French factories to shoulder a greater share of production for the German war economy. In so doing, the chapter makes an important contribution to the literature on business history under Vichy and the question of 'economic collaboration'.

With Chapter 5, the narrative shifts to the French Resistance, particularly the CFLN based in Algiers. With the outcome of the war becoming clearer in 1943 and 1944, the Resistance was forced to consider the question of whether to maintain the Committees created by Vichy for their pragmatic value or to dissolve them due to their obvious association with the regime. The debate was ultimately settled by de Gaulle, albeit for political rather than economic considerations. In the months preceding the Allied landings in Normandy, the CFLN unanimously endorsed the maintenance of Vichy's Committees.

As noted above, the reforms of the Organisation Committees undertaken between 1944 and 1946 remain largely unaddressed in the existing literature. Chapter 6 constitutes the most thorough study to date of the Committees under the Provisional Government of the French Republic. It shows that these reforms were quite limited and the *épuration* strikingly superficial. The most significant reform was the inclusion of labour representation within the Committees, although this had in fact been foreseen in the law of 16 August 1940; ironically, these provisions of the Vichy law were implemented more effectively under the Republican government led by de Gaulle than they had been under Pétain.

The seventh chapter explains the dissolution of the Organisation Committees and the emergence of new, strikingly similar institutions: the Modernisation Commissions (*commissions de modernisation*) of the

Monnet Plan. The influence of the Committees on the new Commissions created by Jean Monnet is discussed, as are institutional and individual continuities between the Committees and the Commissions. It concludes that the Commissions drew on the Committees to a far greater extent than is generally recognised in the literature.

Chapter 8 covers the period between the implementation of the Monnet Plan in 1946 and the successful launch of the ECSC in 1952. Focusing on the struggle between relevant employers' associations and the offices of the Monnet Plan, it reveals the methods used by Jean Monnet and his collaborators to ensure the success of the Monnet Plan and then the Schuman Plan. The influence of the Modernisation Commissions on the ECSC is also discussed, as are continuities in personnel from Vichy to Europe's first supranational institution.

This rigorously researched study of Vichy's Organisation Committees and their successors provides an analysis of the evolution of Vichy's New Industrial Order not only during the war but crucially in post-war France. In so doing, this account provides original insights on industry under Vichy, the Monnet Plan, and Europe's first supranational institution, the ECSC. Furthermore, in addressing the degree of continuity from Vichy to the ECSC, this book challenges two common depictions still prevalent in public debates concerning the history of the EU: the denial of any wartime antecedents of European integration, on the one hand, and the claim that the EU is little more than an amended version of Hitler's New European Order, on the other hand. As such, this study aims both to ameliorate our understanding of the Second World War's legacy in post-war Europe and to inform contemporary debates concerning the EU.

CHAPTER 2

France's New Industrial Order: Reorganising Industrial Production After the Fall of France

The Armistice signed by France and Germany on 22 June 1940 initiated a ceasefire between the two countries and established the context in which cross-Rhine relations would unfold until the Liberation of France four years later. While the crucial matter of French industrial production was not directly addressed in the document, by the end of the summer the French government had fundamentally reorganised the nation's industry. The keystones of Vichy's industrial order were the Organisation Committees, formally established following the law of 16 August 1940, put forward by Minister for Industrial Production René Belin. The existing literature on French industry under Vichy naturally focuses on this law, but in so doing fails to adequately explain why the industrial reorganisation took the shape that it did. In order to answer this question, it is necessary to study the actions of the French authorities in Paris over the month of July, rather than the law written in Vichy in August. Such an analysis reveals not only that the reorganisation of French industry took place weeks earlier than it is generally held, but more importantly that the entire undertaking occurred under German auspices and in the context of broader Franco-German collaboration. Far from being an assertion of French sovereignty in the face of German exigency, Vichy's New Industrial Order created the foundations of durable industrial collaboration in a Europe under German domination.

© The Author(s) 2017

L.-A. Brunet, *Forging Europe: Industrial Organisation in France, 1940–1952*, Security, Conflict and Cooperation in the Contemporary World, DOI 10.1057/978-1-349-95198-7_2

In many ways the single most important stipulation in the Armistice was that, to safeguard German interests, the greater part of metropolitan France would be partitioned into two zones. The first zone covered the northern half of France, stretching from Lorraine to Brittany, including Paris, as well as the entire Atlantic coast, from Belgium to Spain. This area, known as the Occupied Zone, was occupied directly by the Germans, ostensibly to guard the Continent against any invasion by British troops. Germany stated that it would reduce its presence in this zone 'following the cessation of hostilities with England'.[1] The text also included the vague provision that 'in the occupied regions of France, the German Reich enjoys the rights of the occupying power'.[2] This sentence, left open to interpretation, would be used to legitimate a gamut of German actions during its occupation of France.[3] The southern, unoccupied zone remained free of German control and under the full authority of the French government, led by Maréchal Philippe Pétain.[4] This division of France was not merely administrative; crossing from one zone into the other was strictly controlled by the German military, and written permission had to be obtained. This applied to all French citizens, including members of the government, which exacerbated the problem of the absence of the government from Paris, where the civil service remained.

The German occupation of northern and western France, and the imposition of the strictly enforced demarcation line, were features of a broader German policy that eroded France's sovereignty. In addition to the Occupied and Non-Occupied Zones defined in the Armistice, France was partitioned into a further three zones. The eastern provinces of Alsace and Lorraine, which had been part of Germany from 1870 until 1918

[1]'Convention d'Armistice' franco-allemande, 22 June 1940, Chauvel 62, MAE. All translations are the author's unless otherwise indicated.

[2]Ibid.

[3]France interpreted this article along the lines of the Hague Convention of 1907, which clearly delineated what these powers could reasonably include. The German authorities, however, had a Thrasymachean attitude to this clause, and subsequently argued that even the most unjustified requisitions were made legitimate by this article.

[4]This zone is variously referred to as the Non-Occupied Zone or the Unoccupied Zone, or simply as Vichy France. For administrative purposes within French industry, it was often referred to as Centre-Midi. During the war it was often called the Free Zone, but this term has fallen out of favour, largely to distinguish between the de Gaulle-led 'Free France' and the authoritarian regime led by Pétain.

under the Second Reich, were 'restored' to Germany.[5] The two northernmost departments of France, Nord and Pas-de-Calais, were detached from the Occupied Zone by Germany and appended to Belgium, where they were administered by the German Military Administration in Brussels. Lastly, a strip of French territory along the Italian border, from Switzerland to the Mediterranean, was occupied by Italy, following its late entry into the war.[6] While the French government at least formally governed the Occupied Zone, in these three zones it had no powers.

This redrawing of the map of France was significant for industrial production because it placed the two most heavily industrialised areas entirely beyond the control of the French government in Vichy. Most important were Nord and Pas-de-Calais, which together constituted the heartland of French manufacturing and were home to its largest coal deposits, responsible for two-thirds of pre-war domestic production. Nearly as devastating was the loss of the coal and steel industries of Lorraine, the site of France's most modern coal mines and the source of one-eighth of French coal in the 1930s.[7] Most harmful to French industry, however, was the demarcation line that bisected the country; raw materials from one zone could not be transported to a factory in the other without prior authorisation. The Germans also used the demarcation line as a political tool, knowing full well that the Non-Occupied Zone depended on the more industrialised but also more agriculturally productive northern regions of the country.[8]

The cessation of hostilities between France and Germany had an acute effect on French industry. Following the Munich Accord, French industry had been increasingly geared towards the production of war *matériel*. From 3 September 1939, when France declared war on Germany, virtually all domestic production was redirected for the purposes of war.

[5]The three departments of Haut-Rhin, Bas-Rhin (Alsace), and Moselle (half of Lorraine), together referred to as Reichsland, were never formally annexed by Germany, but became de facto territories of the Reich. Alsace was added to the Gau, or province, of Baden, while Lorraine was fused with Saarland, forming Westmark Gau. For a thorough contemporary analysis of the incorporation of Alsace-Lorraine into the Reich by the British Foreign Office, see 'The Problem of Alsace-Lorraine', revised 22 May 1944, FO 371 41988, TNA.

[6]'Convention d'Armistice' franco-italienne, Papiers Rochat 49, P 4325, MAE.

[7]'The Coal Economy of France under German Occupation', WO 219/3752, NA.

[8]See Eric Alary, *La Ligne de démarcation* (Paris: Presses universitaires de France, 1995).

The termination of Franco-German fighting, however, meant the immediate cessation of such production.[9] French factories thus stopped all orders for military purposes, but had no others to replace them. In the uncertain period following the Armistice, French industry ground to a halt.

The paralysis of French industry was exacerbated by another condition imposed by the German authorities. Given that Germany remained at war with Great Britain, the former insisted that all trade between France and Great Britain cease. This extended to the French and British empires, despite vehement objections that this would effectively asphyxiate certain French possessions that were entirely dependent on goods from the British Empire.[10] Of more direct consequence for metropolitan France was the loss of imports from Great Britain. Throughout the interwar period, France was the world's largest importer of coal, and this was the single most heavily imported commodity from Great Britain, accounting for a full third of France's domestic consumption.[11] From September 1939, coal imports from across the Channel had steadily increased, fuelling France's armaments production.[12] From the end of June 1940, however, Great Britain began diverting coal shipments initially bound for France to neutral or other allied countries.[13] From this date, with the loss of imports from Britain, France would have to make do with a maximum of two-thirds of its total 1939 supply of coal. In addition to the loss of coal, which remained the fuel for virtually all heavy industry, the suspension of trade with the British Empire paralysed entire industries that

[9]'Rapport sur l'activité du ministère de la production industrielle et du travail du 15 juillet au 15 novembre 1940', 17 November 1940, F 12 10157, AN.

[10]Among these were the French possessions in India (most notably Pondicherry) and the islands of Saint-Pierre et Miquelon, off the coast of Newfoundland. See 'Séance de la Sous-Commission Finances et Banque du 23 juillet', 23 July 1940 and 'Relations financières et économiques avec la Grande-Bretagne', 11 November 1940, AJ 41 170, AN.

[11]'Note du 31 juillet', 31 July 1940, AJ 41 170, AN.

[12]In March 1940, British monthly coal exports to France exceeded 1,000,000 tons for the first time, and by 3 June provisions were made to raise monthly shipments to 2,250,000 million tons per month. See 'Letter from Sanderson to Tolerton', 11 April 1940 and 'Letter from L.G. Lowry to R.H. Tolerton', 3 June 1940, MT 63 51, TNA. See also 'Report of the Special Sub-Committee of the Anglo-French Coordination Committee constituted to consider the supply of coal from the United Kingdom to France' by Jean Monnet and W.B. Brown, 13 May 1940, AME 4 5 4, FJM.

[13]'Letter from T.G. Jenkins to C.W. Dixon', 17 July 1940, MT 59 148, NA.

were dependent on imports of particular primary goods from British colonies.[14] The need to find new sources of coal quickly became an *idée fixe* of French industrial policy. Not only was British coal inaccessible, but the two largest coalfields in France, in Nord-Pas-de-Calais and Lorraine, had been integrated into Belgium and Germany, respectively. This left only the meagre coal mines in the Loire, which were already thoroughly exploited.[15] Much of the coal extracted from this site was of inferior quality, however, and the small, otherwise unusable pieces could only be used when joined together with pitch to make briquettes, which were functional as fuel for French ships. Even this imperfect option was complicated by the fact that the pitch required had been imported from Great Britain, and was thus no longer readily available.[16]

The shortage of primary materials, compounded by the lack of orders for French factories, was aggravated by a scarcity of labour. From the day of Germany's incursion into France on 10 May, increasingly significant areas of the country had been evacuated, which meant that factories in the most heavily industrialised areas in France, particularly in Nord-Pas-de-Calais and Alsace-Lorraine, but also across the northern Occupied Zone, were in practice inoperable. As a result of this exodus of labour and the general disruption of the economy caused by the German invasion, overall French coal production had decreased from 4.6 million tonnes in April 1940 to a mere 1.2 million tonnes in June.[17]

Aside from these direct difficulties imposed on French industry, the restrictions placed on the French government had serious implications for industrial production as well. The government had fled Paris on 10 June as the Wehrmacht closed in on the capital, relocating first to Tours, then further southwest to Bordeaux. When the Armistice decreed that Bordeaux would fall within the Occupied Zone, the government relocated yet again to Clermont-Ferrand, before settling on the provincial spa town

[14]Textile industries, for example, were deprived of jute and cotton. In this context, it was impossible for them to approach even 30 per cent of 1938 production levels. See 'Lettre de Bessonneau', 4 November 1940, F 60 1539, AN.

[15]Coal production in the Non-Occupied Zone actually exceeded pre-war levels, reaching 135 per cent of 1938 production in 1941 and 150 per cent in 1942. 'The Coal Economy of France under German Occupation', WO 219 3752, TNA.

[16]'Achat de brai en Grande-Bretagne', 19 December 1940, AJ 41 102 and 'Note du Ministère des affaires étrangères', 11 December 1940, AJ 41 170, AN.

[17]'Compte rendu d'un entretien avec M. Fanton d'Anton', May 1941, AJ 41 168, AN.

of Vichy on 1 July. The town had little to recommend it, aside from the absence of any serious political opposition and the abundance of hotels, which were quickly transformed into government offices.[18] The centuries-old tendency towards centralisation in France meant that virtually all administrative services were concentrated in the capital; the government's absence from Paris amounted to decapitation. The Armistice included a provision that the government 'is free to choose any seat in the Non-Occupied Zone, or even, if it wishes, to establish itself in Paris. In the latter case, the German government commits to ensure all necessary facilities to the French government and to its central administrative services, so that it will be able to govern the occupied and non-occupied territories from Paris'.[19] On 8 July, the German administration offered to allow the French government to establish itself in Versailles, with free access to central Paris, which would remain occupied.[20] On this presumption, and in the hopes of reviving French industry, the civil service of the so-called technical ministries, most importantly the Ministry for Industrial Production, returned to their offices in Paris, anticipating the imminent return of the government to the capital. Instead, however, the German administration suspended its approval of the government's return, claiming that 'technical reasons oppose it', but that the government would ultimately return to Paris.[21] As it was, the French government would remain in Vichy until August 1944, when a very different French government, led by Charles de Gaulle, established itself in a Paris liberated from the Nazis.

The absence of the French government from Paris engendered increasing anxieties about French sovereignty. By early July, German industrialists were placing demands for war *matériel* with French

[18]Lyon, the largest city in the region and the obvious candidate for provisional capital, was ruled out because of its Radical mayor, former president Edouard Herriot. See Paul Baudouin, *The Private Diaries of Paul Baudouin* (London: Eyre and Spottiswoode, 1948), 153.

[19]'Convention d'Armistice' franco-allemande, Chauvel 62, MAE.

[20]'Allemagne et Italie', undated note, Papiers Baudouin, MAE. In his diary, Foreign Minister Paul Baudouin records that on 9 July, the Cabinet replied to the German offer, demanding that the ministerial quarter of Paris also be free of occupation troops and that transportation between this quarter and Versailles be guaranteed. He adds: 'We must get back to the capital as soon as possible, and we hope to be there before the end of the month.' See Baudouin, *The Private Diaries of Paul Baudouin*, 153–154, 163.

[21]Baudouin, *The Private Diaries of Paul Baudouin*, 195.

factories in the Occupied Zone.[22] French industrialists were faced with an ultimatum by the German military authorities: they could either fulfil the orders, or be replaced by German industrialists and workers who would complete the orders themselves. A flurry of letters from industrialists flowed to Vichy begging for direction from the government.[23] The government's initial attempts at intervention were of little use, although they were unsure whether this was due to German maliciousness or simply disorganisation – the French government's representative in Paris was unable to discern who among the Germans in Paris was responsible for economic questions.[24] On 30 June, German workers occupied the Renault and Citroën factories in Paris to produce goods intended to contribute to the imminent German offensive against Great Britain.[25] Germany's swelling control of French industry justified fears that, left unchecked, this would lead to direct control of French production by the Reich. Indeed, in Belgium the German Authorities set up *Wirtschaftsgruppen*, economic offices to oversee branches of industry, like those that existed in the Reich.[26]

The increasing command exerted by Germany over French industry was perhaps most shockingly displayed by Germany's attempts to negotiate a trade agreement between France and Yugoslavia – without even informing the French government. The French ambassador in Belgrade learned of the negotiations and was able to warn the government in Vichy, whose objections were sufficient to derail the talks.[27] The incident nevertheless highlighted the extent to which French sovereignty was threatened by Germany's actions, both on and beyond French soil.

[22]'Note', 13 July 1940, AJ 41 529, AN.

[23]'Lettre à Monsieur le Gouverneur Militaire de la Région de Paris', 5 August 1940, AN.

[24]'Rapport Barnaud', 10 July 1940, Guerre de 1939–1945 Vichy, 581, 'Economie française interne', MAE.

[25]'Commandes allemandes de guerre en France, 25 juin 1940–1923 mai 1941', AJ 41 529, AN.

[26]'Kriegestagebuch der Rüstungs-Inspektion Belgien', 31 May 1940, RW 25 1a, BA-MA. For Belgium under the Occupation, see Etienne Dejonghe (ed.), *L'Occupation en France et en Belgique, 1940–1944* (Lille: Revue du Nord, 1987).

[27]'Note pour le Secrétariat général du Conseil supérieur de la défense nationale', 7 July 1940, in 'Notes de principe et convention d'armistice, février–août 1940', Guerre de 1939–1945 Vichy, 609, MAE.

In the weeks following the Armistice, French industry had stalled and the government, isolated in a provincial holiday town 300 kilometres from Paris, appeared disorganised and powerless. Meanwhile, German control of the Occupied Zone seemed to be extending to industrial production. Fearing that its jurisdiction could become permanently reduced to the rump Non-Occupied Zone, the French government realised that the status quo was unsustainable. The government responded decisively by passing the law of 16 August 1940 'concerning the provisional organisation of industrial production'.[28] With this single page of legislation, the French government fundamentally reorganised French industry and established the New Industrial Order that would endure in France for more than four years.

The law of 16 August 1940 was intended to 'reorganise the economy in light of the current situation, and to draw maximum profit from the means of production, from the labour reserves, and from the primary materials at our disposal'. The reorganisation was sweeping indeed. National confederations of trade unions and of employers' associations, deemed too political and inefficient, were dissolved.[29] The same fate was expressly reserved for any organisation that was judged to threaten the state's plans for efficiency, whether by articulating overt opposition or simply by being 'incompatible with the discipline and speed of the decision necessary'.[30] To replace the organisations that had been among the mainstays of the economy of the Third Republic, the French government created so-called Organisation Committees. These Committees formed the central pillars of the New Industrial Order established in the summer of 1940. Instead of representing either workers or employers, these Committees were organised according to particular branches of industry. For example, while steel workers might have belonged to the CGT before 1940 and the owners of those steel firms had gathered in the *Comité des*

[28] *Journal officiel*, 18 August 1940.

[29] The law banned trade union confederations and employers' confederations operating at the national level. With a decree on 9 November 1940, the government explicitly dissolved the *Confédération générale du patronat français* (CGPF) and two specific employers' associations, namely those for coal, the *Comité central des houillères de France*, and steel, the *Comité des forges*, as well as the principal trade union confederations, the *Confédération générale du travail* (CGT) and the *Confédération française des travailleurs chrétiens* (CFTC). This decree was published in the *Journal officiel* on 12 November 1940.

[30] *Journal officiel*, 18 August 1940.

forges, both groups would henceforth be represented in a single Organisation Committee for Steel. Analogous arrangements were made for most industries; while initially limited to 25 vital industries, by 1944 there were over 300 Committees, representing industries as disparate as hairdressing and the entertainment industry.

In keeping with the notion of organising production according to branches of industry rather than by class, the law foresaw the inclusion of representation from employers and workers, although this was to be added at a later date.[31] Moreover, the text of the law specified that 'there can be no question of leaving full freedom to the interested parties. The Minister for Industrial Production will determine the composition of each Committee [. . .] and will exert constant control'.[32] The reorganisation was thus meant to be fundamentally statist, allowing the government to exert unprecedented control over virtually every aspect of industrial production. In place of the liberal order that had 'allowed private, uncontrolled organisms to appropriate for their own profit', the law articulated that 'today, all initiatives and decisions must be taken by the government', and that 'all interests and all activities must be subordinate to the urgency of the revival of the country'.[33]

The Committees were responsible for conducting a thorough inventory of primary materials available to each industry. Based on this information, the Committee would organise which orders would be carried out in which factories, and how primary materials were to be provisioned accordingly.[34] The principal shortcoming of this arrangement, however, was that the Committees had control only over the primary materials that were already in the stocks of various industries. To address this limitation, the government passed a supplementary law on 10 September, establishing the Central Bureau for the Distribution of Industrial Products (OCRPI).[35] This Central Bureau was divided into sections corresponding to branches of industry, similar to the way in which the Committees were organised. Each section had sweeping powers, and controlled the acquisition, distribution, storage, and consumption of particular products. These powers even included the

[31]The composition of the Organisation Committees is discussed in Chapter 3.

[32]*Journal officiel*, 18 August 1940.

[33]Ibid.

[34]Ibid.

[35]*L'Office central de répartition des produits industriels (OCRPI).*

authority to force producers to sell specific amounts of particular products to chosen buyers, and vice versa. While the Committees controlled industrial production, the Central Bureau managed the supply of primary materials on which industry relied. At least one member of each Committee was also a member of the analogous section of the Central Bureau, and the government had a representative present at every meeting.[36] With this law, the construction of France's New Industrial Order was complete.

This new system departed radically from the pre-war liberal order of the Third Republic. While the government had passed a law in July 1938 allowing for greater State involvement in French industries deemed to be strategic, industrial reorganisation had remained firmly in the hands of employers. Another initative from October 1939 championed by René Belin among others, known as the Majestic Accords, had pledged to promote cooperation between employers and workers in armaments factories, but again in practice industrialists had been able to make their decisions with little regard to workers.[37] Given its statist character and the far-reaching responsibilities given to the new offices, the establishment of the Organisation Committees following the Fall of France was thus an unprecedented reorganisation of the nation's industry.

Patriotism or Collaborationism? Explaining the Creation of the Organisation Committees

The paralysis of French industry, coupled with the increasing pressure exerted by Germany on French industrialists, compelled the French government to adopt more direct control over the economy. The economic situation in the summer of 1940 does not, however, explain why the reorganisation of the French economy took the particular form it did. Similar conditions of penury and disorder existed in France in 1944 in the wake of the Liberation. Then, however, the Provisional Government opted to nationalise strategic industries outright (beginning with the coal mines of

[36] *Journal officiel*, 12 September 1940.

[37] According to Talbot Imlay, the Majestic Accords 'proved to be a sham... Dictation, not collaboration, marked wartime industrial relations'. Talbot Imlay, *Facing the Second World War: Strategy, Politics, and Economics in Britain and France, 1938–1940* (Oxford: Oxford University Press, 2003), 285.

northern France in December 1944), an option that was never entertained by French authorities in 1940. Indeed, a number of different economic models had been implemented since the First World War, from Soviet central planning to Roosevelt's New Deal to the Nazi model based on rearmament.[38] The path chosen by the French government was not the only nor even the most obvious one. The reasons for the architecture of the New Industrial Order merit closer attention.

In the existing literature on Vichy France, there are four different explanations of why French industry assumed its peculiar form: continuities between the 1930s and the Vichy era; the National Revolution articulated by Pétain; a patriotic desire to protect French industry from German schemes; and that Vichy's model was simply the German model, transposed to France. Regarding the first, an important stream of scholarship has tended to highlight the continuities between the 1930s and the Vichy era, particularly in the field of intellectual history. This approach draws on the many so-called non-conformist journals published in France over the decade preceding the war that gave voice to critics of the Third Republic and of economic liberalism more generally.[39] Ideas such as economic planning were entertained and advocated, particularly after Henri de Man introduced planning in Belgium in 1933.[40] Interestingly, a number of individuals who would gain prominent positions in the French government in Vichy published articles in the 1930s advocating economic reforms that would be echoed in policies passed under Pétain.

[38]On the Soviet economy under Stalin, Robert C. Allen offers a controversially rosy analysis in *Farm to Factory: A Reinterpretation of the Soviet Industrial Revolution* (Princeton: Princeton University Press, 2003); for a more balanced study of the Soviet consumer economy, see Elena Osokina, *Our Daily Bread: Socialist Distribution and the Art of Survival in Stalin's Russia, 1927–1941* (London: M.E. Sharpe, 2001). For an excellent international history of the New Deal, see Kiran Klaus Patel, *The New Deal: A Global History* (Princeton: Princeton University Press, 2016). The best overview of the Reich's economy in English is Adam Tooze, *Wages of Destruction: The Making and Breaking of the Nazi Economy* (London: Allen Lane, 2006); for a comparison of Soviet and German models, see Peter Temin, 'Soviet and Nazi Economic Planning in the 1930s', *Economic History Review*, 44:4, 1991, 573–593.

[39]Early studies that explored this issue are Michael Marrus, 'Vichy avant Vichy', *Histoire*, no. 3, November 1979, 72–92; and Loubet del Bayle, *Les non-conformistes des années 30* (Paris: Seuil, 1969).

[40]Jean-François Biard, *Le Socialisme devant ses choix: La naissance de l'idée de plan* (Paris: Publications de la Sorbonne, 1985).

Given these continuities, some scholars have concluded that these men implemented a long-fermenting programme developed over the 1930s when they rose to positions of power in Vichy.

In his wide-ranging study, Philip Nord traces continuities in a number of fields through the 'transwar' period from the 1930s to the 1950s.[41] On the economic side, Nord focuses on medium- and long-term economic planning, advocated by some non-conformist writers in the 1930s and later developed under Vichy. It must be noted, however, that such forward-looking planning emerged in Vichy only in 1941 (with the first plan appearing in 1942), well after the New Industrial Order had been established.[42] Moreover, these plans were intended for the post-war period and were therefore never implemented by Vichy. Similarly, Jackie Clarke argues that the creation of the Organisation Committees 'reflected the demand for an organized economy that had grown among a section of France's elite in the interwar years', observing that a speech given by Jean Bichelonne in 1943 'echoed the language that had already been used at Redressement français in the late 1920s'.[43] Claire Andrieu also argues that ideas set out in interwar non-conformist publications, particularly those of Pierre Laroque, decisively shaped the law of 16 August 1940. For Andrieu, 'the ideal of a constantly negotiated social peace' as described by Laroque in 1938 'was at the doctrinal foundation of the Organisation Committees'.[44] This explanation of the origins of the Committees rests on the history of ideas, arguing that interwar debates determined the decisions made in Vichy in 1940.

Interestingly, in his memoirs, René Belin comments on the non-conformist writings of the 1930s. Despite having found them intriguing – and indeed,

[41] Philip Nord, *France's New Deal* (Princeton: Princeton University Press, 2010).

[42] See Philippe Mioche, *Le Plan Monnet* (Paris: Publications de la Sorbonne, 1987) and Richard Kuisel, *Capitalism and the State in Modern France* (Cambridge: Cambridge University Press, 1981).

[43] Jackie Clarke, *France in the Age of Organization* (Oxford: Berghahn, 2011), 133. Jean Bichelonne was Minister for Industrial Production by this time. *Redressement français* was a think tank made up of industrialists that advocated economic rationalisation in the interwar period.

[44] Claire Andrieu, *La Banque sous l'occupation. Paradoxes de l'histoire d'une profession* (Paris: FNSP, 1990), 135. Laroque sets out this ideal in *Les rapports entre patrons et ouvriers* (Paris: Aubier, 1938).

having written some himself[45] – he lamented that the usefulness of these articles was tremendously limited: 'beyond vague principles, nothing concrete, no method, not a shadow of a technique ... Nothing of what had been said or written in France on the matter was useable in the situation in which France found itself [in the summer of 1940]'.[46] Moreover, the preamble of the law of 16 August 1940 explicitly dismisses 'the formulae of "industrial democracy" often advocated in recent years. [To adopt such ideas] would be to misunderstand the particularly imperious necessities of the moment'.[47] This suggests that the economic ideas developed by French intellectuals in the 1930s did not themselves determine the reforms made to French industry in 1940. It would seem that the conditions of the summer of 1940 demanded not the application of idealistic plans from the 1930s, but instead pragmatic action based on the circumstances at hand.

The truth of the matter lies somewhere between the tidy continuities from the interwar years to Vichy, on the one hand, and the lack of any influence of these ideas claimed by Belin, on the other hand. It is undeniable that the particular context of the summer of 1940 determined the shape of the Organisation Committees to a significant degree. Yet it is also difficult to claim that the views held by the architects of this New Industrial Order were immaterial. Indeed, Belin and his collaborators, Jacques Barnaud, Jean Bichelonne, and Pierre Laroque, had all contributed to non-conformist journals in the 1930s and shared a common, if woolly, notion of how to reform the French economy and society. Central to many of these non-conformist writings was a pseudo-corporatist model based on class cooperation, particularly after the tumultuous clashes between workers and employers demonstrated during the government of the Popular Front elected in 1936.[48] While these ideas provided them with a general notion of how the economy might be organised, the fact

[45]See, for example, 'La compréhension ouvrière sera acquise aux nécessités de l'Exposition', *Syndicats*, 25 February 1937, and reprinted in *Nouveaux cahiers*, 15 March 1937. A large number of Belin's pre-war writings on industrial relations can also be consulted at the Fonds Belin, IHS.

[46]René Belin, *Du Secrétariat du C.G.T. au Gouvernement de Vichy (Mémoires 1933–1942)* (Paris: Albatros, 1978), 146.

[47]*Journal officiel*, 18 August 1940.

[48]Julian Jackson, *The Popular Front in France: Defending Democracy, 1934–1938* (Cambridge: Cambridge University Press, 1988).

remains that these interwar intellectual exercises did not constitute a practical blueprint for constructing new institutions in the urgent and completely unforeseen conditions of 1940.

A second explanation of the New Industrial Order's origins attributes the economic decisions to the logic of the National Revolution articulated by Pétain.[49] The official ideology of the Vichy regime, the National Revolution held that France had grown decadent and weak under the Third Republic and had therefore been unable to defend itself against the Nazi threat. France needed a spiritual rejuvenation, a return to the fundamental values on which French greatness had always been based. The Republican motto of *Liberté, Egalité, Fraternité* was accordingly replaced by that of the National Revolution: *Travail, Famille, Patrie*.[50] As part of this vision to renew France, Pétain outlined the characteristics of the economic policy that should guide the nation: 'Faced with the failure of economic liberalism, nearly all peoples have embarked on the path of a new economy. We must engage in this and, through our energy and our faith, make up for lost time.' France's renewal depended on the national economy being organised and controlled by the State, thereby quashing the selfishness inherent in liberalism by subordinating all economic activity to national interests.[51] It is not difficult to recognise this anti-capitalist and statist spirit in the law of 16 August 1940, in which the State did indeed seize control of the economy and reorganise national industry. But it would be a mistake to argue that ideology preceded economic considerations in the summer of 1940. The quotation above is from Pétain's speech of 10 October 1940, and it is on this occasion that the notion of the National Revolution was first introduced to the French public – two months after the law of 16 August established the Organisation Committees. It was only after the law of 10 September, which established the Central Bureau and

[49]See, for example, Henry Rousso, 'L'organisation industrielle de Vichy' in *Vichy. L'événement, la mémoire, l'histoire* (Paris: Gallimard, 1992), 79–109; Henry Michel, *Vichy Année 40* (Paris: Robert Lafont, 1966), 118–137; Jacques Chapsal, *La vie politique en France de 1940 à 1958* (Paris: Presses universitaires de France, 1984), 65–66.

[50]On the National Revolution, see Limore Yagil, *'L'Homme nouveau' et la Révolution nationale de Vichy, 1940–1944* (Paris: Septentrion, 1997) and Debbie Lackerstein, *National Regeneration in Vichy France. Ideas and Policies, 1930–1944* (Farnham: Ashgate, 2012).

[51]Philippe Pétain, 'Discours du 10 octobre 1940' in *Discours aux Français* (Paris: Albin Michel, 1989), 92–93.

completed the new bureaucratic structures of French industry, was already in place that Pétain made any remarks about the organisation of the French economy in any of his speeches.[52] Barely a month after Pétain had received full powers as Head of State, any ideas on economic policy aside from a rejection of the liberalism associated with the Third Republic remained ill-defined.[53] In August 1941, Pétain would call for the reform of the Organisation Committees to bring them in line with the National Revolution, which would hardly have been necessary had they been moulded by the ideology in the first place.[54] While the National Revolution did influence later economic policy, and indeed played a decisive role in projects such as the Labour Charter, there is no evidence to suggest that it decisively influenced the measures taken over the summer of 1940.

The confusion surrounding Vichy's industrial policy and the National Revolution has been exacerbated by the association of the two retrospectively, which can even be found in government documents in Vichy. In his summary report for Pétain prepared three months after the law of 16 August – and one month after the first public announcement of the National Revolution by Pétain – René Belin applies a veneer of National Revolution rhetoric to his account of the creation of the New Industrial Order:

> In your speech, you definitively condemned an economic system in which, because of the game played by trusts, not necessarily French interests created and stifled work. It was therefore impossible to allow such a regime, which perpetuated a situation so injurious to the material and moral interests of the nation, to be restored. It was necessary to organise production, to frame it in legal and moral discipline, in which the dignity of France and French workers experience the eminent reverence that they deserve. Such was the purpose of the law of 16 August…[55]

[52]Ibid.

[53]It is telling that the most extensive study of the National Revolution attributes the creation of the Organisation Committees to immediate pragmatic considerations and not to the regime's nebulous ideology. See Yagil, *'L'Homme nouveau' et la Révolution nationale de Vichy, 1940–1944*, 213–214.

[54]See Philippe Pétain, 'Message du 12 août 1941' in *Discours aux français* (Paris: Albin Michel, 1989), 167.

[55]'Rapport sur l'activité du Ministère de la Production Industrielle et du Travail du 15 juillet au 15 novembre 1940', 17 November 1940, F 12 10157, AN.

In this report, Belin implies that the creation of the Organisation Committees was in reaction to the address of Pétain on the National Revolution, which in fact took place two months later.[56] This deceptive rethinking, which took place even in confidential documents mere weeks after these events occurred, may explain at least in part why some historians continue to view the laws of the summer of 1940 through the lens of the National Revolution first outlined that autumn.[57] In his memoirs, published 34 years after the end of the Vichy regime, Belin bluntly dismisses the National Revolution as 'nothing more than a formula, a slogan, maybe a myth . . . an invention of a quadroon of intellectuals who haunted Vichy's corridors'.[58] It should be noted that he makes no mention of having framed reports for Pétain in the ideological context of this 'invention', but it does seem to be the case that Vichy's nascent ideological project had very limited influence on the regime's earliest industrial legislation.

The third explanation may be called the 'patriotic narrative', as it emphasises the distinctions between the French and German model by contending that the New Industrial Order was created by the French government in Vichy in reaction to German actions and against the wishes of the German authorities. This account is especially prevalent in the literature and is clearly favoured by the actors who created the Organisation Committees, given the obvious appeal of distancing the creation of the Committees from the collaboration with which the offices were associated during the war.[59] René Belin claimed that the law of 16

[56]Belin's statement regarding trusts is a clear reference to Pétain's speech of 10 October: 'The day when coalitions and trusts broke this essential mechanism [free competition], production and prices were left defenceless before the spirit of profit and speculation . . . The coordination of private activities by the State must destroy the strength of trusts and their power of corruption.' See Pétain, 'Discours du 10 octobre 1940' in *Discours aux Français*, 92.

[57]Henry Rousso cites a speech from 1942 that claimed that 'the Organisation Committees form an integral part of this [National] Revolution' as proof of this argument, but the speech he quotes is similarly affected by the retrospection that is clear in Belin's writings from December 1940. See Henry Rousso, 'L'organisation industrielle de Vichy', op.cit., 80.

[58]Belin, *Du Secrétariat du C.G.T. au Gouvernement de Vichy (Mémoires 1933–1942)*, 184.

[59]See Belin, *Du Secrétariat du C.G.T. au Gouvernement de Vichy (Mémoires 1933–1942)*; Pierre Laroque's post-war interviews with historians have done much to entrench the narrative of 'the patriotic inspiration of the Organisation Committees'. See Andrieu, *La*

August 'provoked rage among the Germans, undoubtedly since it pulled the rug out from under their feet'.[60] This narrative is maintained by Arne Radtke-Delacor, who argues that the legislation 'led to a vehement reaction' from the 'furious' German authorities: they imposed a new requirement that all legislation affecting the Occupied Zone be submitted in draft form for German approval beforehand. This, it is argued, was in direct response to the law of 16 August; Belin's assertion of French sovereignty in the face of the occupiers thus 'came at a very high cost'.[61]

This account of the German authority's 'rage' at the creation of the Organisation Committees, however, is not supported by the archival evidence.[62] To the extent that the German Military Administration might have been upset at all, it was principally because, from its perspective, the French government had not followed protocol, namely by failing to submit the draft of the law to Dr Michel for approval prior to its promulgation. Indeed, the requirement that Vichy submit all draft legislation affecting the economy of the Occupied Zone, formally imposed by the Germans after 16 August, was merely a refinement of an earlier German order from 20 July, which stipulated that 'all economic decisions made by the Delegation or its collaborators be submitted to [Dr Michel] for approval'.[63] The supposedly angry reprisal of the German authorities, after having been outdone by the audacious law of 16 August, was in fact merely a clarification that the French government in Vichy should be counted among the collaborators of the French Delegation in Paris, at least when passing legislation affecting the economy of the Occupied Zone, and therefore subject to the order of 20 July. Belin's ex-post facto attempt to assign a patriotic gloss to his actions in 1940 must therefore be treated with some scepticism.

Banque sous l'Occupation, 131 and Michel Margairaz, *L'Etat, les finances et l'économie. Histoire d'une conversion 1932–1952* (Paris: CHEFF, 1989), 513–514.

[60]Belin, *Du Secrétariat du C.G.T. au Gouvernement de Vichy (Mémoires 1933–1942)*, 150.

[61]Arne Radtke-Delacor, 'La position des comités d'organisation face aux autorités d'occupation: la pomme de discorde des commandes allemandes en 1940–1941' in Hervé Joly (ed.), *Les Comités d'organisation et l'économie dirigée du régime de Vichy* (Caen: Centre de recherche d'histoire quantitative, 2004), 63–72.

[62]Radtke-Delacor does not provide any archival evidence to support the claim that any German officials were angered by the law, other than the fact that they put the new requirement in place. This author's research, particularly in the archives German Military Administration, similarly found no evidence of such a negative reaction among the German authorities.

[63]'Résumé des indications données par le Major Burandt', 20 July 1940, F 60 1539, AN.

At the opposite pole, the fourth and final explanation is that the model for organising French industry was basically the German model, transposed to France. Indeed, upon the Liberation of France the Provisional Government of the French Republic denounced Vichy's industrial order as having been 'imported on the backs of invading tanks'.[64] Françoise Berger has argued that Vichy 'establish[ed] a structure consistent with the German system', which she specifies 'cannot have been a coincidence'.[65] This view was also advanced by François Lehideux, Belin's successor as Minister for Industrial Production, who admitted that the French Committees' 'technical methods were the same' as those of the German *Wirtschaftsgruppen*, and that the French model was patterned on the Reich's 'without any great imagination'.[66] Indeed, the industry-specific *Wirtschaftsgruppen* that operated under the Reich's Economic Chamber (*Reichswirtschaftskammer*) were strikingly similar to the institutions developed under Vichy following the Fall of France. Recent studies of the Nazi economic and industrial systems have cast light on the differences between the Organisation Committees and the *Wirtschaftsgruppen*, however, as the French version was much more statist, allowing more direct control over industrial production by the government than was the case in Germany.[67] Yet the similarities between the Reich's established model and the system of Organisation Committees put together in 1940 are striking and not accidental. While the German system was not imposed unaltered upon France, the French authorities did model their own institutions upon Germany's, not least because these seemed to be worthy of emulation following the Reich's decisive victory over the Third Republic. The Organisation Committees were indeed created by French actors – rather than being imposed by the German authorities – but they were clearly inspired by the Reich's economic model and looked to adapt it to the particular circumstances of French industry in 1940.

[64] *Journal officiel*, October 1944. By this time the official publication of the French government was issued by the Provisional Government.

[65] Françoise Berger, *La France, l'Allemagne et l'acier (1932–1952). De la stratégie des cartels à l'élaboration de la CECA* (Paris: Université de Paris I, 2000), 447.

[66] Qtd. in Yagil, *'L'Homme nouveau' et la Révolution nationale de Vichy, 1940–1944*, 221.

[67] On industrial organisation in Nazi Germany, see Johannes Bähr and Ralf Banken (eds), *Das Europa des Dritten Reichs. Recht, Wirtschaft, Besatzung* (Frankfurt: Klostermann, 2005); Daniela Kahn, *Die Steuerung der Wirtschaft durch Recht im nazionalsozialistischen Deutschland. Das Beispiel der Reichsgruppe Industrie* (Frankfurt: Klostermann, 2006); and Avraham Barkaï, *Das Wirtschaftssystem des Nationalsozialismus* (Frankfurt: Fischer, 1988).

There is nevertheless some merit to all of these explanations, and they are by no means mutually exclusive. Indeed, it is likely that Belin and his associates were concurrently motivated by their pre-war beliefs, by a desire to protect French industry, and by an admiration of the German model. Critically, what all four narratives of the establishment of the New Industrial Order have in common is that they take 16 August 1940 as the starting point. Formally, of course, this is faultless – it was indeed this law that established the Organisation Committees. The law, by all accounts, was drafted hurriedly and was largely improvised. Moreover, it is agreed that René Belin, as Minister for Industrial Production, was the author of the law and the originator of its content. This is in no small part confirmed by Belin himself, who later wrote that 'the *ligne générale* of the law of the 16th of August was mine and mine alone'.[68] Consequently, historians have tended to focus on the Ministry for Industrial Production, on Belin, and on the law of 16 August as the source of the Organisation Committees and the consequent reordering of French industry. A thorough analysis of the archival documents available, however, reveals a significantly different narrative. The first proposal for organising French industry according to branch into committees was made on 15 July, the day after Belin was appointed to Vichy's Cabinet, and a full month before the passing of the law that he claimed was entirely his own idea. In order to gain a better understanding of the motivations and influences behind the creation of Vichy's New Industrial Order, it is therefore necessary to examine the developments in the month preceding the 16 August 1940.

Building the New Industrial Order, July-August 1940

As we have seen, by June the German occupation authorities were approaching French factories individually and forcing them to produce materials for the German military, lest they be evicted from their factories. In an attempt to overcome this dilemma, a proposal was made by General Charles Huntziger, the head of the French delegation at the Armistice Commission;[69] in a letter to Pétain dated 15 July, he suggested the creation of an intermediary body attached to the French government.

[68]Belin, *Du Secrétariat du C.G.T. au Gouvernement de Vichy (Mémoires 1933–1942)*, 149.

[69]The Armistice Commission, based in Wiesbaden, was established to oversee the application of the Franco-German Armistice and to resolve any disputes over the interpretation and application of the text.

'This organism would receive the German government's orders and distribute them among the French manufacturers, making no distinction between the Occupied and Non-Occupied Zones.'[70] Huntziger foresaw that this body would have jurisdiction over all armaments production, whether destined for the Wehrmacht, the Luftwaffe, or the Kriegsmarine. Already we can identify the *ligne générale* of the Organisation Committees: the creation of a state-controlled organism that would be placed between the German occupation authorities and French industrialists, distributing orders from the former to the latter. It is also crucial to recognise that Huntziger foresaw that the system would apply equally to both zones. Until this point, the German authorities had not attempted to have factories in the Non-Occupied Zone complete orders for the Reich. Combining both zones for the purposes of industrial production proved to be a double-edged sword: while it gave the French government in Vichy control over industry in the Occupied Zone and improved industrial production by relaxing the demarcation line, it also allowed the German authorities to exert far more influence over the southern zone than had previously been the case.

On the very day that General Huntziger was sketching out the earliest description of the Organisation Committees, the French government in Vichy announced that it had named its new Minister for Industrial Production: René Belin.[71] While Belin was settling into his first days of political office, exchanges between the French authorities and their German counterparts continued. On 21 July, six days after Huntziger's proposal, Léon Noël, Vichy's *délégué general en zone occupée* and head of the French Delegation in Paris, sent a letter to Dr Elmar Michel, head of the Economic Section of the German Military Administration of France, noting that both German and French governments had agreed that their objective was to revive France's economy and to 'ensure good use of production capacities in France'. To this end, Noël stated that 'each industry will form an office that will have contact with the German Economic Delegation' in Paris.[72] This marks the first mention of industry-specific offices created to deal directly with the German

[70]'Lettre de Huntzinger' [*sic*], 15 July 1940, F 60 1539, AN.

[71]Belin was made Minister for Industrial Production and for Labour on 14 July, and the appointment was announced the following day. See Belin, *Du Secrétariat du C.G.T. au Gouvernement de Vichy (Mémoires 1933–1942)*, 125.

[72]'Lettre à Dr Michel', 21 July 1940, F 60 1539, AN.

authorities of behalf of French industrialists, a defining feature of the Organisation Committees. The next day, the French Delegation in Paris spelt out this design in more detail, outlining a proposal for the creation of a 'Liaison Office' that would represent the French chemical industry to the German authorities. The document specifies that this office 'should be in touch with the Liaison Offices of other industries, thereby forming the base of a collective organisation that would permit the eventual creation of a sort of central exchange commission that would ensure financing and facilitate Franco-German compensation'.[73] By 22 July, then, a network of interrelated offices representing different branches of French industry to the German authorities had been delineated by the French authorities in Paris. Noël resigned from his position in August 1940 and later joined the Resistance, but not before making an enduring contribution to Vichy's industrial organisation.[74]

This plan was directly incorporated into the report prepared by Jacques Barnaud, René Belin's *directeur de cabinet*, and presented to the Cabinet in Vichy on 24 July.[75] Since the ministries' civil service was based in Paris, while ministers remained in Vichy, Barnaud shuttled back and forth between the two cities. Assigned to compile a report on the status of French industry in the Occupied Zone, Barnaud painted a bleak picture emphasising the many attempts of the German authorities to seize control over French industry. While his report provided a valuable synthesis of the situation in the Occupied Zone, the most noteworthy section of the report was its recommendation:

> A single solution to this agonising situation seems to present itself. In the face of German organisation, we must set up strong [French] organisation. This cannot exist without the grouping together of different economic activities in obligatory and disciplined professional organisations. These organisations must designate

[73]'Proposition de bureau de contact pour les industries chimiques', 23 July 1940, F 60 1539, AN.

[74]A successful diplomat and a keen supporter of de Gaulle, Noël would later become the first President of the *Conseil constitutionnel* of the Fifth Republic. See Yves Beauvois, *Léon Noël: de Laval à de Gaulle via Pétain (1888–1987)* (Villeneuve-d'Ascq: Presses universitaires du Septentrion, 2001).

[75]Jacques Barnaud was Belin's *directeur de cabinet* as Minister for Labour, but Barnaud worked extensively on projects under the Ministry for Industrial Production, as Belin held both portfolios until February 1941.

> responsible representatives for each branch of activity whose duty it will be to negotiate alone with the German economic authorities. Nevertheless, these representatives will take direction from qualified French authorities beforehand and will remain in contact with them ...[76]

This constitutes the first recorded mention of such an organisation in Vichy. Although he does not identify the origins of the proposal, we do know that Barnaud met with Charles Célier, Noël's deputy, at the French Delegation in Paris on 22 July and he left that meeting with a copy of the Delegation's plans for industrial reorganisation.[77] In his report, Barnaud presented the Cabinet of the French government with a distillation of what the French authorities in Paris and Wiesbaden had been steadily developing over the previous nine days. Nevertheless, it would take three more weeks for Belin to present to the Cabinet the draft of the law that would create the Organisation Committees.[78] In the meantime, the actions taken in Paris would continue to outpace those of the Ministry for Industrial Production in Vichy.

On 26 July, the French Delegation wrote a letter to Dr Michel, informing him that the plans to organise the French chemical industry were now a *fait accompli*. They asked that the German authorities cease to deal directly with individual French industrialists, and instead deal only with the 'Professional Office' created for the chemical industry.[79] That same day, letters were written to French industrialists instructing them to reply to any German orders by explaining that the German authorities must instead address themselves to the relevant Professional Offices.[80] The implementation of effective bodies that would coordinate German orders within different branches of industry had begun.

[76]'Rapport de M. Barnaud', 24 July 1940, Papiers 1940, Papiers Baudouin, MAE.

[77]'Lettre à M. Barnaud', 23 July 1940, F 60 1539, AN.

[78]According to Baudouin, Belin presented the text of the law to the Cabinet on 14 August, two days before it was signed into law by Pétain. Baudouin, *The Private Diaries of Paul Baudouin*, 202.

[79]'Note à Michel', 26 July 1940, F 60 1539, AN. It is worth noting that at this stage the terms Liaison Office and Professional Office were used interchangeably (sometimes within the same document) to refer to the new offices. Curiously, the Organisation Committees would formally revert to the name Professional Offices in 1945, in an attempt to dissociate the institutions from Vichy.

[80]Lettre de Charles Célier, 26 July 1940, F 60 1539, AN.

By the end of July, the French authorities in Paris had succeeded in reorganising French industry in the Occupied Zone. Certainly, the system that existed at the end of July and the one that would exist a month later, after the law of 16 August, had a number of important differences. Most obviously, the Liaison Offices existed only in the Occupied Zone, despite having been initially envisaged for both zones by General Huntziger. Institutionally, the Liaison Offices existed within the existing employers' associations, which made it possible for them to be set up in such a short period of time. The law of 16 August, however, moved the Offices outside of these employers' associations – and soon dissolved several employers' associations. The text of the law put the Organisation Committees firmly under state control and indicated that they would ultimately include labour representation, with less domination by industrial interests. In practice, however, the Organisation Committees would be stacked with representatives of large firms and labour representation was minimal.[81] The Committees were also to be more statist than the Liaison Offices, which received direction from, without being controlled by, the government. Despite these differences, it is clear that the Liaison Offices that emerged in July 1940 constitute the foundation of the Organisation Committees associated with the law of 16 August.

Having examined the evolution towards Organisation Committees that was taking place in the Occupied Zone, it is worthwhile comparing this with the actions of the Ministry for Industrial Production in Vichy in early August. While industry in the Occupied Zone had already been reorganised by this time, René Belin's concerns seem to have been strikingly different. In a report he prepared for Pétain dated 7 August, the minister reveals himself to be perceptibly out of step with the developments made in the Occupied Zone. Much of Belin's report is simply a repackaging of the descriptions of industry in the northern zone provided by Barnaud in his report two weeks earlier, along with a lengthy section on social conditions in the Occupied Zone. His assessment of the Occupied Zone suggests that he was not even aware of the system that had already been put in place nearly a fortnight earlier. He notes that the German authorities had entered into contact with French industrialists in an effort to 'control the economy of the Occupied Zone', but he never mentions any of the measures already taken by the French Delegation in Paris. Moreover, his

[81]'Observations sur le Rapport Belin', 1 December 1940, F 12 10157, AN.

recommendations for Pétain are of strikingly little substance: 'It is indispensable that the government return to Paris and reach political and economic agreements with the occupying power. These two objectives are undoubtedly demanded by the current conditions [in the Occupied Zone]'. To this he adds a short paean to Pétain, whom he urges to 'examine these problems and take the decisions without which the moral and political unity of France will be broken for the foreseeable future'.[82] His recommendations are not only vague but also unoriginal: the French government had been trying to return to Paris since the beginning of July, and was waiting for the German authorities to authorise the relocation. Meanwhile, his suggestion that the government reach 'political and economic agreements', without specifying what these might contain, is similarly ineffective. It is remarkable that only one week before Belin presented the text of the law that would reorganise French industry, the Minister seemed to be ill-informed and without vision.

The turning point in Belin's thinking was a two-day meeting he convened to discuss the situation of French industry. On 9 and 10 August, Belin was joined by Jacques Barnaud, Yves Bouthillier, the Minister for Finance and the Economy, and a small handful of other members of Belin's ministry, including Jean Bichelonne, to produce a solution to the problems being faced in the Occupied Zone.[83] While no records of that meeting exist, we can surmise what took place. Given Barnaud's recommendation to the Cabinet for the creation of Liaison Offices more than two weeks earlier, it is most likely that the idea to establish Organisation Committees was his, derived from his experience in the Occupied Zone. He had been in close contact with the French authorities in Paris since the signing of the Armistice and was keenly aware of the situation in the Occupied Zone and what measures had been implemented. Considering the weaknesses of the report completed by Belin only two days before this meeting, and the conspicuous absence of any plausible solutions to the situation in that report, it is indeed improbable that the idea of creating Organisation Committees was, as he later claimed, his and his alone. Rather more plausible is that Belin, who had been the last minister

[82]'Lettre à Pétain' de Belin, 7 August 1940, Guerre 1939–1945, Economie française interne, MAE.

[83]Belin, *Du Secrétariat du C.G.T. au Gouvernement de Vichy (Mémoires 1933–1942)*, 149.

appointed to the Cabinet and had never held political office, was still learning the ropes less than a month after his arrival. In this context, it is logical that the new minister allowed himself to be influenced by his *directeur de cabinet*, Jacques Barnaud.

While Belin may not have been the originator of the idea, he did influence the final shape of the Organisation Committees. Although his report from 7 August may have revealed the absence of any kind of meaningful industrial reorganisation on his part, it also demonstrated the degree to which social conditions mattered to him. Having spent his career working in trade unions, and simultaneously holding the Labour portfolio in Vichy's government, Belin clearly gave more consideration to the plight of working people than did any other member of the Cabinet. This preoccupation is detectable in the text of the law of 16 August, particularly when juxtaposed with the descriptions of the system of Liaison Offices. While the latter focused on creating a buffer between the German authorities and French employers, the law of 16 August sought to involve workers as well, essentially merging employers' associations with trade unions and arranging them according to branches of industry. This addition certainly bears echoes of the non-conformist writings of the 1930s, but it is important to note that this element was added on to the existing Liaison Offices. These elements were absent from both the system established in the Occupied Zone and the recommendations made by Barnaud to the Cabinet in Vichy on 24 July, in which the Liaison Offices were simply housed in the relevant employers' associations. While Barnaud may have initiated the reorganisation of French industry, it was likely the Minister for Industrial Production who sought to involve labour in the new structure.

A Franco-German Europe?

The law of 16 August did not spring fully formed from René Belin's forehead, but was instead the culmination of a series of measures taken to resist German pressures in the Occupied Zone virtually as soon as the ink on the Armistice was dry. Given how the law of 16 August would appear to derail Nazi plans to occupy or intimidate individual firms, it seems remarkable that they did not simply overrule the law by one means or another. By tracing the origins of the Organisation Committees to July rather than mid-August, however, it becomes clear that the German authorities had been fully informed of the establishment of the Liaison Offices and cooperated with this new regime. The reason for their willingness to work with such a system is explained by the fact that they had their eyes on a far more ambitious prize than the mere occupation of isolated factories in northern France.

At a meeting at the quarters of the French Delegation in Paris on 20 July, Major Burandt of the German Military Administration explained to his French interlocutors that, with Germany still at war against Great Britain, industrial production in Germany and in Occupied France alike had to be mobilised to this end. He stated his vision of comprehensive industrial planning in the Occupied Zone, including the distribution of raw materials in France by Germany.[84] To this end, French industry should be rationally organised. By the first week of August, Célier wrote to Dr Michel to follow up on a letter sent on 26 July stating that the Liaison Office had been established for the French chemical industry: 'I can confirm that the French government desires that relations between French industry and the German authorities be centralised, for each industry, by a Liaison Office . . . This will facilitate the establishment of a common plan to make full use of French and German means of production and to distribute raw materials.'[85] This shows that, for the French Delegation, the reorganisation of French industry was not simply to protect factories from German takeovers, but crucially to facilitate Franco-German collaboration.

Barnaud was well aware of this reasoning. At a meeting on 3 August, Dr Michel stated that he wished 'to establish a Franco-German economic collaboration, notably through the establishment of a common plan for production and distribution corresponding to the needs of both countries and by a certain pooling of raw materials.'[86] At a meeting of representatives from the French and German textile industries, at which Barnaud was present, the Germans proposed 'conducting a census of the entirety of stocks and means of production existing in both zones, in order to establish a Franco-German production programme and, eventually, a distribution of raw materials that would permit German and French factories to work at the same rhythm.'[87] At the meeting, it was also recognised that the organisation of French industrialists into Professional Offices (or

[84]'Résumé des indications données par le Major Burandt', 20 July 1940, F 60 1539, AN. This last dimension anticipates OCRPI, which would be *de facto* controlled by the Germans and would be responsible for the allocation of raw materials to French industry.

[85]Lettre de Célier, 5 August 1940, F 60 1539, AN.

[86]'Questions économiques', 3 August 1940, F 60 1539, AN.

[87]Ibid.

Liaison Offices) had already been a success, and that both sides were dealing with the Offices increasingly.[88] August began with French and German governments and their officials in agreement to construct a harmonised Franco-German production system, founded largely on the Professional Offices that preceded the Organisation Committees.

On 8 August, the day before the meeting at which the law of 16 August was developed in Vichy, another meeting between the French and German economic delegations confirmed the willingness of both sides to embrace collaboration. Responding to the French strides in industrial reorganisation, the German authorities 'accept[ed] in principle collaboration between the French administration authorities, the responsible organisms and their own services for the preparation of an organisational plan applicable to the diverse branches of the French economy.' They also confirmed that as soon as this plan was established, the practice of requisitions would cease. Most importantly, it was agreed that 'the Professional Offices will study under the authority of the Ministry for Industrial Production the stocks and production capacity of firms as well as the needs of the French economy'.[89] This constitutes the mission statement of the Organisation Committees, a week before their creation. While not all of the aspects discussed had yet been implemented, French and German authorities in Paris had agreed to virtually all the elements of the creation of Organisation Committees, right down to the role of Belin's ministry. Barnaud attended this meeting on 8 August before returning to Vichy to meet with Belin for two days, during which they developed the text of the law of 16 August. This discussion of 8 August shows that the German authorities did not see the organisation of French industry into branches as a threat to German interests, as some have claimed,[90] but rather as a constructive path towards a German-led European economy. The French authorities were relieved that the practice of requisitions in the Occupied Zone would end with the institution of this new system. While the Liaison Offices may have initially been conceived as a means to protect French factories, by the beginning of August they were increasingly guided by plans for economic collaboration with the Reich.

[88]Ibid.

[89]'Note sur la situation économique du 7 au 11 août', 12 August 1940, F 60 1539, AN.

[90]Radtke-Delacor, 'La position des comités d'organisation face aux autorités d'occupation: la pomme de discorde des commandes allemandes en 1940–1941'; Belin, *Du Secrétariat du C.G.T. au Gouvernement de Vichy (Mémoires 1933–1942)*.

This vision of an integrated European economic order was publicly outlined by Walther Funk, the German Minister for the Economy, in a speech made on 26 July. He declared that, once German victory had been achieved, the Reich would 'apply the economic methods that ha[d] brought it such great economic and military success' to France and the rest of Continental Europe. He claimed that 'National Socialist economic policy has never allowed itself to be governed by rigid dogma in its methods. We have always used whatever methods seemed most expedient at the time... In the same way the New Economic Order in Europe will grow out of the existing circumstances.'[91] Applied to the French case, this would mean that whatever provisional arrangements were enacted would serve as a foundation for the post-war order. Of course, this was not the European integration promoted by Briand and Laval a decade earlier.[92] Funk made it perfectly clear that the purpose of this New Economic Order was to serve German interests, and that countries such as France would serve as export outlets for German goods.[93] Nevertheless, it did offer an insight into what was in store for French industry. A German victory was not a distant prospect, but was understood to be imminent. The day after Funk's speech, a report was circulated in the French Foreign Ministry noting that Germany had already offered the terms of a negotiated peace to the British government, and was still awaiting a reply.[94] These terms demarcated clear German and British spheres of influence: Germany would control the European continent, Britain would maintain its Empire.[95] If the British were to reject the offer, Germany was ready to attack England 'as soon as weather permits'. The

[91]Walther Funk, 'The Economic Reorganization of Europe' in Walter Lipgens, *Documents on the History of European Integration. Volume 1: Continental Plans for European Union, 1939–1945*, (Berlin: Walter de Gruyter, 1984), 65–70, here 66.

[92]On Germany's economic plans for Europe during the war, the classic study remains Jacques Freymond, *Le IIIe Reich et la réorganisation économique de l'Europe, 1940–1942* (Paris: Leiden, 1974). For the 'European' ideology of the Nazis, see Julien Prévotaux, *Un européisme nazi. Le Groupe Collaboration et l'idéologie européenne dans la Seconde Guerre mondiale* (Paris: François-Xavier de Guibert, 2010) and, for French perceptions of German plans for European integration, Bernard Bruneteau, *'L'Europe Nouvelle' de Hitler, une illusion des intellectuels de Vichy* (Monaco, Du Rocher, 2003).

[93]Funk, 'The Economic Reorganization of Europe'.

[94]'Presse allemande du 26 juillet', 26 July 1940, Papiers 1940, Papiers Baudouin, MAE.

[95]'Copie d'un télégramme du 27 juillet de Havas New-York à Havas Clermont', 27 July 1940, Papiers 1940, Papiers Baudouin, MAE.

Nazis estimated that they would take control of Britain within 30 days of the initial attack.[96] While these estimates look utterly naïve in retrospect, the French had every reason to believe them at the time. On 10 May, the first day of the German attack, France believed that it was protected from Germany by the impenetrable Maginot Line; by 10 June, 30 days later, the French government declared Paris an open city, and the capital fell four days later. After such a decisive victory over France, Germany was seen by many as an invincible force; the choice for Britain seemed to be between a negotiated peace and certain defeat. In either event, German plans for a post-war European economic order were of pressing concern. Subsequent events – and significant opposition to such schemes among some senior Nazis – would ensure that Funk's plans never progressed beyond their theoretical stages, but in the summer of 1940 they were taken very seriously by the French authorities at precisely the time they were developing their new model of industrial organisation.[97]

The French authorities in Paris and the French government in Vichy were both very much aware of Funk's speech, and summaries of the speech were distributed to French officials.[98] Five days after Funk's speech, the French Delegation wrote to Dr Michel that 'the French government is ready to collaborate with the German government to organise a planned economy for Continental Europe'.[99] Shortly after the law of 16 August had been promulgated, Jacques Barnaud wrote to industrialists to explain that until the Organisation Committees were inaugurated, the Liaison Offices would continue to serve as the point of contact between French industry and the German authorities. He further specified that 'the negotiations taken by these Liaison Offices must fit into the framework of a Franco-German economy'.[100] This receptiveness of the French to Nazi

[96]Ibid.

[97]Many initiatives of Nazi ministers were scuppered by rival ministers vying for influence, and by the parallel structures of the German state and the Nazi Party. The classic articulation of this 'Nazi polycracy' is Martin Broszat, *Der Staat Hitlers: Grundlegung und Entwicklung seiner inneren Verfassung* (Munich: Deutscher Taschenbuch Verlag, 1969).

[98]'Discours de FUNCH' (sic), Papiers 1940, Papiers Baudouin, MAE

[99]'Note au sujet des relations financières et commerciales entre la France et ses colonies, d'une part, l'empire britannique, l'Egypte, les Colonies néerlandaises et belges, d'autre part', 31 July 1940, AJ 41 170, AN. The note was from either Noël or his deputy, Célier.

[100]'Note sur l'organisation industrielle', 30 August 1940, AS 40 20, ANMT.

plans for a united European economy led the German authorities to abandon the capricious requisitioning that had characterised the first weeks of the German presence in France, refocusing their energies on restoring the French economy so that it could better serve German interests.[101] General Huntziger, who had been the first to propose creating an entity to coordinate German orders made to French industry, argued that producing war *matériel* for the Reich was inevitable given German dominance, and that the government should at least negotiate concessions in exchange for supplying the German military.[102] While the Germans themselves had originally foreseen the production of component parts of war *matériel* rather than finished armaments in France, they certainly expected France to produce for the German war effort.[103] France's integration into a German-dominated Europe, stretching from the English Channel to the Soviet border, would deepen over the following years and its contributions to the German economy and war effort would be increasingly important. When the Wehrmacht invaded the Soviet Union in June 1941, it did so with tanks made of French steel.[104]

The German motivation for accepting the reorganisation of French industry along the lines of the law of 16 August was thus tied to Germany's desire to harness Europe's economy which could be mobilised towards German interests, including the war against Britain. German occupations of factories ceased and engagement with the Organisation Committees became standard procedure. A French government report noted that German 'intentions to control economic and industrial activity

[101]See Margairaz, *L'Etat, les finances et l'économie. Histoire d'une conversion 1932–1952*, 528–529. Different stages to Germany's economic priorities in France have been identified in the literature, transitioning from simple pillage immediately following the Fall of France to a more institutionalised form of collaboration. Cf. Alan Milward, *The New Order and the French Economy* (Oxford: Oxford University Press, 1970); Arne Radtke-Delacor, 'Produire pour le Reich. Les commandes allemandes à l'industrie française (1940–1944)' in *Vingtième siècle*, no. 70, avril-juin 2001, 99–115; Adam Tooze, *Wages of Destruction*, op.cit.

[102]'Note sur les commandes allemandes de matériel de guerre', 5 August 1940, AJ 41 529, AN.

[103]'Tätigkeitsbericht', 10 August 1940, RW 24/15, BA-MA. Throughout the war, the Reich preferred to have armaments produced on German rather than French territory, a preference that informed the Speer-Bichelonne accords of 1943.

[104]'Commandes allemandes de guerre en France. 25 juin 1940–23 mai 1941', AJ 41 529, AN.

in France is obvious. It appears, however, that whenever the Germans find themselves in the presence of efficient civil servants or industrialists, the Germans quite willingly respect their authority'.[105] As long as French industry served German interests, the German authorities were perfectly willing to allow the French to run their own factories. In other words, there was no need to set up *Wirtschaftsgruppen* in France, as Germany had done in Belgium.[106] The desire that French industry be coordinated and mobilised to German ends explains German acquiescence to the law of 16 August, despite the French transgression of not submitting the text of the law to the German authorities before promulgating it. Indeed, the Germans might also have objected to the decidedly statist character of the Organisation Committees, which distinguished these organisms from the Liaison Offices approved by the Germans a week earlier. While those offices were based in employers' associations, the law of 16 August allowed the Minister for Industrial Production to designate the composition of each Committee and gave the Ministry not only a representative on each committee, but also a veto on virtually all decisions. Yet this 'assertion of sovereignty'[107] on the part of the French government was hollow, since it constituted part of a broader policy of increasing integration into the Continental European economy under German hegemony. While the law was intended in part to safeguard French factories from being taken over directly by Germans, the law itself was entirely compatible with Germany's broader interests.

The reorganisation of French industry was completed with the law of 10 September. While the Organisation Committees dealt with industrial production, it was quickly realised that an initial distribution of raw materials to the various branches of industry had to be carried out before these allocations could in turn be redistributed by the relevant Organisation Committees. This would be the responsibility of the

[105] 'Note sur l'activité de la délégation économique', 12 July 1940, F 60 1539, AN. Underlined in the original document.

[106] 'Kriegestagebuch der Rüstungs-Inspektion Belgien', 31 May 1940, RW 25 1a, BA-MA. For Germany's economic strategy in the countries it had conquered in Europe, see Walter Naasner, *Neue Machtzentren in der deutschen Kriegswirtschaft* (Boppard am Rhein: H. Boldt, 1994); Götz Aly, *Hitlers Volksstaat: Raub, Rassenkrieg und nationaler Sozialismus* (Frankfurt: S. Fischer, 2005); Tooze, *Wages of Destruction*; and Mark Mazower, *Hitler's Empire: How the Nazis Ruled Europe* (New York: Penguin, 2008).

[107] Radtke-Delacor, 'La pomme de discorde . . . ', 65–66.

Central Bureau for the Distribution of Industrial Products (OCRPI), created by the law of 10 September. In his memoirs, Belin confesses that, in the haste in which the law of 16 August was written, he had not foreseen the shortcomings of the Organisation Committees and the need for the Central Bureau. 'In truth I must say that it was Dr Michel and his team, with their long experience with economic planning, that first indicated this flaw to me. The law of 10 September ... completed our purview of the planned economy.'[108] This attribution to Dr Michel is confirmed by the head of the economic section of German Military Administration himself in a report written at war's end. He claims that 'the French government quickly recognised the reasonableness of German demands and, on 10 September, the law for the regulation of raw materials was promulgated.' Michel adds that 'the Military Administration could provide the French government with practical lessons accumulated over several years in Germany.'[109] During the war, Michel had described the role of the Military Administration as the 'management of economic planning' being done by the French; while the Germans provided the French with 'guidance', he insisted that 'control of the French economy remains in the hands of the French State'.[110] Coming from the German authorities, the recommendation to create the Central Bureau was certainly not intended to buttress French assertions of sovereignty or to strengthen the French State. From their creation, each of the sections of OCRPI would include a representative of the German authorities. While the French government had secured tight control over the Organisation Committees, they themselves were dependent on the initial distribution of raw materials by the Central Bureau. Even though the Committees had been created with a view to deepen Franco-German economic collaboration, the increased German influence through the creation of OCRPI exerted further pressure on Vichy to contribute to the German-dominated 'European' economy.

[108]Belin, *Du Secrétariat du C.G.T. au Gouvernement de Vichy (Mémoires 1933–1942)*, 151.

[109]'Rapport final du Dr MICHEL sur l'Administration Militaire en France, 1940–1944', undated (1944), 72 AJ 262, AN.

[110]'Economie dirigée en France', *Berliner Börsen Zeitung*, 10 April 1942, 72 AJ 262, AN. Translated from German into French on 16 April 1942.

Conclusion

The paralysis of French industry following the Fall of France necessitated decisive state action. The French authorities in Paris led the way, setting up Liaison Offices within employers' associations in order to deal with the German authorities on behalf of industrialists. By tracing the development of these offices over the month prior to the law of 16 August, it emerges that collaborating with the Reich to construct a still ill-defined European economy was at the heart of these initiatives. Jacques Barnaud's insistence that 'in the face of German organisation, we must set up strong [French] organisation' reiterates that French officials were looking to the Reich for ideas of how to reorganise the nation's industry. This should hardly be surprising; the military defeat of the Third Republic had discredited its political and economic model, which prompted the Vichy regime to look elsewhere for inspiration. Given the stunning victories of the Wehrmacht across Europe in 1940 and the apparent strength of the German economy behind them, the industrial organisation of the Reich certainly seemed worthy of emulation. The French authorities thus adapted the model of the German *Wirtschaftsgruppen* to the French context, beginning with the Liaison Offices and culminating in the creation of the Organisation Committees and OCRPI. Indeed, given that the Liaison Offices were housed in the existing employers' associations, did not involve the inclusion of labour representation, and were less statist than the Organisation Committees as described in the 16 August law, the Liaison Offices were meticulous imitations of the Reich's institutions. Tellingly, practically every step of the construction of these offices was approved by the Germans well before 16 August, and Walther Funk's musings on an integrated European economy were eagerly taken up by the French government as it sought to secure France a favourable place in the post-war European order.

In this context, it is clear that the literature that describes the creation of the Committees as an audacious and patriotic stroke that reasserted French sovereignty while 'pulling the rug out from [Germany's] feet'[111] does not tell the whole story. Nevertheless, this patriotic narrative is important for pointing out that the motivations of the individuals who set up this New Industrial Order were not necessarily collaborationist. The

[111]Belin, *Du Secrétariat du C.G.T. au Gouvernement de Vichy (Mémoires 1933–1942)*, 150.

protection of French factories from German requisitions or outright occupation was an important motivation, and one that could indeed be described as patriotic. The example of Léon Noël, who instigated the creation of the first Liaison Committees mere weeks before resigning his position in Paris to join the French Resistance in London, is telling. The creation of bodies analogous to the German *Wirtschaftsgruppen*, with whom the German authorities would have to deal, seemed a promising means of defending French economic interests. For others, cooperating more closely with the Germans made sense for economic, practical, or even ideological reasons. Regardless of whether the personal motivations were patriotic or pro-German, however, the result was the same: the institutionalisation of economic collaboration with the Reich and the adaptation of Nazi institutions for French industry.

CHAPTER 3

Twixt the Cup and the Lip: Building the New Industrial Order, 1940–1941

By the end of the eventful summer of 1940, the judicial foundations of the New Industrial Order had been laid. The law of 16 August, based on the developments made in the Occupied Zone during the seven weeks following the Armistice, called for the creation of Organisation Committees that would take inventory of existing stocks and rationally organise production within each industry. The law also denoted that these new bodies would be tripartite, drawing their representatives from amongst employers, workers, and government officials. The law of 10 September created complementary bodies in the Central Bureau for the Distribution of Industrial Products (OCRPI) that would allocate primary materials to the Organisation Committees. These two laws had clearly set out the shape that French industry would take in a German-led Europe.

Despite the straightforward clauses contained in these laws, however, constructing these new institutions proved more difficult than it had been to describe them. Indeed, the law of 16 August built upon the existing Liaison Offices (also called Professional Offices) that had developed immediately following the German presence in France. The greatest innovation of the text itself was the addition of labour and the State to a realm that had hitherto been the reserve of employers.[1] The text of the law, which had been hammered out over a mere weekend in Vichy, took nearly three months to

[1] *Journal officiel*, 18 August 1940.

© The Author(s) 2017

L.-A. Brunet, *Forging Europe: Industrial Organisation in France, 1940–1952*, Security, Conflict and Cooperation in the Contemporary World, DOI 10.1057/978-1-349-95198-7_3

be applied to key industries such as steel and coal. In the meantime, Jacques Barnaud, the Chief of Staff of Minister for Industrial Production René Belin, instructed industrialists to continue using the provisional Liaison Offices until the new Organisation Committees had been consitituted.[2]

On 9 November 1940, the Organisation Committees for Steel and for Coal were inaugurated. Given the tripartite spirit of the law of 16 August, introduced under former trade unionist Belin, the most shocking aspect of the new organisations was the utter lack of labour representation. The Organisation Committee for Steel (CORSID) consisted of four industrialists, while the analogous Committee for Coal (COH) had three; neither included even a token representative from a trade union. This rapid loss of the tripartism enshrined in the text of the law of 16 August 1940 demands further explanation.

Industrial Organisation Under Vichy: acte révolutionnaire or pure façade?

The existing literature on the early stages of industrial reorganisation in Vichy France fails to provide a satisfactory explanation for the rapid fading of tripartism after 16 August 1940. Much of the scholarly debate remains focused on the degree to which 1940 marked a true turning point for French industry, or whether there was instead considerable continuity from the interwar period. Earlier accounts of Vichy tended to emphasise the rupture between the Third Republic and Vichy; this was in no small part nourished by documents that had flowed from the French and German authorities during the war, eager to distance the new regime from the liberal republic dominated by 'trusts', to use Vichy's favoured term for large corporations. Moreover, historians writing before the late 1970s did not have access to the relevant French archives, and the German archives on which many earlier analyses were based tended to emphasise the Fall of France as a breach in French industrial organisation.[3]

[2]'Note sur l'organisation industrielle', 30 August 1940, AS 40 20, ANMT.

[3]This is true of early 'orthodox' scholarship as well as 'revisionist' works from the 1970s. The best of the former include Robert Aron, *Histoire de Vichy* (Paris: Fayard, 1954) and Henry Michel, *Année 1940* (Paris: Robert Laffont, 1966). For the latter, see Robert Paxton, *Vichy France, Old Guard and New Order* (New York: Barrie and Jenkins, 1972) and Alan Milward, *The New Order and the French Economy* (Oxford: Oxford University Press, 1970).

The dissolution of the *Comité des forges*, the employers' association for steel, was singled out in the German press as an '*acte révolutionnaire*', and with its termination, 'new personalities have entered the scene, and the French [steel] industry is henceforth represented not by politicians, but by technicians'.[4] Maréchal Pétain similarly trumpeted the 'universal failure of the liberal economy' and the need for France to 'embark upon the path of a new economy',[5] which was to be achieved through Vichy's National Revolution.

The *Comité des forges* and the *Comité central des houillères de France*, the analogous grouping for the coal industry, were dissolved by decree on 9 November 1940. Both dating from the mid-nineteenth century, these two employers' associations were closely associated with the political power held by the French *grand patronat*; indeed, in addition to their influential lobbying, it was revealed in the interwar period that these two committees were in fact the managers of *Le Temps*, the leading newspaper of record of the Third Republic.[6] Along with the *Comité générale du patronat français* (CGPF), the confederation bringing together employers from across industries, the employers' associations for steel and coal were singled out for dissolution by Vichy.[7] Moreover, their respective leaders were excluded from the newly assembled Organisation Committees, a state of affairs that elicited bitterness towards the regime from the erstwhile leaders.[8] This purposeful targeting of these associations, and the exclusion of their leaders from the successor bodies, indeed suggest discontinuity from the Third Republic.

[4] *Deutsche Allgemeine Zeitung*, 2 November 1942 in 'Décret de fondation du Corsid', F 12 22340, AN.

[5] Philippe Pétain, 'Discours du 10 octobre 1940', *Discours aux Francais* (Paris: Albin Michel, 1989), 92.

[6] See Jean-Noël Jeanneney, *François de Wendel en République: l'argent et le pouvoir, 1914–1940* (Paris: Perrin, 2004).

[7] *Journal officiel*, 12 November 1940. The Organisation Committees for Coal and for Steel were created on the same day, but the law announcing their creation was published one day earlier.

[8] Richard Vinen, *The Politics of French Business, 1936–1945* (Cambridge: Cambridge University Press, 1991), 104–105. Both the President, François de Wendel, and the Delegate General, Lambert Ribot, of the *Comité des forges* were excluded from CORSID upon its creation, while the President of the *Comité central des houillères*, Henri de Peyerimhoff, was absent from the Organisation Committee for Coal.

The radical nature of the law of 16 August, the suppression of trade union confederations and employers' associations, and the introduction of a de jure tripartite industrial order would all suggest that the changes made in the summer of 1940 did indeed constitute a decisive break from the pre-war era. Yet Philippe Mioche, the most prolific historian of the French steel industry during the mid-twentieth century, argues that 'CORSID falls within the history of professional organisation' through 1940, and that 'the men, the debates, and the actions of CORSID continue those of the *Comité des forges*'.[9] He concludes that the institutional changes introduced in 1940 were merely superficial. Marxist historian Annie Lacroix-Riz agrees, asserting that the decree of 9 November amounted to a '*dissolution de pure façade*'.[10] These claims fit into a broader historiographical turn that has sought to highlight the pre-1940 origins of many aspects of Vichy's innovations, with a particular focus on intellectual history.[11]

While the German propagandist lauding of the dissolution of the *Comité des forges* as a revolutionary act can hardly be taken at face value, it is necessary to explore the argument that the *Comité des forges* underwent little more than a change of name in 1940. Given the decidedly radical content of the laws of 16 August and 10 September 1940, had these been implemented as originally articulated, the question of continuity could be answered rather easily. There was, however, a significant evolution between the proclamation of the laws of industrial organisation and the formation of the bodies foreseen in those laws, over the winter of 1940–1941. These developments, and the influences that caused them, reveal a more nuanced explanation.

[9]Philippe Mioche, 'Le comité d'organisation de la sidérurgie: un lieu d'affrontement entre modernisateurs de la sidérurgie et gardiens de la profession?' in Hervé Joly (ed.), *Les Comités d'organisation et l'économie dirigée du régime de Vichy* (Caen: Centre de recherche d'histoire quantitative, 2004), 95–108, here 95.

[10]Annie Lacroix-Riz, 'Les comités d'organisation et l'Allemagne: tentative d'évaluation' in Joly, *Les Comités d'organisation*, 60.

[11]Gérard Noiriel, *Les origines républicaines de Vichy* (Paris: Hachette, 1999); Philip Nord, *France's New Deal* (Princeton: Princeton University Press, 2010); Jackie Clarke, *France in the Age of Organization: Factory, Home and Nation from the 1920s to Vichy* (Oxford: Berghahn, 2011).

The Creation of CORSID: Stillborn Tripartism?

The law of 9 November 1940 formally created the Organisation Committee for Steel along the lines of the law of 16 August. Four members were named, all of them industrialists: Jules Aubrun, who was proclaimed president of the body, Eugène Roy, Léon Daum, and Jean Dupuis. This short decree, signed by Pétain and Belin, established one of the first Organisation Committees.[12] The law retained the strong statist element of the August law, specifying that the decision of which firms would come under the jurisdiction of CORSID would be made by the Minister for Industrial Production. It was therefore possible for firms only marginally involved in steel production to be subject to the Committee's decisions.[13] The new body would organise output for all firms involved in the production of all iron-based metals, not strictly limited to steel. The law gave CORSID legal personality and stipulated that professional confidentiality must by all means be maintained by the Committee.[14] The Organisation Committee for Coal was established the same day, with three members, all of whom were industrialists: Aimé Lepercq, Maxime Bucher, and Emile Marterer.

Also that same day, the pre-war employers' associations for these two industries, the *Comité central des houillères de France* and the *Comité des forges*, were abolished. Hardly ignoring labour, the Vichy regime also explicitly dissolved trade union confederations, particularly the CGT and the CFTC.[15] Given that employers' associations and trade unions were meant to be superseded by Organisation Committees that would represent both industrialists and labour, the list of members of the new Committees raised both eyebrows and objections. Within days, members of the defunct CGT and CFTC issued their famous *Manifeste des douze*, a declaration signed by a dozen trade unionists that openly criticised the

[12]The first Organisation Committee created was the Committee for Automobiles, on 9 September 1940, with François Lehideux as President. Lehideux later served as Minister for Industrial Production in 1941–1942.

[13]In practice, individual firms often had to deal with more than one Organisation Committee, especially as the number of Committees grew to over 300 by 1944.

[14]*Journal officiel*, 11 November 1940.

[15]*Journal officiel*, 12 November 1940. The CGPF, France's principal employers' confederation, was also dissolved on 9 November.

Vichy government and the legislation passed by Belin and Pétain.[16] Others within the labour movement continued to support Belin, however, hoping that having 'one of our own, our friend René Belin' at the helm of what were ultimately rather statist bodies would ensure that workers' concerns were properly addressed.[17] Hopes that Vichy could be a golden age for workers were soon dashed, however, particularly as the National Revolution, with its emphasis on artisans and farmers over industrial workers, began to exert an increasing influence on policy. With the dissolution of the main trade union confederations and the exclusion of labour representation from the new Organisation Committees, the New Industrial Order emerged as a system dominated by employers.

Meanwhile, the composition of the Organisation Committees came under attack from the right. Within weeks of the creation of the Committees for Coal and Steel, an anonymous report was submitted to Pétain accusing Belin of syndicalism; the minister's desire to resolve class struggle through collaboration between the classes and greater consideration for labour issues was labelled as syndicalist, which was opposed by doctrinaire corporatists who sought to transcend the notion of class altogether in favour of guild-like, industry-specific groupings.[18] Clearly, both groups felt that the Organisation Committees could be the vehicle through which they could realise their contradictory projects. In the months that followed, corporatists levelled a remarkable array of accusations against Belin, alleging that he was promoting the CGT's interests within the Vichy Government,[19] that he was part of a supposed

[16]The text, published on 15 November 1940 as '*Manifeste du syndicalisme français*', was written by CGT members Robert Lacoste and Christian Pineau. Both later joined de Gaulle and went on to become government ministers after the war: Robert Lacoste held the portfolio for Industrial Production for most of the period between 1944 and 1950, later becoming Minister Resident of Algeria between 1956 and 1958; Christian Pineau was Minister for Public Works between 1947 and 1950 and then Minister for Foreign Affairs between 1956 and 1958, a tenure marked by the Suez Crisis and the Treaty of Rome.

[17]'Bonne chance, René Belin', *Au travail* (a workers' weekly), 30 November 1940. A copy is kept in the Belin Archives, 98 J 7, IHS.

[18]'Observations sur le Rapport Belin', 1 December 1940, F 12 10157, AN. On corporatism under Vichy, including the tensions between 'corporatist' and 'syndicalist' conceptions, see Jean-Pierre Le Crom, *Syndicats nous voilà!* (Paris: Editions de l'Atelier, 1995).

[19]'Observations sur le Rapport Belin', 1 December 1940, F 12 10157, AN.

'*Mouvement Synarchique d'Empire*',[20] and that he was a freemason.[21] One letter to Pétain in December 1940 attacked the New Industrial Order whose creation Belin had overseen as 'the triumphant realisation of the policies of the Popular Front'.[22] Another report to the Maréchal that same month claimed that by appointing exclusively members of 'trusts' to the Organisation Committees, Belin was seeking to ensure that 'the management of different branches of industry are in the hands of capitalists and not of professionals'.[23] After levelling these accusations of Belin handing over far too much power to the capitalists, the authors conclude that their report 'sheds light on the attitude of M. Belin, which shows that he remained in direct contact with syndicalist militants (with CGT leanings) since his appointment as Minister'.[24] Absurdly, Belin was thus denounced for being at once too accommodating to industrialists, while simultaneously being too close to organised labour. Such accusations continued even after the embattled Minister surrendered the portfolio for Industrial Production in February 1941.

The composition of the Organisation Committees came under further criticism due to the exclusion of small and medium-sized enterprises (SMEs). In the case of some industries, this omission made sense; industries such as steel and coal, for instance, were dominated by a relatively small number of large companies. The omission of SMEs nevertheless led to increasing reproaches, ultimately leading Pétain himself to call for SMEs and artisans to be better represented within the Committees.[25] Yet despite

[20]'Rapport sur la société secrète', (undated) 1941, 98 J 10, IHS. Synarchy was a myth propagated under Vichy that alleged that a group of industrialists and bankers, many of whom held key posts in Vichy, had long plotted to seize power in France. The classic treatment of the question is by Richard Kuisel, 'The Legend of the Vichy Synarchy', *French Historical Studies* (6:3), 1970. The best study is Olivier Dard, *La synarchie, le mythe du complot permanent* (Paris: Perrin, 1998); a revisionist interpretation is provided by Annie Lacroix-Riz, *Industriels et banquiers sous l'Occupation* (Paris: Armand Colin, 1999) and, in relation to the Organisation Committees, 'Les comités d'organisation et l'Allemagne' in Hervé Joly (ed.), *Les Comités d'organisation*.

[21]'Note sur la francmaçonnerie', 15 December 1941, 98 J 10, IHS.

[22]Lettre de Jules Verger et Léonce Raynès à Pétain, 14 December 1940, 2 AG 611, AN.

[23]'Observations sur le Rapport Belin', 1 December 1940, F 12 10157, AN.

[24]Ibid.

[25]'Etude sur les CO', 10 September 1941; 'Discours de Pétain' 21 November 1941, F 37 20, AN. Pétain made similar calls during his speech on 12 August 1941, which is discussed in Chapter Three. See 'Discours du 12 août 1941'in Pétain, *Discours aux Français*, op.cit.

such calls from the head of the authoritarian state, most Organisation Committees, including those for steel and coal, remained exclusively in the hands of representatives of large firms.[26]

The multifarious condemnations of the Organisation Committees' composition beg the question of why the tripartism expounded in August faded by November, leaving only the industrial elite in positions of power. In his memoirs, René Belin, himself the former Deputy Secretary General of the CGT throughout the 1930s, justified his staffing of the Committees against claims that he had handed control of the French economy to 'trusts' and to the Germans: 'The hundreds of men I needed immediately – I emphasise this word – to take inventory and, provisionally, to manage France's industries, where was I to find them?'[27] He writes that neither civil servants, nor politicians, nor trade unionists – 'I knew this better than anyone' – had the necessary expertise to fill the roles. 'We had at our disposal, aside from extremely rare exceptions which were generally unknown to us at the time, only a single source: the men who already had the knowledge of and the experience within their branch of industry.'[28] For the sake of expedience and effectiveness, then, the *patronat* was the only viable choice. As for criticisms levelled at Belin that he had excluded SMEs from the Committees, he responded: 'small- and medium-sized enterprises figured in all the Committees. And they played the role commensurate with their size [. . .] That being said, to lead the Organisation Committee for Coal, was I supposed to ask the corner coalman [*le bougnat du coin*]?'[29] The first sentence of this statement is demonstrably false, since SMEs were clearly not represented in many Committees. In light of this, the role of SMEs 'commensurate with their size' seems to have been nil. His choice of representatives from large firms over the *bougnat du coin* reinforces his explanation that individuals were chosen based on their abilities to administer vast industries. His claim that the need for experience and expertise left only a very small pool of viable candidates, all issued from the *patronat*, is plausible.

[26]An additional member, Pierre Francou, from a smaller steel firm, Marrel Frères, was ultimately added to CORSID in September 1941, although this firm would not be classified as an SME.

[27]René Belin, *Du secrétariat de la CGT au gouvernement de Vichy* (Paris: Albatros, 1978), 152.

[28]Ibid., 153.

[29]Ibid.

Meanwhile, the industrialists themselves were by no means eager to welcome trade unionists into their innermost circle, especially after the experience of the Popular Front government elected in 1936. The industrialists initially had little enthusiasm for the Organisation Committees, which had been created without their consultation and which disrupted their own organisation which stretched back several generations. Understandably, many employers simply wanted a continuation of the system that had served them so well under the Third Republic. François de Wendel, who had been President of the *Comité des forges* from 1918 until its dissolution,[30] expressed his disapproval of the reorganisation of French industry:

> at a moment when everything is disorganised and when when we are lacking all materials, it is clear that only routine and resourcefulness can allow firms to survive. But what do[es the Vichy government] do? [It] prevents routine from being carried out by publishing a new law or decree every day, and we are prevented from fending for ourselves by the creation of the Organisation Committees.[31]

This preference for routine over industrial experiments, coupled with the failure of Belin to consult industrialists before issuing the law of 16 August – not to mention the dissolution of the *Comité des forges* – ensured an unenthusiastic attitude of the *patronat* towards the new Organisation Committees. Needless to say, the projected inclusion of organised labour in the *Comité*'s successor was similarly unwelcome.

Despite the promise of tripartism in the law of 16 August, the development of the New Industrial Order instead led to greater power for the small group of industrialists named to the Organisation Committees, even if the *patronat* was initially unimpressed with these changes. Amidst vitriolic and contradictory accusations that he had, on the one hand, empowered 'trusts' with the new Committees and that, on the other, he was pursuing the interests of the CGT and the Popular Front, Belin stepped down as Minister for Industrial Production in February 1941.

[30] De Wendel and Schneider were the two largest steel companies in France. In addition to his duties at the family firm, François de Wendel was a member of the Assemblée Nationale from 1914 until 1940 and hence exemplified the political power held by the *Comité des forges*. He abstained from the vote to grant full powers to Pétain in July 1940.

[31] Qtd. in Jean Noël Jeanneney, *François de Wendel*, 595.

He would nevertheless remain Minister for Labour until 1942, during which time he managed to promulgate the Labour Charter.[32]

While Belin oversaw the sidelining of labour in the Organisation Committees, it is worth considering the third party that was to be included in this supposedly tripartite structure: the State. In practice, this was limited to a single Director, who belonged to the Ministry of Industrial Production, and who served as a liaison officer between the minister and a given Committee. Technically, the government had the power to veto any decision made by any Organisation Committee, although in the case of the Committees for Steel and Coal, there was not a single instance of a decision made by the industrialists being vetoed by the representative of the ministry. The first Director named to follow CORSID's meetings was Henri Coqueugnot, who had a long career as a steel industrialist himself, having worked as an engineer at both Longwy and Schneider before becoming Director General of the *Société Métallurgique des Terres-Rouges* in Luxembourg. From 1933 until his appointment to the Ministry of Industrial Production in 1940, he was Director General of the *Union des Consommateurs de Produits métallurgiques et industriels* (UCPMI). The Director for Mines, meanwhile, was André Fanton d'Andon, and he attended the COH's meetings throughout the war. He, too, had spent his career as an industrialist, rising to the position of Deputy Director General of the *Mines domaniales de potasse d'Alsace* in 1937 before being appointed to Belin's ministry in October 1940. The common background of Coqueugnot and Fanton d'Anton is telling; both had spent their careers in related industries, and neither had held a position with the State before 1940. Given that the only person at CORSID's or the COH's meetings not representing industrialists would in fact have been an industrialist himself, it is striking how homogeneous the would-be tripartite bodies turned out to be.

With the complete absence of labour representation, and the passive role of the State within the Committees, the new institutions were controlled by employers. Moreover, given Belin's preference for choosing men of experience who had already held great responsibilities over the *bougnat du coin*, the industries were run by representatives of some of the largest firms. The tripartism that had informed the text of the law of 16 August had quickly subsided, as the pre-war industrial elite maintained and even strengthened its control of French heavy industry. To the extent

[32]The Labour Charter is discussed in Chapter 4.

that the steel and coal industries remained in the hands of industrialists, there was a certain degree of continuity through 1940.

'Action, Dynamism, Authority': The New Men for the New Industrial Order

While power remained in the hands of industrialists, it does not follow that the same industrialists who dominated the pre-war employers' associations held the top positions in the new Organisation Committees. Indeed, a closer examination of the individuals appointed to the new Committees reveals an important evolution in the leadership of the key industries under Vichy.

One month before the creation of the Committees for Steel and Coal, the Ministry of Industrial Production released a communiqué describing the kind of people it was looking for to oversee industry under the new regime:

> The [Organisation] Committees [...] are neither deliberative assemblies nor associations representing professional interests, but rather a mechanism for economic action, called upon to make decisions, to decree rules, to impose discipline. These Committees will only be comprised of a few members. They could even consist of a single member only. These members are not chosen with the worry of ensuring an exact representation of the interests of the profession, but rather based on their qualities of action, dynamism, and authority; in a word, based on their ability to decide and to act.[33]

This text drips with the exultation of firmness, strength, and action, qualities typically associated with the National Revolution and with pseudo-fascist regimes more broadly. These values make clear the sort of people Belin and his colleagues were seeking. Above all else, they wanted 'men of action', who knew the industry thoroughly and could be trusted to make sound decisions quickly and firmly; after all, given the chaotic context of 1940 when the Committees were developed, it was likely that important decisions would have to be made under pressure. As the war dragged into the autumn, and the prospect of an imminent victory over Britain receded, these qualities took precedence over the goal of assuring a more equitable tripartite distribution of power in the new committees. It is

[33]Communiqué du ministre secrétaire d'Etat à la production et au travail, *Le Temps*, 6 October 1940.

also worth noting the presence in this passage of the *Führerprinzip*, reinforced by the suggestion that the supposedly tripartite bodies could in fact be comprised of a single individual, provided he was a 'man of action'. The suggestion that the Committee could be made up of a single person, and the dismissal of the need for accurate representation within the Committee, are further indications that the tripartite spirit of August 1940 was quickly waning.

In his post-war memoirs, Minister for the Economy and for Finance Yves Bouthillier describes the individuals chosen to lead the newly created organisms as 'strong personalities who, by their previous jobs, by the regular exertion of command, by their capacity to rapidly create new services', showed themselves to be efficient men of action.[34] This is consistent with the statements issued by Vichy at the time, and indeed with the profiles of the individuals selected. It should also be noted that the German authorities insisted on approving the members chosen for the Organisation Committees, suggesting that any individuals who had been openly critical of Nazi Germany could be excluded a priori.[35] In the case of CORSID and the COH, no objections were raised over the candidates. It should also be remembered that the Organisation Committees were created with a view to further Franco-German economic collaboration, a goal that was openly discussed with industrialists as early as July 1940. On 30 October 1940, following Pétain's meeting with Hitler at Montoire, the Maréchal proclaimed that France was 'entering the path of collaboration'. While this policy led to the resignations of the Minister and Secretary General for Foreign Affairs, it did not deter the nominees for the emerging Organisation Committees from accepting their new positions.[36] Given Vichy's public commitment to collaboration and, more importantly, the fact that the Committees were created in part to deepen Franco-German cooperation, it is clear that the members appointed to the new bodies were conscious of and willing to work within this framework.

[34]Yves Bouthillier, *Le drame de Vichy* (Paris: Plon, 1951), vol. 2, 275.

[35]Richard Kuisel, *Capitalism and the State in Modern France* (Cambridge: Cambridge University Press, 1981).

[36]Paul Baudouin, Minister, and François Charles-Roux, Secretary General, resigned in reaction to Montoire. See Baudouin, *The Private Diaries of Paul Baudouin* (London: Eyre and Spottiswoode, 1948).

In describing the selection process for Committee members, Belin claimed that he sought to 'move aside the old bigwigs (*vieux bonzes*) of the employers' group, to find relatively young men ready to make themselves available to serve the public interest, men with no or very limited commitments to political parties or employers' associations'.[37] This search for relatively young men, untainted by the partisanship of the late Third Republic, who had not been at the centre of pre-war employers' associations like the *Comité des forges*, and who embodied 'action, dynamism, authority' yielded four individuals for the Committee for Steel, who were given control of one of France's most crucial industries.

Jules Aubrun, then 59 years old, was named President of CORSID. He had risen to become Director General of Schneider, France's second-largest steel firm, from 1921 until his departure in 1929. In 1932 he became Arbitrator for the *Comptoir Sidérurgique de France*, a position he left in 1935 to become Consulting Engineer for the Lazard Bank in Paris.[38] While his position at a Franco-American bank made him a curious choice for CORSID, his experience as an Arbitrator made him a strong candidate for president of a Committee whose decisions would have to be accepted by all in the steel industry. He was joined by three high-level members of some of France's most important steel firms. The Committee's Vice-President, Eugène Roy, 56, had been Director General of the Longwy steelworks since 1931, while Jean Dupuis, 54, was Deputy Director of Chatillon-Commentry et Neuves-Maisons. Both companies ranked among the largest in France at the end of the 1930s.

Léon Daum is perhaps the most interesting of the four members. The son of a renowned Nancy glassmaker, Daum married the niece of then president Raymond Poincaré in 1913. Daum pursued a successful career in the steelworks of Marine and Homécourt, rising to the post of Deputy Director General, and he was groomed as the successor of President-Director General Théodore Laurent. He was placed in charge of the French-occupied mines in Saarland after the First World War, and during the French occupation of the Ruhr in 1923, he was called upon by then Prime Minister Poincaré's government to put German heavy industry to

[37]Belin, *Du secrétariat de la CGT au gouvernement de Vichy*, 153.

[38]'Jules Antoine Marie AUBRUN' in *Dossiers individuels d'ingénieurs des mines*, F 14 20693, AN.

work for the French economy.[39] In July 1940, at the age of 53, Daum was invited by Pierre Laval to be Vichy's first Minister for Industrial Production, an invitation Daum eagerly accepted. At the eleventh hour, however, Pétain instead entrusted the portfolio to René Belin, who had only just been offered the position of Minister for Labour. Belin would later recall that he had been appointed due to his career as a trade unionist in an effort to balance out the very right-leaning government, a political tendency that the presence of a *Poincariste* like Daum would only have exacerbated.[40] Daum thus has the rather dubious distinction of being the first individual to be denied a Cabinet position in Vichy for being too right-wing. Despite narrowly missing an appointment as Minister, Daum nevertheless thrived under Vichy and participated energetically in the activities of the new regime, and in early 1941 he was appointed to the *Conseil national*,[41] a non-democratic assembly created as a toothless substitute for the defunct parliament. He purportedly also held significant political sway in Vichy, haunting the corridors of power and having the ears of ministers.[42]

This brief overview of the members chosen for the Organisation Committee for Steel reveals several points of interest. First of all, none of the three largest steel firms in France – Schneider, de Wendel, or Nord – was represented on the Committee. While Belin had been criticised for neglecting SMEs and labour, he also excluded the principal heavyweights of the industry. Moreover, none of the members of CORSID was the president or owner of the firm; rather, the industrialists named to the Committee were all high-level employees and potential successors to the current leaders. In one of the most-cited articles on Vichy's industrial organisation, by Henry Rousso, it is claimed that the president chosen for any given Organisation Committee was 'almost always [. . .] the head of the largest

[39]Mauve Carbonell, *Les Hommes à l'origine de l'Europe*, (Aix-en-Provence: Publications de l'Université de Provence, 2008), 211–212.

[40]Belin, *Du secrétariat de la CGT au gouvernement de Vichy*, 127–128.

[41]'Groupement du Centre et de l'Ouest. Séance du 29 Janvier 1941', 21 January 1941, 139 AQ 82, AN. Daum's participation is also mentioned in Michèle Cointet, *Le Conseil national de Vichy* (Paris: Aux amateurs de livres, 1989), 194–195.

[42]Le Crom, *Syndicats nous voilà!*, 108. Le Crom also refers to Daum as 'an industrialist known more for his dubious practices than for the economic success of his business'.

firm in the sector'.[43] Indeed, the article misidentifies Aubrun as 'the former President of Schneider' and uses this to buttress the argument that the President of an Organisation Committee was usually the sitting president of the industry's largest firm.[44] Yet this was demonstrably not the case with the Committee for Steel, given that Aubrun arrived at CORSID from the Lazard Bank, more than a decade after he had left Schneider. Furthermore, CORSID's members were high-, but not the highest-, ranking figures from three large, but not the largest, steel companies, with its president drawn from a financial institution. Indeed, the 'head of the largest firm in the sector' would have been François de Wendel, who was sacked from his position with the dissolution of the *Comité des forges* and replaced by a Consulting Engineer from a Franco-American bank; in the steel industry, we can observe the very opposite of the trend usually described in the literature. The President of the Organisation Committee for Coal, Aimé Lepercq, similarly confounds this characterisation, as he was Managing Director of a Czech automotive company, Škoda, until 1940.[45] One individual who does seem to fit the standard narrative of the Committee President is François Lehideux, who was Director General of Renault, one of the three largest automotive companies in France, before being named President of the Organisation Committee for Automobiles. Yet even Lehideux does not match the description perfectly, since he had resigned from Renault in the summer of 1940 and thus was not part of the company when he was named to the Committee in September.[46] The assertion that the President of the Organisation Committee was 'almost always [. . .] the head of the largest

[43]Henry Rousso, 'L'organisation industrielle de Vichy' in *Vichy. L'événement, la mémoire, l'histoire* (Paris: Gallimard, 1992), 79–109, here 83.

[44]Ibid., 107. Aubrun had been Director General of Schneider, not President, and left the firm in 1929. As such, the link between Aubrun and Schneider which had been severed for more than a decade is insufficient for Aubrun to be seen as a representative of that firm in 1940.

[45]Aimé Lepercq studied at the Polytechnique and the Ecole des Mines before becoming Director of Prague-based holding company *l'Union européenne industrielle et financière* until 1929. During the war he joined the Resistance but remained President of the COH until August 1943. Lepercq was named Minister for Finance in de Gaulle's first post-Liberation government in September 1944 but died in a car accident two months later.

[46]On his resignation from Renault in August 1940, see François Lehideux, *De Renault à Pétain* (Paris: Pygmalion, 2001), 220–231.

firm in the sector' is simply inaccurate when describing France's heavy industries and obscures the significant changes in industrial leadership brought about with the creation of the Committees.

Given the membership of the new Committees, it would indeed seem that Belin had 'move[d] aside the *vieux bonzes* of the employers' group, to find [. . .] men with no or very limited commitments to political parties or employers' associations'.[47] Of the four individuals appointed to CORSID, Daum was the only one who was a member of the *Comité des forges.*[48] While the continuities were somewhat stronger in the case of the COH – both Bucher and Marterer had been members of the *Comité central des houillères* – the sidelining of Henri de Peyerimhoff and the appointment of a relative outsider, Aimé Lepercq, as President of the COH further demonstrates this trend described by Belin. Moreover, compared to an individual like François de Wendel, who headed the *Comité des forges* while holding a seat in the National Assembly and managing *Le Temps*, the members of the new Organisation Committees in 1940 had 'no or very limited commitments to political parties'. Belin had thus succeeded in excluding the uppermost echelon of the steel industry, the *vieux bonzes* of who dominated the pre-war employers' associations. And as for his aim to supplant them with 'relatively young men'? All born between 1881 and 1887, CORSID's members were decidedly middle-aged, and sometimes hardly younger than those excluded. François de Wendel, for instance, was only seven years Aubrun's senior, although Théodore Laurent, head of Daum's firm, was 77. Only a handful of presidents of the Organisation Committees were under 50, with François Lehideux, Pierre Ricard, and Antoine Pinay being among the youngest.[49] In this last goal of generational change, Belin, only 42 years old himself, succeeded only modestly.

Yet the lack of youth among those appointed to the Committees must not be understood as simply the continuation of the old guard. The highest strata of the industry had been excluded – in the steel and coal

[47]Belin, *Du secrétariat de la CGT au gouvernement de Vichy*, 153.

[48]For a full list of member of the *Comité des forges* in 1939–1940, see Françoise Berger, 'La France, l'Allemagne et l'acier (1932–1952). De la stratégie des cartels à l'élaboration de la CECA', PhD thesis (Université de Paris I, 2000), 226.

[49]François Lehideux was only 36 when he was appointed President of the Organisation Committee for Automobiles. Pierre Ricard (President of the Committee for Foundry) was 41, while Antoine Pinay (President of the Committee for Leather) was 49.

industries, none of the members chosen for the Committees was president of a firm, and the largest firms were left out. Early intimations of this selection may be detected in the interwar writings of Jacques Barnaud, René Belin's Chief of Staff and the father of the Organisation Committees. In an article published in 1937, he decried the industrialists who were at once the owners and the managers of their factories as '*le patron du droit divin*'. He observed that:

> among the employers, those who naturally understand best are the leaders of the public limited companies (*Sociétés anonymes*) who, most of the time, are not shareholders in their companies or, if they do hold shares, they only amount to a miniscule amount of the capital. These, veritable civil servants for the company, cannot have the same reaction to the occupation of their factories as a company head who is at once manager and owner.[50]

This preference for civil servant-like managers over those whom had inherited vast family-run empires informed the selection of members of the Organisation Committees. Gone were the dominant personalities of François de Wendel and the other *patrons du droit divin*[51] who generally dominated pre-war employers' associations; in their stead was placed a group of managerial *fonctionnaires* who would be expected to deal with industrial decisions impartially, akin to 'technocrats' in the private rather than the public sector.[52] The four individuals appointed to run the steel industry had risen towards the top of their field based on their abilities, rather than their lineage, and were equipped with impressive credentials. Jules Aubrun and Léon Daum, for example, had attended the Ecole

[50]Jacques Barnaud, 'L'industriel', *Nouveaux cahiers*, no. 2, 1 April 1937, 12.

[51]Scholars, particularly sociologists, have since used the terms '*patron familial*' or '*patron propriétaire*' to describe the same phenomenon. See, for example, Pierre Bourdieu, *La noblesse d'Etat* (Paris: Editions de Minuit, 1989) and Michel Bauer and Bénédicte Bertin-Mourot, *Les 200: Comment devient-on un grand patron?* (Paris: Seuil, 1987).

[52]For the rise of 'technocracy' in France, and the importance of the Vichy years in this process, see Gérard Brun, *Techniciens et technocratie en France* (Paris: Albatros, 1985), Delphine Dulong, *Moderniser la politique. Aux origines de la Ve République* (Paris: L'Harmattan, 1997), and Olivier Dard, 'Les technocrats: archéologie d'un concept, généalogie d'un groupe social' in Olivier Dard, Jean-Claude Daumas and François Marcot (eds), *L'Occupation, l'Etat français et les entreprises* (Paris: Association pour le développement de l'histoire économique, 2000), 213–228.

Polytechnique and then the highly competitive Ecole des Mines, where they graduated first and second in their class, respectively. Aimé Lepercq had similarly attended the Polytechnique and went on to graduate top of his class from the Ecole des Mines[53]; meanwhile, Pierre Ricard, the President of the Committee for Foundry, followed the same trajectory and was awarded several prizes upon graduating from the Ecole des Mines. More important than passing the direction of the steel industry to a slightly younger generation, Vichy opted for an ostensibly meritocratic leadership equipped with diplomas and managerial training to replace the *vieux bonzes* who had in many cases inherited rather than earned positions of power. This change would endure beyond the end of the war, both in general and particular matters: not only would the Fourth and Fifth Republics trumpet themselves as explicitly meritocratic, but those who achieved seats at the Organisation Committee for Steel in 1940 would retain some of the very highest positions in that industry.

While this change in the leadership on French industry was significant, it is important to qualify how radical it was. The idea that trained managers were preferable to employers who had simply inherited their position was not unique, and was articulated by a number of Barnaud's contemporaries in the 1930s, whether in non-conformist journals like *Nouveaux cahiers* or in organisations like the *Centre des jeunes patrons.*[54] Moreover, the notion that an individual could rise to the top positions within an industry due to his managerial talents rather than his inheritance was hardly unprecedented by 1940. Indeed, several influential positions within French industry in the interwar period were occupied by such individuals, most notably the President of the *Comité central des houillères*, Henri de Peyerimhoff, who has been described as a *fonctionnaire patronal.*[55] In addition,

[53]'Bulletins de notes d'élèves-ingénieurs du corps des mines. Promotions entrées à l'Ecole de 1853 à 1960', annales.org/archives/images/n1, last accessed 5 September 2016.

[54]Olivier Dard, *Le Rendez-vous manqué des relèves des années 1930* (Paris: Presses universitaires de France, 2002); Clarke, *France in the Age of Organization*; on the *Centre des jeunes patrons*, see Florent Le Bot, 'La naissance du Centre des jeunes patrons (1938–1944). Entre réaction et relève' in *Vingtième siècle* 2012/2, numéro 114, 99–116. For contemporary examples from outside of France, see Adolf Berle and Gardiner Means, *The Modern Corporation and Private Property* (New York: Macmillan, 1932); Bruno Rizzi, *La Bureaucratisation du monde* (Paris: Presses modernes, 1939); James Burnham, *The Managerial Revolution* (New York: John Day, 1941).

[55]Peyerimhoff earned a degree in law from Sciences Po and became Vice-President and then President of the *Comité central des houillères* from 1925 until 1940. Atypically, he rose to this

the distinction between a trained manager and an heir to the family company is not always so clear. With his degree from Sciences Po and lacking any family background in the automotive industry, François Lehideux, for example, might be placed in the former category, but his appointment as Director General of Renault at the age of 30 had more to do with his marriage to the niece of Louis Renault, the company's president, than his degree. Furthermore, being due to inherit one's family firm did not necessarily preclude one from attending the Polytechnique or the Ecole des Mines.[56] Indeed, although he was not a *polytechnicien*, François de Wendel attended the Ecole des Mines in the 1890s before assuming control of the family firm and ultimately the *Comité des forges*.

Despite these qualifications, the replacement of the *Comité des forges* by CORSID marked a significant change in the organisation of the French steel industry. The marginalisation of the pre-war leadership of the industry and the promotion of lower-ranking, managerial individuals from smaller (but still large) firms was unprecedented. While CORSID and the pre-war *Comité des forges* were dominated by industrialists, the leadership of the industry had changed hands as education and apparent apoliticism outweighed tradition and privilege. The new leadership would not wait long before exercising its powers.

First Actions of CORSID

Given the significant changes in leadership brought about by the creation and staffing of the Organisation Committees, the first actions taken by the newly created Committee for Steel are of some interest. The very first decision taken by CORSID was to exercise control over the Centre-Midi grouping of the steel industry, corresponding to the Non-Occupied Zone of France, and to place it under Daum's control.[57] To effectively

position without being a director of a particular firm, specialising instead in the management of the employers' association, leading some to consider him a *fonctionnaire patronal*. See Alain Chatriot, 'Henri de Peyerimhoff (1871–1953), le gentleman du charbon' in Olivier Dard and Gilles Richard (eds), *Les permanents patronaux: éléments pour l'histoire du patronat en France dans la première moitié du XXème siècle* (Metz: Université Paul Verlaine de Metz, 2005), 45–73.

[56]See Hervé Joly, 'Fondateurs, héritiers et managers' in Jean-Claude Daumas (ed.), *Dictionnaire historique des patrons français* (Paris: Flammarion, 2010), 777–782.

[57]'Déclaration No. 1 du Corsid', 25 November 1940, 139 AQ 80, AN.

administer the country's steel industry, CORSID decided to carve up the map of France and assign each area to one of its members; accordingly, Roy was put in charge of overseeing the industrialised Meurthe-et-Moselle region, corresponding to the part of Lorraine that had not been annexed by the Reich. The other important region under CORSID's control was the Centre-Ouest, which corresponded to the Occupied Zone. Meanwhile, in the industrialised regions in Nord and Pas-de-Calais which had been administratively appended to Belgium by the Germans, the extension of the Organisation Committees' powers to these two *départements* was vetoed by the German authorities.[58] Nevertheless, French industrialists in the region were allowed to set up a similar body, called SIDENOR, which maintained contact with CORSID.[59]

Early on, CORSID set out to enshrine for itself the powers normally held by the *Comité des forges*. CORSID's second declaration announced the creation of the *Comptoir français des produits sidérurgiques* (CPS), effective from 1 December. This effectively recreated the *Comptoir sidérurgique de France*, created by the *Comité des forges* in 1918. Among other responsibilities, this body was assigned responsibility for the allocation of orders to different factories, a role that had been given to the Organisation Committee.[60] The *Comptoir* was supplemented with a *Commissaire technique* in December, then a body of commercial experts in January,[61] while duties related to resource allocation were assigned to the *Commission des Charbons et des Cokes* (CCC), a CORSID-controlled body established in December 1940.[62] This commission, in particular, seemed to duplicate some of the responsibilities of OCRPI, which prompted the Ministry of Industrial Production to issue a series of documents in early 1941 to clarify what the role of OCRPI was indeed to be, and to what extent the powers of the Organisation Committees were to be curbed accordingly. The need for such declarations reflected attempts by Organisation Committees to seize

[58]'Lettre du Préfet du Nord', undated 1941, F 12 10134, AN and 'Note à M le Préfet du Département du Nord sur la validité de la législation française nouvellement parue', 17 July 1941, F 12 9974, AN.

[59]'Note sur l'application des décisions des CO dans les département du Nord et Pas-de-Calais', 4 March 1942, F 12 9974, AN.

[60]'Déclaration No. 2 du Corsid', 3 December, 139 AQ 80, AN.

[61]'Déclaration No. 4 du Corsid' and 'Déclaration No. 10 du Corsid', 139 AQ 80, AN.

[62]'Déclaration No. 6 du Corsid', 139 AQ 80, AN.

more powers than Vichy was willing to grant them. As OCRPI became fully operational over the first half of 1941, the powers of some of CORSID's newly created institutions were progressively diminished.[63]

Perhaps more significant than these encroachments on OCRPI's responsibilities was the establishment of a consultative commission, named the *Commission générale*, in February 1941. Unlike the CPS, the *Commission générale*'s powers were not defined, aside from the provision that the body could convoke *Commissions d'étude* to investigate issues identified by the *Commission générale*. Meetings of the Commission would be called and chaired by the President of CORSID, Jules Aubrun, and would be attended by the members of CORSID. The rather woolly articulation of the Commission's duties in CORSID's declaration was juxtaposed with a comprehensive list of the members of this new body. This included most of the giants of the French steel industry, who had consciously been excluded from CORSID by Vichy, from François and Humbert de Wendel to Théodore Laurent.[64] There were nevertheless two striking absences from this *Who's Who* of French steel. Schneider, France's second-largest steel firm, was excluded, as was Alfred Lambert Ribot, who had served as Secretary General of the *Comité des forges* until its dissolution in November 1940. The latter's absence was likely linked to criticisms he had levelled against Vichy after July 1940,[65] and both exclusions helped distance the new Commission from the *Comité des forges*. Despite these two absences, however, the creation of the *Commission générale* brought back into the fold most of the prominent members of the pre-war *Comité des forges*, including its president, François de Wendel, if only in a consultative capacity.

These continuities have led some historians to declare that the 'dissolution of the *Comité des forges* is a fabrication' or a 'pure façade'.[66] For Annie

[63]'Compte-rendu de la première plénière des répartiteurs', 19 April 1941, F 12 10134, AN.

[64]'Déclaration No. 15', 5 February 1941, 139 AQ 80, AN. Curiously, Daum's name appeared on the first published list, which was corrected a week later. See 'Erratum', 12 February 1941, 139 AQ 80, AN.

[65]Philippe Mioche suggests this explanation, and Vinen provides an account of his criticism of Vichy. See Mioche, 'Le comité d'organisation de la sidérurgie', and Vinen, *The Politics of French Business, 1936–1945*, 104.

[66]Mioche, 'Le comité d'organisation de la sidérurgie', 98–99. Marxist historian Annie Lacroix-Riz similarly dismisses the dissolution as a '*pure façade*', as the Organisation Committees were dominated by employers. See Lacroix-Riz, 'Les comités d'organisation et l'Allemagne'.

Lacroix-Riz, the Organisation Committees merely 'strengthened the heads of the former employers' associations'.[67] According to Philippe Mioche, this *Commission générale* was 'a reproduction of the *Comité des forges*' and it was here, not CORSID, 'where the decisions were effectively taken'. He also suggests that François de Wendel acted as de facto president of the *Commission générale*, preserving his role from the *Comité des forges*. While the membership of the Commission was strikingly similar to that of the pre-war *Comité des forges*,[68] there is little evidence to support the conclusion that it was in fact the Commission and de Wendel, rather than CORSID and Aubrun, who continued to direct the steel industry throughout the war. Indeed, this characterisation of the Commission rests entirely on François de Wendel's private notebooks from the war, particularly a passage where de Wendel describes turning

> the *Comité des forges* into a slightly enlarged *chambre syndicale*... The only substantial modification [being] that once each month, the transformed *Comité des forges* would hold a meeting to which only the four members of the Organisation Committee would be present, and that Aubrun... would chair instead of me.[69]

This entry, however, was written by de Wendel in October 1940, before the *Comité des forges* had been dissolved and CORSID established in November, and months before the creation of the *Commission générale* in February 1941. His musings on how the Organisation Committee might function after the abolition of the *Comité des forges* must therefore not be taken as conclusive evidence of how it operated in practice the following year. As no minutes of the *Commission générale*'s meetings have survived, it is impossible to confirm whether it was there, rather than in the meetings of CORSID, that the decisions were truly taken. In the surviving minutes of CORSID's meetings, however, no mention of

[67] Lacroix-Riz, 'Les comités d'organisation et l'Allemagne', 61.

[68] Comparing the membership of the Commission and that of the *Comité des forges* in 1939, Mioche calculates that only three new members were added, and five removed, from the *Comité des forges* to create the *Commission générale*. See Mioche, 'Les comités d'organisation et l'Allemagne'.

[69] Qtd in Mioche, 'Les comités d'organisation et l'Allemagne'. The original quotation comes from the Carnets François de Wendel (CFW), 31 October 1940.

the *Commission générale* is ever made.[70] If it was indeed the *Commission générale* that was pulling the strings behind the façade of the Organisation Committee for Steel, it was a well-kept secret that has left no archival trace.

CORSID indeed sought to expand its powers by creating parallel bodies that would, it was hoped, supersede other bodies created by Vichy that would be beyond their direct control, such as CPS replicating some of the responsibilities of OCRPI. This was typical of institutions and individuals alike in Vichy France, as newly created yet ill defined bodies and positions competed for power. Despite reaching out to the pre-war elites of the steel industry through the creation of the *Commission générale*, however, the decision-making responsibilities remained with the Organisation Committee and the new leaders of the steel industry.

Conclusion

The annunciation of the tripartite ideals in the law of 16 August was not followed by the birth of a genuinely tripartite industrial order. The promise of cooperation between organised labour, civil servants, and industrialists with the Organisation Committees quickly gave way to the dominance of the industry by only one of these groups. For the remainder of the war these employers would be responsible for the coordination of their industry.

To the extent that the reins of the steel industry remained in the hands of steel industrialists, the dissolution of the *Comité des forges* does seem like little more than a '*pure façade*'. Crucially, however, the torch had passed from one group of industrialists to another. As such, high-ranking managers of fairly large, but not the largest, steelworks took over from the presidents of the very biggest firms – a significant change that would prove permanent. While pre-war figures from the *Comité des forges* were given a consultative role in the *Commission générale*, the coordination of the steel industry was firmly in the hands of Jules Aubrun and the other members of CORSID.

While this development was most striking in the steel industry, it is in keeping with several broader trends under Vichy. Individuals like de Wendel, whose industrial dominance and political influence epitomised

[70]The minutes of CORSID's meetings can be consulted in 139 AQ 82, AN.

the faults of the Third Republic, was an obvious target of the new regime's anti-capitalist ideology. More importantly, for the group of younger individuals in Vichy focused on modernisation, known as the *jeunes cyclistes*, the replacement of owner-presidents with civil servant-like managers was seen as an important step on the way to modernisation. These *jeunes cyclistes* – which included René Belin and his staff members Jacques Barnaud and Jean Bichelonne – also shared a common background, having graduated from the Ecole Polytechnique. Their preoccupation with replacing the *vieux bonzes* of the *patronat du droit divin*, and their choice of managers with a similar educational background to theirs, suggests that these changes were very much in keeping with their vision of Vichy's project.[71]

While it is clear why Belin and his colleagues chose this group of individuals to run French industry under Vichy, it is worth considering why these industrialists accepted the invitation to join the new Committees. One consideration was the prospect of personal advancement. Given that Vichy selected comparatively junior industrialists to run the important new institutions, this amounted to a significant promotion that placed figures like Jules Aubrun and Aimé Lepercq above dominant leaders like François de Wendel. In many cases, these promotions to the highest ranks within their respective industries in 1940 were maintained by Committee members after the war. Another factor was a certain degree of support for the new regime, at least in 1940 – which was by no means exclusive to the *patronat*. This undoubtedly influenced a figure like Léon Daum to agree to join Pétain's cabinet and later the *Conseil national* as well as CORSID. It must, of course, be remembered that initial support for the Vichy regime did not necessarily entail sympathy for the Third Reich; the fact that Aimé Lepercq became President of the COH in 1940 and went on the lead one of the main organisations of the Resistance is instructive.[72] Most important for those who joined the

[71]On the *jeunes cyclistes*, see Belin, *Du secrétariat de la CGT au gouvernement de Vichy*; Jacques Benoist-Méchin, *A l'épreuve du temps: Souvenirs II, 1940–1947* (Paris: Perrin, 1989) and Gérard Brun, *Technocrates et technocratie en France* (Paris: Albatros, 1985).

[72]Indeed, many supporters of Vichy's National Revolution, notably Maxime Weygand, were French patriots who were at least implicitly anti-German. See Jackson, *France, The Dark Years* and Debbie Lackerstein, *National Regeneration in Vichy France: Ideas and Policies, 1930–1944* (Farnham: Ashgate, 2012).

Organisation Committees, however, was likely a sense of professional duty to ensure the success of their industry. Just as the priority of directors of individual firms was to keep factories running, so too were the employers tasked with coordinating the industry as a whole through the Organisation Committees preoccupied with the survival of factories and the maintenance of production – even if this meant producing for the Reich.[73] Over the next four years, the members of the Organisation Committees would need to balance these various considerations – their degree of support for the regime, their post-war career prospects, and the necessity of keeping factories running – under increasingly difficult circumstances.

[73]These motivations have been called the '*logique du gestionnaire*' or 'managerial logic' in Renaud de Rochebrune and Jean Claude Hazera, *Les patrons sous l'Occupation* (Paris: Odile Jacob, 1995). Annie Lacroix-Riz, in *Les industriels et banquiers sous l'Occupation* (Paris: Armand Colin, 1999), on the other hand, has argued that profits were the primary motivation for industrialists. For a similar consideration of the motivations of civil servants under Vichy, see Marc Olivier Baruch's excellent *Servir l'Etat français. L'administration en France de 1940 à 1944* (Paris: Fayard, 1997). For a discussion of workers under Vichy, see Xavier Vigna, *Histoire des ouvriers en France au XXe siècle* (Paris: Perrin, 2012) and Ludivine Broch, *Ordinary Workers, Vichy and the Holocaust* (Cambridge: Cambridge University Press, 2016).

CHAPTER 4

The Organisation Committees Between Collaboration and Resistance, 1941–1944

It is often lamented by historians of Vichy France that the archives of the Organisation Committees have been destroyed, which inevitably complicates the possibility of writing their history.[1] Fortuitously, a copy of the minutes of the Organisation Committee for Steel (CORSID)'s meetings – spanning from 1940 until 1944 – have been preserved in the archives of the firm Marine-Homécourt. This previously unexploited resource provides an invaluable window into the inner workings of CORSID and the issues they debated during the war. In particular, they allow for an unprecedented assessment of how the Committee members reacted to a range of Vichy's initatives over the course of the regime's existence.[2]

Under the banner of the National Revolution, the official ideology of the Vichy regime, the government issued the Labour Charter in October 1941, intended to help transcend the class struggle by fostering the collaboration

[1]According to Henry Rousso, the archives of the Organisation Committees were preserved by the Archives nationales until the 1970s, at which point they seem to have been destroyed. See Rousso, 'L'organisation industrielle de Vichy' in *Vichy. L'événement, la mémoire, l'histoire* (Paris: Gallimard, 1992).

[2]The minutes of CORSID's meetings can be consulted at the Archives nationales, Pierrefitte-sur-Seine, under 139 AQ 82. While the meetings are officially of the grouping for the Centre-Ouest region – equivalent to the Non-Occupied Zone – a remarkable range of issues were discussed. In addition to issues relating to the French steel industry as a whole, a number of specfic cases in the Occupied Zone were examined in detail.

© The Author(s) 2017

L.-A. Brunet, *Forging Europe: Industrial Organisation in France, 1940–1952*, Security, Conflict and Cooperation in the Contemporary World, DOI 10.1057/978-1-349-95198-7_4

of employers and workers. The following spring saw the introduction of a series of schemes aimed at sending French workers to Germany to work in factories in the Reich – at first voluntarily, later through a labour draft known as the *Service du travail obligatoire* (STO), introduced in February 1943. In September of that year, Minister for Industrial Production Jean Bichelonne went to Berlin and agreed with Nazi minister Albert Speer that French factories would take over a substantial share of civilian production for the Reich to enable German factories to increase armaments. All of these initatives were launched by the Vichy government without prior consultation with CORSID. Yet throughout this period and these shifting policies, CORSID continued to coordinate the French steel industry and to reconcile the interests of the industry, particularly its employers, and the policies of the government.

The National Revolution and the Labour Charter

René Belin's surprise appointment as Minister for Industrial Production in July 1940 was followed by the drafting of the law of 16 August 1940, for which Belin relied heavily on his advisors Jacques Barnaud and Jean Bichelonne. The latter retained central positions in the Ministry of Industrial Production for the remainder of the war, becoming one of two Secretaries General of the Ministry and ultimately becoming Minister for Industrial Production himself. As soon as OCRPI had been created in September 1940, he became the chief French civil servant responsible for it.[3] Meanwhile, Jacques Barnaud left Vichy in February 1941 to become *délégué général* for Franco-German Economic Relations at the Armistice Commission in Wiesbaden. That same month, Belin was relieved of the Industrial Production portfolio, with industrialist Pierre Pucheu taking his place.[4] Pucheu's tenure lasted only until July, however,

[3]The other Secretary General was Henri Lafond. OCRPI was centralised in the Ministry for Industrial Production, although the presence of a German official with veto powers on each OCRPI Section impinged on Vichy's freedom of action.

[4]Pucheu was an industrialist with ties to the far-right *Croix de feu* and *Parti populaire français* (PPF) in the 1930s; his appointment was therefore quite a shift from the trade unionist Belin. Pucheu later served as Minister for the Interior until the return to government of Pierre Laval in April 1942. His ill-fated attempt to join the Resistance in Algeria in 1943 is discussed in Chapter 5.

when he was succeeded by François Lehideux, the President of the Organisation Committee for Automobiles (COA).[5]

Barely a month after becoming minister, Lehideux faced a challenge from an unlikely source. On 12 August 1941, Pétain gave a speech in which he attacked the Organisation Committees, which he claimed were dominated by 'trusts'. This speech came after months of complaints about and attacks on the Committees, many of which were sent directly to the Maréchal.[6] Pétain claimed that the Committees, 'created to correct the errors of capitalism', had been founded with the best of intentions. 'Trusts', however, 'sought to reassert themselves by using the [Committees] for their own particular ends'.[7] Pétain reassured the nation that 'the provisional statute of the organisation of the economy will be rearranged on the basis of the reduction and the merging of Committees [and] of greater representation within [the Committees] of small industry and artisans'.[8] Having spent most of the Vichy period up to that point as President of the the first Committee created and, as newly appointed Minister for Industrial Production, now responsible for the Committees in their entirety, Lehideux had indeed been handed a challenge.

According to his memoirs, Lehideux questioned Pétain privately shortly after the speech, objecting to the use of the 'imprecise, demagogic, lethal' term – 'trusts' – and taking issue with Pétain's 'unfair and inappropriate' speech.[9] Lehideux claims that he made an impassioned defence of the valuable Committees and offered to resign on the grounds of the chasm that existed between Lehideux's and the Maréchal's views on the bodies. In Lehideux's version of events, Pétain sheepishly admitted that he had not meant to criticise the Committees so harshly and that 'perhaps, he admitted,

[5]COA was the first Organisation Committee created, on 9 September 1940, and Lehideux remained its president throughout the war. Having married Louis Renault's niece, Lehideux had been Director General of Renault from 1934 until his resignation in August 1940.

[6]Dozens of letters criticising the Committees are preserved among Pétain's papers, 'Papiers du chef d'Etat, Etat français', 2 AG 611 and 612, AN. Criticisms levelled against the Organisation Committees and the minister responsible for their creation, René Belin, are discussed in Chapter 3.

[7]Pétain, 'Message du 12 août 1941' in *Discours aux français* (Paris: Albin Michel, 1989), 167. In his memoirs Lehideux mistakenly states that the speech was broadcast on 11 August. See Lehideux, *De Renault à Pétain* (Paris: Editions Pygmalion, 2001), 317.

[8]Pétain, 'Message du 12 août 1941', 171.

[9]Lehideux, *De Renault à Pétain*, 317–318.

he had been insufficiently informed on a subject of which he understood little'.[10] He also reassured Lehideux 'that he had confidence in [him]. Before leaving, he invited [Lehideux] to come visit him more often'.[11] Given the implausibility of his account, the lack of any corroborating sources, and the consistently unreliable nature of his memoirs, however, Lehideux's claim that Pétain's attack on the Organisation Committees and his promises of reform were mistakenly articulated and misunderstood can be safely dismissed. Pétain had received letters and reports outlining these criticisms of the Committees since autumn 1940, when they were first created. More importantly, Pétain gave a speech on 1 March 1941 in which he criticised employers on the grounds that their 'selfishness and [their] lack of understanding of the proletarian condition were all too often the best auxiliaries to communism' and called on employers, workers, and technicians to work together in Social Committees.[12] In his speech on 12 August 1941, Pétain referred more explicitly to the National Revolution and some of its projects, such as the Labour Charter, thereby situating his criticisms of the Committees in the broader context of his national project. Pétain's comments in August 1941 were entirely consistent with the policies he was overseeing and the central if still somewhat nebulous project of national revival he was pursuing, and he made similar comments long after his chat with Lehideux.

Due to the nature of the steel industry, greater representation of artisans and small businesses – so revered in the ideology of the National Revolution[13] – never made much sense, but CORSID did its best to answer the call of 12 August 1941 by adding a member from a medium-sized steel firm one month after Pétain's address. Pierre Francou was the Deputy Director General of Marrel Frères, a Loire-based firm that was somewhat smaller than the firms represented by the four original members

[10]Ibid., 321.

[11]Ibid.

[12]Pétain, 'Discours du 1 mars 1941' in *Discours aux français*, 113. Social Committees, a key component of the Labour Charter, are discussed below.

[13]The most comprehensive treatment of the National Revolution is Limore Yagil, '*L'Homme nouveau' et la Révolution nationale de Vichy (1940–1944)* (Paris: Presses universitaires du Septentrion, 1997), while Julian Jackson's chapter on the National Revolution in *France: The Dark Years, 1940–1944* (Oxford: Oxford University Press, 2001) offers the best synthesis.

of CORSID.[14] This change was well-timed, as a study dated 10 September 1941 – one year to the day after the creation of OCRPI – reiterated the criticism that France's Committees were 'led by the industrial elite', arguing that 'some members must be replaced' and that in general 'the make-up of the Organisation Committees must be revised'.[15] The token addition of a fifth member from a smaller firm was as far as CORSID went to assuage such concerns. The inclusion of Francou, however, seems to have been superficial, as the surviving minutes of CORSID's meetings suggest that he was not present at a single meeting.[16]

The project that went furthest in realising Pétain's vision of the renovation of French labour was the Labour Charter, which appeared as the law of 4 October 1941.[17] Belin began work on this Charter in the weeks following 16 August 1940, before the first Organisation Committees were even established. The first draft of the Labour Charter dates from September 1940, and subsequent drafts were produced monthly, taking account of feedback from different experts, ministers, and occasionally Pétain himself.[18] In these early stages one of the chief architects of the Charter was Pierre Laroque.[19] Belin and Laroque based the Charter in

[14]The four original members of CORSID came from some of the largest firms, although the three largest – De Wendel, Schneider, and Nord – were not represented in the Committee.

[15]'Etude sur les CO', 10 September 1941, F 37 20, AN.

[16]The minutes are kept in the archives of the firm Marine and Homécourt, now held by the Archives nationales in the file 139 AQ 82. These meetings were for the Groupement Centre-Ouest, corresponding roughly to the Occupied Zone. Although Léon Daum presided over this grouping, the other original members of CORSID attended nearly every meeting, as did the representative of the Ministry for Industrial Production. Francou's name does not feature among the list of participants for a single meeting.

[17]The best study of the Labour Charter is Jean-Pierre Le Crom's *Syndicats nous voilà!* (Paris: Editions de l'Atelier, 1995), while the classic study remains Jacques Julliard, 'La Charte du travail' in René Rémond (ed.), *Le gouvernement de Vichy, 1940–1942* (Paris: FNSP, 1972).

[18]These can be found in the dossier '"Charte du travail", projets de base 1940–1941' in 98 J 9, Fonds Belin, IHS.

[19]See the dossier 'Charte du travail, projets de René Belin avant decembre 1940, dossier de travail de P. Laroque' in 98 J 7, Fonds Belin, IHS. Laroque had joined the Ministry of Labour in 1931, coincidentally during Pierre Laval's first stint as Prime Minister. He worked closely with Belin until the autumn of 1940, when he was dismissed under anti-Semitic legislation introduced by Vichy. Under de Gaulle, he later became Director General for Social Security in October 1944 and came to be known as the father of social security in post-war France. See Eric Jabbari, *Pierre Laroque and the Welfare State in Postwar France* (Oxford: Oxford University Press, 2012).

part on the Italian Labour Charter introduced under Mussolini in 1927,[20] although given Belin's career as a trade unionist, it is perhaps not surprising that his version offers far more rights to workers than the Italian document, which was meant largely to entrench the support of Italian industrialists for the Fascist regime.[21]

The development of the Charter was fraught with difficulties and internal divisions over its content. At its core, the document was meant to reorganise French society along corporatist lines as a means of transcending the class struggle, a core tenet of the National Revolution. Anti-communism similarly permeated the project, as it was believed that improving conditions for workers and ensuring employment would undermine the appeal of communism.[22] Minister for Finance and for the Economy Yves Bouthillier rejected an early draft of the law in December 1940 because it relied too heavily on Organisation Committees which, 'dominated by heads of "trusts", cannot achieve the social reform' envisaged by Belin.[23] Such criticisms were brought to Pétain's attention throughout 1941 by those whom objected to 'class syndicalism' and urged Pétain to push for 'the fusion of workers, employers and managers in shared bodies', rather than the class cooperation envisaged by Belin.[24] Bouthillier and Foreign Minister Paul Baudouin were among the influential members of Cabinet who lobbied for a more corporatist model that would abolish trade unions and employers' associations altogether.[25]

[20]'Charte du travail italienne, 1927', (undated, but among Belin's papers from his first months as Minister for Industrial Production in summer 1940), 98 J 8, Fonds Belin, IHS.

[21]See Julius Reiter, *Entstehung und staatsrechtliche Theorie der italienischen Carta del Lavoro* (Frankfurt: Peter Lang, 2005).

[22]See Debbie Lackerstein, *National Regeneration in Vichy France: Ideas and Policies, 1930–1944* (Farnham: Ashgate, 2012), 94–102. The strategy of improving workers' rights to undermine the appeal of communism became similarly prevalent in France during the Cold War; see John W. Young, *France, the Cold War, and the Western Alliance, 1944–1949* (Leicester: Leicester University Press, 1990) and Philippe Buton, *Les lendemains qui déchantent. Le Parti communiste français à la Libération* (Paris: FNSP, 1993).

[23]See dossier 'Correspondence avec le ministre des finances, décembre 1940', December 1940, 98 J 9, Fonds Belin, IHS.

[24]Lettre à Pétain (not signed), 28 April 1941, 2 AG 611, AN. On the debate between 'syndicalism' and 'corporatism', see Le Crom, *Syndicats nous voilà!*.

[25]Richard Vinen, *The Politics of French Business, 1936–1945* (Cambridge: Cambridge University Press, 1991), 107–108. Baudouin resigned from Cabinet following Pétain's meeting with Hitler at Montoire in October 1940.

In October 1941, Dr Elmar Michel, the head of the Economic Section of the German Military Administration in Paris, wrote to Belin expressing his authorisation of the Charter, despite some misgivings:

> Reservations concerning certain parts of the project are withdrawn to avoid delaying its publication. The new social organisation must be applied as quickly as possible so as to organise collaboration between workers and employers and, notably, to ensure the representation of workers' interests.[26]

This long-awaited, albeit qualified support from the German authorities allowed the law to be published in full. The Charter was a fundamentally corporatist document and went much further than the legislation of August and September 1940 in breaking down the walls between the classes. Labour unions were banned outright, a step further than the dissolution of the principal trade union confederations realised in the summer of 1940.[27] Moreover, both strikes and lock-outs were outlawed, removing the most provocative weapons of workers and employers, respectively, in the battles between the two groups that had characterised the most rancorous periods of the 1930s. Other, somewhat more progressive measures, such as the first guaranteed minimum wage in France, were also included in the Charter.[28] Crucially, a corporation was to be created for each branch of industry, which would include representatives from employers and workers alike, while the State would be in control of the corporation. Industries were also asked to create Social Committees that would consist of representatives of employers and workers in equal measure.

Unlike the creation of the Organisation Committees, the drafting of the Charter was a slow process and one imbued with the ideology of the

[26]'Réponse de l'administration militaire allemande à la Charte', 21 October 1941, 98 J 9, IHS.

[27]The two largest trade union confederations, the CGT and the CFTC, were dissolved by decree on 9 November 1940.

[28]In the event, the minimum wage was never put into practice due to the context of the war and France's worsening financial position. In 1944 the CFLN abolished the Charter in its entirety, including its more palatable provisions, meaning that the minimum wage provisions were never actually put into practice. Ultimately, minimum wage legislation would be introduced in 1950 in the form of the *salaire minimum interprofessionnel garanti* (SMIG).

National Revolution. While the goals of the law of 16 August 1940 were largely limited to industrial questions, chiefly how to ensure that French industry could continue to function after the Armistice, the Charter was an ambitious project to reorganise French society. Tellingly, it was undertaken by René Belin *qua* Minister for Labour rather than being a project of the Ministry of Industrial Production. As such, Belin remained focused on the Charter after he had left the latter ministry in February 1941. Yet the project of the Charter was obstructed from achieving its goals by the perceived shortcomings of the Organisation Committees that Belin had created the year before. The Charter depended on a certain balance of power between labour and employers. Due to the exclusion of organised labour from the Organisation Committees, however, this balance did not exist, with the employers dominating all decisions related to industry. The Charter was not able to redress this, and in these circumstances it is hardly surprising that labour was not supportive of Vichy's attempts to incorporate workers into Social Committees that – if the nominally tripartite Organisation Committees were any indication – would also be dominated by big business.[29]

Although the final text of the Charter established a broad framework for a new social organisation in France, the legislation in fact changed very little. The law of 16 August 1940 had created the legal framework for the Organisation Committees, but this skeletal system was only fleshed out with the creation of the first individual Organisation Committees in early November. Similarly, the Charter known as the Law of 4 October – despite the numerous changes imposed on the text between that date and its ultimate publication on 26 October[30] – described what would be established. One important innovation echoed Pétain's speech of 12 August, namely the merging of similar existing Committees into 'families' for key industries, which would go some way towards addressing his call to reduce the number of Committees. Each family was to establish a Preparatory Commission that would be responsible for creating the Social Committee for that family, which would include mixed

[29]See Le Crom, *Syndicats nous voilà!*, 392.

[30]A series of alternative drafts and requests for modifications from Belin and others between 4 and 22 October 1941 are preserved among Pétain's papers. See 'Papiers de chef d'Etat, Etat français', 2 AG 611, AN.

representation from employers and workers.[31] Henri Lafond,[32] one of the two Secretaries General for Industrial Production, proposed folding 11 existing Committees related to iron and steel into the family for the production of metals, which would still be presided by Jules Aubrun.[33] Aubrun accepted this in principle in November 1941, although specifying that he would rather limit the number of Committees within the family to eight.[34] The responsibility for the new family was passed on to the President of the largest Organisation Committee in each family. Progress was slow, however, and by 1944, 24 of the 29 families had stalled at the level of creating a Preparatory Commission. In the end, only three families ended up creating Social Committees at all: mining, clothing, and textiles.[35] The belated creation of an Office for Social Committees in March 1944 did little to alter the situation.[36]

For all the Charter's lengthy negotiations and the determined propaganda campaign that accompanied its publication, its impact on economic and production issues in the steel industry was minimal. In every draft of the Charter after December 1940, the existence and independence of the Organisation Committees were guaranteed, and the final text of the law specified that 'questions on economic matters will remain, until further notice, in the competences of the provisional Organisation Committees created in accordance with the law of 16 August 1940'.[37] In discussing the eventual

[31]The 'professional families' were ultimately created in May 1942. See 'Création des familles professionnelles', 16 May 1942, F 12 9953, AN.

[32]Like Bichelonne, Henri Lafond was a graduate of the Polytechnique and the Ecole des Mines. A banker by profession, Lafond worked in the Ministry for Industrial Production between 1940 and 1942, when he returned to banking. He pursued a successful post-war career in the private sector until his assassination by an OAS militant in 1963.

[33]'Projet de répartition des comités d'organisation du Secrétaire Géneral de l'énergie en famille' by Henri Lafond, 12 December 1941, F 12 9953, AN.

[34]'Note pour Monsieur le secrétaire général de l'énergie', 12 November 1941, F 12 9953, AN.

[35]Henry Rousso, 'L'organisation industrielle de Vichy' in *Vichy. L'événement, la mémoire, l'histoire* (Paris: Gallimard, 1992), 79–109, here 99–100. Richard Vinen rightly points out that the last two industries were typically more supportive of the National Revolution, but that the action on the part of the mining industry is surprising. See Vinen, *The Politics of French Business*, 115.

[36]'Création d'un office des comités sociaux', 15 March 1944, F 12 9953, AN.

[37]Titre 1, Article 4, 'Loi relative à l'organisation sociale des professions' (Charte du travail), 4 October 1941.

establishment of Social Committees, CORSID emphasised that these bodies should remain silent 'when it comes to questions of allocation' of raw materials within the industry.[38] Léon Daum, the member of CORSID most involved in the discussions around the Labour Charter, specified that the role of the Social Committees would instead be to focus on 'questions related to the working conditions of the factory, working hours, hygiene, etc.'.[39] By restricting the responsibilities of the proposed Social Committees, CORSID ensured that it would retain its powers in running the French steel industry.

Having ensured that the Social Committees would not encroach on the Organisation Committee's powers, CORSID displayed a certain enthusiasm in setting up the bodies outlined in the Labour Charter. Léon Daum was an early champion of the Charter, emphasising the usefulness of the bodies which would 'lead workers and employers to speak with each other' and discuss matters of mutual interest.[40] He urged industrialists to 'not delay in setting up this instrument of social peace'.[41] Daum was more closely involved with the Vichy regime than the other members of CORSID – Pétain had appointed him to the *Conseil national* in January 1941 and Daum had accepted a cabinet position in Vichy in July 1940, although the government's offer was ultimately withdrawn.[42] In October 1942, CORSID announced that Daum had been named President of the Organisation Commission for the Professional Family of Metal Production,[43] responsible for setting up the Social Committee for the

[38]'Réunion du Groupe Centre-Ouest du 15 juillet 1942', 15 July 1942, 139 AQ 82, AN.

[39]'Réunion du Groupe Centre-Ouest du 21 janvier 1942', 21 January 1942, 139 AQ 139, AN. Based on the minutes of CORSID's meeting, Daum seems to have been the most active member in most areas. Industrialist Roger Martin later wrote of Daum that at meetings, 'when he wasn't asleep, he had a sprightly wit'. See Martin, *Patron du droit divin* (Paris: Gallimard, 1984), 37.

[40]Ibid.

[41]'Réunion du Groupe Centre-Ouest. Séance du 18 février 1942', 18 February 1942, 139 AQ 82, AN.

[42]For Daum's appointment to the *Conseil national*, see 'Groupement du Centre et de l'Ouest. Séance du 29 Janvier 1941', 21 January 1941, 139 AQ 82, AN. On Daum nearly being appointed Minister for Industrial Production in July 1940, see René Belin, *Du secrétariat de la CGT au gouvernement de Vichy* (Paris: Albatros, 1978), 128.

[43]'Groupement du Centre et de l'Ouest. Séance du 13 octobre 1942', 13 October 1942, 139 AQ 82, AN. Although Aubrun remained President of the new 'family', Daum became President of its Organisation Commission, created to oversee the establishment of the National Social Committee.

family of which CORSID would be the leader. Daum claimed that, according to Belin, 'the work of the Commission should last from six months to one year'.[44] It look more than a year, however, for the Provisional National Social Committee to hold its first meeting, in November 1943. Its membership included ten workers and ten employers, in line with the National Revolution's ideals of social harmony, and at the first meeting, wages and apprenticeships were identified as priorities, with commissions being proposed for each. Although progress was finally being made, the second meeting, on 3 March 1944, proved to be its last. A permanent Social Committee was never established and the incoming Provisional Government of the French Republic (GPRF) led by de Gaulle repealed the Labour Charter and its constituent institutions.[45]

While the Social Committee outlined in the Labour Charter proved to be abortive, it is important to note CORSID's reaction to the initiative. The Organisation Committee's initial preoccupation was protecting its existing powers. Once reassured that the Social Committee would not have a say in economic questions or in matters of resource allocation, CORSID was willing and even enthusiastic to set up the new Social Committee that could treat social questions such as working conditions, wages, and apprenticeships. CORSID's chief concern was ensuring that the steel industry continued to function as optimally as possible given the disastrous shortage of raw materials. This motivation led CORSID to oppose the tenets of the National Revolution that would be harmful to its running the steel industry, such as a more equitable representation of SMEs to dilute the power of 'trusts'. Accordingly, CORSID endorsed the elements that would not damage and might even benefit the industry, such as discussing social questions with workers and industrialists, thereby maintaining social peace and avoiding strikes.[46] Yet political and military developments in France similarly affected CORSID's attitude. If Daum was enthusiastic about the Social Committees in early 1942, by 1943 CORSID seemed to be dragging its feet with the implementation of the new Social Committee. While the National Revolution had been running out steam by the spring of 1942, any prospects of national renewal were

[44]Ibid.

[45]See 'Rétablissement de la liberté syndicale et épuration des organisations syndicales de travailleurs et d'employeurs', 13 January 1944, CFLN-GPRF 602, MAE.

[46]Strikes had erupted in the coalfields of northern France in the autumn of 1941.

decisively ended in November 1942 when the Reich occupied the hitherto Non-Occupied Zone which included the town of Vichy. From that point on, with a lack of government pressure to adopt the Labour Charter and with the regime's fading ideological project proving distinctly unpopular among French workers, CORSID had little reason to push for the speedy implementation of the Charter.[47] By then, CORSID was preoccupied with problems far greater than the creation of the Social Committee.

Working in the Reich

The spring of 1942 marked an important turning point in the history of Vichy. On 18 April, Pierre Laval returned as Head of Government and quickly affirmed that France's overriding policy was to integrate itself into a German-led Europe [*l'Europe allemande*]. In a radio address two days after his reinstatement, Laval described the choice facing France: 'either we integrate […] into a new and pacified Europe that will flourish after the war that is currently unfolding, or we resign ourselves to witnessing the destruction of our civilisation' by Bolshevism.[48] Laval's renewed enthusiasm for collaboration with Germany coincided with the sputtering out of the National Revolution. Under Laval, who had always been sceptical of the National Revolution, ambitious plans for a spiritual renewal of the nation were neglected in favour of securing for France a favourable position in post-war Europe through collaboration. Meanwhile, Germany was facing increasing difficulties on the Eastern Front nearly a year after its invasion of the Soviet Union and consequently

[47]In her detailed study of the National Revolution, Debbie Lackerstein observes that 'the Charter [was] totally irrelevant by 1943 [and] most of the structures it prescribed were never constituted, even though some groups worked on them until the end of the Occupation'. See Lackerstein, *National Regeneration in Vichy France*, 100.

[48]Qtd. in Jean-Paul Cointet, *Pierre Laval* (Paris: Fayard, 1993), 368. Laval, a veteran politician of the Third Republic, was Prime Minister under Pétain until his dismissal in December 1940. His reinstatement was largely due to German pressure, as Laval was a strong advocate of closer collaboration with the Reich. On anti-Bolshevism as a unifying factor across Nazi-occupied Europe, see Lorna Waddington, *Hitler's Crusade: Bolshevism and the Myth of the International Jewish Conspiracy* (London: Tauris, 2007), particularly Chapter 13, and Bernard Bruneteau, *L'Europe nouvelle de Hitler. Une illusion des intellectuels de la France de Vichy* (Paris: Editions du Rocher, 2003).

shifted its strategy from Blitzkrieg to trying to develop the economic potential of Europe for its war effort.[49]

The central policy pursued by the Reich in building up the German war economy at this stage was deporting workers from occupied Europe and forcing them to work in German factories. Gauleiter Fritz Sauckel[50] was placed in charge of the scheme, and he was soon demanding hundreds of thousands of French workers from Laval. The French Head of Government proposed the so-called *Relève*, whereby France would send workers to Germany, with the Reich releasing one French prisoner of war for every three French workers sent to Germany. This arrangement, established in June 1942, saw tens of thousands of French volunteers head to Germany, but the numbers fell far short of Sauckel's demands. As a result, Sauckel imposed labour conscription across occupied Europe in August 1942. Laval followed suit with the law of 4 September 1942, which established the labour draft in France. In response to further requests for workers from Sauckel, Laval set up the *Service du travail obligatoire* (STO) on 16 February 1943. Under these laws roughly 650,000 French workers were forcibly deported to Germany.[51] Overseeing the sweeping changes this would bring to French industry was Jean Bichelonne; in the major Cabinet reshuffle that accompanied Laval's return, François Lehideux

[49]Arne Radtke-Delacor, 'Produire pour le Reich. Les commandes allemandes à l'industrie française (1940–1944)' in *Vingtième siècle. Revue d'histoire*, no. 70, April–June 2001, 99–115. For Germany's industrial strategy throughout this period, see Adam Tooze, *The Wages of Destruction: The Making & Breaking of the Nazi Economy* (London: Penguin, 2007).

[50]A member of the Nazi Party since 1923, Fritz Sauckel was appointed General Plenipotentiary for Labour Deployment in March 1942, where he oversaw over 5 million foreign workers arrive to work in German factories. He was found guilty of war crimes and crimes against humanity at the Nuremberg trials and was executed in 1946.

[51]To this number we must add 300,000 who volunteered to go to Germany, of whom 60,000 left before 4 September 1942. These volunteers generally went for economic reasons, as Germany offered higher wages and more hours of work. See Jean-Pierre Azéma's 'Introduction' in *La main-d'oeuvre française exploitée par le IIIe Reich* (Caen: Centre de Recherche Quantitative, 2003). In addition to this excellent collected volume, the classic work on the STO in France remains Jacques Evrard, *La déportation des travailleurs français dans le IIIe Reich* (Paris: Fayard, 1972), while the best recent works are Patrice Arnaud, *Les STO. Histoire des Français requis en Allemagne nazie 1942–1945* (Paris: CNRS, 2010) and Raphaël Spina, *La France et les Français devant le service du travail obligatoire (1942–1945)* (PhD thesis. Cachan: ENS, 2012).

resigned and Bichelonne, his long-time Secretary General, was promoted to Minister for Industrial Production.

The situation would become even more serious after 8 November 1942, when American and British forces landed in Algeria to establish a foothold in the Mediterranean. The Allies thus gained a valuable springboard from which they later worked their way up the Italian peninsula. In response, on 11 November 1942, the Wehrmacht crossed the demarcation line established in June 1940, ostensibly to protect the soft underbelly of Vichy France and its apparently vulnerable Mediterranean coast. Henceforth, the entirety of metropolitan France remained occupied by Germany (or Italy, in the case of the small Italian zone of occupation) until the D-Day landings in Normandy, putting an end to the notion of a 'Non-Occupied Zone'. Two days later, Laval secured from Pétain the powers to pass laws on his own authority, without the need for the Maréchal. As a result, as Julian Jackson has appositely put it, 'Pétain, whose powers had been compared to those of Louis XIV two years earlier, was now more like a Third Republic president'.[52] Meanwhile, the once seemingly invincible Wehrmacht started struggling in Stalingrad. The Soviets launched the first in a series of offensives on 19 November 1942 and by the end of the winter the Germans were in retreat. As the Reich abandoned its Blitzkrieg strategy in favour of harnessing the economic potential of occupied Europe for its war effort, it was clear that France would have an important role.

In terms of increasing German armaments production, the STO does seem to have been successful. In Adam Tooze's assessment, 'the foreign labour programme was clearly by far the most important contribution that occupied Europe made to Germany's armaments effort'.[53] From a French perspective, however, the results were far less impressive. From the time the *Relève* was first instituted, industrial productivity in France dropped, a trend that only worsened as more workers were deported.[54] Perhaps more

[52]Jackson, *France: The Dark Years*, 227.

[53]Tooze, *Wages of Destruction*, 640. It should be noted that Tooze is referring to the German recruitment of labour from across Europe, not only France.

[54]Françoise Berger has calculated that overall steel output in France declined significantly in 1943 compared to 1942. This is consistent with trends in other industries; coal production peaked in 1942, for example, before declining significantly in 1943. For steel, see Françoise Berger, *La France, l'Allemagne et l'acier (1932–1952). De la stratégie des cartels à l'élaboration de la CECA* (Paris: Université de Paris I, 2000), 460–461. For coal, see 'The Coal Economy of France under German Occupation', WO 219 3752, NA. It has also been

important was the negative reaction among the French public. As Richard Vinen notes, 'for the first time, Vichy had an obviously malign effect on the lives of millions of French people, not just on those who left but also on those who endured risk or hardship in order not to go, and on the relatives of both these groups'.[55] Among those in the second group, who opted not to go, joining the Resistance was the logical alternative, and the *maquis* in France swelled from the summer of 1942. As the Resistance grew in strength and more and more of the population turned against the regime, acts of sabotage increased in French factories, disrupting production further still.[56] Of course, the STO was not the only factor causing these phenomena: the scarcity of raw materials slowed production after 1941, as did Allied bombardments of factories, while the increasing probability of an Allied victory convinced many to join the Resistance.[57] While the scheme proposed by Laval did secure the release and return to France of over 90,000 prisoners of war, it had a negative impact on French industry and weakened support for a regime already in decline.

In this broader context, it is worth considering how the Organisation Committees reacted to such initiatives. Based on the minutes of CORSID's private meetings, it is striking not only how staunchly they opposed the idea of sending French labourers to Germany, but indeed how early they made preparations to undermine such schemes. In March 1941, well over a year before the *Relève* was established, CORSID was visibly wary of German attempts to poach unemployed workers from steel firms. By the winter of 1940–1941, the shortage of coal was seriously affecting steel output, and the inconsistent deliveries of coal led to

suggested that the drop in production can be attributed to deliberate under-production (*freinage*) by employers. This argument is advanced by François Marcot in 'Qu'est-ce qu'un patron résistant?' in Olivier Dard et al., *L'Occupation, l'Etat français et les entreprises* (Paris: ADHE, 2000), 277–292, while the best critical discussion of this thesis is provided by Talbot Imlay and Martin Horn in *The Politics of Industrial Collaboration during World War II: Ford France, Vichy and Nazi Germany* (Cambridge University Press, 2014).

[55]Richard Vinen, *The Unfree French: Life under the Occupation* (London: Penguin, 2007), 249.

[56]Denis Peschanski and Jean-Louis Robert (eds), *Les Ouvriers en France pendant la Seconde Guerre Mondiale* (Paris: CNRS, 1992).

[57]For an insightful discussion of the multifaceted nature of 'the Resistance' and the diverse motivations of individuals opposing the Vichy regime, see Robert Gildea, *Fighters in the Shadows: A New History of the French Resistance* (London: Faber & Faber, 2015).

unpredictable periods of underemployment in many firms. In early 1941, Léon Daum urged industrialists to 'prepare for the possibility of employing workers for general work', such as clearing wooded areas and even tending vegetable gardens. Daum stressed that 'we mustn't be lacking in ideas when we are suddenly faced with the question of unemployment. The witnesses of the occupying army are keeping an eye on the availability of our personnel.'[58] Indeed, it emerged at the same meeting that the German authorities had allocated workers from the Hennebont firm in Brittany who were 'not very busy' to work at the nearby port of Lorient, where the Germans were building a submarine base. Despite Hennebont's appeals to the local prefecture, the Germans' decision prevailed, and the steel workers helped build the Nazis' U-Boat base in Brittany.[59]

By the end of April 1941, the local prefecture sent a request to a steel firm on behalf of the *Feldkommandantur* that the working week at the firm be increased to 40 or even 48 hours in order to free up more workers. The firm was also asked to provide a list of workers who had 'become available' due to decreased production levels.[60] Daum reiterated that 'labour that might appear to be surplus must be automatically taken on by us', even if this meant assigning them agricultural or forestry work outside the factory. CORSID was also made aware of a circular distributed by the German authorities in March trying to pursuade workers to volunteer to work in Germany, in return for higher wages and more hours of work. It was specified that such arrangements were done 'of the [workers'] free will and apply only to unemployed personnel in France', to which Daum flatly responded 'we need to ensure that we have no unemployed

[58]'Groupement Centre-Ouest. Réunion du 18 mars 1941', 18 March 1941, 139 AQ 82, AN. The minutes of this meeting state that 'Daum repeats his previous recommendations' on keeping workers busy, but unfortunately the detailed minutes of the previous meetings are not available.

[59]Ibid. While the nature of the work at Lorient is not discussed in the document, the project was undoubtedly the construction of a submarine base under the auspices of Organisation Todt (OT), the Reich's engineering group which oversaw infrastructure projects across Europe. For a discussion of the Lorient project and the OT in France, see Rémy Desquesnes, 'L'Organisation Todt en France (1940–1944)', *Histoire, économie et société*, 11:3, 1992, 535–550. For a more thorough account of the OT in France and a comparison with the Italian case, see Fabian Lemmes, *Arbeiten für das Reich: die Organisation Todt in Frankreich und Italien, 1940–1945* (PhD thesis, European University Institute, 2009).

[60]'Groupement Centre-Ouest. Réunion du 29 avril 1941', 29 April 1941, 139 AQ 82, AN.

personnel'. Daum concluded that 'we must get a head start to ensure that any presence of surplus labour not be revealed. We must also have the charade ready for any situations that may result from the precariousness of our supply of coal'.[61] Even Henri Coqueugnot, the representative of the Ministry for Industrial Production at CORSID's meetings, agreed with the Committee's measures, stating that 'it is not enough to simply inform the relevant authorities of the situation; [firms] must develop further initiatives capable of preventing the unemployment of their personnel'.[62] As a long time industrialist himself, Coqueugnot found himself siding with the employers running CORSID rather than the Reich. By early 1942, however, the small-scale work in forestry and agriculture that could be found for French workers 'appear[ed] to be fairly weak compared to the degree of unemployment'.[63] By the start of 1942, the French steel industry had a growing number of under- and unemployed workers which was becoming increasingly difficult to conceal. Meanwhile, more and more firms were being forced to hang recruitment posters in factories encouraging workers to volunteer to work in Germany; CORSID admitted that they had no choice but to comply.[64]

By the end of 1941, an interesting situation had arisen. The Forges d'Audincourt, in Franche-Comté, part of the Occupied Zone, found itself short of skilled labour and asked whether 50 to 60 rolling mill specialists from other firms could be dispatched to Audincourt. Daum noted that the question was of 'theoretical interest, to let us know whether we can move 50 workers in France'.[65] He encouraged factories to send unemployed specialists to Audincourt, observing that 'we have at the moment factories that are out of work while others are short-staffed, which should mean that we can fill the void at Audincourt'. This example shows how unpredictable production had become due to the inconsistent provision of coal. Although a firm might be suffering from underemployment, an important

[61]Ibid.

[62]'Comité d'organisation de la sidérurgie. Région du Centre et de l'Ouest. Réunion du 27 août 1941', 27 August 1941, 139 AQ 82, AN.

[63]'Réunion du Groupe Centre-Ouest du 21 janvier 1942', 21 January 1942, 139 AQ 82, AN.

[64]'Réunion des Usines du Centre-Ouest du 23 mai 1941', 23 May 1941, 139 AQ 82, AN.

[65]'Réunion du Groupe Centre-Ouest du 21 janvier 1942', 21 January 1942, 139 AQ 82, AN.

order requiring specialised rolling mill workers could suddenly demand 60 specialists. If the French steel industry hoped to be able to fill such orders, it would require sufficient labour when necessary – something made impossible by the deportation of workers to Germany.[66]

What is striking from these discussions is that CORSID was already trying to undermine German attempts to recruit workers for the Reich, more than a year before the *Relève* was formalised. The lack of raw materials had slowed steel production significantly, which in turn reduced the number of man-hours needed; an average working week was thus between 32 and 35 hours in March 1941, being as low as 24 hours in some firms.[67] CORSID's preoccupation seems to have been to maintain the full labour force and prevent outright unemployment. The motivations for this strategy, however, are not entirely obvious. After the war, many employers claimed that any refusal on their part to give up workers to the German authorities was a profoundly patriotic act, or even an act of resistance.[68] Such attempts at self-exoneration in the immediate post-war period, however, must be treated with some scepticism. While there may have been a patriotic dimension to preventing workers from volunteering (or, later, from being conscripted) to work in Germany, the business reasoning against losing one's workers was likely a much stronger factor. Given how inconsistent coal deliveries had become, it was essential that the workforce not be depleted during a shortage of coal, only for industry to find itself short of

[66]The Forges d'Audincourt specialised in sheet metal, but its production was severely disrupted by Allied bombings in July 1943. With production thus affected, more workers were vulnerable to the STO and by 1944 only 650 workers remained at the factory, compared to 1150 at the beginning of the war. See Eric Coulon, *Les Forges d'Audincourt* (Strasbourg: Coprur, 2006), 94.

[67]'Groupement Centre-Ouest. Réunion du 18 mars 1941', 18 March 1941, 139 AQ 82, AN. In May and June 1941 the average working week for the industry fell to 30 hours and dropped below 29 hours for July 1941. See 'Réunion du Groupe Centre-Ouest du 27 août 1941', 27 August 1941, 139 AQ 82, AN.

[68]The best overview of this argument is provided by François Marcot, 'Qu'est-ce qu'un patron résistant?'. For specific examples, see Marcot, 'La direction de Peugeot sous l'Occupation: pétainisme, réticence, opposition et résistance' in *Mouvement social*, no. 189, October–December 1999, 27–46; Christophe Capuano, 'Travailler chez Schneider sous l'Occupation. Les cas des usines du Creusot' in Christian Chevandier and Jean-Claude Daumas (eds), *Travailler dans les entreprises sous l'Occupation* (Besançon: Presses universitaires de Franche-Comté, 2007), 187–207; and Imlay and Horn, *The Politics of Industrial Collaboration during World War II.*

workers when the provision of coal increased.[69] It has also been suggested that 'social fear' motivated some Committees to oppose labour deportations, citing 'a general fear among the patronat that if they did not distance themselves from the deporation of labour to Germany they would suffer the consequences of the workers' anger'.[70] Whatever the motivation, it is clear that CORSID opposed early attempts to relocate French workers to Germany, and at the start of 1942, Daum predicted that in the months to come, 'we will endure phenomena worse than the loss of a few specialist workers'.[71] With the establishment of the *Relève* in June and the labour draft later that summer, Daum's warning proved prophetic.

CORSID's initial reaction to the *Relève* was restrained. Eugène Roy, the Vice-President of CORSID, observed that the situation 'leaves us a certain hope that we will not see calls for labour that are too massive'.[72] CORSID also ensured that each firm provided an updated list of employees who were still prisoners of war in Germany, ranked in order of priority for release, with skilled labourers being at the top of the list.[73] Given that the terms of the *Relève* promised the release of one POW for every three workers sent to Germany, CORSID wanted to ensure that it secured the return of the industry's most useful workers. Following the law of 4 September 1942 establishing compulsory labour drafts, CORSID decided to gather information from its factories before approaching the government, noting that 'information is still imprecise in many cases' and they

[69]De Rochebrune and Hazera have argued that 'managerial logic' informed the decision-making of employers during the war, by far outweighing the patriotic 'logic of the citizen'. See Renaud de Rochebrune and Jean Claude Hazera, *Les patrons sous l'Occupation* (Paris: Odile Jacob, 1995) and the discussion below.

[70]While Vinen includes examples of the COH protesting labour deportations in 1942, his discussion of the motivations for the opposition to these policies focuses on the STO. He notes that by 1943, when the STO was established, 'business calculations were now founded on the assumption of an allied victory'. He adds that 'Resistance to STO ... was in theory the policy of all COs'. See Richard Vinen, 'The French Coal Industry during the Occupation', *The Historical Journal*, 33:1, 1990, 105–130, here 113–114 and 123. This 'social fear' may also explain CORSID's support for Social Committees, which would theoretically have improved relations between workers and employers.

[71]'Réunion du Groupe Centre-Ouest du 21 janvier 1942', 21 January 1942, 139 AQ 82, AN.

[72]'Réunion du Groupe Centre-Ouest du 15 juillet 1942', 15 July 1942, 139 AQ 82, AN.

[73]Ibid. This request was sent out as 'Circulaire du 13 juillet 1942', 13 July 1942, 139 AQ 79, AN.

were not entirely sure what impact the labour draft would have on the industry.[74] To this end, CORSID issued a circular to all factories only hours after the law was passed requesting information so that CORSID could establish statistics on the departure of workers to Germany.[75] A file was opened for each worker sent to Germany in order to keep track of them, and in most cases communication was established between the workers sent to Germany and their firm back in France.[76]

By February 1943, CORSID observed that 'important departures [were] underway in most factories'.[77] Meeting on 16 February 1943, the very day the STO was formally established, Robert Baboin,[78] who had replaced Coqueugnot as representative of the Ministry of Industrial Production, reiterated his request 'that factories inform him of workers who are not employed in their area of specialty', noting that 'the answers received so far are insufficient'.[79] There could be little doubt that such documents would be used to compile lists of workers to be sent to Germany. It is worth noting the evolution of the attitude of the Ministry for Industrial Production regarding sending labour to Germany. While the Ministry's representative, Coqueugnot, had supported CORSID's efforts to frustrate German attempts to acquire volunteers to work in Germany in mid-1941, the Ministry's policy by February 1943, as articulated by Robert Baboin, was to abet the conscription of French workers.[80] The

[74]'Comité d'organisation de la sidérurgie. Région du Centre et de l'Ouest. Réunion du 13 octobre 1942', 13 October 1942, 139 AQ 82, AN.

[75]Ibid.

[76]'Comité d'organisation de la sidérurgie. Région du Centre et de l'Ouest. Réunion du 16 novembre 1942', 16 November 1942, 139 AQ 82, AN.

[77]'Comité d'organisation de la sidérurgie. Région du Centre et de l'Ouest. Réunion du 16 février 1943', 16 February 1943, 139 AQ 82, AN.

[78]After graduating from the Polytechnique and the Ecole des Mines de Paris, Robert Baboin taught at the Ecole des Mines de Saint-Etienne before succeeding Coqueugnot as Director for Steel at the Ministry of Industrial Production. Coqueugnot's health was failing and died in January 1944.

[79]'Comité d'organisation de la sidérurgie. Région du Centre et de l'Ouest. Réunion du 16 février 1943', 16 February 1943, 139 AQ 82, AN.

[80]The replacement of Coqueugnot, an industrialist by profession, with former professor Baboin may in part explain why the Ministry of Industrial Production's representative was no longer in agreement with the industrialists running CORSID on this question. Laval's support for the STO, however, was likely the most important factor.

institutionalisation of the labour draft was decisive in bringing about this shift, but CORSID's position does not seem to have followed the Ministry's conversion, however, since industrialists were primarily concerned with keeping their factories running, which was hardly compatible with the removal of large numbers of their workers. Accordingly, CORSID was decidedly uncooperative with the Ministry over the STO; Baboin renewed his request for lists of workers ripe for deportation again in April, grumbling about how little progress had been made since his request at the beginning of the year.[81] Daum seems to have lobbied the Ministry to ensure that steel was recognised as 'an essential industry to the economic life of the country', which entitled factories to 'be exempt from all departures [of workers] that are not immediately compensated' with replacement workers, thereby keeping the number of workers as constant as possible.[82] In several cases, deported French workers were replaced by the German authorities with workers from North Africa.[83] CORSID also pleaded for the release of several categories of workers. While requests for the repatriation of students, farmers, and women were dismissed, the possibility of repatriation was granted for the fathers of large families (with five or more children), workers older than 50, and workers who were seriously ill and deemed unfit for work.[84] Although these were relatively minor concessions, they demonstrate that CORSID was active in working with the German and French authorities in order to alleviate the effects of the STO. Given how CORSID had opposed German efforts to encourage individual workers to volunteer to travel to Germany for work in 1941, it is not surprising that they opposed the massive labour deportations envisaged by Sauckel. CORSID used its influence to work within the system to ease the

[81]'Comité d'organisation de la sidérurgie. Région du Centre et de l'Ouest. Réunion du 13 avril 1943', 13 April 1943, 139 AQ 82, AN.

[82]'Comité d'organisation de la sidérurgie. Région du Centre et de l'Ouest. Réunion du 18 mai 1943', 18 May 1943, 139 AQ 82, AN.

[83]'Comité d'organisation de la sidérurgie. Région du Centre et de l'Ouest. Réunion du 15 juin 1943', 15 June, 139 AQ 82, AN. The minutes of this meeting report that the factories of Guérigny and Imphy, both in Nièvre (Bourgogne), received North African workers from the German authorities. While not specified in the documents, these workers would likely have come from Tunisia, which was occupied by German forces following the Allied landings in Algeria and Morocco in November 1942 until May 1943.

[84]'Comité d'organisation de la sidérurgie. Région du Centre et de l'Ouest. Réunion du 13 juillet 1943', 13 juillet, 139 AQ 82, AN.

symptoms of the STO most debilitating to the French steel industry. While CORSID tried to act as a shield to protect its firms and their workers, the success of its interventions was limited.

CORSID was by no means alone in its opposition to the STO; indeed, given how decidedly disadvantageous the scheme was for employers, the deportation of workers to Germany was opposed to varying degrees by the majority of the Organisation Committees. The most notable case is likely the Organisation Committee for Coal (COH) and particularly its president, Aimé Lepercq. By 1943, Lepercq was deeply involved with the internal Resistance, namely as President of the *Organisation Civile et Militaire* (OCM). In August 1943, he was dismissed as President of the COH, not due to his activities with the OCM, which remained hidden from Vichy, but because of his opposition to the STO. Lepercq would go on to be celebrated as one of the heroes of the French Resistance and became Minister for Finance in de Gaulle's first government, before dying prematurely in November 1944. Yet the grounds for his dismissal – opposition to the STO – were hardly unique among the leaders of the Organisation Committees. The members of CORSID similarly opposed and frustrated the government's policies of labour deportation and clashed with the representative of the Ministry of Industrial Production over the issue. While Lepercq's activities with the OCM distinguish him from the majority of industrialists in Vichy France, his opposition to the STO as a member of an Organisation Committee was unexceptional.[85] Indeed, in the weeks following Lepercq's dismissal, even the Minister for Industrial Production, Jean Bichelonne, would abandon his support for the STO in favour of a new policy that would gain the support of French industrialists.

Franco-German Integration Under Speer and Bichelonne

The negative effects of the STO in France, particularly in terms of industrial production, were by no means lost on Jean Bichelonne. Production in France was in steady decline: the lack of coal drove down production, which the

[85] Richard Vinen has argued that most of the COH's efforts to resist the STO took place after Aimé Lepercq's dismissal in the summer of 1943 and were instead overseen by his successor Charles Crussard, 'a less high profile resistant than Lepercq'. See Vinen, 'The French Coal Industry during the Occupation', op.cit.

Germans used to justify sending French workers to Germany, reducing production even further. Moreover, the majority of workers removed from French factories never made it to Germany,[86] and a significant number of those fleeing the STO opted to join the Resistance, leading Vichy to cheekily refer to the *maquis* as *l'armée Sauckel*.[87] With shortages of raw material and labour, dwindling production, low morale, and a burgeoning Resistance amongst its consequences, the STO was a disaster for French industry.

It was in this context that Jean Bichelonne travelled to Berlin to meet Albert Speer, the German Minister for Armaments and War Production, in September 1943.[88] The two men had a great deal in common, both generally being described as young, apolitical technocrats.[89] Bichelonne argued that France could produce far more efficiently for the German war economy if French workers could return to French factories and if the labour deportations were to cease. Speer proposed that France focus on 'consumer goods as well as military equipment, rather than armaments'; this would enable German factories 'to stop production of certain civilian goods entirely so as to further develop [its] armaments programme'.[90] In

[86]According to Alan Milward, 'only about ten per cent on average of the men detailed to go to Germany actually arrived there'. See Milward, *The New Order and the French Economy* (Oxford: Oxford University Press, 1970), 153.

[87]There is some debate as to how many conscripted for work in Germany actually joined the *maquis*, with one estimate placing the proportion as low as 19 per cent (for the *département* of Tarn). See Jean-Pierre Azéma and Olivier Wieviorka, *Vichy, 1940–1944* (Paris: Perrin, 2004), 256.

[88]Given that German industry was formally oriented towards armaments and war production, Speer can be considered Bichelonne's opposite number.

[89]This characterisation has been questioned in some recent works. Speer's purported apoliticism is rejected by Tooze as 'self-evidently absurd', given Speer's membership in the Nazi Party since 1931 and the political implications of his actions as Minister – by increasing German production he prolonged the war. The depiction of Jean Bichelonne as apolitical has recently come under similar criticism, notably by Jackie Clarke, who describes Bichelonne's proposals to integrate the French economy into a German-led Europe as 'political choices [. . .] despite the professed apoliticism of technicians'. See Tooze, *Wages of Destruction*, 552–553 and Jackie Clarke, *France in the Age of Organization* (Oxford: Berghahn, 2011), 132–135.

[90]'Procès-verbal de la conférence tenue à Berlin le vendredi 17 septembre 1943 dans le bureau de Monsieur Speer', 17 September 1943, 72 AJ 1926, AN. In Speer's memoirs, he writes favourably of the plan, as it allowed the Reich to gain armaments capacity and 'seemed to be the only way [he] could harness French industrial production to [German] purposes'. He adds that 'Hitler proved content' with the plan. See Albert Speer, *Inside the Third Reich* (New York: Macmillan, 1970), 310–311.

addition, all French factories participating in this scheme would be shielded from Sauckel's labour drafts, giving further incentive for industrialists to take part.[91]

This arrangement marked the most explicit attempt to realise 'the New Economic Order in Europe' outlined by German Minister for the Economy Walther Funk in July 1940.[92] By shifting the production of consumer goods to France, Germany was in effect accepting a degree of interdependence with France, rather than considering it as a stable of workers that could be plundered at will. In Berlin, Bichelonne underlined that 'this joint endeavour entails complete trust between the two administrations',[93] adding that the French government was offering 'economic support for the German war effort'.[94] Crucially, Speer and Bichelonne recognised the key role the Organisation Committees would play in this arrangement.[95] This is hardly surprising, since the Committees were initially created precisely to facilitate this kind of Franco-German integration.[96] The Committees continued to receive orders from German firms and authorities and allocate them to the appropriate French firms. Given the opposition to labour deportations in the French steel industry, CORSID welcomed the agreement and cooperated with the scheme by accepting more German orders after September 1943.[97] Moreover, the agreement would ensure more work for French factories, which would

[91]Bichelonne told his German interlocutors that with this protection, 'the labour problem will disappear quite simply'. 'Procès-verbal de la conférence tenue à Berlin (Wannsee)', 17 September 1943, 72 AJ 1926, AN.

[92]Walther Funk, 'The Economic Reorganization of Europe' in Walter Lipgens (ed.), *Documents on the History of European integration. Volume I: Continental Plans for European Union, 1939–1945* (Berlin: Walter de Gruyter, 1985), 65–70.

[93]'Procès-verbal de la conférence tenue à Berlin (Wannsee)', 17 September 1943, 72 AJ 1926, AN.

[94]'Procès-verbal de la conférence tenue à Berlin le vendredi 17 septembre 1943 dans le bureau de Monsieur Speer', 17 September 1943, 72 AJ 1926, AN.

[95]'Procès-verbal de la conférence tenue à Berlin le vendredi 17 septembre 1943 dans le bureau de Monsieur Speer', 17 September 1943, 72 AJ 1926, AN.

[96]See Chapter 2.

[97]'Comité d'organisation de la sidérurgie. Région du Centre et de l'Ouest. Réunion du 18 avril 1944', 18 April 1944, 139 AQ 82, AN.

prevent them from closing and would increase production.[98] Most importantly, Bichelonne had insisted that all orders carried out by the steel industry under the scheme 'must entail the provision of coal' by Germany; with Germany itself increasingly short on coal, however, the coal deliveries often fell short of what was needed.[99] Finally, the prospect of producing chiefly consumer goods rather than armaments undoubtedly made these orders easier to accept, as they could be presented as civilian production.[100] Of course, in the European economy envisaged by Speer and Bichelonne, shifting civilian production to France freed up German factories to focus on armaments production and thereby contributed significantly to the German war effort.

Although industrialists welcomed the accord, its success is debatable. Tooze dismisses the arrangement as 'a last-ditch effort of little practical significance',[101] although he bases his assessment on whether the accord helped the New European Economy compete with Allied production, which by September 1943 was far outpacing that of the Nazi Empire. Milward concludes that neither the STO nor the Speer–Bichelonne accord was successful, 'since the level of exploitation of the French economy [by Germany] was so high already'.[102] Furthermore, since Hitler never abandoned Sauckel's policy entirely, the two remained in competition until the end of the occupation, which undermined the efficiency of both schemes.[103]

[98]On the motivations of French employers for 'economic collaboration', see Fabian Lemmes, 'Collaboration in Wartime France, 1940–1944', *European Review of History: Revue européenne d'histoire*, 15:2, 2008, 157–177.

[99]'Procès-verbal de la conférence tenue à Berlin (Wannsee)', 17 September 1943, 72 AJ 1926, AN.

[100]A standard defence presented by industrialists after the war was that while they produced extensively for the Reich, they produced civilian rather than military goods. A number of recent studies have accepted this defence. See François Marcot, 'Qu'est-ce qu'un patron résistant?' and, for the case of Schneider in the French steel industry, Christophe Capuano, 'Travailler chez Schneider sous l'Occupation'.

[101]Tooze, *Wages of Destruction*, 640

[102]Milward, *The New Order and the French Economy*, 179–180.

[103]Although the number of deportations dropped significantly, several thousand continued to be deported monthly after September 1943. Milward calculates that 5000 workers were deported in September 1943 and fewer than 4000 in October; see Milward, *The New Order and the French Economy*, 161. Speer cites very similar figures in his memoirs; see Speer, *Inside the Third Reich*, 311. In February 1944, the eligibility criteria for being drafted for compulsory labour were broadened even further, aggravating concerns over additional deportations. On the competition between Sauckel's and Speer's initatives, see Walter Naasner, *Neue Machtzentren in der deutschen Kriegswirtschaft* (Boppard am Rhein: Harald Boldt Verlag, 1994).

Arne Radtke-Delacor, meanwhile, argues that the Speer–Bichelonne arrangement was in fact successful for the Reich, since the amount of French production for Germany did increase following September 1943. Yet this increase was far from revolutionary: the proportion of overall French production for Germany rose from just over 40 per cent in the second quarter of 1943 to between 45–50 per cent by the second quarter of 1944.[104] Production for Germany in the steel industry was in fact much higher: by the second quarter of 1944, a typical proportion of production for the Reich among French steel firms was between 75 and 85 per cent.[105] Over the period covered by the agreement, however, steel production actually dropped slightly, with the output of Martin steel falling from 13,236 tonnes in September 1943 to 12,234 tonnes in May 1944 in the Centre-Ouest region;[106] this was chiefly due to the drastic shortages of coal confronting French industry. Despite taking part in the Speer-Bichelonne programme to produce consumer goods for Germany, the French steel industry in Centre-Ouest received only 7,500 tonnes of coal for April 1944, which came with the caveat that the entire amount had to be allocated to a single factory in order to maximise efficiency.[107] This can be compared to 34,000 tonnes received in September 1942, the month the labour draft was established in France, which itself was a decrease from previous months.[108] Indeed, given the circumstances, ranging from ever worsening shortages of coal to increasingly frequent Allied bombings of French factories, it is striking how much the French steel industry was able to produce, even if there was a real decline in output. From September 1943, we can observe an increase in

[104]Radtke-Delacor, 'Produire pour le Reich', 114.

[105]'France industrie', 25 April 1944, F 12 9971, AN. According to this calculation, the Etablissements Edmond Chevalier in Verneuil-sur-Eure was producing 75 per cent for the Reich, while the Fonderie des Avenues in Pont Audemer was producing 85 per cent for the Reich, with the remainder reserved for the SNCF. Both firms were protected under the Speer-Bichelonne agreement from the STO (*Sperrbetriebe*).

[106]'Comité d'organisation de la sidérurgie. Région du Centre et de l'Ouest. Réunion du 13 octobre, 1942', 13 October 1942 and 'Comité d'organisation de la sidérurgie. Région du Centre et de l'Ouest. Réunion du 13 juin 1944', 13 June 1944, 139 AQ 82, AN.

[107]'Comité d'organisation de la sidérurgie. Région du Centre et de l'Ouest. Réunion du 16 mai 1944', 16 May 1944, 139 AQ 82, AN.

[108]'Comité d'organisation de la sidérurgie. Région du Centre et de l'Ouest. Réunion du 13 octobre 1942', 13 October 1942, 139 AQ 82, AN.

the proportion of production for Germany, even if overall output continued to drop amidst the worsening shortages of raw materials.[109]

The German stipulation that the entirety of its coal deliveries to the steel industry for the month of April 1944 be used by a single factory was part of a broader German effort to impose a certain concentration of French industry. Hans Kehrl, one of Speer's closest collaborators in the Ministry of Armaments and War Production who met separately with Bichelonne in September 1943, criticised the tendency of Organisation Committees to 'spread orders [across its factories] far more than is necessary', a tendency that Bichelonne recognised as well. 'It would be much more practical', Kehrl argued, 'to concentrate production in the hands of a small number of firms'.[110] While Bichelonne accepted the logic behind this reasoning, he insisted that 'we must maintain the firms where production is suitably efficient', regardless of their size.[111] With worsening shortages of raw materials, Bichelonne argued that efficient use of coal should determine whether a factory should be closed. This tendency to 'spread orders' amongst the firms in a given industry had been pursued by the Organisation Committees from the very beginning, and with good reason. If the primary motivation of Committee members was to keep the factories in their industry running, then concentrating production in a handful of factories at the expense of the rest could not be tolerated. Given that in many cases the largest firms in a given sector were excluded from the relevant Organisation Committee, concentrating production in a small number of 'champions' was similarly unlikely to win over the Committees. Moreover, such attempts at concentration would lead not only to the closure of factories, but to the loss of those workers, who would predictably be conscripted for work in Germany. Given the lengths to which

[109]Writing on the French automotive industry in this period, Talbot Imlay has similarly noted 'if the Germans captured a large part of the productive pie, it was a pie that had considerably shrunk'. See Imlay and Horn, *The Politics of Industrial Collaboration during World War II*, 267.

[110]'Procès-verbal de la conférence tenue à Berlin le vendredi 17 septembre 1943 dans le bureau de Monsieur Speer', 17 September 1943, 72 AJ 1926, AN. Kehrl summarises Bichelonne's visit to Berlin in his memoirs in a chapter tellingly entitled 'The Concentration of the War Economy'. See Kehrl, *Krisenmanager im Dritten Reich* (Düsseldorf: Droste Verlag, 1973), 310–318.

[111]'Procès-verbal de la conférence tenue à Berlin (Wannsee), 17 September 1943, 72 AJ 1926, AN.

CORSID went to undermine labour deportations, it is hardly surprising that the German prescription of industrial concentration held little appeal. Finally, with the intensification of aerial bombardments of French factories by the Allies, concentrating production in a few, easy-to-target sites risked paralysing the entire industry.[112] Bichelonne and CORSID managed to resist the German pressure to concentrate French industry, even while French production for the German war effort intensified.

More important than his disagreement with Kehrl over concentration was Bichelonne's opposition to further deportations of workers to Germany, a position supported by Speer. Following Bichelonne's trip to Berlin in September 1943, the policy of the Ministry of Industrial Production was thus to accept as many orders for the Reich as possible, thereby contributing to the German war economy by producing consumer goods rather than providing workers. Not surprisingly, this policy was promoted by the Organisation Committees that operated under the Ministry; indeed, this broad policy of keeping factories running by producing for Germany had been at the foundation of the Committees, which had never been enthusiastic about the mass deportations of their labour force. At the governmental level, meanwhile, Laval resisted Sauckel's further requests for labour, signalling support for the Bichelonne-Speer agreement as an alternative to the STO. From September 1943 until the end of the Vichy regime, the French government opposed further deportations and focused its energies on increasing production for the Reich as a way of contributing to the German war effort.[113]

Harmonising Franco-German Industry

By February 1942, with the worsening shortage of coal taking its toll on the steel industry, officials began discussing, apparently without irony, the prospect of melting down the Eiffel Tower to recycle its 7,200

[112] On opposition to industrial concentration in the French steel industry due to fears of bombardment, see Christophe Capuano, 'Travailler chez Schneider sous l'Occupation'. The issue of concentration in the French steel industry in the post-war period is discussed in Chapter 8.

[113] Despite the opposition of Laval and Bichelonne, Hitler supported Sauckel's calls for more labour in early 1944 and the law of 4 September 1942 was consequently broadened on 1 February 1944 to include more categories, such as men up to 60 years old and women between 18 and 45.

tonnes of steel.[114] The right-wing intellectual Thierry Maulnier went further, suggesting that the much smaller Vendôme Column be recycled as well, not only for its raw materials but also 'in the name of perspective and harmony'.[115] The Column was famously made from the cannons captured from German armies by Napoleon at Austerlitz, and it was thought that destroying this monument to the French victory over German forces might please the Nazis. Fortunately for Paris' skyline, neither of these schemes came to fruition, although French steel mills shipped many times the weight of the Eiffel Tower in steel products across the Rhine each month.[116]

The majority of the work done by CORSID throughout the war was rather mundane and usually fairly technical,[117] with its principal task being to distribute the raw materials allocated to the industry by OCRPI to the appropriate steel firms. Its other main responsibility was to receive and process orders from the German authorities, passing along the relevant order and the appropriate share of raw materials to a given steel firm. The Committees had after all been established in the summer of 1940 to stand between individual French firms and intimidating German authorities. The coordination of orders from Germany was assigned to the *Comptoir des*

[114]In one of the better-known anecdotes about Jean Bichelonne, the Minister was told of a German plan to melt down the Eiffel Tower for its steel. Bichelonne was able to spontaneously provide the figure for the exact tonnage of steel in the Tower, which was reassuringly small enough to make the scheme impractical. This is recounted in Kuisel, *Capitalism and the State in Modern France: Renovation and Economic Management in the Twentieth Century* (Cambridge: Cambridge University Press, 1981).

[115]'Bulletin d'information', 9–11 February 1942, F 12 10933, AN. This was requested by Thierry Maulnier, a future member of l'Académie française, in the pro-Vichy daily *l'Action Française*.

[116]7,500 tonnes of steel would be comparable to a month's output at a single steel mill during the war. Schneider's large factory in Creusot, for example, produced an average of 11,376 tonnes of steel per month in 1941; the monthly average for 1942 was 9,590 tonnes. For the production figures, see 'Relations avec l'occupant allemand', 1941–1942, 187 AQ 575, AN.

[117]During the war, Committees' work was criticised for being arcane and unclear. One article claimed that employers affected by Committees' decisions were 'incapable of understanding anything of the jumble of often contradictory memoranda' emitted by the Committees, with the result of the memoranda simply being ignored. See *L'Espoir Français*, 10 November 1942 in 'Revue de presse. Partie économique (du 23 au 29 Novembre)', compiled by OCRPI, F 12 10931, AN.

Produits Sidérurgiques (CPS), created by CORSID in December 1940.[118] It largely inherited the role of the pre-war *Comptoir sidérurgique de France* (CSF), which had been responsible for receiving and centralising orders and deliveries for the industry. The new CPS functioned in a fundamentally different conext, however, as the Committees, CORSID chief among them, had been created with a view to institutionalise and deepen economic cooperation between France and the Reich. CORSID found it useful to adapt the pre-war CSF to this end in the form of the new CPS; the latter would deal extensively with German authorities and industrialists, receiving orders from and producing extensively for them. CORSID even published a bilingual technical vocabulary list to help German and French steel industrialists ensure they were placing and receiving orders for the correct products.[119]

In addition to receiving German orders, CORSID also oversaw attempts to 'harmonise' French and German steel production. In reality, this involved adapting French practices to German ones. This was largely carried out by the *Bureau de normalisation de la sidérurgie* (BNS), another body established by CORSID and placed under the leadership of Eugène Dupuy, a professor at the Ecole des Mines.[120] Its role was formally to standardise steel production across France, ensuring that various steel products were uniform and thus interchangeable.[121] This is broadly in line with much of the literature that emphasises Vichy's attempts to rationalise the French economy.[122] Crucially, however, the BNS took the specifications used in

[118]Indeed, the creation of this body was only the second formal action CORSID took, on 25 November 1940. 'Déclaration no. 2', CORSID, 3 December 1940, 139 AQ 80, AN.

[119]'Circulaire du 7 août 1941', 7 August 1941, 139 AQ 79, AN. CORSID issued this circular to ask how many copies of the French–German and German–French technical vocabulary list each factory wanted to receive.

[120]On Eugène Dupuy, see Philippe Mioche, 'Un tournant dans l'histoire technique de la sidérurgie: la création de l'Irsid', *Histoire, économie et société*, 8:1, 1989, 119–140, 124.

[121]'Circulaire du 27 octobre 1941', 27 October 1941, 139 AQ 79, AN.

[122]Attempts at rationalisation under Vichy included the development of economic planning, the creation of a research centre for the steel industry, the development of comprehensive statistics and economic data for France, and the emergence of 'technocracy'. Indicatively, Richard Kuisel, 'Vichy et les origines de la planification économique (1940–1946)', *Le Mouvement social*, no. 98, January 1977, 77–101; Philippe Mioche, 'Un tournant dans l'histoire de la sidérurgie'; Delphine Dulong, *Moderniser la politique. Aux origines de la Ve République* (Paris: L'Harmattan, 1997); Olivier Dard, 'Les technocrats: archéologie d'un

Germany as its point of reference, and sought to harmonise France's steel products in line with these dimensions. This started in earnest in March 1942, when the BNS informed all steel firms of the new 'standard dimensions for thin sheet metal [*tôles minces*]'.[123] These dimensions were confirmed throughout the war and while they had initially been 'recommended', they later became obligatory. These specifications remained in place after the Liberation and were confirmed in April 1945.[124]

Adopting German practices and specifications made sense in this context. Given that by 1944 the overwhelming majority of French steel production was geared towards filling German orders, it was logical to export products that could be used immediately by the German war economy without modification. Since French factories had replaced German ones in producing a variety of non-military goods for the German market, many French steel mills had become little more than branch plants of the Reich's economy by the late stages of the war, and so their products were made as if they were in Germany. Yet these developments had been underway for some time, as CORSID received orders from German firms and oversaw the adoption of German specifications well before the Speer–Bichelonne agreement was reached, since production for the Reich still accounted for the majority of the steel industry's orders. The BNS had been active in this process of adopting German standards since 1941 and by June 1943 the CPS had compiled an extensive list of prices for products with German specifications that had been approved by the Reich authorities.[125] In December 1943, by now under the aegis of the Speer–Bichlonne agreement, the Reichsbahn ordered large sheet metal [*larges plats*] made according to German specifications,[126]

concept, généalogie d'un groupe social' in Olivier Dard, Jean-Claude Daumas and François Marcot (eds), *L'Occupation, l'Etat français et les entreprises* (Paris: Association pour le développement de l'histoire économique, 2000), 213–228; Philip Nord, *France's New Deal* (Princeton: Princeton University Press, 2010); Clarke, *France in the Age of Organization*.

[123]'Lettre d'Eugène Dupuy', 17 March 1942, 139 AQ 79, AN.

[124]See, for instance, 'Note du BNS sur l'épaisseur des tôles minces', April 1945, 139 AQ 80, AN.

[125]'Prix, produits selon les spécifications allemands homologués', 4 June 1943, 104 AQ 113, ANMT.

[126]'Larges plats satisfaisant à des specifications allemandes', December 1943, 104 AQ 113, ANMT.

while Stahlunion, a subsidiary of Otto Wolff, made numerous orders in 1944 for sheet metal [*larges plats* and *tôles fortes, moyennes et minces*], all explicitly following German standards and specifications.[127] The CPS continued to send price lists and other documents to Stahlunion until at least mid-July 1944. In other words, CORSID was continuing to supply the Reich with French steel products even as the German army was fighting Allied troops on French soil. In November 1944, two months after Charles de Gaulle had re-established a Republican government in Paris, Otto Wolff, one of the leading armaments producers for the Wehrmacht, complained to the CPS that one of its orders had still not arrived.[128]

In Nord and Pas-de-Calais, meanwhile, the 'harmonisation' of French and German steel production happened in a far more direct way. SIDENOR, the organisation analogous to CORSID in the two northernmost departments, reported that the German authorities there forced all steel firms in the region to adopt the German method for producing Thomas steel. Unsurprisingly, the Nazi authorities judged the German production method superior to the one used by the French.[129] Annexed to Belgium by Germany and in the midst of a crippling shortage of coal, Nord and Pas-de-Calais had little choice but to assimilate to the production methods imposed on it by Germany.

This standardisation in the French steel industry is significant. Not only did the BNS standardise steel products across France, but it harmonised Franco-German specifications, albeit by unilaterally accepting Germany's, which facilitated the easy transfer of French steel products to the German market. Importantly, this standardisation occurred before the Speer–Bichelonne agreement, demonstrating that even while CORSID was protesting against the deportation of French workers, it continued to integrate the French steel industry into *l'Europe allemande*. Given that the Organisation Committees were first created to facilitate the realisation of a 'New Economic Order in Europe', their progress in standardising French

[127]See, for example, 'Larges plats suivant norme allemande', 19 January 1944 and 'Tôles fortes, moyennes et minces satisfaisant à des spécifications allemandes', 28 April 1944, 104 AQ 113, ANMT. The French names of these steel products have ben included since both *plat* and *tôle* would be rendered into English as 'sheet metal'.

[128]Letter on behalf of Otto Wolff (signature illegible), 9 November 1944, 106 AQ 14, ANMT.

[129]'Note', April 1942, in 'Dossier Lille', F 12 10935, AN.

production to German norms is not surprising. Furthermore, by the time that Speer and Bichelonne agreed to deeper cross-Rhine economic cooperation, the French steel industry was already well prepared to produce for Germany. The advances made by CORSID in this respect reveal that while they opposed the deportation of workers to Germany, they were entirely willing to produce for the Reich and to 'harmonise' the industrial production of the two countries.

Conclusion

The question of whether French industrialists 'collaborated' or 'resisted' during the Second World War has been fiercely debated since the end of the Vichy regime. Since the 1990s in particular, new taxonomies have been introduced in an attempt to more accurately categorise individuals' actions under Vichy. Accordingly, the action of producing goods for the Reich in order to keep one's factory running has variously been labelled 'collaboration for survival',[130] 'coerced accommodation',[131] and 'coerced adaptation',[132] while producing civilian goods for the Reich, rather than armaments, has been described as an act of 'resistance'[133] – despite the fact that such production was demanded by Speer as a means of freeing up German industrial capacity to increase the Reich's armaments production. Opposition to the STO, broadly shared among members of the Organisation Committees, has similarly been vaunted as 'resistance'.[134]

[130]See Robert Frank, Jean-Marie Flonneau and Robert Mancherini, 'Conclusion' in Alain Beltran, Robert Frank and Henry Rousso (eds), *La vie des entreprises sous l'Occupation* (Paris: Belin, 1994). This label is also used in Fabian Lemmes, 'Collaboration in wartime France, 1940–1944', *European Review of History*, 15:2, 2008, 157–177.

[131]Philippe Burrin, *La France à l'heure allemande* (Paris: Seuil, 1995), especially 468–470. In this influential study, Burrin proposed the term 'accommodation' to describe a huge range of actions between the extremes of collaboration and resistance. Accordingly, producing for the Reich in order to protect one's factory is considered by Burrin to be 'accommodation' rather than 'collaboration'.

[132]François Marcot, 'Qu'est-ce qu'un patron résistant?', op.cit., 278\280.

[133]Christophe Capuano, 'Travailler sous Schneider sous l'Occupation' and Marcot, 'La direction de Peugeot sous l'Occupation'. Both authors identify individual employers whom they argue privileged civilian over military production.

[134]A discussion of the claims made by COH members after the war that opposition to the STO constituted resistance is provided by Vinen, 'The French Coal Industry during the Occupation'.

In the case of CORSID, it is clear that its preoccupation with keeping its factories running determined its response to the gamut of Vichy's initatives, from the Labour Charter to the STO to the Speer–Bichelonne agreement. With regard to the Labour Charter, CORSID insisted that the proposed Social Committees would not impinge upon the responsibilities of the Organisation Committees. Once this concession had been gained, Daum and his colleagues supported the Charter insofar as it could improve relations between employers and workers. By 1943, however, with the entirety of France occupied and the regime's illusions of sovereignty in tatters, it was clear that support for the Labour Charter and the broader National Revolution would not be an effective means of improving labour relations; CORSID's brief enthusiasm for the Social Committees thus waned markedly.

The reaction of the Organisation Committees to the STO was consistent with the Committee's priorities. In order to keep factories running, employers need a labour force. Any scheme to deplete this labour force and hence the productive capacity of a factory would inexorably be opposed by the Committee. Strikingly, CORSID undermined any attempt to lure workers away from their factories, even if the workers were to volunteer, from the very beginning. The lengths to which CORSID went to disguise under- and unemployment to keep steel workers in place was remarkable. In their opposition to the STO, the members of CORSID were very much in agreement with Aimé Lepercq.

If CORSID's negative response to labour deportations was logical, so too was its positive reaction to the Speer–Bichelonne agreement and indeed to producing goods for the Reich in general. The maintenance of factories depended on receiving a steady stream of production orders and in the context of a Nazi-controlled Europe, those orders would inevitably come from Germany. This reality had prompted the creation of the Organisation Committee in the first place; they were to receive orders from the Reich and allocate them to factories within their industry. CORSID's efforts to have factories adopt German specifications thus made good business sense. Similarly, the prospect, offered by the Speer–Bichelonne agreement, of producing civilian goods for Germany in exchange for protection from the STO, was irresistible. Conversely, Hans Kehrl's insistence that production be concentrated among a small handful of factories was rejected by CORSID on the same grounds – such a policy would inescapably lead to the closure of countless factories.

After the war, advocates of dissolving the Organisation Committees justified their stance by arguing that the Committees had collaborated during the war, claiming that they 'produced for the enemy for four years' and that it was 'thanks to the Organisation Committees, [that French] workers were deported' to Germany.[135] The above study shows, however, that labels such as 'collaboration' or 'resistance' are ultimately unhelpful for understanding the wartime actions of the members of the Organisation Committees. Committee members sought, above all else, to keep their factories running, and this remained the primary motivation of their actions under Vichy. Paradoxically, this logic meant that an act that could be considered as collaborating – such as providing 'economic support for the German war effort'[136] – was carried out in part to realise what could be seen as an act of resistance: 'ensur[ing] that any presence of surplus labour not be revealed'[137] in order to undermine attempts to deport French workers to Germany. While these may be considered political choices, they did not display a consistent position with regard to the Vichy government or even the Reich that could neatly be categorised as either 'collaboration' or 'resistance'. What remained constant was rather CORSID's business reasoning or 'managerial logic',[138] which determined how the members of the Committee navigated the volatile waters of the *années noires.*

[135]'Il faut un meilleur ravitaillement et des salaires suffisants pour obtenir un renforcement de la capacité de production', *L'Humanité*, 28 March 1945 for the first quotation and, for the second, 'Suppression des Comités d'organisation', *L'Humanité*, 24 April 1946.

[136]'Procès-verbal de la conférence tenue à Berlin le vendredi 17 septembre 1943 dans le bureau de Monsieur Speer', 17 September 1943, 72 AJ 1926, AN. This quotation comes from Jean Bichelonne in a meeting with Albert Speer.

[137]'Groupement Centre-Ouest. Réunion du 29 avril 1941', 29 April 1941, 139 AQ 82, AN. This quotation comes from Léon Daum.

[138]This term, or '*logique de gestionnaire*', is proposed by Renaud de Rochebrune and Jean Claude Hazera in *Les Patrons sous l'Occupation* (Paris: Odile Jacob, 1995).

CHAPTER 5

Nous serons les successeurs, sinon les héritiers de Vichy: Maintaining the New Industrial Order in Post-Vichy France

As the final outcome of the Second World War in Europe became increasingly certain, various groups within the French Resistance began to intensify their efforts to develop coherent plans for the post-war period. Whereas the Fall of France had come as a surprise to virtually everyone, not least to Germany, and was followed by a flurry of relatively improvised legislation over the summer of 1940, the reconquest of France was a long-anticipated process, and the country's post-war economic, domestic, and foreign policies had already been debated extensively by the time Paris was liberated in August 1944. The standard narrative of this process highlights the re-establishment of the French Republic and the abolition of all Vichyste legislation, closing the bracket definitively on the *années noires*.[1] Meanwhile, the unity of the Resistance is commended in accounts of the

Louis Vallon, 'Note sur l'organisation professionnelle de la vie économique', 2 June 1944, MAE, CFLN 687. Vallon was de Gaulle's *directeur adjoint de cabinet*, having joined the London-based Resistance in 1942.

[1]See, for example, Fondation Charles de Gaulle, *Le Rétablissement de la légalité républicaine* (Paris: Editions Complexe, 1996) and Jean Lacouture, *De Gaulle. Le rebelle, 1890–1944* (Paris: Seuil, 1984). De Gaulle famously claimed that, since Vichy was illegitimate, the Republic had never ceased to exist and therefore did not need to be proclaimed. See Charles de Gaulle, *Mémoires de guerre. L'unité: 1942–1944* (Paris: Plon, 1956).

© The Author(s) 2017

L.-A. Brunet, *Forging Europe: Industrial Organisation in France, 1940–1952*, Security, Conflict and Cooperation in the Contemporary World, DOI 10.1057/978-1-349-95198-7_5

post-war programme issued by the *Conseil national de la Résistance* (CNR) on 15 March 1944, which is said to represent 'a major trace of the transitory but real solidarity that existed among the French resistants'[2] and 'an historic consensus unique in French political history',[3] suggesting a certain unanimity in its commitment to wipe out Vichy's undemocratic legislation, to re-establish the French Republic, and to pursue the policies agreed upon in the CNR Programme.[4]

This chapter will examine how the question of maintaining Vichy's industrial organisation figured in the discussions of post-war policy in the Resistance, particularly the *Comité français de Libération nationale* (CFLN).[5] By 1943, a debate had emerged over whether the Organisation Committees and offices of the Central Bureau for the Distribution of Industrial Products (OCRPI) created by Vichy in 1940 should be abolished or maintained by the new regime. On the one hand, these bodies were originally created to facilitate economic collaboration between Vichy France and Nazi Germany in the context of a 'New Economic Order in Europe'.[6] Moreover, the Organisation Committees were dominated by the *patronat* and excluded labour representation, while largely overlooking the interests of small and medium-sized enterprises (SMEs). Given the profound implication of these institutions in France's contribution to the Third Reich's war economy and the widespread unpopularity of the bodies, it was clear to

[2]Claire Andrieu, *Le programme commun de la Résistance. Des idées dans la guerre* (Paris: Editions de l'Erudit, 1984), 135.

[3]Isser Woloch, 'Left, Right and Centre: the MRP and the Post-war Moment', *French History*, 21:1, 2007, 85–106, 90.

[4]A document issued by the CFLN in April 1943 affirmed that its first objective, shared by all in the Resistance, was 'the abolition of all Vichy legislation'. See 'Note du Comité National Français', 21 April 1943, CFLN 297, MAE. The standard Gaullist narrative has been challenged, notably in Henry Rousso, *Le syndrome de Vichy. De 1944 à nos jours* (Paris: Seuil, 1987), although Rousso does not discuss the CNR Programme in great detail.

[5]Created in June 1943, this was the main external Resistance organisation and soon evolved into a government-in-waiting. Based in Algiers, it was led by de Gaulle and was renamed the *Gouvernement provisoire de la République française* (GPRF) on the eve of the Allied landings in Normandy in June 1944.

[6]Walther Funk, 'The Economic Reorganization of Europe' in Walter Lipgens, *Documents on the History of European integration. Volume 1: Continental Plans for European Union, 1939–1945*, (Berlin: Walter de Gruyter, 1984), 65–70, here 66.

many that they should be swept away with the re-establishment of the French Republic. On the other hand, the Committees and OCRPI had been established to deal with conditions of penury and chaos following the Fall of France – conditions that would continue and indeed worsen following the reconquest of metropolitan France. In this light, a pragmatic argument in favour of maintaining the existing institutions until French industry was on sounder footing appealed to many. Despite differing opinions in 1943, by the spring of 1944 a consensus had been reached within the CFLN, and an uneasy agreement on the question was soon reached involving individuals from across the French political spectrum, from Communists to former Vichy ministers. By the time de Gaulle arrived in Paris in August 1944, the fate of the Organisation Committees had long been decided.

Post-War Programmes, Organisation Committees, and the Division of the French Left

The French Resistance during the Second World War began even before the Franco-German Armistice was signed, with de Gaulle's famous *appel* of 18 June 1940 broadcast while the two countries were still fighting.[7] Over the following months and years, resistance to the Vichy regime and to the German occupation developed steadily. The Free French, led by de Gaulle and based in London, developed into a government-in-exile comparable to those from other countries which had been conquered by the Reich. Meanwhile, within France itself, a variety of groups which opposed the Vichy regime appeared and are collectively known as the interior Resistance. Efforts to unite these disparate and often-disorganised factions of Vichy's opponents intensified in 1943, leading to the creation of the *Conseil national de la Résistance* (CNR) under Jean Moulin in May 1943. By the time of the Allied landings in Normandy in June 1944, virtually all Resistance groups in France had pledged their support to de Gaulle and the CFLN.[8]

[7] De Gaulle's celebrated radio speech was broadcast by the BBC on 18 June 1940. While Pétain had urged the French to lay down their arms on 17 June, the Armstice was only signed on 22 June.

[8] For a wide-ranging discussion of the historiography on the Resistance, see Laurent Douzou, *La Résistance française: une histoire périlleuse* (Paris: Seuil, 2005). On the question of what actions constituted resistance, an illuminating discussion is provided by Jacques Semelin,

Throughout the war, Resistance groups issued myriad declarations concerning policies that ought to be followed in a post-Vichy France. By 1943, a number of substantial post-war programmes, setting out the broad direction of policies to be followed once the Vichy regime had been swept away, began to appear. The first such programme of any importance was issued by the *Comité d'action socialiste* (CAS) in January 1943.[9] A socialist group within the Resistance, the CAS called for widespread nationalisations and the end of 'trusts[…], competition, and profits'.[10] Despite these socialist economic ambitions, however, no mention was made of the Organisation Committees or of how nationalised industries were to be organised in the still-hypothetical post-war era. The lack of details on this question is typical of early declarations on post-war France, issued at a time when a German defeat seemed a distant, even if inevitable prospect. By the autumn of 1943, however, the advent of a post-war Europe seemed increasingly plausible. The Allies landed in North Africa in November 1942, and Algeria, still considered an integral part of France, was under Allied control. Over the summer of 1943 the Allies took Sicily, and in September landed on mainland Italy. As the defeat of Nazi Germany, and the accompanying fall of the Vichy regime, seemed to be approaching, the post-war programmes issued by the Resistance became more detailed in their policies. As the outcome of the war became clearer, more and more civil servants fled the ill-fated Vichy regime and joined the Resistance in Algiers,

'Qu'est-ce que "résister"?', *Esprit* 198 (1994). On the Free French, see Jean-Louis Crémieux-Brilhac, *La France libre: De l'appel du 18 juin à la Libération* (Paris: Gallimard, 1996); for two studies that explore the heterogeneity of 'the Resistance', see Robert Belot, *La Résistance sans de Gaulle* (Paris: Fayard, 2006) and Robert Gildea, *Fighters in the Shadows: A New History of the French Resistance* (London: Faber & Faber, 2015).

[9]This section is indebted to the work of Claire Andrieu, Richard Kuisel, and Michel Margairaz. In particular, see Andrieu, *Le programme commun de la Résistance*, Kuisel, *Capitalism and the State in Modern France* (Cambridge: Cambridge University Press, 1981), and Margairaz, *L'Etat, les finances et l'économie. Histoire d'une conversion, 1932–1952* (Paris: CHEFF, 1991).

[10]'Notre programme', in *Le Populaire*, 16 janvier–1 février 1943, qtd in Andrieu, *Le programme commun de la Résistance*.

bringing with them their expertise and their intimate knowledge of Vichy's institutions.[11]

In September 1943, two comprehensive post-war programmes were generated by Resistance groups. The first, known as both the Laffon Report and the Guizot Report,[12] is a lengthy document that included an economic and social charter for post-Vichy France, as well as recommendations for domestic and foreign policy. The report echoes the CAS's call for nationalisations and the elimination of 'trusts', so much so that Claire Andrieu has argued that Laffon derived his report from the CAS programme issued in January of that year.[13] While the earlier report had remained silent on the question of industrial organisation, however, Laffon was explicit: the Organisation Committees and OCRPI must be maintained, lest 'France's depleted economy [...] lose itself in anarchy.' Yet this support was not unconditional: the Committees had to be purged of their current leadership, be reduced in number, and be brought firmly under the control of the Ministry of Industrial Production. Furthermore, those who had engaged in economic collaboration – left undefined – were to be barred from serving the French state after the Liberation.[14] This formulation, calling at once for the maintenance and the purge of the Organisation Committees, indicates the balance sought by the author between economic pragmatism, on the one hand, and the demands of ideology and justice, on the other. The report, including its unequivocal call for the preservation of Vichy's industrial organisation bodies, enjoyed broad support from most of the interior Resistance, trade unions, and the remnants of the SFIO. It was nevertheless vehemently

[11]The German occupation of the hitherto Non-Occupied Zone in November 1942, itself in reaction to the Allied landings in Algeria, effectively put an end to Vichy's supposed sovereignty. This development prompted a number of civil servants to leave their posts in Vichy. See Marc Olivier Baruch, *Servir l'Etat français. L'administration en France de 1940 à 1944* (Paris: Fayard, 1997).

[12]Guizot was the Resistance name of the author, Emile Laffon. A graduate of the Ecole des Mines, Laffon was a lawyer before the war and joined de Gaulle in London in 1942.

[13]Andrieu, *Le programme commun de la Résistance*, 38.

[14]Margairaz, *L'Etat, les finances et l'économie*, 735–737.

opposed by the Communists and the *Front national*,[15] as well as by the right-wing factions of the Resistance.[16] The Communist opposition to the report hinged on the plans to maintain Vichy's industrial bodies, which were condemned as collaborationist. Despite significant support, the plan failed to achieve the consensus hoped for by the leaders of the Resistance.

That same month, the *Confédération générale du travail* (CGT) issued its *Programme d'action d'après-guerre*, although the long-standing divisions within the trade union confederation made it difficult to articulate a coherent policy. As with the contemporaneous Laffon Report, on the question of Organisation Committees the CGT remained divided. The Communists within the CGT, known as the *unitaires*, demanded the 'suppression of the Organisation Committees, whose malfeasance is obvious to all, and which constitute a strengthening of trusts'.[17] The *confédérés*, the more moderate wing of the organisation, meanwhile, advocated the reform of the Organisation Committees, while recognising that maintaining them would be useful.[18] They suggested that the State should exert more control over the bodies, and be responsible for choosing Committee presidents from the ranks of the civil service. Moreover, the 'trusts' would be stripped of their supposed monopoly within the bodies, while a 'democratic representation of the elements of production', with members to be named by trade unions such as the CGT, would determine the composition of the Committees. There was thus a certain willingness to embrace a model of 'industrial democracy' in the form of post-war Organisation Committees.[19] While this proposal to give greater powers to the State and to labour, at the expense of employers and factory owners, won favour with the *confédérés* who supported Léon Jouhaux and generally backed the Socialists, it was unambiguously rejected by the Communist wing of the CGT. There are some significant

[15]The *Front national* was a communist group within the Resistance, founded in May 1941. It has no link to the current French political party of the same name, which was founded in 1972.

[16]Margairaz, *L'Etat, les finances et l'économie*, 734.

[17]Andrieu, *Le programme commun de la Résistance*, 43.

[18]It is worth noting that René Belin, who created the Organisation Committees in August 1940 as Minister for Industrial Production and Labour, belonged to the latter group and rose to the rank of Deputy Secretary General of the CGT before resigning in 1940.

[19]Andrieu, *Le programme commun de la Résistance*, 43.

similarities in how these two post-war programmes issued in September 1943 were received by the French Left. In both cases, the Socialists supported the maintenance and reform of Vichy's Organisation Committees, with this proposal also enjoying broad support among the rest of the Resistance. The Communists, meanwhile, refused to endorse such plans, and insisted on the abolition of the Organisation Committees altogether. This division between the Communists and the rest of the French Left on the question of the Organisation Committees would continue over the following months.

That particularly fruitful autumn produced yet another programme for post-war France, the so-called Courtin Report. Issued by the *Comité général d'études de la Résistance* (CGE), it was named after René Courtin, the former university professor who led the small team of experts who drafted the document.[20] The communists were intentionally excluded from this committee, although the Left was represented by Robert Lacoste, a socialist who would later replace Jean Bichelonne as Minister for Industrial Production following the Liberation.[21] In an earlier draft of the report, Courtin touched on the fate of the Organisation Committees and OCRPI: they would have to be maintained, despite their unpopularity, out of necessity and because Courtin concluded that French industrialists would prefer the maintenance of Vichy's system to an even more statist one.[22] The final report, published in November 1943, suggested provisionally maintaining the Committees and OCRPI, allowing for their abolition once the economy was in a better state. It was suggested that Vichy's institutions could be substituted by a *Conseil des Investissements*, '*véritable bureau du Plan*', which was described as an independent body run by a small team of civil servants that would develop

[20]This team consisted of Courtin, Paul Bastid, Robert Lacoste, François de Menthon, Alexandre Parodi, and Pierre-Henri Teitgen.

[21]Robert Lacoste spent his pre-war career with the CGT; in November 1940, he co-authored the *Manifeste des douze* and became involved with the Resistance. He was Minister for Industrial Production in 1944–1945 and again from 1946–1950, although he is most notorious for his time as Minister Resident in Algeria from February 1956 until May 1958. His only biography is Pierre Brana and Joëlle Duseau, *Robert Lacoste (1898–1989). De la Dordogne à l'Algérie, un socialiste devant l'histoire* (Paris: L'Harmattan, 2010).

[22]Kuisel, *Capitalism and the State in Modern France*, 163–172.

a *plan d'équipement* for the post-war years.[23] Yet the Courtin Report also failed to gain broad support: the communists, who had been excluded from its drafting, dismissed it as too liberal, as did many socialists, while the liberals derided it as overly *dirigiste*. The report ultimately failed to gain the CFLN's endorsement and was never directly implemented. Michel Margairaz has criticised the report for being plagued with internal contradictions, which also explains its failure to enjoy widespread support.[24] It is nevertheless important to note that at this stage, Lacoste, the future Minister for Industrial Production, was promoting the strategy of maintaining Vichy's Organisation Committees. Moreover, the similar recommendations made in the Laffon report were generally received favourably by the Socialist wing of the CGT. Over the following months, this argument would increasingly gain traction, as socialists and liberals alike opted for the preservation of Vichy's industrial institutions.

These post-war programmes are useful for identifying the divisions within the French Left before the Liberation of the country. By the end of 1943, two distinct strategies were being pursued regarding French industrial policy. On the one hand, the centre-left saw in the existing Organisation Committees the tools for realising a strong, State-led economy with a greater role for workers in deciding on the direction of the nation's industry. On the other hand, the Communists remained steadfast in their opposition to maintaining Vichy's industrial organisation, and sought to abolish the Committees upon the Liberation of the country. Indeed, the Communist Party made it clear that the 'radical *épuration* of the civilian and military administration' in France was a *sine que non* for its support.[25] As the Allied landings in France approached, these differences would be debated with increasing urgency within the Resistance.

[23]Margairaz, *L'Etat, les finances et l'économie*, 729–730. The *Conseil des Investissements* of the Courtin Report has similarities with what would ultimately emerge as the *Conseil Général du Plan* (CGP) under Jean Monnet's leadership. For the origins of the Monnet Plan, see Philippe Mioche, *Le plan Monnet. Genèse et élaboration 1941–1947* (Paris: Publications de la Sorbonne, 1987).

[24]Margairaz, *L'Etat, les finances et l'économie*, 733.

[25]Philippe Buton, *Les lendemains qui déchantent. Le Parti communiste français à la Libération* (Paris: FNSP, 1993), 36–38.

The Long Shadow of Vichy

The post-war programmes from late 1943 are generally the beacons by which French historians are guided in their accounts of the evolution of the Resistance's post-war programmes. The role played by figures who had thrived in Vichy and who defected to the Resistance in 1943, however, has received less attention.[26] The examples of two figures – Maurice Couve de Murville and Pierre Pucheu – who both held key economic posts in Vichy before fleeing metropolitan France to join the Resistance in North Africa, is instructive. For both men, preserving what had been established by Vichy was a priority, and they supported the maintenance of reformed Organisation Committees and OCRPI rather than their outright abolition. While many on the centre-left within the Resistance were favouring this option, they received vital support and expertise from those who had been immersed in the system in Vichy, who made their contributions to the debate in the crucial months before the Laffon report and the CGT's programme were completed.

Maurice Couve de Murville had served as Director of External Finances, a top job in the civil service, in Vichy until February 1943. As the outcome of the war became clear, and as the Allies established themselves in North Africa, Couve de Murville defected to Algiers and joined the CFLN, where he was quickly appointed Commissioner for Finance. It was in this capacity that, on 13 May 1943, Couve de Murville presented an early report on how the Organisation Committees ought to be reformed.[27] While the report dedicates 13 pages to outlining specific reforms that should be imposed on the existing system, the most obvious reform is striking in its absence. Never is the possibility of dissolving the

[26]Jean-Pierre Azéma and Olivier Wieviorka have suggested the term 'vichysto-résistant' to describe individuals who supported Pétain's regime until 1943 and who then defected to the resistance. See *Vichy, 1940–1944* (Paris: Perrin, 1997). Much of the literature on this category of *résistants* has focused on François Mitterrand, who supported Vichy and was even decorated with the regime's *francisque* before joining the Resistance in the latter half of 1943; see Pierre Péan, *Une jeunesse française: François Mitterrand, 1934–1947* (Paris: Fayard, 1994). For a lesser known example, see Johanna Barasz, 'Un vichyste en Résistance, le général de La Laurencie', *Vingtième siècle*, 2007/2, no. 94, 167–181.

[27]'Projet d'instruction de la réforme de l'organisation professionnelle et de la répartition', 13 May 1943, CFLN 631, MAE.

existing Vichy institutions entertained. This is all the more remarkable when one considers that, according to a CFLN document written only weeks earlier, the first and most important goal unifying all *résistants* was 'the abolition of all Vichy legislation'.[28] Yet Couve de Murville proposed the replacement of only the elements of Vichy's industrial legislation seen as incompatible with some of the most obvious ideals of the Resistance, rather than annulling the entire canon of Vichy's industrial legislation a priori. Having held a senior position in Vichy, Couve de Murville was well-placed to judge which elements of the existing system could be improved upon, and which should be left in place. This report helped reframe the question of France's industrial organisation, and provided a technical roadmap for how Vichy's New Industrial Order, first established to facilitate collaboration with the Reich, could be adapted for the post-war Republic.

Couve de Murville's trajectory after he left Vichy for Algiers was a long and successful one, and he would go on to serve as Minister for Foreign Affairs for the first decade of the Fifth Republic before becoming Prime Minister in 1968. His post-Vichy career contrasts markedly with that of his one-time associate, Pierre Pucheu. From 1941, Pucheu held several portfolios in Vichy, notably as Minister for Industrial Production and for the Interior. After being shuffled out of the Cabinet following the return of Pierre Laval in April 1942, Pucheu contacted General Giraud, a leader of the Algiers-based Resistance and at the time a rival to de Gaulle.[29] Pucheu expressed his interest in joining the Resistance, and Giraud invited him to North Africa, which Pucheu accepted in 1943. Such a changing of sides was not uncommon at this stage in France; indeed, Pucheu's predecessor as Minister for the Interior in Vichy, Marcel Peyrouton, was by this point Governor General of Algeria under Giraud.[30] Upon his arrival in Morocco from Spain, Pucheu was indeed met by members of the Resistance – who placed him under arrest for treason. He was imprisoned in Algeria while awaiting trial, which took place in March

[28]'Note du Comité National Français', 21 April 1943, CFLN 297, MAE.

[29]Giraud's title at this time was 'Civilian and Military Commander-in-Chief'.

[30]Marcel Peyrouton had been Vichy's Minister for the Interior in 1940–1941, where he passed a series of anti-Semitic measures such as the infamous law of 3 October 1940, which removed Jews from a range of positions in the public sector. Appointed Vichy's ambassador to Argentina in 1941, he was brought to Algeria at the insistence of the Roosevelt Administration and appointed Governor General. He was forced to resign from this position in June 1943 and was then arrested and imprisoned in December as part of *l'épuration*. See Marcel Peyrouton, *Du service public à la prison commune. Souvenirs* (Paris: Plon, 1950).

1944 under the watch of General de Gaulle. Pucheu did indeed have blood on his hands – as Minister for the Interior he passed heinous anti-Semitic legisla tion – and he was found guilty. On 20 March 1944 he was executed by firing squad in the first case of formal *épuration*.[31]

The example of Pucheu reveals a number of themes related to *épuration*: the harsh penalty meted out early in 1944 compared to the relatively lighter sentences that were issued later in the year, for example, and the glaring dissimilarity between the fates of two Vichy figures – one a high-level civil servant, one a minister – who changed sides at approximately the same time.[32] Perhaps most intriguing of all, however, is just how pervasive the idea of preserving Vichy's industrial order was becoming in Algiers. At the time of Pucheu's arrest, the CFLN had not formally articulated its position on the post-war fate of the Organisation Committees. De Gaulle was chronically reluctant to make any promises regarding post-war policy, insisting instead that only a future assembly chosen by the electorate of liberated France would have the legitimacy to pronounce such policies.[33] To this effect, de Gaulle created the Provisional Consultative Assembly on 17 September 1943 to recreate a pseudo-parliamentary system and strengthen his claims to democratic

[31]'Procès Pucheu', MAE, CFLN 619. Pucheu's trial and execution were widely condemned by the international press, the consensus being that the former minister was not given a fair trial. De Gaulle justified the trial and the sentence in his memoirs, on the grounds that 'it was necessary that our combatants, and our enemies, had immediate proof that culprits would have to answer for their actions'. See de Gaulle, *Mémoires de guerre*, vol. 2, 213.

[32]On France's *épuration*, the classic study in English remains Peter Novick, *The Resistance versus Vichy: The Purge of collaborators in Liberated France* (London: Chatto & Windus, 1968); the best recent synthesis is Jean-Paul Cointet's *Expier Vichy: l'épuration en France 1943–1958* (Paris: Perrin, 2008), while a helpful overview is provided in Henry Rousso, 'L'Epuration en France: Une histoire inachevée' in *Vichy. L'événement, la mémoire, l'histoire* (Paris: Gallimard, 1992), 489–552. For more specific studies, see François Rouquet, *L'Epuration dans l'administration francaise. Agents de l'Etat et collaboration ordinaire* (Paris: CNRS, 1993) and Marc Bergère (ed.), *L'épuration économique en France à la Libération* (Rennes: Presses universiatires de Rennes, 2008). For a regional approach to the first, most brutal purges, see Philippe Bourdrel's *L'épuration sauvage, 1944–1945* (Paris: Perrin, 2002).

[33]De Gaulle's insistence on republican legitimacy developed in part as a means of securing his own position in the face of the reactionary Giraud. It was also hoped that such democratic overtures would reassure Roosevelt that de Gaulle was not, as the US President feared, a budding dictator. See Serge Berstein, *Histoire du gaullisme* (Paris: Perrin, 2001).

legitimacy.[34] By the spring of 1944, however, an apparent consensus had been reached within the CFLN to maintain Vichy's industrial committees. It is therefore worthwhile to examine how the conversations between the former Minister for Industrial Production and the CFLN's leaders may have contributed to the latter's industrial policies for post-war France.

In his prison journal, Pucheu recorded that he met with a number of individuals from the leadership of the Resistance. Together they discussed industrial policy for post-war France, and after Pucheu's death and the Liberation of France, some of those individuals would accede to key ministerial posts in the Provisional Government.[35] Pucheu definitely spoke at length with Couve de Murville, and he also had conversations with Paul Leroy-Beaulieu and especially René Mayer about how industry should be organised in liberated France.[36] While no transcripts of these meetings exist, Pucheu's views on industrial questions are clearly expressed in his journal, which suggests the lines of argument he pursued in his conversations with the CFLN figures. In his journal, he frames the issue:

> With regard to the economy, what exactly will be France's organisation following its liberation? If the current framework remains in place, we will be faced with an economy that is almost entirely 'managed' [*dirigée*]. In addition to the role of relevant ministries, the system responsible for this economic management

[34]This Assembly included the 80 members of the National Assembly who voted against handing full powers to Philippe Pétain on 10 July 1940. In his memoirs, de Gaulle criticised the Assembly's 'harsh and extended debates' on *épuration*, and for their avoidance of 'the most pressing issues' related to French foreign policy. Nevertheless, he noted the importance of the Assembly's recognition of his legitimacy as leader of the French Republic. See de Gaulle, *Mémoires de guerre*, 185–190.

[35]Unlike most memoirs by Vichy-era figures, Pucheu composed his before the end of the war and died in 1944. While his writings reflect the broad strategy of exoneration typical of such memoirs, they were not altered by the author in light of post-war events, although the text was edited by his heirs. See Pierre Pucheu, *Ma Vie* (Paris: Amiot-Dumont, 1948).

[36]Pucheu, *Ma Vie*, 117. These meetings occurred in August 1943, although it is probable that other such meetings with CFLN figures took place between Pucheu's arrest in May 1943 and his execution in March 1944. Leroy-Beaulieu was an *Inspecteur général des finances* who held top posts at NATO and at the French Embassy in Bonn after the war. René Mayer held a number of portfolios in the Fourth Republic, including Economic Affairs and Finance, and became Prime Minister in 1953. In 1955 he succeeded Jean Monnet as President of the High Authority of the European Coal and Steel Community, where he sat alongside Léon Daum.

> consists of the Organisation Committees and OCRPI. These entities were created in August and September 1940. Were they in response to the implementation of a new economic doctrine? Not in any way. They were in response to the exigencies of war, or rather of the Armistice and of the Occupation. Moreover, the laws that created the[se entities] were described as 'provisional' in their preamble. For this reason, and notwithstanding their extreme impopularity [. . .] and the current bias favouring the systematic denigration of all that was done by the governments of the Maréchal, these cannot be seen – unless we are being intellectually dishonest – as the expression of a doctrine deliberately created or adopted by the men in Vichy. I can say this especially freely as I took no part in the drafting of these laws and as I simply inherited the state of affairs that they brought about, when I became Minister for [Industrial] Production several months later, in the final days of February 1941.[37]

In 1943, Pucheu made the case for maintaining the Organisation Committees and the New Industrial Order that had been erected in the months following the Fall of France by appealling to practicality. By arguing that the Committees had been created out of pragmatism and not ideology, Pucheu advanced that they could be maintained because they had not been informed by the now-discredited National Revolution.[38] Moreover, by highlighting that he had arrived in the Ministry and used the already created Committees to direct French industry, Pucheu argued that the future Provisional Government should do the same. Given the economic constraints in which France found itself in the summer of 1940, and which would again be the case following the Liberation, the Committees would be an invaluable and practical tool. He also emphasised the depth of experience that those in charge of the Organisation Committees had accumulated over four years, and that these would be a precious resource for the new administration:

> If these new men can overcome ideological differences, they will have access, in the ministries as well as in the Sections [of OCRPI] and the Committees, to an operating staff and to senior and middle management, trained through

[37]Pucheu, *Ma Vie*, 336–337.

[38]This statement is confirmed in previous chapters, which show that the creation of the Organisation Committees was not decisively influenced by the National Revolution (Chapter 2) and that the bodies were not significantly reformed in line with Vichy's official ideology (Chapter 4).

> a long and difficult experience [...] many of whom will have developed sound expertise which could be adapted immediately to the new situation.
>
> More importantly, rather than beginning from scratch when establishing priorities, operating procedures, and action plans, these new individuals responsible for running the economy will have at their disposal precious documentation. Thanks to the statistical archives of the Sections [of OCRPI] and the Committees, they will know immediately, for all branches of industry and commerce, all aspects of pre-war economic activity and also how things have changed under the challenges of the Occupation. With full knowledge of the facts, they will be able to deal with immediate challenges and to seamlessly manage the implementation of their own economic management model in accordance with the doctrinal pillars they will have developed for the post-transitional period.[39]

Pucheu advised maintaining the Organisation Committees and OCRPI in order to manage French industry at a tumultuous time of regime change and penury. He emphasised the expertise and experience of those who had worked in the Vichy-era bodies of industrial organisation, and how these formally apolitical bodies and their employees would be just as helpful to any post-war government as they had been to Vichy. Indeed, when Jean Monnet developed his eponymous Plan in 1946, production targets were based on the 'precious documentation' compiled by the Organisation Committees under Vichy.[40] Pucheu also noted that the economic tools established by Vichy would need to stay in place until France's coal shortage – more severe in 1944 than it had been in 1940, when the Committees had been created, and which was exacting a heavy toll on French industry and transportation – had been resolved.[41]

In addition to Couve de Murville and Pucheu, many individuals who had spent the war in Vichy or working with its institutions supported their survival in a post-war France.[42] The expertise of those who had run French

[39]Pucheu, *Ma Vie*, 344.

[40]'Projet de résolution soumis au Conseil du Plan. Objectifs généraux pour l'activité française', 13 March 1946, AMF 2 3, FJME.

[41]Pucheu, *Ma Vie*, 345. France suffered prolonged coal shortages from 1940, when imports from its traditional supplier, Great Britain, became impossible.

[42]René Belin and François Lehideux, the two Ministers for Industrial Production who survived the war, defended the New Industrial Order in their post-war accounts, as did Yves Bouthillier, Minister for the Economy in Vichy. See Belin, *Du secrétariat de la CGT au*

industry, from former Ministers for Industrial Production to leaders of the Organisation Committees, were not lightly dismissed by the new leaders of France.[43] The claim that these bodies were apolitical and improvised pragmatically and not ideologically was made by virtually every official who had been associated with French industry during the war, and this defence worked to exonerate individuals and institutions alike.[44] It should also be noted that it was primarily Pucheu *qua* Minister for the Interior who was tried and convicted in Algiers. The racist and reprehensible laws he passed while responsible for that portfolio contrast with his competent handling of Industrial Production, which undoubtedly gave his advice concerning the latter more weight.

Ultimately, the direct influence of Pucheu on the CFLN's post-war programmes is difficult to measure. It is clear that he was discussing questions of economic and industrial organisation with those responsible for such issues within the CFLN at precisely the time when the Resistance was working to develop its own post-war programmes. While Pucheu was discussing Organisation Committees with Couve de Murville and René Mayer, for instance, the CGT and Laffon were drafting their post-war programmes. The CFLN was reluctant to publish any plans for liberated France, in large part due to de Gaulle's insistence on democratic legitimacy and his aversion to tying his hands with particular policy commitments. After two aborted committees established at the end of 1943 and February 1944, respectively, the *Comité économique interministériel* (CEI) was established by the CFLN at the end of April 1944, more than a month after the CNR Programme had been published. It was within this Committee that the future of French industry was discussed until the creation of the Provisional Government in August 1944. While the exchanges recorded within the CEI are enlightening, no series of documents seems to exist today that can clearly demonstrate the CFLN's attitudes towards the Organisation Committees in 1943 and

gouvernement de Vichy (Paris: Albatros, 1978); Bouthillier, *La drame de Vichy* (Paris: Plon, 1951); Lehideux, *De Renault à Pétain* (Paris: Pygmalion, 2001).

[43]According to François Lehideux, de Gaulle lamented that the former had been appointed minister by Pétain, since de Gaulle wanted to make him a minister in his own Cabinet. It should be noted, however, that Lehideux makes a number of highly questionable claims in his memoirs, so this should be treated with scepticism. See Lehideux, *De Renault à Pétain*, 459.

[44]On the role of pragmatism in the creation of the Committees, see Hervé Joly (ed.), *Les Comités d'organisation et l'économie dirigée de Vichy*, 2000.

early 1944. Given these limitations, Pucheu's exchanges with the CFLN are important rather in demonstrating the pervasiveness of the argument in favour of maintaining Vichy's industrial organisation. Whether the various members of the CFLN were influenced by former Vichy ministers, by trade unionists, by socialists, by liberals, or by nationalists is ultimately less important than the fact that all these incongruent groups were pressing for the same policy. Regardless of which of these groups was most influential, the result was the CFLN's joining this consensus. Despite the formal promise to destroy all of Vichy's legislation,[45] it was increasingly understood that this need not apply equally to all of Vichy's laws.

Both Couve de Murville and Pucheu saw in Vichy's industrial organisation indispensable tools to ensure the proper functioning of France's economy. They recognised the pragmatic value of maintaining the Organisation Committees and OCRPI and hoped to use them to ward off penury and industrial stagnation. In this respect, they shared the motivations of the creators of the New Industrial Order, albeit without the objective of closer Franco-German collaboration that marked the creation of the Committees. The reforms that Couve de Murville and Pucheu proposed were in part technical adjustments to improve the efficacy of the system, and in part political concessions to distance the bodies from the wartime regime. We can clearly observe the trend of those who had worked with Vichy's industrial organisation wanting to keep the system in place, albeit with some modifications. This would continue to be the case in liberated France, as industrialists such as Jules Aubrun, President of the Organisation Committee for Steel (CORSID) for the duration of the war, pleaded with the new government to maintain the Organisation Committees and to minimise reforms that would make the bodies more representative.[46] Indeed, Aubrun's position was shared by his opposite number in the Organisation Committee for Steel (COH), the celebrated *résistant* Aimé Lepercq. In May 1943, Lepercq and a few close collaborators in the *Organisation Civile et Militaire* (OCM) produced a cahier on

[45]'Projet sur le rétablissement de la légalité républicaine', 3 July 1944, CFLN, MAE.

[46]'Observations de la Chambre syndicale de la sidérurgie', 29 December 1944, F 12 10062, AN. Given that virtually all the active industrialists were still in France (and indeed working within the system of the Organisation Committees), they did not take part in the debates that unfolded in Algiers on the maintenance of the Committees.

economic and social reform for post-war France where they, too, called for the maintenance of Vichy's Committees, such as the one Lepercq was still directing.[47] Such an endorsement from Lepercq further strengthened the case for keeping Vichy's institutions in place.

As the year 1943 drew to a close, an unlikely agreement was forming between quondam Vichy officials and the more moderate members of the French Left. Both groups saw the value of maintaining what Vichy had erected and using this system to provide a relatively smooth transition for post-war France. Individuals as disparate as Pierre Pucheu and Léon Jouhaux embraced this strategy, despite the repeated promises of the Resistance to abolish all Vichy legislation. These groups would join together with others in the debate that would determine the political economy of post-war France.

Abolishing the New Industrial Order in North Africa

Over the course of the year 1943, there was a discernible trend within the Resistance towards a growing if sometimes grudging acceptance that Vichy's Organisation Committees would need to be maintained after the war. One illustrative example of this tendency is given by General Henri Giraud and his advisor Jean Monnet.[48]

The first legal measures regarding the fate of the Organisation Committees were in fact taken as early as May 1943. At this time, General Giraud was Civilian and Military Commander-in-Chief in North Africa, although de Gaulle would soon displace him as leader of the Resistance in Algiers. The first Organisation Committees in Algeria had been established in December 1941, more than a year

[47]See Maxime Blocq-Mascart, *Chroniques de la Résistance* (Paris: Corréa, 1945) and Kuisel, *Capitalism and the State in Modern France*. Kuisel argues that 'the OCM, perhaps more than any resistance movement, wanted to rebuild with the materials of Vichy's corporatist construction', 166. Lepercq remained President of the COH until his dismissal in August 1943 for opposing the STO.

[48]Jean Monnet began the war overseeing the coordination of the French and British economies in London; after the Fall of France he was sent to the United States as a member of the British Supply Council and soon started advising President Roosevelt. Like Roosevelt, he initially supported Giraud over de Gaulle, although he helped negotiate the creation of the CFLN by the two generals in June 1943.

after their counterparts in metropolitan France.[49] On 15 May 1943, Giraud issued a decree abolishing Vichy's 'laws and decrees concerning professional organisation', namely the Organisation Committees in Algeria.[50] The decree allowed for a transition of three months by the end of which the Organisation Committees and OCRPI would cease to exist. This was thought to be sufficient time 'to set up a liberal system that takes account of the pressing necessities of the moment'. Giraud justified the decision by attacking the law of 16 August 1940, which he argued introduced 'into French legislation a theory that is foreign to it: that of the Führer in charge, placed at the head of each organisation. We therefore had to abolish these laws.'[51] This decree would mean that by 15 August 1943, almost exactly three years after their creation in France, the Organisation Committees would cease to exist, albeit only in the territories under the control of Giraud, namely Algeria, Morocco, and Tunisia.[52] In practice, however, the dismantling of Vichy's institutions in North Africa did not go as smoothly as Giraud might have hoped. The 'liberal system that takes account of the pressing necessities of the moment' did not spring forth as soon as the Committees' abolition was declared. By August, days away from the expiry of the three-month transitional period inaugurated by the May decree, the CFLN had to decree the re-establishment of union rights [*liberté syndicale*] in North Africa.[53] While the Organisation Committees had replaced trade

[49]For a discussion of the Organisation Committees in Algeria, see Jacques Cantier, *L'Algérie sous le régime de Vichy* (Paris: Odile Jacob, 2002), 170–172 and Daniel Lefeuvre, 'Vichy et la modernisation de l'Algérie: Intention ou réalité?', *Vingtième siècle*, no. 42 (avril-juin 1994), 7–16. While the first Committees in Algeria were only set up in December 1941, this was nevertheless done within the framework of the law of 16 August 1940.

[50]'Ordonnance du 15 mai 1943 portant abrogation des lois et décrets concernant l'organisation professionnelle', published in the *Journal officiel*, 16 May 1943, AME 34 6, FJME. That same day Giraud also decreed the repeal of Vichy's corporatist Labour Charter. See 'Ordonnance du 15 mai 1943 portant abrogation de la loi du 4 octobre 1941 relative à l'organisation sociale des professions', published in the *Journal officiel*, 16 May 1943, AME 34 6, FJME.

[51]'La révision des lois de Vichy. Le général Giraud abroge les dispositions concernant l'organisation professionnelle', *La Dépêche Algérienne*, 19 May 1943, AME 34 6, FJME. Underlined in the original.

[52]'Déclaration et ordonnance du commandant en chef français civil et militaire concernant la validité de la législation en vigueur dans les territoires relevant de son autorité', March 1943, AME 34 2, FJME.

[53]'Note sur l'Organisation syndicale de la Régence', 4 August 1943, CFLN 875, MAE.

unions and employers' associations, Giraud had failed to order the recreation of these organisations when he called for Committees' abolition. This experience in North Africa revealed the difficulties the CFLN might face in trying to replace the Committees in metropolitan France. As de Gaulle's consellor on economic affairs, Raymond Offroy, later recalled, 'it was easy to abolish [the Committees], but experience in North Africa had shown that one needs to know what will take their place'.[54]

Giraud's decree abolishing the Organisation Committees in North Africa reflects the prevailing mood of those opposed to Vichy in early 1943. While small committees of technicians drew up plans arguing for the necessity of keeping Vichy's industrial bodies, and former Vichy officials extolled the benefits of the institutions, many in the Resistance remained opposed to prolonging the life of the unpopular Committees. Giraud was not alone in wanting to abolish the Committees at this stage, and he was counselled on this decree by his chief advisor on economic matters, Jean Monnet. Indeed, in a speech delivered by Giraud on 14 March 1943, which Monnet claims to have 'negotiated word by word', Monnet insisted that Giraud declare that Vichy's 'legislation is now considered null and void, which is crucial'.[55] In the spring of 1943, Monnet and Giraud agreed that the Organisation Committees should be abolished; by September of that year, however, Monnet's opinion had changed dramatically. Monnet argued that 'according to all reports from France', including Pucheu's, 'a significant part of the [Vichy] administration has been courageous, competent, and, overall, managed extremely complex and difficult problems very well'. He added:

> *I think that we should therefore plan on using the existing administrative apparatus in its entirety.* In this case, insofar as it is necessary, we should study how to adapt the organisation of the Committees so that, following the liberation, any new managers can be neatly slotted into the existing administration. We should also consider which individuals currently in key positions should be maintained and which should be replaced and, if possible, by whom.[56]

[54]Kuisel, *Capitalism and the State in Modern France*, 182. Offroy was writing in February 1944.

[55]Jean Monnet, *Mémoires* (Paris: Fayard, 1976), 271.

[56]'Note sur la première étape de la reconstruction en France', 22 September 1943, AME 33 1, FJME. Emphasis added.

Monnet went on to justify maintaining Vichy's institutions using a line of argument similarly employed by Pucheu: that Vichy's system of industrial organsiation was bereft of ideology. France had found itself faced with a shortage of raw materials, a situation that Monnet insisted had been shared by 'all the countries in the war' and to which 'the solution had inevitably been the same: complete control by the State of the economy, of production, and of allocation [and] control of exports and imports'. Given how widespread this economic approach was, Monnet argued, 'it is not a question of opting for one economic system or another. We must make France flourish with resources inferior to her needs. No other solution is possible' aside from maintaining Vichy's institutions.[57]

While Monnet had insisted six months earlier that Giraud declare all Vichy legislation, including laws on industrial organisation, 'null and void', and had advised Giraud on the dissolution of the North African Organisation Committees, by the end of the summer of 1943 Monnet was demanding the maintenance of Vichy's 'existing administrative apparatus in its entirety'. This dramatic *volte-face* was likely informed by the difficulties encountered when trying to abolish the Committees in North Africa earlier that year. Yet his conversion to the cause of maintaining Vichy's economic bodies on pragmatic grounds was only one of a growing number within the CFLN; Monnet's call for maintaining the Organisation Committees was made the same month as the completion of the Laffon Report and the CGT's post-war programme, both of which advocated the same policy regarding the Committees.

Debating the New Industrial Order: '*Suppression ou Transition?*'[58]

The first half of 1944 featured a number of discussions within the CFLN about the fate of Vichy's Organisation Committees and OCRPI. There was broad consensus that the Labour Charter, René Belin's crowning achievement as Minister for Labour that sought to implement a comprehensive, corporatist organisation of the French economy, should be scrapped, and that union rights [*liberté syndicale*] had to be re-established;

[57]Ibid.

[58]Blum-Picard, 'Discussion de réforme des Comités d'Organisation', 14 April 1944, CFLN 686, MAE.

these changes were proclaimed by the CFLN in January 1944 and echoed Giraud's decrees of the previous year.[59] These were uncontroversial decisions within the Resistance, since the Labour Charter was explicitly developed within the framework of Pétain's National Revolution and had little effect on the running of the French economy; indeed, by 1944 the Charter had been largely abandoned by the Vichy government itself.[60] For the members of the CFLN, the return to republicanism entailed the restoration of the proper functioning of trade unions and, perhaps more grudgingly, employers' associations. On such matters, there was indeed a unified position within the CFLN. On the question of the Organisation Committees and OCRPI, however, the debate had far more gradations. As with the post-war programmes produced in the autumn of 1943, unanimous agreement on the question proved elusive. In January 1944, a report on Vichy's industrial bodies was produced in order to inform the debate within the CFLN. Leprince, the author of the report, admitted that the Organisation Committees were 'anti-democratic [and] the creations most characteristic of the Vichy administration'.[61] But, he asked in his introduction, 'should we to destroy them on principle?'[62] In the coming months, a significant majority within the CFLN would definitively make up their minds.

By early 1944, a consensus was emerging within the CFLN that maintaining the Organisation Committees was the only viable option for France. The greatest obstacle to this plan, however, was the Commissioner for Production and Supply,[63] André Diethelm.[64] An esteemed civil servant in the interwar years, he was an early supporter of de Gaulle and held key positions in the French Resistance from early 1941. Diethelm mounted a strong opposition to the maintenance of legislation

[59]'Note', 13 January 1944, CFLN 602, MAE.

[60]The best study of the Labour Charter is Jean-Pierre Le Crom, *Syndicats nous voilà!* (Paris: Editions de l'Atelier, 1995). For a recent detailed study, see Debbie Lackerstein, *National Regeneration in Vichy France: Ideas and Policies, 1930–1944* (Farnham: Ashgate, 2012).

[61]Rapport Leprince, 26 January 1944, CFLN 686, MAE.

[62]Ibid.

[63]In the CFLN, *Commissaire à la production et au ravitaillement* was analogous to Minister for Industrial Production.

[64]An *Inspecteur des finances*, Diethelm joined de Gaulle in London in 1941. The best biography of this lesser-known figure of the CFLN is Frédéric Turpin's *André Diethelm 1896–1954. De Georges Mandel à Charles de Gaulle* (Paris: Les Indes savantes, 2004).

from Vichy, and took issue with the policy of maintaining Vichy's industrial organisation towards which the CFLN seemed to be drifting. As early as July 1943, he called for the unqualified abolition of Vichy's Organisation Committees during a meeting of the CLFN, and his draft law to enact this was approved by the CFLN on 6 July 1943.[65] On 9 February 1944, he circulated a report among the CFLN that unequivocally demanded the dissolution of the Committees:

> The decree known as the 'law of 16 August 1940' established, for both industry and commerce, a corporatist system that ensures unlimited power for economic oligarchies. The unpopularity of these approximately 300 bodies, their never-ending quarrels over [resource] allocation, [and] the tyranny they exert on the small- and medium-sized enterprises in their industry leave no doubt as to the answer that the Assembly must give to the question of abolishing and liquidating the Committees.[66]

If members of the CFLN had supported abolishing the Committees in July 1943, their opinion had been very much reversed by February 1944. The day after Diethelm's report was issued, the CFLN's General Secretariat, run by Louis Joxe,[67] produced a response to the report that criticised Diethelm's conclusions, and sent it to de Gaulle. While Diethelm had called for an open debate in the Assembly on whether Vichy's institutions should be maintained, Joxe dismissed this idea, claiming that closed-door decisions by the relevant Cabinet members were preferable to democratic debate in the Assembly, as only the former would present a 'clear and precise programme', while a parliamentary-style debate would only be 'confused, riddled with contradictions, and would bring no effective contribution to resolving France's current problems'. The report concluded that it is the role of the government, and not of the Assembly, to consider such questions and to determine the industrial policy of the nation.[68] On the question of

[65]Turpin, *André Diethelm 1896–1954*, 128–129.

[66]'Note du Commissaire au ravitaillement et à la production', 9 February 1944, F 60 914, AN.

[67]A teacher, journalist, and civil servant before the war, Joxe was named Secretary General of the CFLN in 1942. After the war, he pursued a successful career as a dipomat and a minister and led the negotiations culminating in the Evian Accords in 1962, which granted independence to Algeria.

[68]'Note pour le général de Gaulle', 10 February 1944, F 60 914, AN.

Organisation Committees, Joxe suggested that they be reformed or, if they had to be abolished, that they be replaced with similar institutions. The author also argued that OCRPI must be maintained, albeit purged of its current leadership, despite the fact that its sections 'were and remain the instrument used by the Germans to carry out their decrees'.[69]

These rival reports set out the two sides of the debate over the maintenance of Vichy's industrial organisation. On the one hand, Diethelm argued that they should be abolished, following an open, democratic debate. On the other hand, Joxe made the case for maintaining the institutions regardless of their role in the Nazi war effort. While de Gaulle did not issue any formal endorsement of either position at the time, his actions spoke volumes. On 3 March, three weeks after the two reports had been sent to de Gaulle, Diethelm was dismissed as Commissioner for Production and Supply, and instead given the portfolio for War. He was replaced by Paul Giacobbi, a member of the National Assembly for the centrist Radical Party before the war and one of the 80 who had voted against granting Pétain full powers on 10 July 1940.[70] More importantly, Giacobbi had previously argued that the Committees and OCRPI should be maintained after the war. With this single reshuffle, de Gaulle had replaced the most significant opponent of Vichy's industrial organisation with one of its more vocal proponents. By reversing the policy of the Commissioner for Production and Supply, de Gaulle quietly determined the ultimate outcome of the debate within the CFLN.[71] Meanwhile, the issue was not raised in the Consultative Assembly until July 1944, when it

[69]Ibid.

[70]Interestingly, a certain Giacobbi worked as director of legal services for OCRPI as late as September 1943 and worked closely with Jean Bichelonne. For the Giacobbi at OCRPI, see 'Note', April 1943, and 'Note de Bichelonne', September 1943, F 12 10932, AN.

[71]This Cabinet reshuffle is mentioned in the memoirs of both Joxe and de Gaulle. Curiously, Joxe makes no mention of Diethelm, noting only that Giacobbi 'took on the difficult tasks of Supply and Production', while de Gaulle misidentifies Giacobbi's portfolio as the Economy (which was held by Pierre Mendès France at the time). Both de Gaulle and Joxe present Giacobbi's promotion as part of a general reshuffle that saw the addition of two Communists (Fernand Grenier and François Billoux) to the CFLN, but in fact their appointment happened one month later, on 4 April, weeks after the CNR Programme was released. Overall, Diethelm is strikingly absent from Joxe's narrative, as the Minister for War is not once mentioned in the chapter on the Liberation. See Louis Joxe, *Victoires sur la nuit* (Paris: Flammarion, 1981), 188 and de Gaulle, op.cit., 181.

was announced that the members of the CFLN were in 'absolute agreement' on maintaining the Committees and OCRPI.[72] By that point, the Assembly could do little but comment on the *fait accompli*. Joxe's recommendation that the decision be taken by the CFLN rather than the Assembly was chosen over Diethelm's calls for a more transparent process.

It is unlikely that De Gaulle's intervention had much to do with his own preferences for post-war France's industrial policies. Consistently more interested in political, diplomatic, and military issues, de Gaulle was notoriously lackadaisical when it came to economic questions. In the months preceding the Liberation of French territory, de Gaulle avoided making clear promises regarding France's economic policies, since any firm policy pronouncement would inevitably upset some element within the Resistance which might then put further strain on the fragile coalition de Gaulle was leading. Consequently, he 'practiced purposeful ambiguity on economic issues in order to focus attention on the war effort and to avoid dissension'.[73] The sacking of Diethelm was thus most likely a means of stamping out dissent within the CFLN rather than the expression of a clear partiality of de Gaulle's regarding the fate of the Organisation Committees. By reassigning Diethelm to an unrelated portfolio, de Gaulle managed to ensure that there was finally a consensus among those within the CFLN responsible for economic matters.

The need for such agreement within the CFLN had more to do with de Gaulle's political and diplomatic priorities. Still struggling to be recognised as France's legitimate representative by Roosevelt, Churchill, and Stalin, de Gaulle was seeking to consolidate the Resistance under his command to strengthen his hand with the Allied leaders.[74] One of the most significant advances in this respect

[72] The issue was first introduced to the Consultative Assembly by Paul Giacobbi on 21 July 1944. Despite criticism of the decision by Vincent Auriol, the future President of the Fourth Republic, Giaccobi concluded the session by exclaiming that 'there is an absolute agreement on the foundations of the economic doctrine of the Government and of the Nation'. See 'La politique économique du gouvernement', 22 July 1944, C I 591, AN.

[73] Kuisel, *Capitalism and the State in Modern France*, 180.

[74] The 'Big Three' would ultimately recognise de Gaulle as France's legitimate leader only on 23 October 1944, two months after the liberation of Paris. He would continue to be excluded from crucial international summits, most notably the Yalta Conference in February 1945.

coincided with Diethelm's dismissal. On 29 February 1944, de Gaulle was sent the text of the CNR Programme, finally agreed by the members of the CNR, ranging from the Communists to the Christian Democrats. This long sought-after but hitherto elusive agreement unified the disparate factions of the internal Resistance around a common set of policies that has been described as 'an historic consensus unique in French political history'.[75] For de Gaulle, the document's most important passage was the call for all *résistants* to remain united 'to establish a provisional government of the Republic under the leadership of General de Gaulle'.[76] With the CNR Programme, de Gaulle's claim to speak for the French nation received a dramatic boost. Despite its clarity on some issues, such as the agreement to nationalise key industries after the war, the Programme remained silent on the fate of the Organisation Committees.[77] Given how divisive the question had been within the Left when earlier post-war programmes had been attempted within the Resistance, raising the issue at this point might well have scuppered the tenuous but politically invaluable agreement within the CNR.

By the time the final version of the CNR Programme was agreed upon a fortnight later, Diethelm had been reassigned far from any economics portfolio and was instead, somewhat surprisingly for a civilian given the context, named Minister for War. Diethelm maintained his hard-line approach in his new role; indeed, such was his zealousness that in September 1944 he had Robert Schuman sacked from his first post-war post, demanding the 'immediate dismiss[al of] this product of Vichy'. France's future Foreign Minister and 'Father of

[75]Isser Woloch, 'Left, right and centre: the MRP and the post-war moment' in *French History*, 21:1, 2007, 85–106, 90.

[76]Qtd in Andrieu, op.cit., 157. This version of the programme was agreed by the CNR on 28 February 1944 and a copy was relayed to de Gaulle the next day by Bingen, the CFLN's representative at the CNR. The final text of the programme was approved on 15 March 1944, in which the quoted passage remained unchanged.

[77]The vagueries on specific policies suited the PCF, as it wanted to avoid 'hav[ing] its hands tied by a detailed political programme or by precise measures that would be too constraining'. Given the 'radical' policies contained in the CNR Programme, Philippe Buton concludes that it was a 'success for the PCF'. See Buton, op.cit., 53. Prior to March 1944, the SFIO had been the staunchest supporter of the nationalisation of key industries, of which the PCF was sceptical.

Europe' would have to wait until September 1945 for his case to be dismissed.[78] Yet despite the seemingly important portfolio Diethelm had been given, he was a junior minister and in practice his powers were surprisingly limited. Upon arriving in Paris on 25 August 1944, de Gaulle opted to set up his headquarters in the office of the Minister for War, while Diethelm remained in Algeria.[79] The titles of '*chef des armées*' and 'President of the Committee for National Defence', meanwhile, were held not by Diethelm, but by de Gaulle.[80] Predictably, General de Gaulle sought to play an overriding role in the military reconquest of metropolitan France. While Diethelm drew up detailed proposals on the reform of the French land army and sent them to de Gaulle, the general did not even bother to read them[81]; de Gaulle instead oversaw military reforms on his own, without the input of Diethelm.[82] While it was always unlikely that General de Gaulle would have taken advice from a civilian such as Diethelm on such matters, de Gaulle's dominance of defence-related issues effectively demoted his Minister for War to an ancillary role and curtailed Diethelm's influence considerably.[83]

After the playing field was decisively tilted with the replacement of Diethelm by Giacobbi as Commissioner for Production and Supply, the debate on Vichy's industrial organisation became effectively one-sided. No significant opposition to maintaining the Organisation Committees and OCRPI was voiced within de Gaulle's entourage after Diethelm's dismissal, although this was due in no small part to

[78]Frédéric Turpin, op.cit., 142. Schuman had voted full powers to Pétain on 10 July 1940 and did not actively participate in the Resistance, which explains Diethelm's statement. Schuman's position in September 1944 was Political Counsellor for issues related to Alsace-Lorraine.

[79]De Gaulle visited the Ministry of War and then the police prefecture before making his public appearance at the Hôtel de Ville. See de Gaulle, *Mémoires de guerre*, 358–359.

[80]Lettre du général Valin au général de Gaulle, 7 November 1945, 3 AG 4 30, AN. Diethelm remained Minister for War until 21 November 1945, when he was succeeded by de Gaulle himself, who took on the portfolio for National Defence in addition to his role as President.

[81]'Nouveau projet d'ordonnance soumis en septembre par M Diethelm au Chef du Gouvernement', undated (September 1944), 3 AG 4 32. 'This text was not read by de Gaulle' was hand-written on the document by a member of de Gaulle's staff.

[82]'Réorganisation des armées terre, air, mer', 28 May 1945, 3 AG 4 30, AN.

[83]Diethelm was ultimately dropped from Cabinet for good in the autumn of 1945.

the exclusion of communist members of the Resistance. Following the successful reception of the CNR Programme, two Communists were appointed to the CFLN in April 1944: Fernand Grenier was named Commissioner for the Air and François Billoux was named Secretary of State without portfolio. Despite this gesture, no communist members of the Resistance were invited to the meetings at which France's industrial policies were discussed. At a meeting of the *Commission d'étude des problèmes économiques d'après-guerre*, presided by Lambert Blum-Picard,[84] the Socialist Albert Gazier[85] suggested that it might be sensible to invite a representative of the PCF to take part in the meetings. No response to his suggestion is noted in the minutes, but the fact that the PCF remained unrepresented in future meetings is a clear indication of the Commission's reaction.[86] The exclusion of dissidents on this question ensured that the bodies created by Vichy in 1940 would be maintained by the post-war regime.[87]

The debate in the Provisional Consultative Assembly demanded by Diethelm ultimately took place at the end of July 1944, long after the decision regarding the Committees had been made by the CFLN. Giacobbi presented the economic policies of the Provisional Government and noted that France 'is turning towards a system of a planned economy [*économie dirigée*], regardless of the nation's thirst

[84]Blum-Picard, an *Inspecteur général des Mines* before the war, joined de Gaulle in London in December 1943 and became his Economic Advisor in 1943 before being named Secreatry General for the Commissariat for Industrial Production in 1944.

[85]A trade unionist with the CGT before the war, Albert Gazier signed his name to the *Manifeste des douze* in November 1940 and joined de Gaulle in Algeria in 1943. Elected to the National Assembly with the SFIO in 1945, he held a number of ministerial positions under the Fourth Republic.

[86]'Commission d'étude des problems économiques d'après-guerre. Procès-verbal de la séance du 17 avril 1944', 17 April 1944, CFLN 686, MAE.

[87]In his memoirs, de Gaulle describes how meetings of the CFLN were organised. Assisted by Joxe, de Gaulle would decide on the matters to be discussed and would ask ministers for their opinions. 'Then, I would conclude by formulating the resolution of the Council and, if need be, providing a final decision to resolve any disputes.' If this were the case, opposition from either of the Communist members of the CFLN, or indeed from Diethelm *qua* Minister for War, could have been easily overruled by de Gaulle, particularly as Giacobbi supported maintaining the Committees. See de Gaulle, *Mémoires de guerre*, 210.

for liberty'.[88] Crucially, the economic policies were presented as a package, based on the CNR Programme that had already been endorsed by representatives of all major Resistance groups within France. The debate in the Assembly was thus not focused on the maintenance of the Organisation Committees alone, but on the entire post-war programme agreed upon in March 1944, which consciously avoided weighing in on the question of the Committees. By asking the Assembly to ratify the Provisional Government's economic policies, the GPRF was in fact seeking approval not only of the CNR Programme, but also of policies too divisive to have been included in that agreement in the first place in a kind of omnibus bill. Chief among these was the maintenance of Vichy's Committees. Predictably, a number of deputies opposed the preservation of the Organisation Committees, with Socialist Roger Mistral decrying that 'it would be madness to maintain [Vichy's] system. France wants a new economic regime'.[89] André Marty, a senior member of the PCF, criticised the studied ambiguity of the economic policies outlined by Giacobbi, stating that 'the Communist delegation can only deplore the inadequate precision of these declarations'.[90] Despite these reproaches, however, support for the CNR Programme and the economic priorities it outlined was remarkably strong and the Assembly consequently endorsed the overall economic policies of the Provisional Government. Giacobbi enthused that 'all the speakers demonstrated that there exists absolute agreement on the foundations of the economic doctrine of the Government and of the Nation'.[91] Such an outcome would have been unlikely had Giacobbi not replaced Diethelm as Commissioner for Production and Supply.

Within the CFLN, meanwhile, the discussion had long since turned to the nature of the reforms that should be implemented on the Organisation Committees, rather than whether the Committees should continue to exist at all.[92] By mid-April, Pierre Mendès France, by now Commissioner for the National Economy, was able to declare that 'the CFLN has discussed the question and the majority of its members

[88]'La politique économique du gouvernement', 21 July 1944, C I 591, AN. The debate took place over two days, 21–22 July 1944.

[89]Ibid., 22 July 1944.

[90]Ibid., 21 July 1944.

[91]Ibid., 22 July 1944.

[92]The reform of the Organisation Committees and OCRPI are discussed in Chapter 6.

seems to have decided, as I have, to maintain these institutions after the [Allied] landing' in France. He justified this decision by noting that 'it seems to me that it would be very dangerous to dissolve these institutions at the very moment when a planned economy would require us to rely on effective organs of action. The disappearance of these institutions would create a serious void that could only be filled after a long delay needed to reconstruct new institutions that would be impossible to improvise'.[93] With the removal of Diethelm and the exclusion of the Communists from the debate, the decision to maintain Vichy's undemocratic and unpopular institutions was made without opposition. The debate in the Provisional Consultative Assembly at the end of July merely added credibility to the decision, particularly crucial to de Gaulle's strategy of legitimising himself as the rightful leader of the French Republic. Within the Assembly, meanwhile, even those who questioned the decision to maintain the Committees supported the Provisional Government's overall economic policies.

In his influential study of post-war France, William Hitchcock argues that the fall of Mendès France – marked by his resignation as Minister for the National Economy in April 1945 – was due to his support for maintaining Vichy's institutions, particularly the Organisation Committees and a strong Ministry for the National Economy. Moreover, it is suggested that Mendès France was alone in his defence of the Organisation Committees and OCRPI:

> While still in Algiers, [Mendès France] had argued in the CEI that the organizational committees established by Vichy to exert control over the economy would have to be maintained [. . .] As time wore on, it appeared to his colleagues that Mendès France wanted to maintain the same kind of control that Vichy had exercised, but now through the means of a powerful Ministry of the National Economy. This was perhaps his greatest sin. He wanted to use the political channels of an outmoded and inefficient administration to institute economic change.[94]

[93]Lettre de Pierre Mendès France, 'Objet: Groupements économiques institues par l'autorité de fait de VICHY', 20 April 1944, F 60 914, AN. A copy of this letter can also be found in F 60 896, AN.

[94]William Hitchcock, *France Restored: Cold War Diplomacy and the Quest for Leadership in Europe, 1944–1954* (Chapel Hill: University of North Carolina Press, 1998), 28–29.

According to this account, Mendès France's 'greatest sin', for which the only absolution was his resignation as minister, was his desire to maintain parts of Vichy's 'outmoded and inefficient system'. But this overlooks the fact that support for maintaining the Organisation Committees was virtually unanimous within the CFLN. Furthermore, the Organisation Committees continued to operate in France well beyond Mendès France's resignation; similarly, the State continued to intervene heavily in the economy, even more so after the series of nationalisations that only intensified after Mendès France's departure.[95] Maintaining Vichy's Organisation Committees to serve a more interventionist French State was a broadly shared goal explicitly supported by every major party in post-war France – with the significant exception of the PCF. The claim that a notable minister, namely Mendès France, was forced to resign for holding precisely such views has more in common with the Gaullist myth of a decisive break between Vichy and post-war France than with the reality of the CFLN's position on the matter. Indeed, as the case of André Diethelm demonstrates, it was not support for the maintenance of Vichy's organisms that threatened a ministerial career, but rather opposition to their maintenance.

Conclusion

By the time the Allies landed in Normandy in June 1944, the French government-in-waiting had developed a coherent political economy for post-war France. Aside from the celebrated post-war programme of 15 March 1944, however, the debates that evolved over 1943 and 1944 are essential to understand the CFLN's plans for France's industrial organisation. Throughout 1943, the question of whether Vichy's Organisation Committees and OCRPI should be maintained divided the French Left. These institutions were created to facilitate France's

[95]While France's coal mines were nationalised in December 1944 and certain companies, notably Renault, in early 1945, the majority of nationalisations occurred after Mendès France's resignation on 6 April 1945. These included the Banque de France as well as the largest banks in the country, and key sectors such as gas and electricity. The best study of the post-war nationalisations remains Claire Andrieu, Lucette Le Van, and Antoine Prost (eds), *Les nationalisations de la Libération* (Paris: FNSP, 1987).

collaboration with the Reich and afforded a small handful of industrialists unprecedented power over French industry. This was enough for their abolition to be unwaveringly demanded by the Communist elements of the Resistance. Yet the more moderate members of the French Left argued that these bodies could be reformed and thereby maintained for their pragmatic value. The latter opinion was increasingly shared by virtually all CFLN members in Algiers, a position reinforced by their conversations with former Vichy officials and by the practical difficulties encountered when trying to abolish the Committees in North Africa. De Gaulle himself intervened to remove the most significant obstacle to an agreement on the matter by replacing Diethelm with Giacobbi, although the general was motivated more by political and diplomatic factors than by economic ones. While the fate of the Organisation Committees was intentionally omitted from the 15 March post-war programme, barely a month later the CFLN formally agreed that Vichy's industrial apparatus would be maintained. The consensus on this question ran the gamut from socialist *résistants* such as Robert Lacoste to purportedly apolitical technicians like Jean Monnet to pseudo-fascist former Vichy ministers such as Pierre Pucheu.

On 3 July 1944, the CFLN, by then calling itself the Provisional Government of the French Republic (GPRF), drafted a law re-establishing the legality of the Republic. 'All laws and decrees' passed by Vichy, it declared, were henceforth 'null and void'.[96] This would, of course, nullify the laws of 16 August and 10 September 1940, which created the Organisation Committees and OCRPI, respectively. Yet this was not the case. The CFLN preferred to amend these laws rather than to actually abolish them, and the first article of the law of 16 August 1940 was overturned in January 1944.[97] The apparent contradiction of amending a law that was declared 'null and void' in the first place was deliberately

[96]'Projet sur le rétablissement de la légalité républicaine', 3 July 1944, CFLN 603, MAE.

[97]'Rétablissement de la liberté syndicale et épuration des organisations syndicales de travailleurs et d'employeurs', 21 January 1944, CFLN 602, MAE. The first article of the law abolished national confederations of trade unions and employers' associations, although individual confederations, notably the CGT, the CFTC, and the CGPF, were not formally dissolved until 9 November 1940. The re-establishment of union rights necessitated the removal of this clause, but the remaining articles remained valid.

overlooked. Anticipating this inconsistency in April 1944, Leprince had suggested that the CFLN could 'appeal to the law of 11 July 1938, *which might mask the fact that we would be using Vichy's organisations from the time of the Liberation*'.[98] Leprince was right to recognise that the French public would not look favourably upon the maintenance of Vichy's Committees.

The Provisional Government had succeeded in maintaining Vichy's industrial organisation, but it now faced two challenges to this policy. The Communists, who would emerge from the first elections in liberated France as the largest party in the National Assembly, never renounced their opposition to these bodies and continued to criticise them openly following the Liberation. Despite the 'historic consensus' reached with the CNR Programme, this agreement had only been achieved by avoiding specific technical questions like the maintenance of Vichy's Committees. As resisting the Vichy regime was replaced by governing the French Republic, such differences among the parties as those consciously ignored in the CNR Programme inevitably resurfaced. The second threat to the Organisation Committees was public opinion – the maintenance of deeply unpopular institutions that were enduring symbols of Vichy and collaboration was never destined to please the electorate. With the return of open, democratic debate, the continued existence of Vichy's industrial organisation was called into question. Ultimately, the Provisional Government's success in preserving Vichy's New Industrial Order would prove to be similarly provisional.

[98]'Commission d'étude des problems économiques d'après-guerre. Sous-commission des Comités d'organisation. Séance du 21 avril 1944', 21 April 1944, CFLN 686, MAE. Emphasis added. The law of 11 July 1938 'on the general organisation of the Nation for wartime' included articles on 'economic organisation in wartime', but these fell far short of what had been established with the law of 16 August 1940. The 1938 law granted relevant ministers the possibility of managing the trade, use, and rationing of resources deemed to be vital to the needs of the country. No new institutions were foreseen in the legislation, as the Organisation Committees would only be created in 1940.

CHAPTER 6

Conserver la forme en réformant l'esprit: Reforming Vichy's Industrial Order, 1944–1946

By the spring of 1944, the CFLN had agreed that the institutions created by Vichy in 1940 to manage French industry, namely the Organisation Committees and OCRPI, should be maintained yet subjected to a number of reforms. These bodies consequently continued their work until the National Assembly ultimately voted to dissolve them in April 1946. In the existing historiography on the Organisation Committees, however, this crucial period of the Provisional Government between 1944 and 1946 is generally ignored, as almost all studies of the Committees conclude with the end of the Vichy regime.[1] Writing in 1990, Claire Andrieu lamented

'Si l'on conserve la forme du comité d'organisation, il faut en réformer l'esprit' ('If we maintain the form of the Organisation Committee, we must reform its spirit'), in 'Maintien éventuel du CO du bâtiment et des travaux publics', by Leprince, 26 January 1944, CFLN 686, MAE.

[1]The only book-length study of the Organisation Committees, a volume edited by Hervé Joly, focuses on the period 1940–1944, as do virtually all other studies of the Committees. See Hervé Joly (ed.), *Les Comités d'organisation et l'économie dirigée du regime de Vichy* (Caen: Centre de recherché d'histoire quantitative, 2004) and, indicatively, Henry Rousso, 'L'organisation industrielle de Vichy: perspectives de recherche', *RHDGM*, October 1979; Adrian Jones, 'Illusions of Sovereignty: Business and the Organization of Committees of Vichy France', *Social History*, January 1986; and Olivier Dard, Jean-Claude Daumas and François Marcot (eds.), *L'Occupation, l'Etat français et les entreprises* (Paris: Association pour le développement de l'histoire économique, 2000).

© The Author(s) 2017

L.-A. Brunet, *Forging Europe: Industrial Organisation in France, 1940–1952*, Security, Conflict and Cooperation in the Contemporary World, DOI 10.1057/978-1-349-95198-7_6

'the forgetting of the final act of the drama, namely the survival of the Committees in liberated France, from 1944 until 1946',[2] yet this gap remains unfilled. Even wide-ranging studies that consider the French economy in 1944–1946 in a broader context, and which summarise the debate within the CFLN regarding the maintenance of the Committees, offer no more than a passing allusion to the actual reforms carried out over the next two years.[3] The existing literature thus recognises that the survival of the Committees agreed in 1944 was conditional on their post-war reform, yet fails to provide a satisfactory account of these reforms between the Liberation and the dissolution of the Committees in 1946. This chapter thus constitutes the first detailed study of the reform of the Organisation Committees under the Provisional Government, focusing particularly on the Committee for Steel.

By Any Other Name: Unveiling the Professional Offices

The most conspicuous reform of the Organisation Committees was carried out at the beginning of 1945. Robert Lacoste, Minister for Industrial Production in de Gaulle's first post-Vichy government, was briefed on the systematic attacks against the continued existence of the Organisation Committees in the French press. *L'Humanité*, the Communist daily, was the most tenacious critic of the Committees, stating that the government 'had not done away with the fascist bureaucracy' set up during the war and demanding that the 'rotten edifice of Vichy be knocked down in its entirety', including what they dubbed the 'disorganisation committees'.[4] Moreover, many blamed the ongoing

[2]Claire Andrieu, *La Banque sous l'Occupation. Paradoxes de l'histoire d'une profession* (Paris: FNSP, 1990), 128.

[3]Three of the most important books on the subject offer no more than a paragraph each on the reforms, and these tend to simply reiterate what had been agreed within the CFLN in Algiers, providing no specifics on how the reforms were actually carried out. See Richard Kuisel, *Capitalism and the State in Modern France* (Cambridge: Cambridge University Press, 1981), 216; Andrew Shennan, *Rethinking France* (Oxford: Clarendon, 1989), 272; and Michel Margairaz, *L'Etat, les finances et l'économie. Histoire d'une conversion, 1932–1952* (Paris: CHEFF, 1991), 775–776.

[4]'A Japy, Maurice Thorez fait acclamer les mots d'ordre "s'unir, combattre et travailler"', 2 February 1946; 'Ravitaillement: Problème politique, problème national', 25 March 1945; 'A Angers avec André Marty', *L'Humanité*, 27 March 1945.

shortages of various goods and raw materials experienced in France that winter and the existence of a thriving black market on the supposed incompetence of the Organisation Committees, asserting that 'things will only improve once we have toppled the offices set up by Vichy'.[5] Lacoste, a long-time supporter of the Committees,[6] was 'anguished by this state of affairs' and decided to launch a counter-campaign in the press explaining the necessity of the Committees. He supplemented this strategy with the obvious renaming of the institutions, with the hope that a new name would give the institutions a new lease on life.[7] It was agreed that at the end of February 1945, a decree would rename the Organisation Committees, which would be henceforth known as 'Professional Offices'.[8] Ironically, this was one of the names first used in July 1940 for the nascent Organisation Committees, although the reprise of this name by the GPRF is likely coincidental.[9] An update on the transformation of the Organisation Committees into Professional Offices was given in August 1945,[10] although staff of the Offices and of the Ministry alike continued to refer to the institutions by their Vichy-era names, an embarrassing slip exacerbated by the continued use of the Organisation Committees' letterhead.[11] That autumn, the renamed Professional Office for Steel (OPSID) had to send reminders to industrialists across France to stop using the office's previous name, the

[5]'Assurer le ravitaillement de la capitale? Ce n'est pas uniquement une question de transports!', *L'Humanité*, 7 February 1945. On the black market in France during this period, see Paul Sanders, *Histoire de marché noir, 1940–1946* (Paris: Perrin, 2001) and Fabrice Grenard, *La France du marché noir (1940–1949)* (Paris: Payot & Rivages, 2008).

[6]Lacoste co-authored the Courtin Report, published in 1943, which advocated maintaining the Organisation Committees and OCRPI in liberated France.

[7]'Procès-verbal de la réunion des directeurs', 11 January 1945, F 12 10025, AN.

[8]'Note. Objet: réforme des CO', 16 February 1945, F 12 10025, AN.

[9]The French Delegation in Paris used this term as early as 26 July in a letter to Elmar Michel, the Head of the Economic Section of the German Military Administration in Paris. The other name used for the proto-Organisation Committees discussed in Chapter 2 was 'Liaison Offices'. See 'Note à Michel', 26 July 1940, F 60 1539, AN.

[10]'Réunion des directeurs. Ordre du jour: Offices professionnels', 8 August 1945, F 12 10027, AN.

[11]A paper shortage in France at this time meant that the Republican government awkwardly continued to use stationery with Vichy's letterhead well after the demise of the regime.

Organisation Committee for Steel (CORSID), but to little effect.[12] Despite the obvious continuities between the Organisation Committees and the Professional Offices – the new name belied the fact that they were in fact the same institutions – the Ministry of Industrial Production denied even the most remote similarity between the institutions. In the autumn of 1945, one ministry official insisted to a businessman that 'the Professional Offices have nothing in common with the organisations of the Vichy regime aside from the extreme shortage of primary materials that they have to manage'.[13] The businessman was by no means the only individual who found the purported dissociation of the new Professional Offices from Vichy's Organisation Committees unconvincing.

While some reforms to industrial organisation were foreseen in the early post-war period, it was seen as necessary to establish an *Ecole Supérieure d'Organisation Professionnelle* (ESOP), under the auspices of the Ministry of Industrial Production, to 'oversee the training of economic executives both for the existing institutions and [ultimately] for the establishment of a new organisation'.[14] Just as 1944–1945 saw the overhaul of Sciences Po and the creation of the *Ecole nationale d'administation* (ENA) to train the new generation of civil servants, the Provisional Government decided to create the ESOP to train France's post-war executives who would be working within the Organisation Committees and their successor institutions. This decision shows that France's leadership expected Vichy's system of industrial organisation, with inevitable reforms, to last well into the post-war years – it would hardly have made sense to establish a school to train executives for bodies that were to be imminently dissolved. In an influential report to de Gaulle in February 1944, CFLN Secretary General Louis Joxe observed that even if the Organisation Committees were abolished, the government would need to organise bodies 'to take over the duties entrusted to the Organisation Committees by Vichy, which cannot be surrendered to private initiative'.[15] It was clear that the

[12]'Circulaire d'OPSID', 16 October 1945, AQ 139 83, AN.

[13]'Lettre de Piette au Président de la Chambre de métiers de l'Ain', 18 October 1945, F 12 10031, AN.

[14]'Note sur la formation des cadres économiques', 30 October 1944, F 12 10031.

[15]'Note sur les questions d'ordre économique et de ravitaillement', 10 February 1944, F 60 914, AN.

Committees or institutions very much like them would endure well into the post-war years.

Reforming Vichy's Committees

Politically, the most important reform to be made to the post-war Organisation Committees was the removal of 'collaborators', understood by many to mean the individuals who had run the Committees during the war. This was an essential condition of maintaining the Organisation Committees, and was accepted unanimously throughout the CFLN and then the GPRF.[16] On 7 October, a government decree annulled all appointments to Organisation Committees, effectively sacking the entire industrial leadership of the Vichy era, regardless of the extent to which they might have engaged in various forms of collaboration.[17] As their final act, the members of CORSID submitted their resignation on 9 October 1944.[18] With this simple letter, which simply confirmed the government's decree, the vital step of purging the Committee of its wartime leadership was complete.

Finding successors for the wartime presidents of the Organisation Committees, however, proved to be a difficult task. Nominations were sought within the Ministry of Industrial Production, although such recommendations had to include an explanatory report justifying the nomination, the candidate's CV, no less than six copies of the completed nomination form, and perhaps most daunting of all, written approval from the CGT.[19] Due to the stringent conditions involved in the nomination process, civil servants from the Ministry of Industrial Production ended up running most of the Organisation Committees for months after the

[16]'Projet d'ordonnance relative aux organismes industriels dits comités d'organisation', 29 May 1944, CFLN 602, MAE. Indeed, the 'radical *épuration* of the civilian and military administration' was a non-negotiable condition of the PCF's support for de Gaulle and the GPRF. See Philippe Buton, *Les lendemains qui déchantent: Le Parti communiste français à la Libération* (Paris: FNSP, 1993), 36–38.

[17]'Ordonnance du 7 octobre 1944' in *Journal officiel*, 8 October 1944.

[18]Lettre de Jules Aubrun, 9 October 1944, 139 AQ 80, AN.

[19]'Note', 24 November 1944, F 12 10024, AN.

dismissal of the wartime leadership in November 1944. Furthermore, it was routinely highlighted that, in the context of the *épuration* that marked late-1944, the new leaders of the Organisation Committees had to be 'unassailable figures' [*personnalités inattaquables*].[20] The Ministry ran CORSID, formally renamed OPSID in February 1945, until the appointment of Alexis Aron as Provisional Commissioner of OPSID on 8 March 1945.[21] Aron had been an original member of CORSID's *Commission générale*, a consultative commission of steel industrialists established by CORSID in February 1941.[22] In this capacity, Aron was included in the early organisation of the steel industry under Vichy. With the imposition of anti-Semitic legislation by Vichy, however, Aron, himself the son of a rabbi, was dismissed from the Commission and he spent the remainder of the war in Savoie, which was in the Non-Occupied Zone until November 1942. He remained in close contact with CORSID, which sent him money during the war, and they exchanged draft projects for the French steel industry.[23] He was thus kept abreast of CORSID's actions, participated in the debates on the organisation of the industry, and maintained a close personal friendship with Aubrun in particular.[24] Given his initial position within CORSID's *Commission générale* and his ongoing involvement with CORSID regarding the organisation of the industry, the appointment of

[20]'Procès-verbal de la réunion [des directeurs] du 26 septembre 1944', 28 September 1944, F 12 10024, AN.

[21]'Rapport sur la situation du CO de la sidérurgie fin 1944–début 1945. Note du Commissaire provisoire', 27 April 1945, F 12 10063, AN. The title of President was replaced with that of Provisional Commissioner. Aron would retain this 'provisional' role until the formal abolition of OPSID in mid-1946.

[22]'Déclaration No. 15 du CORSID', 5 February 1941, 139 AQ 80, AN. Philippe Mioche has argued that it was in fact the Commission générale, rather than CORSID itself, that made the important decisions regarding the steel industry during the war, a claim that is discussed in Chapter 3. See Mioche, 'Le comité d'organisation de la sidérurgie: un lieu d'affrontement entre modernisateurs de la sidérurgie et gardiens de la profession?' in Hervé Joly (ed.), *Les Comités d'organisation et l'économie dirigée du régime de Vichy* (Caen: CRHQ, 2004), 95–108.

[23]Philippe Mioche, 'Une vision conciliante du futur de l'Europe: le plan d'Alexis Aron en 1943' in Michel Dumoulin (ed.), *Plans des temps de guerre pour l'Europe d'après-guerre, 1940–1947* (Brussels: Bruylant, 1995), 307–323. Mioche argues that Aron's was the most significant plan for the modernisation of the steel industry developed during the war.

[24]Françoise Berger, 'Alexis Aron, ingénieur sidérurgiste', *Archives Juives* 1/2011 (Vol. 44), 136–139.

Aron to succeed his friend Aubrun as head of CORSID serves as an example of continuity within the management of the French steel industry.

In March 1945, newly-appointed Commissioner Aron commended the 'considerable work accomplished by the former Committee' and to the 'independence and the courage unwaveringly displayed by the Committee in the face of the ever-increasing demands of the Occupation authorities'.[25] Moreover, he reiterated Aubrun's pleas from December 1944 to maintain 'an effective leadership, centralised in the hands of a single, responsible individual, namely the Provisional Commissioner': Aron himself. He also made the case for 'the necessity of a strong, uninterrupted Professional Office [with] sufficient latitude' to rule itself.[26] Aron was perhaps the ideal candidate for those who sought the appearance of *épuration* yet the reality of continuity from the Vichy years. Undeniably a victim of some of Vichy's most heinous legislation – it must be remembered that Vichy's anti-Semitic laws caused the deaths of 75,000 Jews – Aron did indeed fit the bill as an 'unassailable figure'. Yet his involvement with CORSID throughout the war is impossible to ignore, even if his formal participation in the *Commission générale* was forcibly ended in 1941. His unsevered contact with CORSID throughout the war, and his praise of Aubrun upon succeeding him, show that Aron sought to continue and defend the work of the Vichy-era leadership in the steel industry.

While the palpable change in leadership did indeed replace the five wartime Committee members with an 'unassailable figure', the changes in staff ended there. The remainder of those who had worked at CORSID during the war retained their roles in the newly-rechristened OPSID. The Under-Secretary of CORSID, Jean Latourte, retained his position and continued to incorrigibly refer to the new Office by its wartime name.[27] Similarly, Eugène Dupuy, who as President of the *Bureau de normalisation de la sidérurgie* (BNS) worked tirelessly to bring French steel products in line with German specifications, stayed put. The technical staff employed by the Committee continued their work, which would later be used by Jean Monnet as the foundation of his plans for

[25]'Rapport sur la situation du CO de la sidérurgie fin 1944–début 1945. Note du Commissaire provisoire', 27 April 1945, F 12 10063, AN.

[26]Ibid.

[27]Latourte, a graduate of the Polytechnique and then the Ecole des Mines de Paris, was Deputy Director of the Ecole des Mines de Saint-Etienne (where Robert Baboin also taught) before joining CORSID.

modernising French industry.[28] This continuation was similarly noticeable in OCRPI, which remained part of the Ministry for Industrial Production. While the Minister and Secretary General, Robert Lacoste and Blum-Picard respectively, arrived at rue de Grenelle from Algiers, OCRPI's staff remained unchanged. René Norguet, who had worked closely with Jean Bichelonne, Vichy's Minister for Industrial Production from 1942 until 1944, now wrote his memos to the former CFLN members.[29] Even the practice of Christmas bonuses that had developed during the war was maintained by OCRPI.[30] More troublingly, CORSID's allocation of raw materials to firms remained based on wartime production figures, which resulted in the largest quantities of raw materials being sent to those firms which had produced most extensively for the Reich during the war – a controversial point that led some industrialists to decry that the system in place under the GPRF 'rewarded industrialists who collaborated with the Germans'.[31]

If *épuration* was indeed an essential condition for maintaining Vichy's industrial bodies, it turned out to be very slight for members of those Committees. This was largely because the nature of *épuration* changed significantly over the course of 1944. From the latter half of 1943, purging France of 'collaborators' and 'traitors' became a dominant theme within the CFLN; this period saw the arrest of Pierre Pucheu as well as some former Vichy officials who had previously been welcomed by the CFLN. Following the execution of Pucheu in March 1944 and peaking that summer following the Allied landings in France, a period known as *l'épuration sauvage* was unleashed, characterised by punishment meted out to supposed 'collaborators' largely by mobs and generally without a trial.[32] By September,

[28]'Projet de résolution soumis au Conseil du Plan. Objectifs généraux pour l'activité française', 13 March 1946, AMF 2 3, FJME.

[29]Norguet's case is particularly interesting: having spent most of the war working in the ministry, he was arrested on suspicion of anti-Vichy resistance in February 1944, and was ultimately reinstated by the GPRF.

[30]'Note', 14 December 1945, F 12 10028, AN.

[31]The system of sub-allocation developed during the war, which allocated greater quantities to firms producing heavily for the Reich, remained in place at the end of 1944. See 'Procès-verbal de la 20e réunion des directeurs', 20 December 1944, F 12 10024, AN.

[32]The best study on this phase in Philippe Bourdrel, *L'Epuration sauvage, 1944–1945* (Paris: Perrin, 2002). On the punishment of women accused of 'horizontal collaboration' with the enemy, see Fabrice Virgili, *La France 'virile'. Des femmes tondues à la Libération* (Paris: Payot, 2000).

however, de Gaulle sought to end the destabilising forces of these purges by reasserting the supremacy of the State, and placed national reconciliation above punishment for those who had supported the regime. Courts were set up in September, and the result was a slower, more judicial process that spared virtually all members of Vichy's Organisation Committees from being tried.[33] All but the members of the Committee for Steel itself – a total of five individuals – retained their positions, for example.[34] Moreover, of those five who were forced to resign, none was tried for collaboration, and they were able to continue their careers as leaders of the French steel industry.

Jules Aubrun, who had served as CORSID's only president from its establishment in November 1940 until his forced resignation in October 1944, was named President of the *Chambre syndicale de la sidérurgie française* (CSSF), a revived version of the *Comité des forges*, that autumn. While the creation of Vichy's Organisation Committees had abolished and superseded the employers' associations for coal and steel (as well as the main employers' confederation, the CGPF) and trade union confederations, the re-establishment of *liberté syndicale* in 1944 facilitated their return. While CORSID under Aubrun had presumed to combine employers' associations and trade unions alike, in the post-war era he contented himself with representing only the former. It is important to note that the

[33]Jean-Paul Cointet, *Expier Vichy: l'épuration en France, 1943–1958* (Paris: Perrin, 2008). On the purges in the French administration and among employers, see François Rouquet, *L'épuration dans l'administration française. Agents de l'Etat et collaboration ordinaire* (Paris: CNRS, 1993) and Marc Bergère (ed.), *L'épuration économique en France à la Libération* (Rennes: Presses universitaires de Rennes, 2008). In his memoirs, de Gaulle describes his approach to *épuration* at this stage: 'to limit the punishment to the individuals who played a leading role in Vichy's policies and to the men who were in direct collusion with the enemy'. See de Gaulle, *Mémoires de guerre. L'unité: 1942–1944* (vol. 2) (Paris: Plon, 1956), 186.

[34]This list could be expanded to include Vichy's last Minister for Industrial Production, Jean Bichelonne, under whose ministry the Committees and OCRPI operated. Bichelonne died in Berlin in 1945, however, and hence was not subjected to formal *épuration* in France. Needless to say, the German representatives on the Sections of OCRPI were not invited to remain. Vichy's previous Ministers for Industrial Production, René Belin and François Lehideux, were both sought out after the Liberation: Belin fled to Switzerland while Lehideux was arrested in August 1944 and released two years later; both cases were formally dismissed in 1949 thanks to both men's claims of having committed 'acts of resistance' during the war. Belin went on to be elected mayor of Lorrez-le-Bocage while Lehideux became President of the *Association pour défendre la mémoire du maréchal Pétain*.

interwar leaders of the *Comité des forges*, de Wendel and Lambert Ribot, were not returned to their positions in the new CSSF, but that instead Aubrun was maintained as the leader of the industry's employers' association; the dramatic replacement of the leaders of the *Comité des forges* with Aubrun in 1940 thus proved to be permanent. His power within the industry was further increased in 1946, when the resurrected *Conseil national du patronat français* (CNPF)[35] named Aubrun President of its Association for the Steel Industry. Meanwhile Eugène Roy, the Vice President of CORSID, had a similarly successful post-war career. At the end of 1944, the Ministry for Industrial Production asked professionals from various industries to recommend representatives for French industry to participate in the work of the *Commission d'études générales pour l'Allemagne*. An overwhelming endorsement from the steel industry converged around Roy, who only two months earlier had been forced to resign from his position as Vice President of CORSID. The ministry accepted the nomination, and Roy was given the first of a series of important roles in post-Vichy France.[36]

The Ministry of Industrial Production, for its part, tried to temper the attempts to purge Vichy-era industrialists. The director of the Firminy coal mines, in the Loire, was arrested in November 1944. The Ministry pleaded for his release, citing his 'technical, social, and patriotic role' during the Occupation.[37] Even in January 1944, the CFLN acknowledged that, while factory owners had supported the Vichy regime and produced for the Reich, 'it would be unjust to consider filling German

[35]The *Conseil national du patronat français* (CNPF) was established in December 1945 to take the place of the pre-war *Confédération générale du patronat français* (CGPF) that was abolished by Vichy in 1940. Although the CFLN had agreed that the reconstitution of the CGPF would be (politically) impossible after the war, this did not prevent the employers from proceeding with this plan. See 'Rétablissement de la liberté syndicale et épuration des organisations syndicales des travailleurs et d'employeurs', 13 January 1944, CFLN 602, MAE.

[36]'Note du secrétaire général à la production [Blum-Picard] au directeur du commerce extérieur, ministère de l'économie nationale', 15 December 1944, F 12 10024, AN.

[37]'Note', 30 November 1944, F 12 10024, AN. Richard Vinen cites an example of the head of the COH in Loire, Perrin Pelletier, who was similarly arrested and put before a *Commission Régionale d'Epuration*. Here too, Robert Lacoste sent a letter on 30 November 1944 asking for the industrialist's release on the grounds of his 'patriotic attitude'. See Richard Vinen, 'The French Coal Industry During the Occupation' in *Historical Journal*, 33:1, 1990, 105–130, here 122–123.

orders as necessarily expressing an attitude of collaboration'.[38] This fine distinction between 'expressing an attitude of collaborating' and producing for the Reich while supporting the Vichy regime informed the State-managed purges that followed the brief and bloody *épuration sauvage* and what Céline derided as its '*divines raisons d'assassiner*'[39] of the early months following the Liberation.[40] The claim that the French steel industrialists acted patriotically in the war, however, is offset by the selective silence of the industrialists themselves on this question. In November 1944, the Ministry of Industrial Production asked industrialists to nominate candidates amongst themselves for the *Croix de la Libération* and the *Médaille de la Résistance*, decorations to acknowledge patriotic actions associated with the Liberation and the Resistance. The coal industry nominated ten, including Aimé Lepercq, Aubrun's counterpart in the Organisation Committee for Coal who was then briefly Minister for Finance before his premature death at the end of 1944. The chemical industry, despite being tainted with its collaboration with the Reich through IG Farben and other Franco-German ventures, nominated nine patriotic industrialists.[41] The steel industry was unable to produce the name of a single nominee from within its ranks.[42] While hardly conclusive in itself, this example does suggest that the steel industrialists themselves did not see themselves or their peers as having participated actively in either the Resistance or the Liberation. This stands uneasily next to the rhetoric surrounding this purportedly 'technical, social, and patriotic' group.

[38]'Rétablissement de la liberté syndicale et épuration des organisations syndicales de travailleurs et d'employeurs', 13 January 1944, CFLN, 602, MAE.

[39]Céline, *D'un château l'autre* (Paris: Gallimard, 1957), 49. Louis-Ferdinand Céline, one of the greatest French authors of the century, had supported the Vichy regime and published anti-Semitic pamphlets during the war, leading to his being found guilty (in absentia) of collaboration.

[40]The best recent overview of *l'épuration* in France is Jean-Paul Cointet's *Expier Vichy: l'épuration en France 1943–1958* (Paris: Perrin, 2008). Philippe Bourdrel's *L'épuration sauvage, 1944–1945* (Paris: Perrin, 2002) provides regional studies of the early, violent purges of 1944–1945, demonstrating the extent to which *l'épuration* varied across France.

[41]On IG Farben and Franco-German economic collaboration, see Peter Hayes, 'La stratégie industrielle de l'IG Farben en France occupée', *Histoire, économie et société*, 11:3, 1992.

[42]'Propositions d'attribution de la Croix de Libération ou de la Médaille de la Résistance', 30 November 1944, F 12 10024, AN.

In the autumn of 1944, with the war still raging in Europe and French industry in tatters, the Ministry of Industrial Production was clearly more interested in maintaining even the minimal levels of production at that time than in purging vital industries of their leadership. One month earlier the Ministry had revealed its more pragmatic reasoning in demanding the immediate release of another industrialist: '[This arrest] is susceptible to impede the proper functioning of this factory, and we therefore ask that he be released without further delay, or at least that he appear before the *épuration* committee immediately.'[43] Clearly, the value of an industrialist in contributing to timely production outweighed any potential punishment for wartime actions. Henry Rousso has characterised the *épuration* as 'incoherent, notably by leaving the most extensive form of collaboration, that is to say economic collaboration, out of reach'.[44] More recently, Hervé Joly has argued that the purging of French business did indeed take place, claiming that while industrial leaders 'were not rejected by their profession and left with neither employment nor subsistence, they never regained their leading positions' within the industry. According to Joly, the Vichy-era leaders of French industry were permanently demoted after the Liberation, amounting to a moderate but nonetheless real form of *épuration*.[45] In the case of the steel industry, however, the handful of industrialists promoted to leadership positions within CORSID in 1940 continued to thrive after the Liberation, while the demotion of figures like François de Wendel and Lambert Ribot from their pre-war positions proved to be similarly permanent.[46]

Barely a year after the first Allied landings in France, the leaders of the wartime Organisation Committees had been fully reintegrated into

[43]'Note', 30 October 1944, F 12 10024, AN.

[44]Henry Rousso, 'L'épuration en France: une histoire inachevée' in *Vingtième siècle. Revue d'histoire*, no. 33, 1992, 101.

[45]Hervé Joly, 'Mobilités patronales dans l'après-guerre et impact de l'épuration' in Marc Bergère (ed.), *L'épuration économique en France à la Libération* (Rennes: Presses universitaires de Rennes, 2008), 83–100.

[46]Henri de Peyerimhoff, the President of the *Comité des houillères* until its dissolution in 1940, similarly failed to regain any influential position within the coal industry after the war. He nonetheless wrote to de Gaulle in October 1944 urging him in vain not to nationalise the industry. See 'Un document sur le patronat. Une lettre de Henri de Peyerimhoff au général de Gaulle du 15 octobre 1944'in Claire Andrieu et al. (eds), *Les nationalisations de la Libération* (Paris: FNSP, 1987).

France's industrial elite. On 1 August 1945, the Tripartite Commission on Steel met in Brussels, with the purpose of coordinating the steel industries of the Benelux and France, in terms of both domestic production and the policy to be pursued with regard to German steel production. France chose its most qualified representatives from the French steel industry: Jules Aubrun, Léon Daum, and Jean Raty. While Aubrun and Daum had spent the war running CORSID, Jean Raty had been President of the *Chambre Syndicale des Mines de Fer* from 1941.[47] The French delegation was completed by Aron, Aubrun's friend, colleague, and successor as leader of OPSID. Together, these four individuals represented France at these early negotiations on a coordinated steel policy for post-war Western Europe. So important was their presence at the negotiations that Blum-Picard even wrote directly to the Minister for the Interior and to the French police prefecture to ensure that they all received their passports in time to attend the meeting in Brussels.[48] Far from being subjected to the kind of de facto *épuration* described by Joly – let alone the more radical *épuration* demanded by the PCF – the French steel industry continued to be managed and represented by the same small group of industrialists first promoted to these positions by Vichy in 1940. This handful of industrialists would negotiate on behalf of France with its Western European neighbours and play key roles in the European project.

In the final assessment, the *épuration* of CORSID demanded as a condition of maintaining Vichy's Organisation Committees consisted of shifting its leaders to other influential positions representing the same industry. The new Provisional Commissioner, Alexis Aron, had indeed fled from Vichy's repressive and odious anti-Semitic laws. For this reason, he was a seemingly 'unassailable figure' fit to rehabilitate Vichy's unpopular institutions. Yet he was himself closely involved with the Organisation Committee, explicitly in its early stages, clandestinely for the final years of the war. He had developed plans for the modernisation of the industry in consultation with CORSID and remained a close friend of Aubrun

[47]Raty held this position from 1941 until 1949, during which time the name of the *Chambre syndicale* remained the same. He ultimately became President of the CSSF in 1956 after the deaths of Aubrun and Pierre Ricard.

[48]'Lettre de Blum-Picard au Préfet de police', 27 July 1945 and 'Lettre de Blum-Picard au Ministre de l'Intérieur', 26 July 1945, F 12 10027, AN.

throughout the period. In itself, placing Aron at the helm of OPSID, while keeping the rest of the Vichy-era staff in place, was barely more significant than changing the name 'Organisation Committee' to 'Professional Office'. The wartime leaders of France's steel industry were merely laterally relocated to other key posts within the industry. Before the fighting in Europe had even finished, CORSID's President and Vice-President were enjoying plum jobs at the *Chambre syndicale de la sidérurgie française* and the *Commission d'études générales pour l'Allemagne*, respectively.

From Dictatorship to Triumvirate

As we have seen, a consensus had emerged within the Resistance, and indeed among many who had served Vichy, that the regime's industrial organisation ought to be maintained for pragmatic reasons. This maintenance, however, was conditional on significant reform of Vichy's industrial institutions. While the Organisation Committees would continue doing what they had done since their creation in 1940, the new members had to be drawn not only from large firms, but also from organised labour and the State.

The support for these reforms was not unanimous. Predictably, the loudest objections came from industrialists, who enjoyed significant powers under the Vichy-era structure, which disregarded organised labour and SMEs, despite Pétain's faltering attempts to bring them in line with the National Revolution.[49] In his new role as President of the CSSF, Jules Aubrun did all he could to retain the Organisation Committees as they had been during the war. In December 1944, he argued that any reorganisation of the steel industry must only be carried out by the industrialists themselves, who would then place themselves under the authority of the State, whose role it would be to oversee the proper functioning of the employer-forged system. Moreover, Aubrun demanded that the profession 'remain in the framework of the law of 16 August 1940' – in other

[49]Although Mioche has argued that the Vichy era was not advantageous to the *patronat* in the steel industry, they nevertheless sought to maintain the Vichy-era system for as long as possible, since they were overrepresented compared with organised labour and SMEs. See Philippe Mioche, 'Les entreprises sidérurgiques sous l'Occupation' in *Histoire, économie et société*, 1992, 11:3, 397–414.

words, to maintain Vichy's legislation and that regime's system of Organisation Committees which were dominated by industrialists. In what was perhaps a Freudian slip, Aubrun wrote that 'the profession would like to see the appointment of a *collège dictatorial* composed of three people chosen by the profession [i.e. the CSSF] and granted public powers' – the word '*dictatorial*' was then crossed out in favour of '*directorial*'.[50] Trying his hand at compromise, Aubrun noted that if the government insisted that Organisation Committees had to include labour representation, then he could accept a tripartite representation, but only if the *patronat* would be assured 50 per cent of the seats, with the remaining half to be divided amongst workers, technicians, and the State.[51] Rejecting talk of a more equally distributed tripartite arrangement, he defended the autocratic structure of the Organisation Committee: 'we reject the idea of a triumvirate, a method that can only weaken the authority of the leader'.[52] In May 1943 Henri Giraud had denounced the law of 16 August 1940 for having introduced 'into French legislation a thory that is foreign to it: that of a Führer in charge, placed at the head of each organisation'; after having enjoyed unprecedented authority under Vichy, the steel industrialists and their unwavering representative, Jules Aubrun, were reluctant to surrender any of their power to the State or to organised labour.[53]

[50]'Projet d'organisation des groupements sidérurgiques, observations de la Chambre syndicale de la sidérurgie', 29 December 1944, F 12 10062, AN. 'Collège directorial' translates as 'board of directors'.

[51]Surprisingly, a similar ratio, guaranteeing 50 per cent representation for the *patronat*, was entertained by Blum-Picard as early as April 1944, before the CFLN had discussed the matter with French industrialists. Blum-Picard justified his proposal on the grounds that 'the conduct of the workers and the technicians in 1936–1937 does not inspire great optimism'. See 'Discussion de réforme des CO', 14 April 1944, CFLN 686, MAE.

[52]'Projet d'organisation des groupements sidérurgiques, observations de la Chambre syndicale de la sidérurgie', 29 December 1944, F 12 10062, AN. General Giraud denounced the law of 16 August 1940 for having 'introduced into French legislation a theory that is foreign to it: that of a Führer in charge, placed at the head of each organisation'. See 'La révision des lois de Vichy. Le général Giraud abroge les dispositions concernant l'organisation professionnelle', in *La Dépêche Algérienne*, 19 May 1943, AME 34 6, FJME. Underlined in the original.

[53]Aubrun continued to pursue a heavy-handed approach in defending the steel industry's interests against government initatives, particularly following the Schuman Declaration in 1950, which is discussed in Chapter 8.

Aside from the reticence among the *patronat* to embrace any system in which they were not themselves dominant, further difficulties emerged from the trade unions. Allotting a portion of the seats of the new Professional Offices to organised labour ran into trouble quite quickly. The wartime cooperation of the labour movement soon splintered as the antagonistic turf wars between the various labour unions re-emerged. The CGT, already divided between the *confédérés* and the *unitaires*, sought to take advantage of the prestige and popularity of the PCF in the immediate post-war era, and the leading role of communists in the interior resistance.[54] Meanwhile, the Catholic CFTC saw that it could increase its popularity by aligning itself more closely with the moderate Christian Democrats of the MRP, preferring this to collaboration with the CGT.[55] As a result, the government's directive that a third of the seats in the new Offices be filled by trade unions opened the door to bickering among the CGT, the CFTC, and others, each eager to ensure that its own interests were represented in the new organisation. By April 1945, the Ministry of Industrial Production was visibly concerned that the inclusion of labour in the Professional Offices could paralyse their development.[56] Further difficulties were encountered when trying to name representatives from among company executives and employers to the reformed Offices.[57]

While the Ministry of Industrial Production was overseeing the reform of Vichy's Organisation Committees, the re-emergence of employers' associations and strong trade unions – whose functions had initially been folded into those of the Committees – further complicated the role of the Professional Offices. External factors played a major role in this as well:

[54]The CGT contained supporters of both the Socialist SFIO and the Communist Party (PCF). This division had already split the CGT in 1921, when the pro-Communist *unitaire* wing broke away to create the CGTU. The two factions were reunited in 1935, although the emergence of the Cold War in France would lead the *unitaires* to again separate from the CGT, creating CGT-Force ouvrière (FO) in December 1947. See Michel Dreyfus, *Histoire de la CGT: cent ans de syndicalisme en France* (Brussels: Editions Complexe, 1995).

[55]Guy Groux and René Mouriaux, '1944. Les syndicats, la légalité républicaine et le pluralisme' in Fondation Charles de Gaulle, *Le rétablissement de la légalité républicaine* (Paris: Editions Complexe, 1996), 755–765.

[56]'Note pour Messieurs les secrétaires généraux et directeurs', 20 April 1945, F 12 9974, AN.

[57]'Procès-verbal de la 20e réunion des directeurs', 20 December 1944, F 12 10024, AN.

Germany continued to fight until May 1945, almost a full year after the Allied landings in Normandy. This led to deliveries of German coal essential for French steel production and already insufficient at the most collaborative of times under Vichy – dropping off off dramatically, while imports from the Allies remained inadequate. The worsening shortage of coal for French industry was a constant predicament of the Ministry of Industrial Production. Coal extraction had worsened under Vichy, particularly from 1943, and the first trimester of 1944 yielded the lowest amount of coal to date. By the last quarter of 1944, however, liberated France could barely produce 75 per cent of that disappointing amount. This inevitably affected the steel industry, which in November 1944 could produce only 20,000 tonnes, compared to 50,000 the previous November and 65,000 in an average month in 1938.[58] By 1945, the shortage of coal was so acute that swimming pools were closed and rail transport reduced, while blast furnaces at steel mills were unable to be lit due to the lack of coal.[59] In the short term, the reformed Professional Offices were unable to staunch the declining output of the French steel industry.[60]

From Autarky to Planned Production

The reform of the New Industrial Order was completed with some vital changes to OCRPI. When René Belin first signed the law creating Organisation Committees on 16 August 1940 Elmar Michel, the Head of the Economic Section of the German Military Administration in France, promptly informed him that such bodies would only be effective if there were complementary bodies that performed an initial allocation of materials to each branch of industry. Within weeks, OCRPI was created, which oversaw the allocation of resources to each branch of industry before the individual Organisation Committees distributed the resources to its various firms. OCRPI was closely controlled by the

[58]'Note hebdomadaire sur la situation de l'industrie', 28 December 1944, F 12 10024, AN.

[59]'Note', 23 November 1945, F 12 10028, AN.

[60]See Jean-Pierre Rioux's discussion of the '*économie étranglée*' of the immediate post-war period in *La France de la Quatrième République. L'ardeur et la nécessité, 1944–1952* (Paris: Seuil, 1980), 32–39.

Germans, who were thereby able to influence French industry throughout the war.[61]

Germany's influence over OCRPI informed Blum-Picard's stance towards reforming Vichy's industrial organisation. In Algiers, he had championed maintaining the Organisation Committees, arguing that these were 'created by the French'. OCRPI, however, was 'imposed on France by the Germans' as a means of controlling French industry, and he argued that it should consequently be abolished.[62] As Belin had discovered in the summer of 1940, however, it was not possible to have the Organisation Committees without a body responsible for an initial allocation of materials to the various branches of French industry, and OCRPI was maintained. In October 1944, the sections of OCRPI were placed directly under the control of the Secretary General for Industrial Production, Blum-Picard.[63] Despite his earlier objections, he readily assumed control over OCRPI and oversaw their reform. It was also agreed that a representative of the Ministry would sit on each Section, and have a right of veto.[64] While the Organisation Committees were always meant to have a State representative equipped with a veto, in practice the veto was never used.[65] OCRPI, meanwhile, had always had a veto-wielding representative of the State – albeit of the German State rather than Vichy. The reforms thus restored the powers originally provided for the Organisation Committee in the law of 16 August 1940, while handing the veto power within the OCRPI Sections from German to French representatives.

Further reforms were prompted in 1945 when OCRPI's directors and distributors noted that the system of allocation established during the war was somewhat backward. They observed that in other countries that had

[61]See René Belin, *Du Secrétariat de la CGT au Gouvernement de Vichy* (Paris: Albatros, 1978), 151 and 'Rapport final du Dr MICHEL sur l'Administration Militaire en France, 1940–1944', undated (1944), 72 AJ 262, AN.

[62]'Procès-verbal de la sous-commission des CO', April 1944, CFLN 686, MAE. This same juxtaposition of 'French' Organisation Committees and 'German' Sections of OCRPI was also promoted by Pierre Laroque, who worked with Belin in 1940 when the Committees were established. His account has informed important studies on the topic, such as Andrieu, *La Banque sous l'Occupation* and Margairaz, *L'Etat, les finances et l'économie*.

[63]'Note sur la réforme d'OCRPI', 28 October 1944, F 12 10024, AN.

[64]'Exposé des motifs', 29 May 1944, CFLN 602, MAE.

[65]The text of the law of 16 August 1940 explicitly foresaw a representative of the government with a veto. See *Journal officiel*, 18 August 1940.

adopted industrial planning, the plan begins with the finished industrial products desired, then traces what raw materials would be needed for this outcome, allocating those materials to the appropriate industries. The existing system in France, on the other hand, took note of the limited amount of raw materials, and apportioned amounts based on the importance and needs of various branches of industry, who were then obliged to produce what they could with what they had been allotted. Indeed, Richard Kuisel has described 'economic survival' as 'the dominant motive of Vichy's political economy'.[66] By the spring of 1945, this approach was condemned as the 'fundamental error' of the wartime system, and the alignment of allocation with production goals was agreed.[67] This greater emphasis on 'manufacturing programmes' fit quite well with the increased interest in post-war industrial planning, a responsibility which had been assigned to the Ministry of the National Economy in November 1944.[68] This also marked a shift away from Vichy's autarkical political economy, which took a shortage of raw materials as its starting point, and sought to manage the scarcity as effectively as possible. The switch to a production-based political economy was only possible, however, once France had access to massive export markets. The French steel industry emerged from the war with the capacity to produce 12 million tonnes of steel, even if barely a quarter of this amount was produced in 1945; in these circumstances, increasing steel production fourfold could, in theory, be accomplished simply by increasing the amount of coal at that industry's disposition.[69] The German policy initially pursued by de Gaulle and the Provisional Government was in large part motivated by the desire to ensure that the defeated country's coal production would nourish the revival of French heavy industry.[70] While France was forced to do without

[66]Kuisel, *Capitalism and the State in Modern France*, 130.

[67]'Procès-verbal de la séance de la 5e réunion des directeurs et répartiteurs', 26 March 1945, F 12 9974, AN.

[68]The responsibility for drawing up a national plan for the French economy was ultimately passed on to Jean Monnet at the end of 1945.

[69]'Rapport de la Commission de Modernisation de la Sidérurgie', November 1946, 80 AJ 11, AN.

[70]France's German policy until at least 1947 was centred on limiting Germany's productive capacity and ensuring the France would have uninhibited access to coal from the Ruhr. This strategy is outlined by Jean Monnet in 'Note de Jean Monnet sur le premier rapport de remise en marche de l'économie française en 1945, sur les objectifs pour 1946 et sur le but

coal imports from Britain and most other countries during the war, the Liberation of France gave the country renewed access to Allied markets and, by 1945, a measure of influence over German coal production.[71] Freed from its wartime constraints, the French economy could be reoriented towards large-scale production rather than wallowing in autarkical penury. The OCRPI Sections were well suited to harness this change of direction, and the reformed bodies contributed to France's post-war recovery. It is worth remembering that this shift in French political economy occurred in 1945, well before the instauration of the Marshall Plan.[72] Indeed, this shift demonstrated by the reform of OCRPI in 1945 facilitated the success of the Marshall Plan from 1947.

Consolidating Vichy's Committees

One of the central reforms demanded by the Resistance as a condition of maintaining Vichy's Organisation Committees was that their number be drastically reduced. This idea of reducing the overall number of Organisation Committees by integrating related committees into larger ones was by no means new. It had figured in Pétain's notorious 12 August

final à atteindre', 11 November 1945, AMF 1 6, FJME. For an overview of France's German policy during this period, see Raymond Poidevin, 'Frankreich und die Ruhrfrage 1945–1951', in *Historische Zeitschrift*, 228:2, April 1979, 101–119 and, in the context of France's broader foreign policy objectives, William Hitchcock, *France Restored* (Chapel Hill: University of North Carolina Press, 1998).

[71]British coal exports to France never returned to anything approaching their pre-war levels, however, due to a decline in British output and a corresponding drop in exports. See D.W.J. Johnson, 'Britain and France in 1940', *Transactions of the Royal Historical Society*, 5:22, 1972, 141–157 and John Gillingham, *Coal, Steel and the Rebirth of Europe, 1945–1955* (Cambridge: Cambridge University Press, 1991).

[72]It should be noted that it was the Marshall Plan that ultimately permitted France to pay for these imports to develop its industry. According to Frances Lynch, it was thus the Marshall Plan that saved the Monnet Plan; see Lynch, *France and the International Economy from Vichy to the Treaty of Rome* (London: Routledge, 1997). While the goal of increasing production rather than managing scarce resources succeeded after 1947, the reorientation of France's political economy towards increasing production can be observed in 1945. Alan Milward, meanwhile, has argued that the French economy had already begun its recovery before the implementation of the Marshall Plan, and that France's goal in this period was to supplant Germany as Europe's leading producer of steel. See Milward, *The Reconstruction of Western Europe, 1945–1951* (London: Routledge, 1984).

1941 speech, less than a year after the law creating the Committees had been passed. In late 1941 Henri Lafond, Secretary General for Industrial Production, circulated plans to concentrate the spiralling number of Committees into six 'families', corresponding to six key sectors of the French economy: water, gas, and electricity; metals and minerals; quarries; petrol; coal; and steel.[73] The steel 'family' would consist of 11 Organisation Committees related to the production and sale of steel and steel-related products, and thereby help reduce the overall number of Organisation Committees.[74] This project was endorsed by Jules Aubrun, president of CORSID, although he requested that the Committees dealing with mechanical industries such as automobiles and bicycles not be included in steel's 'professional family'.[75]

The reduction in the number of Committees from its peak of over 300 down to a more manageable size of a few dozen is sometimes presented as constituting a shrinking of their power, suggesting that many industries were consequently freed from control by the wartime Committees.[76] This strictly quantitative approach belies the reality that although the number of Committees was reduced, this was done by consolidating several related Committees into fewer, yet much more powerful ones. The elimination of ten of the 11 Committees related to steel would not free the industry from central organisation; on the contrary, it would hand additional powers to the surviving Committees, which could henceforth function even more efficiently with their increased powers. In the end, this concentration of powers ultimately took place in October 1944 under the auspices of the Provisional Government of the French Republic. Six existing Organisation Committees were ultimately folded into the Organisation Committee

[73]Jean Monnet later based the modernisation and reequipment of the French economy around six core industries, including coal, steel, electricity, and petrol. See Philippe Mioche, *Le plan Monnet. Genèse et élaboration 1941–1947* (Paris: Publications de la Sorbonne, 1987).

[74]'Projet de répartition des comités d'organisation du secrétaire général de l'énergie en famille' by Henri Lafond, 12 December 1941, F 12 9953, AN.

[75]'Note pour Monsieur le secrétaire général de l'énergie' from Jules Aubrun, 12 November 1941, F 12 9953, AN. These reforms involving the consolidation of 'families' are discussed in Chapter 4.

[76]See, for example, Henry Rousso, 'Les élites économiques dans les années 1940: Epuration et transition' in *Vichy. L'événement, le mémoire, l'histoire* (Paris: Gallimard, 1992), 553–593.

for Steel, which created a stronger, centralised body to control the whole of France's steel industry.[77]

Return to First Principles: Applying Vichy's Laws in Post-War France

To assess the degree of reform that actually took place following the Liberation, it is worthwhile to re-examine the text of the law of 16 August 1940. The preamble emphasised the pressures on French industry with the division of the country, the Nazi occupation of northern and western France, the sudden stoppage of military production following the Armistice, and the virtual cessation of trade imposed on the country. In this context, 'it was not possible to immediately establish a system that ensured effective and complete representation of employers and workers', but reassuringly 'we will strive to ensure [such representation] later'.[78] Citing the current difficulties facing French industry, Belin and his colleagues justified the 'statist character' of the proposed organisation, which for the time being was necessary instead of a system 'more oriented towards the formulae of 'industrial democracy' often advocated in recent years'. Again, the law alluded to future reforms, promising that '[o]nce the current difficulties have been overcome, it will certainly be possible to increase the role of the interested parties in the management of the economy'.[79]

Indeed, an earlier draft of the law included a stipulation that there must only be 'a single employers' association and a single workers' union' for the whole of France, and which would participate in the Organisation Committees.[80] While this article was omitted from the final text of the law, it does reveal that the authors of the law were considering a formalised representation of both employers and workers within the new system, as would ultimately emerge in 1944. The allusion to future reforms of the law that would bring the French system closer to ideas of 'industrial democracy' would come to fruition with the GPRF's reforms. Belin

[77]'Projet de répartition des CO', 30 October 1944, F 12 10024, AN. CORSID was renamed OPSID in February 1945.

[78]*Journal officiel*, 18 August 1940.

[79]Ibid.

[80]'Premiers projets de la loi du 16 août 1940', 98 J 7, Fonds Belin, IHS.

himself had favoured such reforms in his pre-war writings, notably in the journals *Syndicats* and *Nouveaux cahiers*.[81] Given his career in the CGT and his publications in the 1930s, it is probable that this expressed desire to increase workers' representation within the Organisation Committees as soon as this was feasible was indeed genuine.

Notably, the anticipated representation of workers in the Organisation Committees contained in the law was picked up by the CFLN during their discussions on industrial organisation in post-war France. A report from January 1944 which was discussed by the CFLN that spring even claimed that the law foresaw the participation of employers and workers 'within several weeks'[82] – an overly generous estimate that is not actually contained in the text of the law. Leprince, the author of the report, insisted that the reforms desired by the CFLN could be carried out within the framework of Belin's legislation. He argued that 'if we maintain the form of the Organisation Committee, we must reform the spirit; we must abolish the exclusively employer-led model and hand leadership to a Government Commissioner surrounded by others. This would be possible *simply by applying the text of the Vichy law*.'[83] Surprisingly, he was absolutely correct. While the report did not provide further details, a close reading of the 16 August law reveals that just such provisions were included in the initial legislation. Article 3 of the law declares that 'in the event of inefficiency on the part of the Committee, the Government Commissioner will assume all the powers held by the Committee'.[84] Following the forced resignation of Aubrun and the other members of CORSID, the Government Commissioner from the Ministry of Industrial Production did indeed

[81]See, for example, 'La compréhension ouvrière sera acquise aux nécessités de l'Exposition' in *Syndicats*, 25 February 1937, and reprinted in *Nouveaux cahiers*, 15 March 1937. An extensive array of Belin's pre-war writings on industrial relations can be consulted at the Fonds Belin, IHS.

[82]'Maintien éventuel du CO du bâtiment et des travaux publics', 26 January 1944, CFLN 686, MAE.

[83]Ibid. Emphasis added. Given how problematic supporting Vichy legislation could be for the new regime, Leprince suggested that the Provisional Government could appeal to a 1938 law related to French industry in order to 'mask the fact that we would be using Vichy's organisations'. See 'Commission d'étude des problèmes économiques d'après-guerre. Sous-commission des Comités d'organisation. Séance du 21 avril 1944', 21 April 1944, CFLN 602, MAE.

[84]*Journal officiel*, 18 September 1940.

assume the powers of the Committee. Similarly, the eventual addition of workers' representation on the Committees was foreseen in and legitimated by the text of the law itself, although this provision was not applied under Vichy. In this sense, while the CFLN reformed the spirit of the Organisation Committees as they existed in 1944, they did so in accordance with the Vichy law that had created those bodies in the first place.

The restoration of union rights was the most notable reform of the Committees, and the one that explicitly departed from the text of the law. Although labour representation within the Committees had been anticipated, the text of the law itself impeded their immediate inclusion. For this reason, the CFLN agreed to 'suppress Article 1 of the law known as the "law of 16 August 1940", which dissolved' national trade unions and employer's associations.[85] As we have seen, however, this reform is consistent with the CFLN's reading of the law as outlined by Leprince. More important is the fact that the remaining nine articles of the law were left untouched, and that only the first article was repealed. The CFLN had no qualms with abolishing Vichyste laws and decrees with which they disagreed – the Labour Charter, seemingly Belin's crowning achievement as Minister for Labour, was abolished altogether, as was the corporatist organisation of agriculture that had been implemented by Vichy.[86] The fact that the CFLN abolished only the first article of the law of 16 August reveals that they sought to keep the remaining sections intact.

The remaining reforms implemented in 1944 and 1945 were entirely in accordance with the August 1940 legislation. It is incredibly unlikely that Belin had foreseen that hundreds of Organisation Committees would be created within four years; no numbers are explicitly mentioned in the law, but fewer than 20 Committees had been created by the end of 1940. The concern that there were already too many Committees was voiced by Pétain in 1941, and plans to reduce their number by concentrating similar Committees into 'families' were developed from 1941, as we have seen. By

[85]'Rétablissement de la liberté syndicale et épuration des organisations syndicales de travailleurs et d'employeurs', 21 January 1944, CFLN 602, MAE. In fact the law of 16 August only announced that these organisations would be dissolved; this ultimately took place in November 1940 with the dissolution of the largest trade union confederations and a small number of employers' associations.

[86]'Ordonnance déclarant nuls les textes relatifs a l'organisation corporative de l'agriculture', 25 April 1944, CFLN 602, MAE.

whittling down the number of Committees closer to the number established under Belin's watch, the GPRF's actions were consistent with the spirit of the August law.

The half-hearted shuffling of CORSID's members to other key positions within the steel industry, and placing a close collaborator of theirs at the helm of the Committee, was similarly done in accordance with the 16 August law. The legislation stipulates that members of the Committee could be suggested by unions and employers, but that the individuals would be appointed by the government, who would make the decision unilaterally. Moreover, sitting members could be removed from the Committee at the government's discretion. This process was followed with the forced resignation of the five wartime members and the subsequent appointment of Aron as Provisional Commissioner, as well as the invitation to trade union confederations to recommend representatives to sit on the reformed Organisation Committees.

The remaining reforms taken in 1944 would certainly have appealed to Belin in 1940, but they were simply impossible to enact in the context of a defeated and half-occupied France. The measures set out in the 16 August law were intended to control industry in all of France, including occupied and even annexed regions, but in practice this was vetoed by the German authorities.[87] Similarly, the establishment of OCRPI under German tutelage precluded the possibility of having the Sections under the direct authority of the Ministry of Industrial Production; rather, the German representative in each section enjoyed the most power. Yet the law itself only mentioned veto power for the French representative. The extension of the Vichy-era legislation to all of French territory as it was reconquered by the Allies, and the replacement of a German veto with a French one, were desired by the authors of the law, but impossible in the context of a German-dominated Europe.

Lastly, the guiding principles behind Belin's law were echoed within the CFLN. Blum-Picard recalled that in reforming Vichy's industrial organisation, they 'must not forget the difficulties of the pre-war system'.[88] De Gaulle himself promised in March 1944 that his government 'will not

[87]In practice, CORSID's jurisdiction extended to the Occupied Zone as well as the Non-Occupied Zone, but did not include either Nord-Pas-de-Calais (Nordfrankreich) or Alsace-Lorraine (Reichsland).

[88]'Procès-verbal', 14 April 1944, CFLN 686, MAE.

tolerate coalitions of shareholders, private monopolies, trusts',[89] using language that echoes the rhetoric of Pétain and the National Revolution. Belin and his colleagues were critical of the pre-war, laissez-faire system, and ruled out 'giving a free hand to the interested parties [...] to re-establish a destroyed equilibrium'.[90] The 1940 law denotes that 'only the State has the means and the authority'[91] to run this industrial system, and the CFLN confirmed their adherence to this shift away from pre-war liberalism, noting that 'France's economy will remain managed [*dirigée*] for quite some time', even if liberals within the Resistance 'conceded regretfully that such economic management would be necessary' in the years following the Liberation.[92] A return to the economic *status quo ante bellum* was simply not on the table, and maintaining Vichy's *dirigiste* industrial order was an effective way of pursuing a statist political economy.

Conclusion

Debating the shape of post-war economic reforms prior to the Liberation, the CFLN had looked to other countries' models of industrial organisation for inspiration. The French Communist Party predictably suggested borrowing from the Soviet model, but also spoke positively of Britain's Joint Production Committees and Franklin Delano Roosevelt's innovations in the United States.[93] Of these options, the British model proved most popular within the CFLN, perhaps unsurprisingly given that many of its figures had spent time in London during the first half of the war. André Philip, who served as Commissioner for the Interior in the CFLN, drafted several studies of the Joint Production Committees, which were advanced as an alternative to the existing Organisation Committees.[94] In November

[89]'Exposé de de Gaulle sur la politique du Gouvernement français', 18 March 1944, CFLN 297, MAE.

[90]*Journal officiel*, 18 August 1940.

[91]Ibid.

[92]'Rôle de la Commission économique', 7 April 1944, CFLN 686, MAE.

[93]'Procès-verbal de la séance de l'Assemblée Consultative Provisoire du 5 janvier 1944', 5 January 1944, C I 591, AN. These British committees were known in French as *comités mixtes de production*.

[94]'Etudes d'A. Philip sur les Comités mixtes de production', F 60 895, AN; see also 'Etude sur les Joint Production Committees', 28 June 1944, CFLN 687, MAE. Philip was one of

1944, the Secretary General for Industrial Production, Lambert Blum-Picard, requested copies of William Beveridge's influential report from 1942 on social insurance (known as the Beveridge Report, which led to the creation of Joint Production Committees in wartime Britain) as well as his most recent work, *Full Employment in a Free Society*, published earlier that year. He also requested a copy of the 'Bretten-Woods accords' [*sic*] and the Lend-Lease Agreement.[95] Finally, to make sense of it all, he asked for a copy of the *Oxford English Dictionary*.[96] He received all these documents in February 1945, with one curious exception: the *Oxford English Dictionary* proved 'impossible to find in England', so the Secretary General had to make do with his tenuous grasp of English.[97] Despite the language barrier, it is clear that the Secretary General for Industrial Production, as well as others in his ministry and in the government, were interested in the British alternative to France's Organisation Committees.[98]

The influence of Britain's innovations in French plans for post-war economic reform have been emphasised by a number of historians. Richard Kuisel argues that 'John Maynard Keynes, William Beveridge, and the example of wartime economic and social policy in Britain informed' economic plans within the Resistance, while Andrew Shennan highlights how the 'various attempts which had been made to bring workers and managers together with a view to increasing

the 80 deputies who voted against handing full powers to Maréchal Pétain on 10 July 1940 and he joined de Gaulle in London in July 1942. The best assessment of his career and legacy is Christian Chevandier and Gilles Morin (eds), *André Philip, socialiste, patriote, chrétien* (Paris: CHEFH, 2005).

[95]Beveridge, although never a Fabian or a Socialist, was influenced by Sidney and Beatrice Webb's writings on industrial democracy and advocated social security in the 1920s. See Brian Abel-Smith, 'The Beveridge Report: Its Origins and Outcomes' in John Hills et al. (eds), *Beveridge and Social Security: An International Retrospective* (Oxford: Clarendon, 1994).

[96]'Note', 30 November 1944, F 12 10024, AN

[97]'Note', 20 February 1945, F 12 10025, AN.

[98]For an overview of interwar debates regarding the modernisation of the economy in Britain, see Chapter 2 of Richard Overy, *The Morbid Age: Britain between the Wars* (London: Penguin, 2009). For related discussions on economic planning in Britain, see Daniel Ritschel, *The Politics of Planning: The Debate on Economic Planning in Britain in the 1930s* (Oxford: Clarendon, 1997).

productivity – in particular the wartime Joint Production Committees[99] in Britain and America – were carefully studied by France's post-Liberation elites' and informed the policies of the Provisional Government.[100] Jean Monnet similarly claimed that Britain's tripartite Working Parties influenced the shape of the Monnet Plan under the GPRF.[101] The idea of involving workers and the State alongside employers in tripartite institutions thus gained currency within the CFLN, as it did in Britain and America.[102] While this interest in tripartism within the CFLN was undoubtedly fostered by London-based *résistants*' greater exposure to British and indeed American models during the war, the existence of tripartite institutions to oversee French industry had another, less politically palatable source: the text of Vichy's law of 16 August 1940. Ironically, the realisation of these seemingly British-inspired reforms proved 'possible simply by applying the text of the Vichy law'.[103]

In early spring 1944, André Philip neatly summarised the consensus within the CLFN regarding the reform of Vichy's industrial order. 'We recognise that we must reduce the number of Committees, assure the authority of the State and the effective participation of labour

[99]These Committees were small-scale groupings that existed within individual factories, gathering workers, technicians, and employers 'on the shop floor'. By the time of the Liberation of Paris, nearly 4,500 such committees existed in the UK, a far cry from the 300 or so overarching Organisation Committees that oversaw entire branches of industry instead of isolated factories. See Arthur McIvor, *A History of Work in Britain 1880–1950* (Basingstoke: Palgrave, 2001), 105–107.

[100]See Kuisel, *Capitalism and the State in Modern France*, 162 and Shennan, *Rethinking France*, 58–64 and 191–201. Kuisel focuses on Hervé Alphand's plans drawn up in London from 1942. The influence of Beveridge on the political economy debates within the Resistance is also highlighted by Georges Boris in his post-war writings. See Boris, *Servir la République* (Paris: Julliard, 1963), 324–326.

[101]Monnet wrote that the Modernisation Commissions of the Commissariat Général du Plan (CGP), the institution created to develop and implement the Monnet Plan, were based on Britain's tripartite Working Parties. This claim is discussed in Chapter 7. See Monnet, *Mémoires* (Paris: Fayard, 1976), 342.

[102]The policies of France, Britain, and the United States in the immediate post-war period are discussed in Isser Woloch, *The Postwar Moment: The Allied Democracies in the Aftermath of World War II*, forthcoming.

[103]'Maintien éventuel du CO du bâtiment et des travaux publics', 26 January 1944, CFLN 686, MAE.

unions.'[104] To this list must be added the *épuration* of the Committees, replacing those tainted by their palpable collaboration with the Vichy regime with 'unassailable figures'. On the surface, the GPRF seemingly succeeded in realising these objectives. The wartime membership of CORSID was swept out, to be replaced by an industrialist who had survived the heinous anti-Semitic legislation of the loathed regime. The number of Committees dropped from hundreds to dozens and the bodies were overseen by a veto-wielding representative of the Ministry for Industrial Production. Union rights were re-established, and organised labour was included in the Committees, ending the longstanding monopoly of employers. It seemed as though the bodies created by Vichy had been purged of any incriminating elements and that the parenthesis could be closed on the *années noires*.

Yet this narrative, however expedient for the leaders of the GPRF, does not withstand close scrutiny. The *épuration* of CORSID amounted to shifting wartime leaders into other similarly prestigious and influential positions, in which they continued to represent the industry both domestically and internationally. The 'unassailable figure' of Alexis Aron, who succeeded Aubrun at the helm of CORSID, had participated actively in the undertakings of the Committee during the war, and from 1945 he carried through with the work he and the members of CORSID had started under Vichy. Meanwhile, the consolidation of Organisation Committees into a smaller number of more powerful bodies, first envisaged in 1941 during François Lehideux's time as Minister for Industrial Production, was finally realised by the GPRF. With the withdrawal of German forces from French territory, the role exerted by the representative of the French Ministry of Industrial Production could finally match what had been foreseen in the law of 16 August 1940. With some slight circumstantial changes, all of these reforms could just as well have occurred under Vichy as under the Provisional Government.

Studying the reform of the Organisation Committees following the Liberation, done here for the first time, reveals a significant degree of continuity in industrial organisation through 1944. It also shows that the most important reform carried out in 1944, and the only one that wavered in any significant way from the text of the law of 16 August 1940, was the

[104] Ibid.

restoration of union rights [*liberté syndicale*]. Not only did this permit the existence of national trade union confederations – notably the CGT and the CFTC – but it also opened the door to the resurrection of the national employers' confederation. From their establishment in autumn 1940, the Organisation Committees had superseded national trade unions and employers' associations yet were run exclusively by employers. The return of union rights and the inclusion of labour in the Committees transformed them into properly functioning tripartite bodies – and marked a notable break from the Vichy era in this respect.[105]

Even this substantial reform, however, was not without foundation in the Vichy law itself. While an earlier draft called for the inclusion of trade unions and employers' associations, the final text of the law nonetheless foresaw the inclusion of workers' representation, but at a later date, once the immediate and extraordinary challenges facing French industry had been resolved. The fact that these conditions – foreign occupation, virtual cessation of trade, excruciating shortage of raw materials – endured for years rather than months meant that the provisional composition of the Committees remained unchanged until the Liberation. Only then could the inclusion of labour representation alluded to in the August 1940 law be realised. While this marked an important step in the development of French industrial relations, it was hardly the radical programme of a group that had declared all of Vichy's legislation 'null and void'.[106] On the contrary, in practice much of the law of 16 August 1940 was implemented more fully under de Gaulle than it had been under Pétain.

[105]It should be remembered that the only article of the law of 16 August 1940 that was repealed (Article 1) was the one banning national confederations of trade unions and employers' associations and was therefore incompatible with the re-establishment of *liberté syndicale*.

[106]'Projet sur le rétablissement de la légalité républicaine', 3 July 1944, CFLN 603, MAE.

CHAPTER 7

From Organisation Committees to Monnet's Modernisation Commissions

In the year following the Liberation of metropolitan France, the nation's Organisation Committees were reformed under the energetic leadership of the Minister for Industrial Production, Robert Lacoste. By the autumn of 1945, the Committees (now officially known as 'Professional Offices') included representatives from employers and trade unions, as well as the State, and the Vichy-era leaders had been replaced by 'unassailable figures'. Despite these developments, the Committees remained unpopular reminders of the Vichy regime and scapegoats for the privations experienced by the French population in the early post-war period. Meanwhile, details for a wide-ranging national economic plan to revive French industry were being drawn up by Jean Monnet. The first months of 1946 saw two developments that would have a profound impact on the organisation of France's economy: the establishment of the Monnet Plan and the abolition of the Organisation Committees. This chapter will explore the dynamics between these two processes, and how they transformed industrial organisation in post-war France.

The Conversions of Paul: Nationalising French Industry

The legislative elections on 21 October 1945 were the first held in France since the Popular Front's victory in 1936. The PCF took the largest share of the vote, winning 26.2 per cent of the ballot and 159 of the 586 seats in

© The Author(s) 2017

L.-A. Brunet, *Forging Europe: Industrial Organisation in France, 1940–1952*, Security, Conflict and Cooperation in the Contemporary World, DOI 10.1057/978-1-349-95198-7_7

the National Assembly, while the Christian Democratic MRP and the Socialist SFIO secured 150 and 146 seats, respectively. Unlikely bedfellows though they were, the three parties formed a governing coalition that endured until the eviction of the PCF from government in May 1947.[1] De Gaulle remained President and divided the ministries among the three parties, a delicate process which took a full month to complete. Wary of handing control of any of the 'three levers that control [France's] foreign policy', namely Foreign Affairs, Defence, and the Interior, to the PCF, de Gaulle offered the Communists positions that he considered to be secondary: what he tellingly referred to in his memoirs as 'merely the "economic" portfolios'.[2] As a result, PCF ministers were given the portfolios for the National Economy, Labour, Armaments, and Industrial Production.[3] De Gaulle thus took this last portfolio from Robert Lacoste, who had spent the past year overseeing the reform of the Organisation Committees and attempting to shore up their flagging popularity, and handed it to Marcel Paul.[4]

The outcome of the elections, and the month-long period of uncertainty between election day and the appointment of a new minister, initially paralysed the Ministry for Industrial Production. As the various parties wrangled over portfolios in the soon-to-be-created coalition government, ministries were unable to make key decisions without knowing whom their minister might be. Lambert Blum-Picard, who had worked closely with Lacoste in Algiers and then served as Secretary General for Industrial Production, kept his position as the chief mandarin in the ministry. Nevertheless, he had to postpone important

[1]For a discussion of the expulsion of Communist ministers from the Ramadier government, see Philippe Buton, 'L'éviction des ministres communistes' in Serge Berstein and Pierre Milza (eds), *L'Année 1947* (Paris: Presses de Sciences Po, 2000), 339–372.

[2]Charles de Gaulle, *Mémoires de guerre. Le salut: 1944–1946* (Paris: Plon, 1959), 517 and 327. De Gaulle appointed himself as Minister for Defence, removing hitherto Minister for War André Diethelm from Cabinet for good.

[3]The Ministry for Finance, however, remained firmly in the hands of the liberal René Pleven.

[4]A trade unionist and member of the PCF since 1923, Marcel Paul was captured as a POW by the Nazis but managed to escape in 1940. An active member of the interior resistance, he organised a failed assassination attempt against Hermann Göring in August 1941, for which he was arrested and tortured by Vichy that November. He spent the remainder of the war in prisons and concentration camps, being transferred to Auschwitz in April 1944 and to Buchenwald the following month.

decisions until Lacoste's successor was named. Shortly after the election, but before the Cabinet had been formed, Blum-Picard received a proposal to dissolve the Organisation Committee for Salt. While he agreed that this particular Committee ought to be dismantled, the decision was postponed 'until the general policies of the future government with regard to professional organisation have been decided upon'.[5] Given the likelihood of the arrival of a minister with a very different political agenda, the ministry was unable to continue the route it had charted for itself following the Liberation. This state of uncertainty was finally dissipated on 21 November with the appointment of Marcel Paul as Lacoste's replacement. Paul certainly had a different approach than Lacoste. The ministerial archives show that while every month under Lacoste contains hundreds of notes, reports, and letters, under Paul fewer than 70 pages exist for the first three months of 1946 combined; whether this was due to drastically less communication between Paul and his civil servants, or whether Paul kept or destroyed most of the files that passed through his hands, it was clear that Paul's arrival marked a change in the working relationship between the Minister for Industrial Production and his staff. [6] His position on industrial questions also differed considerably from those of his predecessor.

Despite the considerable ideological differences among the three ruling parties, they managed to broadly agree on a number of policies, based in large part on the CNR Programme of March 1944. For Paul's ministry, the most important passage in that document was the commitment to 'return to the State' France's key industries.[7] The first wave of nationalisations had been completed over the winter of 1944–1945, with the State taking control of the coalfields of Nord and Pas-de-Calais, Renault's factories, and a number of smaller companies.[8] In collaboration with the

[5]'Note. Objet: Dissolution du CO du sel', 31 October 1945, F 12 10028, AN.

[6]These are contained in the folder F 12 10028, AN.

[7]The CNR Programme of March 1944 outlined broad policies to be pursued in post-war France and was endorsed by all major political parties. Among the central policies was the 'return to the State', a euphemism for nationalisation, of France's strategic industries. The best study of this programme is Claire Andrieu's *Le programme commun de la Résistance. Des idées dans la guerre* (Paris: Editions de l'Erudit, 1984). See also Isser Woloch, 'Left, Right and Centre: the MRP and the Post-war Moment', *French History*, 21:1, 2007, 85–106.

[8]Richard Vinen has noted that the nationalisation of the coal mines was not punitive – as the nationalisation of Renault had been – and that 'the preamble to the act of nationalization stressed economic strategy not business misbehaviour'. See Vinen, *The Politics of French*

Ministry for the National Economy, headed by François Billoux, Paul oversaw a second wave of nationalisations representing an even more significant swathe of the French economy.[9] On 2 December 1945, less than two weeks after being named Minister, Paul voted to nationalise the Banque de France and the country's credit organisations, creating the *Conseil national du crédit*. This was followed by the nationalisation of insurance companies on 25 April. As Minister for Industrial Production, Paul's most significant project in early 1946 was the nationalisation of electricity and gas and the concomitant establishment of EDF and GDF.[10] Paul also extended the nationalisation of France's northern coalfields to those of the entire country, with the creation of Charbonnages de France to oversee national coal production.[11]

From the nationalisations of 1944–1946 the steel industry was spared in large part due to the deft diplomacy of the industry's representative: Jules Aubrun. Already President of the industry's employers' association, the *Chambre syndicale de la sidérurgie française* (CSSF), he was also appointed President of the Commission for Private Enterprise of the *Conseil national du patronat français* (CNPF), France's resurrected employers' confederation. This Commission's chief task was to oppose 'all the ravages resulting from the idea of nationalisation and *étatisation*, and to study all the consequences, direct and indirect, on the sectors that are still free, of the already executed nationalisations'.[12] Aubrun had long argued against the nationalisation of the steel industry – one of the most strategic industries in France, and therefore an

Business, 1936–1945 (Cambridge: Cambridge University Press, 1991), 198. The PCF criticised this first wave of nationalisations as 'furthering the interests of capitalists' private interests rather than those of the State', and demanded that priority be given to 'the confiscation of goods from the traitors who are numerous among the managers of trusts'. See 'Note de MM Billoux et Tillon sur les projects de nationalisation soumis par M le Ministre de l'Economie nationale', 3 March 1945, 3 AG 4 26, AN.

[9]Claire Andrieu argues that while the first wave of capitalisations was 'insurrectionary', the second, 'parliamentary' wave of nationalisations overseen by Marcel Paul was in fact more anti-capitalist. See 'Les nationalisations disparates' in Claire Andrieu, Lucette Le Van and Antoine Prost (eds), *Les nationalisations de la Libération* (Paris: FNSP, 1987), 250–266.

[10]Energie de France and Gaz de France. This project was proposed by Paul in the National Assembly on 27 March 1946 and was approved by parliamentary vote on 8 April.

[11]'Loi relative à la nationalisation de l'industrie des combustibles minéraux', 19 April 1946, Assemblée nationale.

[12]'Procès-verbal, Assemblée générale du 12 juin 1946', CNPF, AS 72 835, ANMT.

obvious candidate to be 'returned to the State'.[13] Indeed, calls to nationalise the industry were voiced at the very first meeting of the Provisional Consultative Assembly, the forerunner of the reconvened National Assembly, in Algiers in January 1944. André Marty, a leading PCF representative, denounced the leaders of the steel industry as opportunists who had collaborated with and supported Vichy, whom he alleged were only beginning to support the CFLN in early 1944 as the outcome of the war was becoming increasingly certain. He encouraged France to follow the Soviet model, claiming that 'what they have achieved there we could achieve here, if only fewer of the leaders of our economy belonged to the Schneider group', referring to the second-largest steel company in France.[14] He also insisted that the Commissariat for Production and Supply – the forerunner to the GPRF's Ministry for Industrial Production – must have absolute power, and that 'no other department must intervene in this domain'.[15] Nationalisations were a key part of the CNR Programme of March 1944, endorsed by all parties, and a review of the economic policies of the government-in-waiting in July 1944 confirmed cross-party agreement to 'limit the power of trusts' and to pursue 'nationalisations in certain cases'.[16] Aubrun's success in keeping steel private was undoubtedly aided by his four years' experience leading CORSID, during which he adroitly dealt with Vichy and Nazi officials while undermining initatives of theirs such as the STO.[17] Aubrun continued to argue for the maintenance of the Vichy system in post-war France, in part as a means of preventing the outright nationalisation of the steel industry.[18]

[13]See, for instance, 'Projet d'organisation des groupements sidérurgiques, observations de la Chambre syndicale de la sidérurgie', 29 December 1944, F 12 10062, AN.

[14]'Procès-verbal de la première séance [de l'Assemblée Consultative Provisoire]', 5 January 1944, C I 591, AN. Interestingly, Aubrun had worked for Schneider in the interwar period before pursuing a career with the Lazard Bank, although Marty does not seem to be referring to Aubrun in particular.

[15]Ibid.

[16]'La politique économique du gouvernement', 21 July 1944, C I 591, AN. The SFIO was initially the most enthusiastic supporter of nationalisations, while the PCF was reluctant to endorse the policy since the overall economy would remain capitalist. By the time the PCF was given control over the 'economic portfolios', however, the party was firmly in favour of nationalising key industries.

[17]See Chapter 4.

[18]'Projet d'organisation des groupements sidérurgiques, observations de la chambre syndicale de la sidérurgie', 29 December 1944, F 12 10062, AN.

In February 1945, while nationalisations were proceeding apace, Aubrun and the CSSF celebrated the supposed independence and patriotism of the steel industry before and during the war. They argued that they had actively supported the Third Republic in its final years, but their project remained unfinished in 1940, and they sought to continue their work that had been interrupted by the war. They claimed to have acted in the collective interest of France, and maintained that they should therefore be accorded a free hand to run the industry.[19] Aubrun's intervention proved to be effective: two days later the PCF tabled a motion to nationalise the steel industry, along with the chemical industry and the merchant marine, but the Assembly never voted on it.[20] Aubrun's line of argument was reiterated by Alexis Aron once he was named head of OPSID, as CORSID was renamed, in March 1945. He commended the 'independence and courage' of the wartime leaders of CORSID, Aubrun chief amongst them, and insisted on 'the necessity of a strong Professional Office' with 'sufficient latitude' to run the industry.[21] The *Commission de sidérurgie* meanwhile argued that the nationalisation of the steel industry was inadvisable, because of the significant differences that existed between the industry in the Loire and in Lorraine. Rather than trying to forcibly harmonise the two, it concluded, it would be far better to let each region be run in its own way under the guidance of industrialists.[22] Similar appeals did not dissuade the government from nationalising the French coal industry, however, beginning in Nord and Pas-de-Calais before enlarging the strategy to include the entire country.[23] This second wave of nationalisations troubled many in the private sector, and in January 1946 Jean Monnet

[19]'Organisation de la sidérurgie francaise', 26 February 1945, F 12 10062, AN. Cf. Philippe Mioche, 'Les entreprises sidérurgiques sous l'Occupation' in *Histoire, économie et société*, 1992, 11:3, 397–414.

[20]This motion was tabled by the PCF on 28 February 1945 but not voted on. The PCF would introduce similar motions to nationalise the steel industry well after the end of the 'second wave' of nationalisations, on 5 September 1946 and again on 12 December 1946, but neither motion was voted on. See Andrieu at al., *Les nationalisations de la Libération*, 262–265.

[21]'Rapport sur la situation du CO de la sidérurgie fin 1944–debut 1945', 27 April 1945, F 12 10063.

[22]'Rapport de la Commission de sidérurgie', 6 September 1945, F 12 10027, AN.

[23]Henri de Peyerimhoff, President of the Comité des houillères until its dissolution by Vichy in 1940, wrote to de Gaulle imploring him not to nationalise the coal industry. De Peyerimhoff held very little influence in post-war France, however, while Aubrun's opposite number as President of the Organisation Committee for Coal, Aimé Lepercq, had died in

argued that 'it is essential that the government quickly and definitively draw up a list of industries to be nationalised' on the grounds that investment in the modernisation of industries would be stifled if there were a chance that they would soon be nationalised.[24] Eventually, the elections of June 1946, which saw the MRP emerge as the largest party, brought the nationalisations to an end.[25]

With the nationalised industries firmly in State hands, Paul proceeded to issue some clearly politically motivated orders – in September 1946, for instance, he introduced legislation forcing all nationalised companies to rehire all certified workers [*salariés licenciés*] who had been sacked following the strike of 30 November 1938.[26] Government involvement with such directives infuriated French employers, who by 1946 had organised themselves in the revived CNPF.[27] Such decisions by Paul stoked the embers of the confrontation between workers and employers that had raged in the final years of the Third Republic. Predictably, the leaders of French industry were at odds with the Communist Minister for Industrial Production.

The End of the New Industrial Order?

Throughout the period 1944–1946, the need to revive key industries quickly during a chaotic period led to many Vichy-era officials remaining in their posts for the sake of expediency. Yet just as the PCF had

1944, depriving the coal industry of a possibly more effective defender. For de Peyerimhoff's letter to de Gaulle, see 'Un document sur le patronat. Une lettre de Henri de Peyerimhoff au général de Gaulle du 15 octobre 1944' in Claire Andrieu et al., *Les nationalisations de la Libération*.

[24]'Note sur les impressions préliminaires retirées des consultations que le Commissaire Général au Plan a été amené à avoir avec les représentants de l'administration et de la production', 23 January 1946, AMF 1 6, FJME.

[25]Andrieu et al., *Les nationalisations de la Libération*, 253.

[26]'Note. Objet: Réembauchage des salariés licenciés à la suite de la grève du 30 novembre 1938', 11 September 1946, F 12 10009, AN. The CGT-organised general strike on 30 November 1938 was to protest against the repeal of some of the Popular Front's social legislation, notably the 40-hour work week, by Edouard Daladier's government. Given that striking workers were technically in breach of their contracts, employers had the right to sack them, and many employers took the opportunity to dismiss 'troublemakers'. For a discussion of the consequences of this strike, see Vinen, *The Politics of French Business, 1936–1945*, 68–87.

[27]'Procès-verbal, Assemblée générale du 12 juin 1946', CNPF, AS 72 835, ANMT.

pleaded all along for a deeper *épuration* following the collapse of the Vichy regime, Paul insisted that the new management of France's economic bodies be drawn from the Resistance.[28] Practically, the best way of doing this would be to remove the existing system of Organisation Committees maintained by Lacoste, which left the representatives of the wartime *patronat* with considerable control over French industry, even if labour representation had increased under the Provisional Government. This fit neatly with the PCF's broader agenda of thoroughly purging France of Vichy's individuals and institutions.[29] The PCF never renounced their wartime condemnation of the Committees and continued to criticise the 'parasitic bureaucracies' under Lacoste, demanding the removal of 'the entire Vichyste apparatus of the Organisation Committees and [the] purge of these administrations of Vichy's men'.[30] Now that the party held four key economic portfolios, including the one directly responsible for industrial organisation, they had the ideal opportunity to implement their desired reforms.

The morning of 23 April 1946, only four days after the National Assembly had approved the nationalisation of the country's coalfields, an immediate debate on Marcel Paul's proposal to abolish the Organisation Committees and OCRPI was requested. The motion referenced a number of proposals advocating the dismantling of the bodies from across the political spectrum: Albert Rigal, of the PCF, Edouard Frédéric-Dupont and Jean-Marie Bouvier O'Cottereau, both of the right-wing *Parti républicain de la liberté* (PRL), and Jean Palewski of the MRP. Palewski's proposal made the case for abolishing the existing order and to instead 'establish a system based on liberty'.[31]

[28]See Jean-Pierre Rioux, *La France de Quatrième République. L'ardeur et la nécessité 1944–1952* (Paris: Seuil, 1980), 110. For the PCF's position on *épuration*, see Philippe Buton, *Les lendemains qui déchantent. Le Parti communiste français à la Libération* (Paris: FNSP, 1993),

[29]See Buton, *Les lendemains qui déchantent. Le Parti communiste français à la Libération*, and Stéphane Courtois and Marc Lazar, *Histoire du Parti communiste français* (Paris: Presses universitaires de France, 1995).

[30]'A Anger avec André Marty', 27 March 1945 and 'Il faut un meilleur ravitaillement et des salaires sufisants pour obtenir un renforcement de la capacité de production', 28 March 1945, *L'Humanité*.

[31]'Séance du mardi 23 avril 1946', 23 April 1946, C I 594, AN. Jean Palewski's younger brother, Gaston, was de Gaulle's *chef de cabinet* under the GPRF and both brothers participated in the creation of de Gaulle's *Rassemblement du Peuple Français* (RPF) in 1947.

The debate that followed was remarkably one-sided. O'Cottereau was the only person to take the floor to speak in favour of the proposal, claiming that 'we are all in absolute agreement that the Professional Offices that succeeded the Organisation Committees should be abolished'.[32] His brief remarks justified the need for a debate, rather than to simply pass the legislation without discussion, noting that a question 'as important as the reorganisation of our economy must not be treated lightly'. Yet the call for a parliamentary debate proved to be a mere formality, since not a single voice was raised to oppose the motion. As the Speaker of the Assembly confirmed, 'nobody else wishes to speak?' – a query that was met with silence – he proceeded to read aloud each of the 17 articles of the law, which were all adopted unanimously. The first article, stipulating the 'abolition of the Organisation Committees [and] of OCRPI and its Sections', seemingly sounded the death knell of what remained of Vichy's New Industrial Order.[33] It was agreed that the existing system would remain in place for up to six months, until legislation to replace it had been passed. The discussion then swiftly moved on to the issue of publicly posting transcripts of certain speeches made in the National Assembly, which soon descended into representatives trading accusations of having supported Pétain.[34] In such an Assembly, the issue of abolishing Vichy's Organisation Committees was an uncommonly calm and widely supported affair.

The introduction of the text, and particularly the insistence that the motion be discussed immediately and voted upon that same day, could suggest that Marcel Paul and his allies may have been seeking to take advantage of favourable absences from the Assembly that day to push

[32]Ibid. This can be contrasted with Paul Giacobbi's statement in the Provisional Consultative Assembly in July 1944 that there was 'absolute agreement on the foundations of the economic doctrine of the Government and of the Nation', which included the maintenance of the Organisation Committees. See 'La politique économique du gouvernement', 21 July 1944, C I 591, AN.

[33]'Séance du mardi 23 avril 1946', 23 April 1946, C I 594, AN. It is worth noting that the law referred first and foremost to 'Organisation Committees', even though these had formally been renamed 'Professional Offices' over a year earlier, in February 1945. This reflects the fact that the new label had never caught on, while it also associates the bodies more closely with Vichy.

[34]'Rappel au règlement' in 'Séance du mardi 23 avril 1946', 23 April 1946, C I 594, AN.

through the legislation. Yet only six members were reported to be absent on 23 April, meaning that such erstwhile defenders of the Organisation Committees as Robert Lacoste were indeed in the Assembly that day.[35] Moreover, it was standard practice at this time for a proposal to be introduced, debated, and voted upon in a single day; on 25 April, for example, two days after the law abolishing the New Industrial Order was discussed, there were 10 separate requests for immediate discussion of draft bills.[36] The complete and utter absence of opposition to the legislation shows that it was not a controversial measure to be squeezed through the legislature by a single, decisive vote, but rather that by April 1946 it had become unanimously accepted that the Organisation Committees ought not to remain part of France's industrial organisation.[37]

While nationalisations and dictated hires figured among the chief complaints of the *patronat* in 1946, the abolition of the Organisation Committees gave rise to exceptional objections. The action was denounced by employers as a blatantly political move by the Ministry for Industrial Production. They were stunned by 'the abrupt decision, obviously based on electoral considerations, to abolish, over the course of the month of June, a great number of Organisation Committees and [OCRPI] Offices'.[38] Employers believed that the system established under a regime to which electoral considerations were of no importance favoured the employers far more than the emerging one did, particularly with a Communist Minister for Industrial Production. The employers decried Paul's actions, and likened them to the worst policies of Léon Blum's Popular Front government of the 1930s.[39]

[35]Those who were absent from the National Assembly that day were MM Solinhac, Deyron, Rencurel, Soustelle, Emmanuel d'Astier, and Barthélémy Ott. 'Séance du mardi 23 avril 1946', 23 April 1946, C I 594, AN. Robert Lacoste won a seat in the October 1945 elections but was not made a member of the Cabinet.

[36]Ibid.

[37]Andrew Shennan has observed that candidates from all three governing parties had campaigned against the Organisation Committees ahead of the October 1945 elections, demanding their dissolution. See Shennan, *Rethinking France* (Oxford: Oxford University Press, 1989), 274.

[38]'Assemblée générale du 12 juin 1946', 12 June 1946, CNPF, AS 72 835, ANMT.

[39]Ibid. At this meeting of the CNPF in June 1946, Blum was roundly criticised as well, despite his recent success in negotiating the Blum–Byrnes Accords the previous month.

Moreover, the decision to abolish the Committees, like the decisions to create and later to reform the bodies, was taken without consulting employers, which further fuelled their protestations.

Despite the shock at the sudden abolition of the Organisation Committees, the recently reconstituted CNPF was soon able to make the most of the legislation to increase its members' powers. While Paul's draft law called for the abolition of the remaining Vichyste industrial bodies, it did not outline what bodies if any would succeed them. However, Article 7.2.b of the legislation stated that, 'for large firms, sub-allocation is entrusted to the most representative employers' association', a clause that was not lost on the CNPF.[40] By nature of the industry, virtually all steel firms fell under the provisions for 'large firms', although separate arrangements were advanced for SMEs and for nationalised industries. Within six weeks of the introduction of the legislation, the CNPF was able to celebrate that they had 'secured a number of amendments which ensure[d] a greater role for employers' associations in the functioning of sub-allocation'.[41] The CNPF was also convinced that 'this law will not be applied without many delays by the Minister for Industrial Production', which allowed industrialists time to adapt to the changes.[42] Despite the evident worries engendered by a Communist minister and by what they saw as rash legislation, employers succeeded in securing a decisive role in the sub-allocation of raw materials to their industry, a power that had previously been in the hands of the tripartite Organisation Committees. For Jules Aubrun, then President of the employers' association for steel, the CSSF, this was a particularly ironic turn of events. Aubrun had been forced to resign as President of CORSID in October 1944 as part of the *épuration* of the wartime leadership of the Committees. In April 1946, some of the most crucial powers of the Organisation Committees were restored to Aubrun as head of the CSSF. Furthermore, the *Comptoir français des produits sidérurgiques* (CPS), set up by CORSID in 1940 to assign production orders to particular factories, was also inherited by the CSSF following the dissolution of OPSID. In light of such continuities, many historians

[40]'Séance du mardi 23 avril 1946', 23 April 1946, C I 594, AN.

[41]'Exposé de M. Ricard, Président de la Commission économique du CNPF', 12 June 1946, AS 72 835, ANMT.

[42]Ibid.

justifiably describe the CSSF as the successor to Vichy's Organisation Committee for Steel.[43]

This skilful manoeuvring by the CNPF and by employers' associations like the CSSF undercut some of the expected advantages of Paul's project. The PCF's opposition to the Organisation Committees was in large part based on their perceived dominance by the employers whom PCF leader Maurice Thorez denounced as 'the big industrialists, the magnates of trusts, who, due to their hatred of the people and of democracy... wallowed in the muck of collaboration, and are now trying to divide the Nation'.[44] But this long-standing opposition failed to take into account the significant reforms the Committees had undergone in 1944 and 1945. Far from being bastions of power of the *grand patronat*, as they were seen to have been under Vichy, by 1946 the Committees were regulated, tripartite bodies in which trade unions were represented, under the control of a Communist Minister. Yet the abolition of those loathed bodies ended up handing more power directly to employers' associations, which represented the *patronat* exclusively. Moreover, it returned key functions to the wartime President of CORSID, who had been forced to resign them in October 1944. Ironically, organised labour had more control over French industry as long as the reformed Organisation Committees continued to exist. With the dismantling of the Committees, responsibilities previously shared between employers, workers, and the State were transferred to the former exclusively. Despite his intentions, Paul's legislation ended up weakening the voice of organised labour while strengthening that of the largest employers in France, those derided as the 'magnates of trusts'.

This notable victory for the CNPF and employers' associations was not lost on the Socialists, some of whom soon regretted the disappearance of the Organisation Committees and OCRPI. In December 1946, André Philip, a long-time supporter of maintaining Vichy's industrial bodies and a proponent of *planisme* since the 1930s, admitted that 'we committed a

[43]See, for example, Matthias Kipping, *La France et les origines de l'Union européenne. Intégration économique et compétitivité internationale* (Paris: CHEF, 2002) and Philippe Mioche, 'Les comités d'organisation de la sidérurgie: un lieu d'affrontement entre modernisateurs de la sidérurgie et gardiens de la profession?' in Hervé Joly (ed.), *Les comités d'organisation et l'économie dirigée de Vichy* (Caen: CRHQ, 2004), 95–108.

[44]'A Japy, Maurice Thorez fait acclamer les mots d'ordre «S'unir, combattre et travailler»', 2 February 1945, *L'Humanité*.

grave error in accepting Marcel Paul's proposal to abolish the Organisation Committees. They have resulted in the State no longer controlling allocations [of raw materials], and this power being passed to employers' associations. *Dirigisme* remains the only solution to this problem'.[45] For Philip, by then Minister for the National Economy, and many of his colleagues in the SFIO, the lengthy reforms to the Organisation Committees overseen by Robert Lacoste to ensure labour and the State a proper portion of industrial control had come to nought; Paul's move to abolish the remnants of Vichy's industrial organisation had paradoxically strengthened the hand of employers at the expense of the State and trade unions. In this context, *dirigisme*, or the economic planning being undertaken by the General Commissariat for the Plan (CGP), represented the best way of salvaging what the SFIO and their allies had achieved with the reformed Committees. This gave mourners of defunct Organisation Committees further reason to support the most promising embodiment of economic planning: the nascent Monnet Plan.[46]

The Monnet Plan

Much has been written on the Vichy-era antecedents of economic planning in France. Studies have focused principally on the *Délégation générale à l'équipement national* (DGEN), established by François Lehideux in 1941, which produced two plans for the French economy: the Plan for National Equipment, a ten-year plan produced in 1942, and the *Tranche de Démarrage* completed in early 1944. Richard Kuisel was the first historian to suggest that these projects drawn up under Vichy should be

[45]'Procès-verbal de la séance des Comités directeurs de la SFIO', 3 December 1946, quoted in Michel Margairaz, *L'Etat, les finances et l'économie: Histoire d'une conversion, 1932–1952* (Paris: CHEFF, 1991), 827. In January 1947, Philip asserted that 'the [principal] mistake of the Gouin government was abolishing the Organisation Committees'. Qtd in Margairaz, 'La reconstruction matérielle: crise, infléchissement ou ajustement?' in Serge Berstein and Pierre Milza (eds), *L'Année 1947* (Paris: Presses de Sciences Po, 2000), 24.

[46]While André Philip and Jean Monnet both advocated economic planning, they disagreed over the degree of State intervention needed. Philip pressed for a more Statist version, directed by his Ministry for the National Economy, while Monnet proposed a more liberal system in which markets played a greater role. See Philippe Mioche, *Le Plan Monnet: Genèse et élaboration 1941–1947* (Paris: Presses de la Sorbonne, 1987).

seen as 'a crucial step in the history of economic planning' in France.[47] This claim has been challenged by Adrian Jones on the grounds that these two isolated plans are rather 'the exception that proves the rule', since neither plan was treated with great interest by any Vichy ministers and that the regime eschewed economic planning overall.[48] Philippe Mioche, like Michel Margairaz, emphasises the roots of Monnet's plan in the French Resistance and downplays the importance of Vichy's fruitless plans.[49] Most historians today agree that these planning documents drafted by a minor office under Vichy were not decisive in shaping Monnet's plans,[50] although some note that the detailed statistical data gathered by the Organisation Committees did facilitate the successful realisation of the Monnet Plan.[51] It is also important to note that the DGEN's plan ignored both the coal and steel industries, preferring to focus on textiles, automobiles, and chemical products.[52] As such, its influence on the Monnet Plan, with its initial focus on six core industries, was limited. It is certainly true that in May 1944, technicians at the DGEN set out how, after the end of the war in France, the nation's economy could be revived, yet the plan was ignored by the Vichy leadership. Interestingly, this *Tranche de démarrage* was later read by Jean Monnet, who found much to agree with in its pages. He circulated the document approvingly in November

[47]See Richard Kuisel, 'Vichy et les origines de la planification économique, 1940–1946', in *Mouvement social*, 98, January–March 1977, 77–101. A less detailed discussion is also included in his monograph, *Capitalism and the State in Modern France* (Cambridge: Cambridge University Press, 1981), 256–270.

[48]Adrian Jones, 'Illusions of Sovereignty: Business and Organization of Committees of Vichy France', *Social History*, January 1986, 1–31.

[49]Mioche, *Le Plan Monnet*. Although this monograph covers the years between 1941 and 1947, fewer than 20 pages are devoted to the Vichy period. See also Margairaz, *L'Etat, les finances et l'économie*.

[50]Unsurprisingly, this is the view promoted by Monnet in his *Mémoires* (Paris: Fayard, 1976). See also William Hitchcock, *France Restored: Cold War Diplomacy and the Quest for Leadership in Europe, 1944–1954* (Chapel Hill: University of North Carolina Press, 1998), 23–24 and Philip Nord, *France's New Deal* (Princeton: Princeton University Press, 2010).

[51]See, for example, Mioche, 'Un tournant dans l'histoire technique de la sidérurgie: la creation de l'Irsid. Compétition et collaboration entre l'Etat et l'industrie' in *Histoire, économie et société*, 1989 (8:1), 119–140.

[52]This oversight is highlighted in Kuisel, 'Vichy et les origines de la planification économique', 87, and is apparent in the 'Plan d'équipement national, tranche de démarrage', November 1944, 80 AJ 11, AN. A copy can also be consulted in F 60 659, AN.

1944, with only one subtle change: while the title and the content of the plan remained intact, the date of the document was changed from May 1944 to November 1944, presumably to avoid the plan being too closely associated with the previous regime.[53] The historiographical debate, however, has tended to focus on continuities in economic planning as such from Vichy to Monnet. Institutional continuities from Vichy to the Monnet Plan, and particularly the role of the Organisation Committees in the development of the CGP, however, are seldom considered, constituting an important lacuna in the literature.[54]

Shortly after Marcel Paul's appointment as Minister for Industrial Production in November 1945, Jean Monnet submitted a proposal to de Gaulle for the *Plan de modernisation et d'équipement* – better known as the Monnet Plan. The text made the case for using the context of post-war reconstruction to effect a rapid modernisation of French industry. This would facilitate an increase of domestic consumption, but more importantly allow France to pay for its imports of raw materials – particularly coal – by increasing its exports of industrial products.[55] Perhaps most convincing for de Gaulle was the warning that if France failed to embrace such a rapid modernisation the country would 'be reduced to the rank of a second-rate power'.[56] By bolstering France's economic clout, Monnet claimed that his Plan would strengthen the nation's hand in international power politics.[57] He found in de Gaulle and his famous obsession with France's *grandeur* a receptive audience.

The first weeks of 1946 proved decisive for Monnet's initiative. On 3 January, de Gaulle formally approved the Monnet Plan and the establishment

[53]'Plan d'équipement national, tranche de démarrage', November 1944, 80 AJ 11, AN.

[54]The existing works which do compare the Organisation Committees and the Modernisation Commissions are discussed below.

[55]The best detailed study of the Monnet Plan remains Mioche, *Le Plan Monnet.* For a discussion of the Monnet Plan in the broader context of the French economy in this period, see Frances Lynch, *France and the International Economy: From Vichy to the Treaty of Rome* (London: Routledge, 1997). Lynch argues that the first version of the Monnet Plan was drawn up to show the United States that greater American loans were needed. See Lynch, *France and the International Economy*, 40, and Gérard Bossuat, *L'Europe occidentale à l'heure américaine, 1944–1952* (Brussels: Complexe, 1992).

[56]'Mémorandum sur le Plan de Modernisation et d'Equipement', 13 December 1945, 80 AJ 1.

[57]On the role of the Monnet Plan in France's international relations, see Irwin Wall, *The United States and the Making of Postwar France, 1945–1954* (Cambridge: Cambridge University Press, 1991) and Hitchcock, *France Restored.*

of the General Commissariat for the Plan (CGP). The text approved by de Gaulle set out how the Plan and the CGP would operate. Given the importance of the success of the Plan for France, it was 'indispensible that all vital elements of the Nation participate in its elaboration. It is for this reason that the proposed organisation will bring together, for each branch [of industry], the Administration in charge, the most qualified Experts, and Representatives from professional Syndicates (workers, management, and employers)'.[58] These representatives would together constitute a Modernisation Commission for each branch of industry. In addition, 'a representative from the General Commissariat will sit on each Modernisation Commission as President, Chairperson, or Secretary to ensure the coordination of the Commission's work'.[59] One cannot ignore the striking similarities between the proposed Modernisation Commissions and the existing Organisation Committees. In both cases, a body was organised for each key branch of French industry that included representation from employers, management (*les cadres*), and workers. Also in both cases, the body was completed with the addition of a representative of the State. The crucial difference, however, was which part of the State that individual represented. In the Organisation Committees, he represented the Ministry for Industrial Production and was responsible to the Minister – by now Marcel Paul. In the emerging Modernisation Commissions, however, the representative would be from the General Commissariat for the Plan, led by Jean Monnet and directly responsible to the head of the government.[60] The formation of Modernisation Commissions alongside existing Organisation Committees therefore marks the creation of rival committees with overlapping functions and representation, but overseen by the purportedly apolitical and technical CGP instead of the Ministry for Industrial Production, whose leadership was susceptible to change depending on the results of the latest elections.

[58]'Mémorandum sur le Plan de Modernisation et d'Equipement', 13 December 1945, 80 AJ 1.

[59]Ibid.

[60]Under the Provisional Government of the French Republic (1944–1946), de Gaulle was both Head of State and Head of Government, functions that would be divided under the Constitution of the Fourth Republic (approved in October 1946) between the President and the Prime Minister (officially known as the President of the Council). Under the Fourth Republic, the CGP was responsible to the latter. For a discussion of the Monnet Plan being situated under the Prime Minister rather than the Ministry for the National Economy, see Frances Lynch, 'Resolving the Paradox of the Monnet Plan: National and International Planning in French Reconstruction', *Economic History Review* 37:2, May 1984, 229–243.

Signing the decree creating the CGP was one of de Gaulle's most significant acts in the opening weeks of 1946, but his involvement by no means ended with his signature on 3 January. In a document written by Monnet, marked 'secret' and addressed only to his two closest collaborators, Robert Marjolin[61] and Etienne Hirsch,[62] he detailed the significant work that had to be completed on an unusually pressing deadline. The document, dated 13 January, specified that the membership of the Council for the Plan, which would involve a number of relevant ministers as well as Monnet and his staff, would need to be finalised and prepared as an ordinance for de Gaulle to sign by 17 January, only four days later. The first five Modernisation Commissions then had to be 'constituted, their presidents chosen and confirmed, their chairmen appointed', for Saturday 19 January. 'Jean Monnet must present the constitution of these commissions to General de Gaulle for his signature on this date', with the content of the document to be announced to the Council for the Plan at its first meeting, scheduled for 21 January.[63] The haste in which these documents would have to be drawn up recalls that surrounding the drafting of the law of 16 August 1940, particularly when one considers that Monnet had been able to work for several weeks in December on the text of the initial proposal signed on 3 January.[64]

[61]Robert Marjolin, an economist, worked closely with Monnet in Washington during the Second World War on securing supplies for France following the Liberation. Monnet chose him as his deputy at the CGP, and Marjolin ultimately became Vice-President of the European Commission under Walter Hallstein.

[62]After beginning his career in the chemical industry, Etienne Hirsch joined de Gaulle in London and worked closely with Monnet in Algiers from 1943. He succeeded Monnet as Commissioner for the Plan in 1952 and later became President of Euratom in 1959.

[63]'Note pour MM. Marjolin-Hirsch. Agenda des choses à faire avant le Conseil du Plan', 13 January 1946, AMF 1 0, FJME.

[64]In their respective memoirs, Marjolin and Hirsch use almost identical phrasing when stating that 'on 3 January 1946, the [Commissariat for the] Plan was created by decree' (the text in square brackets is in Hirsch's version only), and neither makes any reference to the activity that went on between that date and the first meeting of the Council on 21 January. Hirsch does, however, note that 'the proposals we submitted to General de Gaulle became, without the slightest modification, the instructions given' to the members of the CGP, which suggests that whatever Monnet gave to de Gaulle to sign before his resignation was approved without amendment. See Robert Marjolin, *Le travail d'une vie* (Paris: Robert Laffont, 1986), 163 and Etienne Hirsch, *Ainsi va la vie* (Lausanne: Fondation Jean Monnet pour l'Europe, 1988), 89.

The frantic pace at which the fundamental institutions of the CGP were developed was likely influenced by a decision that de Gaulle claims in his memoirs he made on 1 January 1946: to resign as President of the Republic.[65] Between de Gaulle's formal approval of the creation of the CGP on 3 January and the secret note Monnet drafted on 13 January, a Sunday, the two men agreed on a very tight schedule during which the essential components of the CGP would be formally endorsed by and backed with ordinances from the President. These had to be presented to de Gaulle for his signature on 19 January for a very simple reason: the following morning he resigned as President.[66] One of his very final acts as President was therefore the approval of the establishment of the first Modernisation Commissions, which were presented to the Council for the Plan as a *fait accompli* the day after de Gaulle's resignation. At that meeting the Commissions were described as 'the keystones of the whole project'.[67] Just as de Gaulle's quiet removal of André Diethelm from his post in the CFLN assured the survival of the Organisation Committees following the Liberation,[68] de Gaulle's cooperation with Monnet in the final days before resigning as President ensured that the Monnet Plan and its 'keystones', the Modernisation Commissions, would survive long after de Gaulle's resignation.[69]

Given that the creation of the Modernisation Commissions resulted in institutions parallel to the Organisation Committees but under the control

[65]De Gaulle, *Mémoires de guerre. Le salut, 1944–1946*, 334. 'Leaving the Palais Bourbon [the National Assembly] the evening of 1 January [1946], I had already made up my mind to resign. All that remained to do was to choose the date.'

[66]In de Gaulle's papers at the Archives nationales, the folder pertaining to his resignation contains no documents concerning the decrees he signed on 19 January. A surprising number of the documents deal with de Gaulle's efforts to exchange his presidential Cadillac for four French-made cars, which had to be authorised by Marcel Paul. Lettre du colonel Allegret à Monsieur le Ministre de la Production industrielle, 25 February 1946, 3 AG 4 97, AN.

[67]'Note pour MM. Marjolin-Hirsch. Agenda des choses à faire avant le Conseil du Plan', 13 January 1946, AMF 1 0, FJME.

[68]See Chapter 5.

[69]As with the removal of Diethelm in 1944, de Gaulle's decision was informed by political rather than economic factors. In his correspondence with de Gaulle, Monnet presented his Plan as a means of restoring France's power and influence as a great nation.

of the CGP rather than the Ministry for Industrial Production, it is worth considering Marcel Paul's reaction to Monnet's proposals. On 4 December, two weeks after Paul's appointment, Monnet sent his proposal for the establishment of the Plan to de Gaulle; by 13 December de Gaulle had responded with a draft memorandum summarising Monnet's plans that was sent to Paul.[70] This document was then discussed at an interministerial meeting on 14 December, where 'the broad lines of M Monnet's memorandum' were endorsed by ministers including Paul and François Billoux, although they made it clear that their support for Monnet's proposal was based on 'the temporary nature of the Commissariat'.[71] In the following weeks, however, Paul made repeated requests to meet with Monnet to discuss the development of his Plan in more detail – to no avail. Given that Paul wrote de Gaulle in December 1945 outlining his proposals to reform his ministry, including the 'disappearance, as quickly as possible, of the Organisation Committees and the Offices of' OCRPI, it is likely that Paul sought to discuss such plans in relation with the emergence of the new CGP.[72] Paul charged Blum-Picard, Secretary General for Industrial Production, with the task of arranging a meeting between the minister and Monnet. This meeting never came about. On 10 January 1946, a week after de Gaulle had approved the Monnet Plan, details of the project including a description of the Modernisation Commissions were made public. Meanwhile, by 18 January Blum-Picard was still unable to arrange any kind of meeting between Monnet and Paul. An exasperated Blum-Picard informed Paul that Monnet 'seem[ed] to systematically evade any meeting with' either Blum-Picard or Paul.[73] Of course we know that on 18 January Monnet was scrambling to finalise all the ordinances that de Gaulle would have to sign the next day. Having secured support for 'the broad lines' of his project, Monnet proceeded to develop the Modernisation Committees with only his closest allies and with the ongoing support of de Gaulle, while

[70]Jean Monnet, *Mémoires* (Paris: Fayard, 1976), 346.

[71]The backing of Billoux, the Communist Minister for the National Economy, was especially important, since France's economic planning was originally intended to be done by his ministry rather than by the CGP. He also expressed his support for the tripartite structure of the proposed Modernisation Commissions. 'Compte-rendu de la séance du vendredi 14 décembre 1945. Organisation du Commissariat au Plan', Comité Economique Interministériel, 14 December 1945, F 60 901, AN.

[72]Lettre de Marcel Paul à Charles de Gaulle, 26 December 1945, 3 AG 4 55, AN.

[73]Note de Blum-Picard à Marcel Paul, 18 January 1946, F 12 10028, AN.

systematically avoiding any kind of meeting with the Minister for Industrial Production. Marcel Paul was one of 12 ministers who attended the first meeting of the Council for the Plan on 21 January, and it was only then that he was briefed on the creation of the new Modernisation Commissions created two days earlier.

Shortly after de Gaulle's departure, Monnet found himself having to defend the decrees concerning the Plan. In his very first meeting with Monnet after succeeding de Gaulle as President, Félix Gouin[74] informed Monnet that he planned to modify the statute of the CGP by attaching it to the Ministry for the National Economy. Politically, this made more sense than it would have a month earlier, since Gouin had given that portfolio to fellow Socialist André Philip, who replaced the Communist Billoux on 26 January. Monnet flatly told the new President that attaching the CGP to the Ministry would be 'a mistake that would compromise the success of the whole undertaking'. The principal reason he gave to justify his argument was that 'it is always bad to modify the conditions in which a project operates once it is already underway'.[75] In other words, the decrees signed by de Gaulle during his last day as President created a *fait accompli* which Monnet seized upon and defended in the weeks and months that followed. Indeed, Monnet drafted a letter of resignation to Gouin to dissuade him from placing the CGP under the auspices of the Ministry for the National Economy. Faced with this ultimatum, Gouin reconsidered and, in June of that year, was succeeded as President by Georges Bidault of the MRP. As Gouin had done, Bidault swiftly appointed one of his own party colleagues, François de Menthon, as Minister for the National Economy. The fact that the first six months of the year saw this portfolio change hands from a Communist to a Socialist to a Christian Democrat does indeed lend credibility to Monnet's insistence on 'placing the CGP above these [partisan] polemics'.[76] Aside from the justification of the Commissariat's structure, it is important to note Monnet's strategy in creating the CGP, namely rushing the plans so that they could be signed into law by de Gaulle,

[74]One of the 80 deputies of the Third Republic who did not vote in favour of giving full powers to Pétain, Félix Gouin was an active participant in the Resistance, co-founding the Comité d'Action Socialiste (CAS) in 1941 and later being elected President of the Provisional Consultative Assembly in Algiers in 1943. He remained a deputy in the National Assembly until 1958.

[75]'Lettre de Monnet au Président', dated 7 February 1946 but not sent, AMF 1 3, FJME.

[76]Ibid.

then defending the status quo against challenges by de Gaulle's successor. It proved to be a successful formula and one that ensured the independence of the CGP vis-à-vis the Ministry for the National Economy, much to the chagrin of André Philip.[77]

From CORSID to CMSID: Institutional Metempsychosis?

On 9 March 1946, barely two months after the creation of the CGP, the Modernisation Commission for Steel (CMSID) was created.[78] This was one of the first Commissions established within the CGP, following the creation of the first five by de Gaulle the day before his resignation.[79] Moreover, steel was highlighted as the single most important industry by Monnet, who granted it 'absolute priority' for access to coal and insisted that 'in effect, it is steel that controls all other activities'.[80] Its composition mirrored that of the reformed Organisation Committee: five of its 15 members were employers drawn from steel firms, with the remaining members being drawn from labour (three), management (two), experts (two), and administrators (three).[81] The leadership of the Commission contained some familiar names. Eugène Roy, who had served as Vice-President of CORSID for the duration of the war, was promoted to President of the new Commission.[82] Jean Latourte, who had worked as Under-Secretary of CORSID and remained in that role in the renamed OPSID, was named Chairman of CMSID. Albert Bureau, another

[77]Monnet used similar tactics when developing the Schuman Plan and during the negotiations for the Treaty of Paris creating the ECSC, which are discussed in Chapter 8.

[78]'Arrêté du 9 mars 1946', 9 March 1946, 80 AJ 1, AN.

[79]The first five Commissions, all approved by de Gaulle on 19 January 1946, were for coal, electricity, construction materials, animal farming, and agriculture.

[80]'Présentation des programmes de base', 9 September 1946, AMF 5 9, FJME.

[81]Despite the vaunted tripartite composition of the Modernisation Commissions, it is worth noting that labour received only one-fifth of the seats in the Commission. Following the expulsion of the PCF from government in May 1947, the CGT refused to take part in the activities of the Commissions, which weakened the voice of labour even further.

[82]Curiously in his memoirs Jean Monnet remembers having appointed 'Etienne Roy' to the post. While this might have been an attempt to distance the Monnet Plan from the Vichy figure, it was more likely an oversight on Monnet's part. See Monnet's *Mémoires*, 357. Industrialist Roger Martin similarly misidentifies CMSID's president in his memoirs, this time as 'Jules Roy', seemingly confusing Roy and Jules Aubrun. See Martin, *Patron du droit divin* (Paris: Gallimard, 1984), 37.

CORSID veteran, was poached from OPSID and named Vice-President of the Commission.[83] Given that the three top positions were awarded to individuals who had worked together closely within CORSID under Vichy, it was hardly surprising that the Commission bore more than a passing resemblance to that institution. It was also stated that the Commission would work closely with two other institutions: the CSSF, of which Jules Aubrun was President, and OPSID, still led by Alexis Aron.[84] This arrangement thus reunited the President and Vice-President of CORSID, along with their wartime ally Aron, to coordinate and manage the French steel industry as they had for the duration of the Vichy regime.[85] It is worth remembering that the appointment of Aubrun and Roy to the top positions of CORSID in 1940 had marked a decisive break from the leadership of the pre-war *Comité des forges*. The replacement of factory owners and pre-war giants like François de Wendel by managerial directors from the industry proved to be an enduring change, as Aubrun's and Roy's post-1944 careers demonstrate.[86] With the staffing of CMSID, and indeed that of other Modernisation Commissions, the leaders of pre-war employers' associations like de Wendel and Henri de Peyerimhoff were passed over in favour of individuals who had earned their influential positions under Vichy.

In the first six months following the Liberation, the preoccupation of steel industrialists was the modernisation of their machinery.[87] After four years of strenuous production with limited access to spare parts, let alone the latest innovations in production, the industry's hardware was in poor shape. While the period during the Second World War had been one of great technological innovation, particularly for the Allies, France had been shut out from such advances. To bring France up to speed, the Ministry for Industrial Production commissioned the *Centre national de la recherche scientifique* (CNRS) to work

[83]'Dossier de presse', March 1947, 80 AJ 2, AN.

[84]'Rapport de la commission de modernisation de la sidérurgie', February 1947, 80 AJ 11, AN.

[85]As we have seen earlier in this chapter, the dissolution of OPSID, completed in autumn 1946, transferred that body's powers of sub-allocation back to Aubrun at the CSSF. Although Aubrun and Roy had worked together closely in CORSID, they nevertheless clashed over a number of issues pertaining to the modernisation of the industry in the late 1940s; see Chapter 8.

[86]See Chapter 3.

[87]'Programme d'organisation de la sidérurgie française', undated but from between September 1944 and February 1945, F 12 10062, AN.

with researchers in London to learn the latest technological advances, including in industrial methods.[88] When the government announced the creation of the CGP and the Monnet Plan on 10 January 1946, Monnet stressed that 'the reconstruction of France does not merely mean repairing the destruction from the war, but also the modernisation of our equipment and our production methods', concluding that 'modernisation and reconstruction must be pursued simultaneously'.[89] This mission imbued the CGP and its constituent Modernisation Commissions.[90]

The role of the Modernisation Commissions was defined by Monnet as 'to coordinate, to manage [*diriger*], but at all costs not to suffocate or sterilise the efforts of the technicians'.[91] Within ten days of its creation, the Commission for Steel was given the task of 'defining all measures that would permit [the French steel industry] to produce ... 6 million tonnes of steel in ingots ... for direct consumption'.[92] They were also to develop a plan to enable the industry to increase that production to 10 million tonnes of steel within three years, thereby matching 1929 production levels, to be increased to 12 million after another two years.[93] Crucially, the plans drawn up by the Commission to meet these targets were based on the data compiled by CORSID since 1940.[94] The Council for the Plan recognised that, despite the best efforts of the Commission, the single

[88]'Note. Objet: Le Centre national de la recherche scientifique française', 16 December 1944, F 12 9974, AN.

[89]'Instructions envoyées par M. le Président du Gouvernement Provisoire de la République à M. le Commissaire Général du Plan, après décision du Conseil des Ministres', 10 January 1946, 80 AJ 1, AN. Although this document was issued by the President, de Gaulle, the text is virtually identical to that of the memorandum written by Monnet and submitted to de Gaulle in December 1946. We may therefore attribute the statement to Monnet.

[90]Monnet's strategy was consequently to use funds, such as those provided by the Marshall Plan, on investing in modern wide-strip steel mills like those set with USINOR and SOLLAC, rather than on short-term spending on food and reconstruction of pre-war buildings. See Mioche, *Le Plan Monnet*.

[91]'Rapport de la commission de modernisation de la sidérurgie', February 1947, 80 AJ 11, AN.

[92]'Résolution adoptée le 19 mars par le Conseil du Plan pour la Sidérurgie', 19 March 1946, 80 AJ 1, AN.

[93]Ibid.

[94]'Projet de résolution soumis au Conseil du Plan. Objectifs généraux pour l'activité française', 13 March 1946, AMF 2 3, FJME.

greatest obstacle to increasing French steel output was 'the insufficient coal supply, in particular imports of coke and coke fines from the Ruhr'.[95] The Modernisation Commission was therefore advised to 'take into consideration the necessity of minimising the use of coal and labour as much as possible'.[96] The Commission for Steel would issue its first report, including projected output and recommendations for the modernisation of the industry, in November 1946.[97] Insofar as the leaders of the Commission had spent the war running the industry while struggling with shortages of coal, their 74-page report built on the work done by CORSID during the war. Given the dramatically different situation of France by 1946, however, the Commission's priority was to increase overall production to levels unseen since before the Great Depression, rather than trying to eke out enough industrial activity to prevent factories from shutting. Yet in 1946, as it had been under Vichy, the French steel industry's preoccupation was obtaining more coal from Germany. Accordingly, the Commission's report emphasised one conclusion in particular: 'Of course, in waiting for the realisation of this long-term endeavour, which after all remains merely a possibility, France can and must continue to rely on the Ruhr, as before the war, for the fuel needed for our steel industry'.[98] This insistence on receiving greater quantities of German coal to fuel France's economic recovery would be a central characteristic of the post-war period.[99]

Replacing the Organisation Committees

The first five Modernisation Commissions, which replicated much of the work of the Organisation Committees, were signed into law by de Gaulle on 19 January 1946. Only five days later, Monnet was already moving to resolve this redundancy by having his Commissions replace the

[95]'Résolution adoptée le 19 mars par le Conseil du Plan pour la Sidérurgie', 19 March 1946, 80 AJ 1, AN.

[96]Ibid.

[97]'Rapport de la Commission de Modernisation de la Sidérurgie', November 1946, 80 AJ 11, AN.

[98]Ibid.

[99]See Alan Milward, *The Reconstruction of Western Europe 1945–1951* (London: Routledge, 1984) and Matthias Kipping, *La France et les origines de l'Union européenne.*

Committees altogether. He noted that there was a 'psychologically disastrous environment which risks indirectly compromising [France's] economic recovery',[100] referring to the unpopularity of the Committees and of certain measures still in place, such as price controls.[101] Explaining the situation, Monnet recognised 'the legitimacy of the maintenance, at least provisionally, of certain regulations', but added that 'the French are unanimous in objecting to the maintenance of many of these regulations more than a year after the Liberation [and] to the administrative carelessness of the Offices responsible for their application'. The solution, he concluded, was 'the abolition or at least the transformation of certain regulations' which could be done 'immediately or in the very near future'. Referring to the various 'administrative offices' responsible for allocating materials to different industries – the Organisation Committees and Sections of OCRPI – Monnet called for a 'transfer [of responsibilities] to bodies that are genuinely professional and democratic'. Monnet recognised that the 'profession will not reform itself', and proposed the creation of a 'provisional Commissariat with absolute powers', whose leader could, 'for a period of four to five months', introduce 'all the simplifications he deems necessary'.[102] While this last suggestion was rejected by the Council for the Plan, it does reveal that Monnet was trying to convince the Council, which included all ministers related to the French economy and industry, of the need to 'simplify' the existing system of industrial organisation. By referring to the measures and offices which were maintained after the Liberation, including the Organisation Committees, and adding that the population unanimously opposed their continued existence – politicians from all three governing parties had campaigned on a pledge to abolish the Organisation Committees during the October 1945 elections[103] – Monnet was making the case for dissolving the Committees. His suggestion that the system be 'simplified' by transferring their powers to 'genuinely professional and democratic' bodies is a clear reference to the Modernisation Commissions he had

[100]'Simplification de la réglementation économique', 24 January 1946, AMF 1 6, FJME.

[101]Kenneth Mouré explains the administration's need to maintain price controls and the unpopularity of this decision in 'Economic Choice in Dark Times: The Vichy Economy', *French Politics, Culture & Society* (25:1), Spring 2007.

[102]'Simplification de la réglementation économique', 24 January 1946, AMF 1 6, FJME.

[103]See Shennan, *Rethinking France*, 274.

just established, which he consistently described as democratic and representing the interests of the industry as a whole through the 'essential collaboration of the State, workers, and [employers from] the industry'.[104] Having created Commissions that largely replicated the existing Committees, albeit under the authority of the CGP, Monnet suggested that the Committees be dispensed with altogether. In this Monnet found common cause with the Communist Minister for Industrial Production, Marcel Paul.

The morning of 23 April 1946, Marcel Paul proposed in the National Assembly that the Organisation Committees be abolished, a motion that received unanimous support. Paul had made no secret of his desire to dismantle the Committees, and had outlined his plans to do so to de Gaulle in December 1945.[105] This agreement was undoubtedly helped by Monnet's suggestion to the key ministers from all three governing parties that the Organisation Committees' powers ought to be transferred to the Modernisation Committees. With the PCF, the SFIO, and the MRP all criticising the Committees during the election campaign the previous autumn, it was increasingly clear that the political will to maintain Vichy's bodies was sagging. Yet some worried that, despite the obvious political complications of maintaining them, 'it will always be necessary to maintain bodies equivalent to' the Committees to coordinate industry.[106] By proposing to take the place of these problematic institutions with the 'genuinely professional and democratic' Modernisation Commissions of the promising new CGP, Monnet would have reassured those apprehensive of rashly dismantling the Committees without establishing equivalent bodies.[107]

The day that this vote in the National Assembly took place, Monnet argued for the necessity of maintaining the Council for the Plan and the

[104]'Note de Jean Monnet sur le premier rapport de remise en marche de l'économie française en 1945, sur les objectifs pour 1946 et sur le but final à atteindre', 11 November 1945, AMF 1 6, FJME.

[105]Lettre de Marcel Paul à Charles de Gaulle, 26 December 1945, 3 AG 4 55, AN.

[106]'Note pour M. le Secrétaire Général à la Production', undated note, but certainly between March and October 1945, F 12 10063, AN.

[107]Indeed, General Giraud's decision, supported by Monnet, to abolish the Organisation Committees in North Africa in 1943 proved disastrous, since no equivalent bodies had been set up to take their place. See Chapter 5.

Modernisation Commissions indefinitely. The ordinances signed by de Gaulle in January had in fact created only a provisional Commissariat and provisional Modernisation Commissions, which were to be dissolved after six months; indeed, it was on the strength of this explicit commitment that the Communist Ministers holding the 'economic portfolios' had been persuaded to accept the Plan.[108] Monnet unambiguously recognised this, admitting in February that 'the Administration only accepted this method because it knows that the Commissariat and the Commissions will disappear in six months [. . . and] because they consider them to be temporary'.[109] The very day the National Assembly voted to abolish the Organisation Committees, however, Monnet abruptly changed his tune and began insisting that 'it is necessary to maintain the Council for the Plan and the Modernisation Commissions and to give them permanent status', and that they continue to operate within the CGP. Having set out to the Council for the Plan how the Modernisation Commissions should take the place of the Organisation Committees, Monnet sought to reassure any ministers apprehensive about dissolving the latter. As soon as this decision was made in the National Assembly, however, Monnet insisted that the Commissions must be made permanent to effectively and enduringly replace the Organisation Committees that were abolished that same day.[110] Monnet's demands were met in practice as the Commissions continued their work well beyond their original six-month shelf life, before the permanence of the CGP and its the Commissions was confirmed by presidential decree in January 1947.[111]

[108]'Compte-rendu de la séance du vendredi 14 décembre 1945. Organisation du Commissariat au Plan', Comité Economique Interministériel, 14 December 1945, F 60 901, AN.

[109]Untitled document by Monnet beginning with 'Les raisons pour lesquelles je considère qu'il n'est pas possible de rattacher le Plan à l'Economie nationale sont les suivants', 12 February 1946, AMF 1 3, FJME.

[110]'Note sur l'élaboration et l'exécution du Plan, ainsi que sur les questions qui doivent y concourir', 23 April 1946, AMF 5 2, FJME.

[111]Interestingly, Monnet's preferred shape of the CGP was once again ensured by presidential decree hours before the president's resignation. Then President Léon Blum decreed the permanent institutionalisation of the CGP on 16 January 1947 before resigning later that same day. The Minister for the National Economy during this period, André Philip, criticised the abolition of the Organisation Committees as a mistake and opposed Monnet's attempts to establish the CGP as a permanent body beyond the control of Philip's ministry.

Despite the striking institutional and individual continuities between the Organisation Committees and the Modernisation Commissions, Monnet insisted on the novelty of the Plan and its Commissions in his memoirs: 'I took nobody's place . . . I occupied a territory that had until that time been with neither name nor master.'[112] According to Monnet, the Commissions had entirely original functions, while in reality they replicated many of those of the existing Organisation Committees. He also claimed the innovation of the tripartite composition of the Commissions: 'administration, producers, and workers had never been gathered around the same table. If they ever did negotiate, it was in a climate of confrontation. There was a winner and a loser, to the detriment of production or the currency',[113] a tendency exemplified by the bitter labour disputes of the 1930s. Monnet explains that he had observed the Working Parties of wartime Britain, which had gathered industrialists, technicians, and labour union representatives, but he found them 'seriously limited by the absence of civil servants representing the public interest and by the lack of general objectives'.[114] He makes the further claim, often repeated in the secondary literature, that he was the first to gather labour union representatives, employers, and civil servants around the same table to discuss and plan their common industry. In his memoirs, Etienne Hirsch makes an almost identical reference to Britain's Working Parties and adds that 'it was necessary to add [. . .] representatives from the civil service. This is how the concept of the Modernisation Commissions came about, which constitutes the originality and indeed the foundation of French planning'.[115] Yet Monnet and Hirsch conveniently ignore the Organisation Committees of 1944–1946, which indeed gathered administration, producers, and workers around the same table, along with civil servants. The expunction of the Committees from his narrative certainly makes Monnet's own efforts seem all the more revolutionary, yet it ignores the important and very real continuities in industrial organisation in *l'entre-deux-républiques*.[116]

[112]Monnet, *Mémoires*, 347.

[113]Ibid., 342.

[114]Ibid.

[115]Hirsch, *Ainsi va la vie*, 89.

[116]Monnet's tendency to exaggerate how innovative his method was has been noted by Andrew Shennan, although he does not address continuities between the Organisation Committees and the Modernisation Commissions. See Shennan, *Rethinking France*, 247–249.

This version of the Modernisation Commissions' origins has also come to dominate the literature on the Monnet Plan. In his influential study of the French economy in the twentieth century, Richard Kuisel claims that the idea for the Modernisation Commissions came directly from Hirsch's observations on Britain's wartime Working Parties, while 'Vichy's [Organisation Committees] seem to have had little or no influence on the CGP in creating the commissions'.[117] Yet Kuisel bases his assessment on an interview conducted with Hirsch, who unsurprisingly reiterated the same account advanced in his memoirs.[118] Henry Rousso similarly argues that Monnet's Commissions had little in common with Vichy's Committees; indeed, he felt the need to justify comparing the two institutions, admitting that associating them 'may seem incorrect'.[119] He also underlines the fundamental differences between the two institutions, describing the Commissions as 'tripartite', in contrast to the 'exclusively employer-led' Committees.[120] More recently, Philip Nord has similarly noted that 'trade unionists . . . played a role on the Commissions de modernisation that they had been denied outright by Vichy', citing this as the key difference between the two institutions.[121] Yet this distinction is based on the Organisation Committees as they existed under Vichy and

[117]Richard Kuisel, *Capitalism and the State in Modern France* (Cambridge: Cambridge University Press, 1981), 227. This explanation is reiterated in Sherrill Brown Wells, *Jean Monnet: Unconventional Statesman* (London: Lynne Rienner, 2011). François Fourquet reaches a similar conclusion based on his interview with Jean Ripert, another collaborator of Monnet. See Fourquet, *Les Comptes de la puissance* (Paris: Recherches, 1980), 56–57.

[118]Elsewhere in the same study, Kuisel describes a proposal advanced by Hirsch in 1942 to reorganise French industry, which was so similar to Vichy's Organisation Committees that André Philip rejected it as overly Vichyste. Kuisel himself labels Hirsch's wartime plans as 'technocorporatist'. See Kuisel, *Capitalism and the State in Modern France*, 279–280.

[119]'La comparaison *a priori* peut paraître abusive.' Henry Rousso, 'Les Elites économiques dans les années 1940: Epuration et transition', in *Vichy: L'événement, la mémoire, l'histoire* (Paris: Gallimard, 1992), 573.

[120]Ibid., 574.

[121]Philip Nord, *France's New Deal* (Princeton: Princeton University Press, 2010), 156–157. Claude Gruson has suggested that Monnet's gathering civil servants and employers within the Modernisation Commissions was 'facilitated' by the previous existence of the Organisation Committees, but he makes no mention of labour representation, nor does he explore any possible links between the two sets of institutions. See Gruson, *Les Origines de la planification française* (Paris: Dunod, 1968).

ignores the significant reforms imposed on the Committees between the end of the Vichy regime and the establishment of the CGP. By 1946, when the first Commissions were established, the Organisation Committees had long ceased to be 'exclusively employer-led', and had instead become 'tripartite' themselves, with 'administration, producers, and workers' indeed sitting around the same table. The dissimilarities between the Organisation Committees and the Modernisation Commissions claimed by Monnet and Hirsch have been amplified by the absence of any thorough study of the reforms of the Committees under the Provisional Government. While the chasm between the Committees of 1944 and the Commissions of 1946 is clear, it is discernibly bridged by the reforms of the Committees overseen by the GPRF.[122]

The continuities in personnel between the Committees and the Commissions has similarly been downplayed in the literature. Based on his interview with Hirsch, Kuisel concluded that 'there was rather little overlap between the [Committees] and the commissions... because Monnet's team, who had lived outside the country for the war's duration, had had few contacts with Vichy personnel and simply recruited elsewhere'.[123] Rousso meanwhile used a quantitative approach to calculate that 'of 57 individuals placed at the head of the Modernisation Commissions, only 5 came from Organisation Committees', suggesting only negligible continuities, with fewer than 9 per cent of Commission presidents having served in Vichy's Committees.[124] Yet a more qualitative approach shows that the opposite is true in the case of the steel industry: Eugène Roy, the Commission's president, was the Organisation Committee's vice-president from 1940 to 1944, having held an important post advising the French government on German industry between the two appointments. Furthermore, Rousso focuses on the heads of the Commissions and the very limited leadership on the Committees, which obscures the fact that the Commission's Vice-President, Jean Latourte, and Chairman, Albert Bureau, both held important positions in CORSID's secretariat. Additionally, the post-war roles of Committee presidents are overlooked – Jules Aubrun, for instance, was quickly appointed President of the CSSF, in which he was called

[122]See Chapter 6 for a study of the reforms to the Organisation Committees under the Provisional Government.

[123]Kuisel, *Capitalism and the State in Modern France*, 227.

[124]Rousso, Les Elites économiques dans les années 1940: Epuration et transition', 575.

upon to collaborate with the newly-formed Modernisation Commission for Steel. Moreover, Aubrun gained further powers of sub-allocation from the Organisation Committees following their abolition, thus recovering some of the key responsibilities he had held as President of CORSID. The two institutions worked together closely under the Monnet Plan, as the Modernisation Commission for Steel asked the CSSF for a briefing on the latter's latest work programmes and expressed its desire 'to associate to our work the great majority of the personnel of the steel industry'.[125] While never formally part of the new Commission, Aubrun was nevertheless invited to play an active part in its activities.[126]

The continuities in individuals from CORSID to CMSID were by no means unique. In the case of the Modernisation Commission for the oil industry, for example, fully two-thirds of its members from among employers had been members of the analogous Organisation Committee under Vichy. Meanwhile, the wartime President of the Committee for the electrical industry, Roger Boutteville, was promptly selected to be President of the Commission for the same industry under the CGP. While Nord has dismissed Boutteville's as 'an anomalous case',[127] the numerous continuities among individuals who had served on Vichy's Committees and then on Monnet's Commissions show that such trajectories were far from exceptional.

The argument that there was little overlap between the Committees and the Commissions because Monnet's team 'had had few contacts with Vichy personnel and simply recruited elsewhere'[128] must be reassessed. While Monnet's closest advisors at the CGP, Hirsch chief amongst them, had generally spent the war as part of the Resistance overseas, this was not true of the employers chosen to sit on the Modernisation Commissions. Very few employers had anything to do with the internal Resistance, and virtually none joined de Gaulle in London – a fact the general allegedly

[125]'Rapport de la Commission de Modernisation de la Sidérurgie', February 1947, AJ 80 11, AN.

[126]Despite this initial invitation, differences soon emerged between the CSSF and CMSID; these are discussed in Chapter 8.

[127]Nord, op.cit., 157. Boutteville was indeed the most glaring example of continuity from Committees to Commissions, as he was the only individual to serve as President of both institutions in a given industry.

[128]Kuisel, *Capitalism and the State in Modern France*, 227.

pointed out at his first post-war meeting with employers.[129] As early as September 1943, Monnet insisted that the CFLN must 'consider which individuals currently in key positions [in the Organisation Committees] should be maintained and which should be replaced and, if possible, by whom'.[130] Such considerations show that Monnet already recognised the necessity of recruiting from amongst employers who were then working for Vichy's Committees. Given the expertise such employers developed by running these institutions for four years, and just how difficult 'recruiting elsewhere' would be given that nearly all employers remained in France for the duration of the war, it should hardly be surprising that Monnet and his colleagues welcomed many from the Committees to join the new Modernisation Commissions.

It is by no means shocking that Monnet and his colleagues would not be eager to highlight any association between the Modernisation Commissions and the Organisation Committees. By 1945, the latter were widely unpopular and regularly attacked in the press, due to their association not only with Vichy but with the ongoing shortages that plagued France in the early post-war period. Indeed, these factors had prompted then Minister for Industrial Production Robert Lacoste to change the name of the Committees to 'Professional Offices', which his ministry insisted 'had nothing in common with the organisations of the Vichy regime' – a blatant lie given that they were the very same institutions.[131] Despite the pragmatic value the Committees may have had, public opinion had clearly turned against them, which helped ensure that they were abolished by unanimous vote in the National Assembly in April 1946. Both Lacoste and Monnet were eager to dissociate the Professional Offices and the Modernisation Commissions,

[129]The quotation from de Gaulle, perhaps apocryphal, is 'I did not see many of you in London, gentlemen'. Qtd in Julian Jackson, *De Gaulle* (London: Haus, 2003), 24. The best study of French employers during the war is Renaud de Rochebrune and Jean Claude Hazera, *Les patrons sous l'Occupation* (Paris: Odile Jacob, 1995); for a revisionist interpretation, see François Marcot in 'Qu'est-ce qu'un patron résistant?' in Olivier Dard et al., *L'Occupation, l'Etat français et les entreprises* (Paris: ADHE, 2000), 277–292.

[130]'Note sur la première étape de la reconstruction en France', 22 September 1943, AME 33 1, FJME. In this note, Monnet was focused on which employers should be maintained within the post-war Organisation Committees, which he contended should be maintained.

[131]'Lettre de Piette au Président de la Chambre de métiers de l'Ain', 18 October 1945, F 12 10031, AN.

respectively, from Vichy, although Lacoste's efforts were ultimately unsuccessful.

One lesson Monnet may have learned from the post-war Organisation Committees is the importance of securing public support for key institutions and projects. Despite their pragmatic value, of which Monnet was well aware as early as 1943, the Committees were the target of merciless criticism from politicians and journalists alike. No matter how practical or even how technical and seemingly apolitical an institution might be, public opposition could force their abolition, as the fate of the Committees revealed. Convincing the public of the value of the Monnet Plan and of the Modernisation Commissions in particular was thus a priority for Monnet from the very beginning. In a note to Marjolin and Hirsch on 13 January 1946, Monnet identified the priorities pertaining to the Modernisation Commissions; 'publicity' was named as one of the most important.[132] In June 1946, Monnet outlined the need 'to bring into public opinion and to make the Government accept a number of ideas', notably that private industry 'such as the steel industry' should execute the elements of the Plan already agreed upon. He also singled out the Modernisation Commissions, writing on the need to 'make them popular among the public and within the administration'.[133] By December 1946, Monnet was developing strategies for promoting the Plan to the public, including the distribution of 'a popular leaflet on the Plan' and even 'propaganda in schools'.[134] Clearly, Monnet was willing to go to great lengths to ensure that his initiative enjoyed broad public support, from government ministers to schoolchildren. Monnet's insistence that public opinion be 'informed' of the virtues of the Plan quickly reached then President Félix Gouin, who in March 1946 stated that 'we will elicit the enthusiasm and cooperation of the country, provided we define and explain to French opinion what we expect of the [Plan] that we are asking

[132]'Note pour MM. Marjolin-Hirsch. Agenda des choses à faire avant le Conseil du Plan', 13 January 1946, AMF 1 0, FJME.

[133]'Objectifs pour le 30 juin', document dated 22 December 1946, but clearly from before 30 June 1946, AMM 2 1, FJME.

[134]'Note du 7 décembre', dated 8 December 1946, AMM 2 1, FJME. The term used by Monnet, '*brochure populaire*', connotes that it was intended for the *classes populaires*, or the working class. Monnet specifies that the Plan should be promoted at both universities and elementary schools.

them to support'.[135] With such a concerted campaign to ensure the popularity of the Monnet Plan and of its 'keystones', the Modernisation Commissions, any mention of the unpopular Organisation Committees as a precursor to the Commissions was to be studiously avoided, in favour of the extollment of the novelty of the Monnet Plan and the 'democratic' composition of its Commissions.[136]

Conclusion

In 1945, a study was prepared for Blum-Picard regarding the future of the Organisation Committee for Steel (CORSID). Notably, it stressed that 'regardless of political developments in the months ahead, it will always be necessary to maintain bodies equivalent to [CORSID] in order to execute its functions'.[137] This recognition of the necessity of an Organisation Committee, or an analogous body, to organise French steel production is telling. Alluding to the modernisation of French industry, the study added that the State must 'invest tens of thousands of francs to reorganise and modernise the steel industry, for this, we will need such an institution [CORSID]'.[138] This document reveals the view that, while CORSID could indeed be dissolved due to 'political developments in the months ahead' – notably the legislative elections of October 1945, ahead of which candidates from all three main parties called for the abolition of the Committees[139] – a successor institution with essentially the same powers and mandate would still be needed. By the time Marcel Paul assumed his responsibilities as minister in November 1945, his Secretary General was well aware of the argument for the necessity of maintaining the bodies

[135] 'Discours prononcé par M. Félix Gouin, Président du Gouvernement provisoire de la République française, le 16 mars, à l'occasion de la première séance du Conseil du Plan', 16 March 1946, AMF 2 4, FJME.

[136] While Monnet successfully mobilised public opinion in favour of the Monnet Plan and, later, for the Schuman Plan, his failure to do so for the Pleven Plan to create the European Defence Community was a decisive factor in the latter's failure. See Edward Fursdon, *The European Defence Community* (London: Macmillan, 1980) and Michel Dumoulin (ed.), *La Communauté européenne de défense, leçons pour demain?* (Brussels: Peter Lang, 2000).

[137] 'Note pour M. le Secrétaire Général à la Production', undated document, but certainly between March and October 1945, F 12 10063, AN.

[138] Ibid.

[139] Shennan, *Rethinking France*, 274.

created by Vichy or, at the very least, of replacing them with analogous institutions.

The benefit of such institutions was by no means lost on Jean Monnet as he developed plans for the architecture of the CGP. Creating tripartite, industry-specific bodies to coordinate production was a logical means of developing and putting into practice the Monnet Plan. In 1943, following the messy dissolution of the Organisation Committees in North Africa without having created institutions to take over their functions, Monnet advocated maintaining the Organisation Committees and their staff in post-war France. By early 1946, amidst growing calls to abolish the Committees in France, Monnet created parallel bodies with a familiar design, overlapping functions, and significant continuities in personnel in the form of his Modernisation Commissions. There were certainly important differences between the two sets of institutions: the Commissions were placed within the supraministerial CGP, answerable directly to the head of the government, rather than under a single ministry; responsibilities for the sub-allocation of raw materials to individual firms were taken over by employers' associations rather than by the Commissions; and, perhaps most importantly, the Commissions were focused largely on modernising equipment and practices to increase production, whereas the Committees had been preoccupied with keeping factories running amidst chronic shortages of raw materials and other disruptions which continued to plague post-war France. Despite these distinctions, the Committees and the Commissions are far more similar than are generally recognised, not least due to the fact that by 1946 the Committees included labour representation, and that Monnet and his colleagues recruited extensively, if by no means exclusively, from veterans of Vichy's institutions. Moreover, Monnet explicitly called for powers to be transferred from the Committees to his 'genuinely professional and democratic' Commissions, suggesting that the latter were indeed meant to supplant the former. If employers' associations such as the CSSF are widely considered to be the successors of the Organisation Committees, the case for the Modernisation Commissions of the CGP to be seen as the Committees' successors is equally strong.

The vote to abolish the Organisation Committees elicited a range of reactions. While employers were initially furious, particularly as they had not been consulted beforehand, they quickly manoeuvred the power vacuum left by the removal of the Committees and OCRPI to gain further control over the allocation of raw materials to their industries.[140] For others, like André Philip, disapproval of the disappearance of the Committees set in later, as it became apparent that, paradoxically, the Communist minister's insistence on destroying Vichy's bodies in fact gave more power to the *grand patronat* while weakening the influence of organised labour. Monnet, for his part, seized the initative within hours of the vote to entrench his Modernisation Commissions as permanent fixtures of the French economy. In this he was successful, and consequently it was these institutions that oversaw ambitious plans to modernise French industry under the Fourth Republic.

[140]The CNPF would later unanimously endorse the creation of the CGP and the Monnet Plan. See 'Assemblée générale du 21 juin 1947', CNPF, 21 June 1947, AS 72 836, ANMT.

CHAPTER 8

L'Unité de l'Europe est à ce prix: The Struggle Between CORSID's Successors and the Creation of the ECSC

With the abolition of the Organisation Committees and OCRPI in April 1946, it seemed that the remains of Vichy's New Industrial Order had been swept away. The Committees' responsibilities were divided between two institutions. One was the Modernisation Commissions of the General Commissariat for the Plan (CGP), the central administrative apparatus of the Monnet Plan, which inherited the staff and much of the documentation of the defunct Organisation Committees, in addition to the responsibility for overseeing the modernisation of the industry's equipment. The other was the main employers' associations, such as the *Chambre syndicale de la sidérurgie française* (CSSF) and the concomitant *Comptoir français des produits sidérurgiques* (CPS), which inherited the Committee's powers over the allocation of raw materials for the industry and the allocation of orders to particular firms. Over the following years, the CGP and the CSSF would struggle to impose their own vision of industrial organisation in France, and ultimately Europe, through the Monnet Plan and then the Schuman Plan. By exploring the clashes between these two groups in light of the discussion of the previous chapters, we can better appreciate the

'This is the cost of European unity'. Lettre de Robert Schuman à Jules Aubrun, 19 June 1951, 81 AJ 135, AN.

© The Author(s) 2017

L.-A. Brunet, *Forging Europe: Industrial Organisation in France, 1940–1952*, Security, Conflict and Cooperation in the Contemporary World, DOI 10.1057/978-1-349-95198-7_8

legacy of Vichy on the organisation of France's and indeed Western Europe's post-war steel industry, culminating in the creation of the European Coal and Steel Community (ECSC).

Modernisation or Decadence: The War of Succession Between the Modernisation Commission for Steel and the CSSF

On 26 April 1946, the National Assembly unanimously endorsed the liquidation of the Organisation Committees and OCRPI, which had been created in the early months of the Vichy regime in the summer of 1940. The law of 26 April granted employers' associations greater control over the sub-allocation of raw materials within their industry and over the awarding of orders to particular firms – heretofore responsibilities of the Organisation Committees since their creation. Simultaneously, Jean Monnet sought to coopt the Committees' powers over planning and modernisation of key industries with the creation of his Modernisation Commissions, the 'keystones' of the CGP. By the dawn of 1947, these new powers had been fully absorbed by the Committees' respective successor institutions.[1]

The ongoing struggle between the CSSF and the Modernisation Commission for Steel – and the CGP more broadly – has been observed in other studies of the period.[2] Yet historians have tended to characterise this as a clash between the old guard of the pre-war *Comité des forges* and the young modernisers working with Monnet. According to members of the Modernisation Commission for Steel (CMSID), this amounted to a

[1]See Chapter 7.

[2]Indicatively, John Gillingham, *Coal, Steel and the Rebirth of Europe, 1945–1955* (Cambridge: Cambridge University Press, 1991); Matthias Kipping, *La France et les origines de l'Union européenne. Intégration économique et compétitivité internationale* (Paris: CHEF, 2002); Françoise Berger, *La France, l'Allemagne et l'acier (1932–1952). De la stratégie des cartels à l'élaboration de la CECA*. PhD thesis. (Paris: Université de Paris I, 2000). For a *longue durée* study of the conflicting protectionist and free market impulses in Western Europe over the nineteenth and twentieth centuries, see Eric Bussière, Michel Dumoulin, Sylvain Schirmann (eds), *Europe organisée, Europe du libre-échange? Fin XIXe siècle – Années 1960* (Brussels: Peter Lang, 2006).

'quarrel between the *anciens* and the *modernes*' or a 'clash between generations'.[3] The post-war CSSF has thus been presented as the simple continuation of the pre-war *Comité des forges*, with CORSID as merely an intermediate step.[4] This characterisation has led to attributes of the *Comité des forges* being projected onto the post-war CSSF; the claim that they 'had long been used to influencing the government',[5] for example, had not been true of steel industrialists since 1940. Consequently, the disagreements between the CSSF and the CMSID have been presented as a conflict between the old guard of the '*patronat du droit divin*' and the young, modernising technocrats leading the charge of what some enthusiastically deemed a 'Second French Revolution'.[6] Indeed, such a depiction echoes the terms from the Monnet Plan's own propaganda, as the choice between 'modernisation or decadence', with the CSSF being unfavourably associated with the latter.

Such a characterisation, however, is incomplete. Crucially, the CSSF was not simply the *Comité des forges* under another name; myriad important changes, from its leadership to its loss of political influence, distinguish

[3]The first quotation is from Roger Martin, Deputy Rapporteur for the Commission for Steel, while the second is from Commission member Henri Malcor. Both are quoted in Kipping, *La France et les origines de l'Union européenne*, 41, as well as in Philippe Mioche, 'Les plans et la sidérurgie: du soutien mitigé à l'effacement possible (1946–1960)' in Henry Rousso (ed.), *De Monnet à Massé. Enjeux politiques et objectifs économiques dans le cadre des quatre premiers Plan (1946–1965)* (Paris: CNRS, 1986), 127–138, 131 and 132.

[4]Philippe Mioche, 'Les comités d'organisation de la sidérurgie: un lieu d'affrontement entre modernisateurs de la sidérurgie et gardiens de la profession?' in Hervé Joly (ed.), *Les comités d'organisation et l'économie dirigée du régime de Vichy* (Caen: Centre de recherche d'histoire quantitative, 2004). See also Pierre Gerbet, *La construction de l'Europe* (Paris: Imprimerie nationale, 1983), 129.

[5]Gerbet, *La construction de l'Europe*, 129. A similar claim is made by Jean Baumier regarding the supposed political influence of the *maîtres de forges*; see Baumier, *La fin des maîtres de forges* (Paris: Plon, 1981). The lack of political influence of CORSID and the CSSF is discussed in the earlier chapters of this book.

[6]The term 'patronat du droit divin' was used by Jacques Barnaud to describe the owner-presidents who dominated the *Comité des forges*, and who were shut out of the Organisation Committees designed by Barnaud in 1940. See Barnaud, 'L'industriel', *Nouveaux cahiers*, no. 2, 1 April 1937, 12. The 'Second French Revolution' was a journalistic label used, among others, by the *New York Herald Tribune*. See, for example, George Slocombe, 'France's Political Changeover', *New York Herald Tribune*, 20 April 1946.

it significantly from its pre-war antecedent.[7] Moreover, the depiction of the struggle between the CSSF and the CMSID as a 'clash between generations' rings hollow given that the presidents of both institutions were born in the early 1880s.[8] This disagreement between the CSSF and the CMSID must not be seen as a clash between young and old or between 'Malthusianism' and modernisation,[9] but rather as a struggle between the two successor institutions of the Organisation Committee for Steel created in 1940. A closer look at the leadership of these two bodies is instructive. Jules Aubrun, President of the CSSF since its creation in 1944, served as President of CORSID under the Vichy regime from 1940 until 1944. The CPS, meanwhile, was directed by Jean Dupuis, one of the other four members of the wartime Committee. The Modernisation Commission for Steel, on the other hand, was presided over by Eugène Roy, who had served as Vice President of CORSID from 1940 to 1944, while the Vice President and Chairman of the Commission, Albert Bureau and Jean Latourte respectively, had both spent the war working for CORSID. The presidents of the CSSF and the CMSID were thus among the men of 'action, dynamism, and authority'[10] appointed by René Belin to Vichy's Organisation Committees to oversee French industry under Pétain. In 1940, the four members of the Organisation Committee for Steel – Aubrun, Roy, Dupuis, and Léon Daum – replaced the *vieux bonzes* of the pre-war *Comité des forges* and represented a new form of industrial organisation.[11] The conflict between Aubrun's CSSF and Roy's Modernisation Commission for Steel must thus be seen as a disagreement within this group of industrialists over who would supplant CORSID and determine the direction of the steel industry under the Fourth Republic, rather than a simple

[7]On the rupture between the *Comité des forges* and the Organisation Committee for Steel, see Chapter 3. The reforms of the Organisation Committees following the Liberation are discussed in Chapter 6.

[8]Jules Aubrun, President of the CSSF, was born in 1881 and Eugène Roy, President of the CMSID, in 1884.

[9]See, for example, Baumier, *La fin des maîtres de forges*, Gerbet, *La construction de l'Europe*, Kipping, *La France et les origines de l'Union européenne*, and Anthony Daley, *Steel, State, and Labor* (Pittsburgh: University of Pittsburgh Press, 1996). Malthusianism in this context refers to the supposed practice of industrialists of limiting production in order to drive up prices, also known as under-production (*freinage*).

[10]Communiqué du ministre secrétaire d'Etat à la production et au travail, *Le Temps*, 6 October 1940.

[11]See Chapter 3.

generational confrontation between young modernisers and the creaking hold-overs of the *Comité des forges*.

In the months following its creation, the Modernisation Commission for Steel busied itself drawing up an extensive plan to modernise the equipment of the steel industry across France. Drawing on the production figures initiated by CORSID and maintained until its dissolution in 1946,[12] the Modernisation Commission developed seemingly ambitious production targets for the steel industry. In March 1946, at a time when France was producing only 2.5 million tonnes of steel per annum, the Modernisation Commission pledged that this output would be quadrupled to 10 million tonnes within just three years. In the following two years, production would be raised further to 12 million tonnes per annum, with a subsequent target of 15 million tonnes per annum to be strived towards soon thereafter.[13]

In its first report, released in November 1946, the Modernisation Commission for Steel revealed that the bold plan to increase production fourfold in three years was entirely realistic, given that the maximum capacity of the French steel industry in 1946 was already 12 million tonnes per annum. In theory, all the CGP needed to do was to ensure the industry had sufficient raw materials and labour to meet the production targets, and the French steel industry could already begin producing at a markedly greater pace. The reality of the situation, however, was not so simple. The Modernisation Commission recognised that, 'in the current state of things, the possibility of receiving sufficient raw materials, particularly coal, and the availability of labour will not allow us to reach this maximum of 12 million tonnes'.[14] Indeed, the Commission's projections were predicated on the industry receiving significantly increased quantities of coking coal from the Ruhr, the *sine qua non* for a major revival of France's steel

[12]'Projet de résolution soumis au Conseil du Plan. Objectifs généraux pour l'activité française', 13 March 1946, AMF 2 3, FJME.

[13]'La première session du Conseil du Plan', 16–19 mars 1946, 80 AJ 1, AN. The figure of 12 million tonnes per annum was especially significant as this was the output for 1929, a total which the industry had been unable to match during the Depression, the war, or the early post-war years.

[14]Rapport de la Commission de Modernisation de la Sidérurgie', November 1946, 80 AJ 11, AN.

production.[15] Such an increase, however, was not forthcoming. In 1947, the lack of coal from Germany led to increased importations of coal from the United States – a costly import given the distance it had to travel. More paralysing still was the scarcity of dollars then available in France, a problem exacerbated by Britain's devaluation of sterling in 1947 that prompted the French government to reduce bread rations to levels not seen since 1940.[16] The shortage of coal was aggravated further still by industrial action in France over the course of 1947, culminating in the strikes of November which drastically cut France's domestic coal production in the final months of the year. Nevertheless, the CSSF acknowledged that their industry could indeed meet the high targets set by the CGP, at least in theory, but they preferred that a programme be developed with a target of 8 to 9 million tonnes per annum rather than 12 to 15, arguing that such a programme 'would be of more immediate and genuine interest'.[17] Nevertheless, they agreed to work within the framework established by the Modernisation Commission for Steel, and acknowledged that the CMSID's projections 'do not seem irreconcilable with our material or financial resources'.[18]

If there was agreement between the CGP and the CSSF on the broad lines of the modernisation of the industry's equipment, the opposite was true of the Modernisation Commission's plans for the concentration of the steel industry, involving the merging and even the closure of a number of factories. This was fiercely resisted by industrialists and the CSSF protested vocally on their behalf.[19] In September 1947 Alexis Aron

[15]Ibid.

[16]In June 1947, over 71 per cent of France's coal imports came from the United States. The CGP made it clear that 'this situation is untenable' and that it was imperative that 'coal from the Ruhr and the Saar replace imports from the United States as soon as possible'. 'Plan de modernisation et d'équipement. Objectifs généraux du Plan', July 1947, 80 AJ 1, AN. The bread ration was reduced to 200 grams per week after the devaluation of sterling in August 1947 as part of a policy of putting all non-essential imports on hold. See Michel Margairaz, 'La reconstruction matérielle: crise, infléchissement ou ajustement?' in Serge Berstein and Pierre Milza (eds), *L'Année 1947* (Paris: Presses de Sciences Po, 2000).

[17]'Rapport de la Commission de Modernisation. Position de la Sidérurgie', report written by Alexis Aron on behalf of the CSSF, 19 September 1947, 139 AQ 85, ANMT.

[18]Ibid.

[19]According to industrialist Henri Malcor, the CSSF's reaction to CMSID's plans to close factories was so violent that Roy retreated; a number of firms were accordingly saved from closure and CMSID watered down its plans to restructure the French steel industry. See Mioche, 'Les plans et la sidérurgie', op.cit., 135.

protested that 'we fear – and past experience justifies our worries – that [the Modernisation Commission's] abstract studies will lead to premature and serious decisions that we will regret in the very near future'.[20] Interestingly, a similar debate had occurred a few short years earlier when Hans Kehrl, one of the closest collaborators of Nazi Armaments Minister Albert Speer, pressured French industrialists to concentrate their productive capacity in a handful of large factories during the war to increase efficiency.[21] Just as Aubrun had resisted such pressure as President of CORSID, so too did he oppose similar projects from Monnet and the Modernisation Commission for Steel.[22] In both cases, the most obvious motivation for opposing concentration – keeping many factories open in order to further the interests of those factories' owners – was cloaked in rhetoric of concern for their workers and even the patriotic defence of France. CORSID and the CSSF consistently argued that industrial concentration would lead to huge numbers of workers losing their jobs, which threatened to destabilise communities. In the context of the Second World War, CORSID had resisted pressure to concentrate production in fewer, larger factories on the grounds that these would create attractive targets for Allied bombarment and that concentration would thus make steel production more vulnerable. Astonishingly, steel industrialists in the Loire made this same argument in 1951 to the Modernisation Commission for Steel on the grounds that 'in the eventuality of armed conflict […] dispersal [of factories] is still, after all, the best means of defence', adding that keeping each of their factories in operation was thus 'an imperative of National Defence'.[23] Although the nationality of prospective bombers had changed in the context of the Cold War, the line of

[20]'Ibid. Alexis Aron, a close friend of Aubrun, had succeeded the latter as head of OPSID (as CORSID was renamed in 1945) in March 1945. Following OPSID'S dissolution in 1946, Aron joined Aubrun at the CSSF.

[21]'Procès-verbal de la conférence tenue à Berlin le vendredi 17 septembre 1943 dans le bureau de Monsieur Speer', 17 September 1943, 72 AJ 1926, AN. These efforts are also recorded in Kehrl's memoirs, *Krisenmanager im Dritten Reich* (Düsseldorf: Droste Verlag, 1973), 310–318.

[22]See Chapter 4.

[23]'Rapport sur la modernisation de la sidérurgie de la Loire et les problèmes qu'elle se pose', October 1951, 80 AJ 11, AN. By this stage it was feared that Soviet rather than British bombers might choose to attack French steel mills, particularly against the backdrop of the Korean War, which had reached a stalemate a year earlier.

argument and industrialists' opposition to concentration remained strikingly consistent.

While the CSSF was understandably resistant to the CGP's prescription of industrial concentration, industrialists were far more amenable to the project of investing millions of francs in the modernisation of the industry's equipment.[24] The CSSF nevertheless criticised the approach of the CGP, accusing the Commissariat of basing important decisions – the closure of a factory, for instance – on subjective figures which were prone to change depending on a drop in the provision of coal for a given month, possible labour action, or a devaluation of the franc. These criticisms and the unresolved matter of industrial concentration would resurface in the following years.

It is important to note that the CSSF and the CMSID agreed on a number of important issues following the launch of the Monnet Plan. Not only were they both ultimately interested in increasing production, but their targets were compatible and not nearly as bold as they are often presented, given the existing capacity of the industry at the time. Similarly, both were fixated on maximising production while using as little coal as possible – a central preoccupation of CORSID since 1940 which marked the beginning of the shortage of raw materials that would characterise the decade. Also like CORSID, they both saw the simplest solution to their predicament being far greater deliveries of coking coal from Germany, a solution that seemed far more plausible in 1946–1947 than during the war. The question of who should benefit from this more efficient production, however, was contested between the two institutions. If the CSSF was enticed by the prospect of making products more cheaply while maintaining a similar selling price – and therefore seeing employers' profits increase significantly – those within the CGP saw cheaper and more efficient production as a means of allowing the French steel industry to lower its selling prices and thereby become more competitive on the international market. While rendering production more efficient continued to be a dominant goal, the intended result differed markedly between the two organisations. The distance between the CSSF and the CMSID was perhaps

[24]Between 1947 and 1951 roughly one-third of total investments in the French steel industry came from public funds, chiefly from the CGP and associated Marshall funds. See Henry Ehrmann, *Organized Business in France* (Princeton: Princeton University Press, 1957), 289.

greatest on the question of the rationalisation and concentration of the industry. While the CMSID saw the closing of the least efficient factories as a positive step towards making the nation's industry more competitive, the CSSF resisted all attempts to close the factories of any of its representatives. This disagreement would similarly reemerge as a bone of contention between the two institutions.

The Early Difficulties of the Monnet Plan

While CORSID's successors disagreed over the future direction of the organisation of the French steel industry, political developments in France were affecting the nation's industry as well. The first government of the Fourth Republic, led by Léon Blum, was in its final days by mid-January 1947. Amidst the uncertainty, the Minister for the National Economy, André Philip, sought to move the core of the CGP's functions to Philip's ministry, repeating his attempt to do so the previous year. Again, Monnet protected the supraministerial position of the CGP by threatening to resign.[25] Again, the French Premier sided with Monnet and Blum decreed the institutionalisation of the CGP on 16 January 1947 before resigning later that day. In addition to protecting the CGP's existence outside of any ministry, it also made the Monnet Plan a permanent fixture of France's economic architecture – the CGP had originally been approved as a provisional measure. While this marked another victory for Monnet, relations with the ministries worsened. By March 1947, former minister Albert Gazier described the state of 'relations between the CGP and the ministries' as 'not very good [. . .] indeed, downright bad'.[26] The obvious solution, he noted, was the 'constitution of a veritable Ministry for the National Economy' with control over the CGP, but lamented that due to 'the personalities involved this solution is not possible for now'.[27]

[25]Indeed, Monnet wrote to the British economist James Meade explaining that he 'could not leave Paris during the formation of the new government in January 1947 for fear that 'his plan' would be stolen by another ministry'. See Frances Lynch, 'Resolving the Paradox of the Monnet Plan: National and International Planning in French Reconstruction', *Economic History Review* 37:2, May 1984, 229–243, 241.

[26]Procès-verbal de la séance de la Commission des Affaires Economiques, Assemblée Nationale, séance du 4 mars 1947, C/15329, AN.

[27]Ibid.

One minister who found it particularly difficult to work with Monnet's CGP was Robert Lacoste. As Minister for Industrial Production from the Liberation until November 1945, Lacoste had tirelessly defended the Organisation Committees and was responsible for the unsuccessful attempt to bolster their popularity by rechristening them 'Professional Offices' after the war.[28] During his year out of Cabinet, he watched helplessly as his successor Marcel Paul abolished the Organisation Committees and Monnet erected the CGP with its Modernisation Commissions. By the time Lacoste reclaimed the portfolio for Industrial Production in December 1946, the Organisation Committees the ministry had inherited from the Vichy era had been abolished and largely absorbed by the CGP and by employers' associations.

One saving grace for Lacoste was that the dismantling of Vichy's New Industrial Order had not been entirely completed by the time he returned to the ministry. While the key Organisation Committees had been dissolved and their responsibilities passed to the analogous Modernisation Commissions and employers' associations such as the CSSF, much of Vichy's OCRPI, responsible for the allocation of raw materials to different industries, remained in place. On 9 April 1947, the government passed a law extending the deadline for dismantling OCRPI further.[29] Although the law of 26 April 1946 had called for the abolition of all Organisation Committees and OCRPI within six months, Lacoste was able to gain an extension the following April that pushed the deadline for the abolition of the remaining Committees to the autumn of 1947. That summer, Lacoste admitted that the system of Organisation Committees and OCRPI 'is not satisfactory and can be considered obsolete. Nevertheless, nobody can deny that the shortage [of raw materials] is long from being over and that necessity demands that we maintain the allocation of energy, of raw materials, and of numerous finished products'. As such, he advocated preserving the remnants of OCRPI under his ministry.[30] In his view, the Committees had been abolished prematurely given that the shortages of raw materials which they were so helpful in managing continued well into the late 1940s. He was also critical of the way in which the Organisation

[28]For the post-war reforms of the Organisation Committees under Lacoste, see Chapter 6.

[29]*Journal officiel*, 10 April 1947

[30]Procès-verbal de la séance de la Commission des Affaires Economiques, Assemblée Nationale, séance du 13 août 1947, C/15329, AN.

Committees had been abolished and decried the fact that 'employers' associations seized too much power' – power which he claimed 'should be restored to' his ministry.[31] In the event, many Sections of OCRPI still in operation when Lacoste became Minister for Industrial Production in December 1946 remained in place for years; the fate of the remaining Sections was still being debated in June 1949, more than three years after the National Assembly had voted to abolish them.[32]

Although a long-time supporter of economic planning, Lacoste criticised the Monnet Plan and particularly the figures produced by the CGP.[33] As early as March 1947, Lacoste declared that the production targets set out in the Plan were not going to be attained. While the Modernisation Commissions had set a target of 73.5 million tonnes of coal for 1947, for example, by mid-March they were projected to produce only 63 million. 'The allocation of coal for the steel industry should have been set well below what was set out in the plan', Lacoste noted, and the reduced amount of coal at that industry's disposal would necessarily mean that the production targets for the French steel industry would consequently be missed as well. Addressing a group of parliamentarians, Lacoste explained that

> our situation remains unchanged since the Liberation, namely that of a great power in a state of ruin that must make patient efforts to recover without surrendering to illusions… This entails the hard work of revising and adapting the targets of the Monnet Plan. This work must be undertaken seriously, just as all work by those who take account of reality. This revision is currently being done jointly by the Commissariat for the Plan, by the Ministry for the National Economy, and by my department.[34]

[31]Ibid. Fellow SFIO minister André Philip expressed similar regrets in December 1946, lamenting that 'the State no longer control[s] allocations, and this power [has been] passed to employers' associations'. Qtd in Margairaz, *L'Etat, les finances et l'économie*, 827.

[32]Procès-verbal de la séance de la Commission des Affaires Economiques, Assemblée Nationale, séance du 15 juin 1949, C/15330, AN.

[33]Lacoste advocated economic planning in France as early as 1933 in publications such as *Nouveaux cahiers*. See Pierre Brana and Joëlle Dusseau, *Robert Lacoste (1898–1989)* (Paris: L'Harmattan, 2010).

[34]Procès-verbal de la séance de la Commission de la Production industrielle, Assemblée Nationale, séance du 13 mars 1947, C/15402, AN.

On this issue Lacoste found himself on the side of the CSSF, which had urged the CMSID to adopt lower production targets that could be reliably attained. The disappointingly inaccurate figures also allowed Lacoste and Philip to exert more influence over the direction of the Plan.[35]

The First Plan was adopted by the French government in mid-January 1947; within two months it was clear that the production targets set by the CGP would be missed by a significant margin. This would prove to be a characteristic of the early stages of the First Plan: it chronically missed its targets and the much vaunted recovery of the French economy kept being postponed.[36] One reason was the economic situation in France at the time. With its widespread shortages of raw materials, and still in the midst of reconstruction, increasing overall production was inevitably difficult. While the Marshall Plan facilitated the modernisation of French industry, the overall economic situation remained fragile.[37] Moreover, Monnet had predicated the recovery of French industry on the nation's unfettered access to coking coal from the Ruhr.[38] While this made economic sense from France's perspective, it was fundamentally a political decision. Monnet had long advocated the separation of the Ruhr from Germany and the creation of an 'internationalised' territory

[35]Henry Rousso has argued that Lacoste's involvement in such 'revisions' of the Plan's targets 'clearly shows [his] desire to cooperate with the officials from the Plan'. Given his criticisms of Monnet's figures and that this amounted to an attempt by Lacoste and Philip to exert more control over the Plan, however, Lacoste's 'desire to cooperate' with the CGP must not be seen as an unconditional endorsement of Monnet or his methods. See Rousso, 'Le ministère de l'industrie dans le processus de planification: une adaptation difficile (1940–1969)' in Henry Rousso (ed.), *De Monnet à Massé*, op.cit., 27–40, 30.

[36]Ultimately, the target set by the Modernisation Commission for Steel for the period 1946–1952 was nearly met. While the objective had been to increase production by 15 per cent over this period, 14.29 per cent was attained, largely due to higher growth in the final two years. According to Michel Margairaz, in December 1947 Jean Monnet was obliged to 'propose a second Plan in order to save the first'. See Margairaz, *L'Etat, les finances et l'économie*, 993.

[37]According to Frances Lynch, the Marshall Plan 'saved' the Monnet Plan by providing it with the funds necessary to realise the modernisation of French industry. See Lynch, *France and the International Economy* (London: Routledge, 1997).

[38]'Note de Jean Monnet sur le premier rapport de remise en marche de l'économie française en 1945, sur les objectifs pour 1946 et sur le but final à atteindre', 11 November 1945, AMF 1 6, FJME.

that would supply coal to other states, France chief among them.[39] While the United States and Britain had considered similar plans during the war, most famously in the form of the Morgenthau Plan, by the late 1940s such schemes had little appeal for the Big Three who occupied the majority of post-war Germany.[40] With the emergence of the Cold War in Europe, the British and Americans quickly developed a preference for rebuilding a unified (West) German state with a strong economy as a bulwark against communism and an eventual ally against the Soviet Union. These developments were anathema to Monnet's initial plan of crippling Germany economically so that France's industry could thrive. This situation prompted Monnet to develop a new plan to ensure unfettered access to German coal for French industry: the Schuman Plan.[41]

The Schuman Declaration: A New Battle Between the CGP and the CSSF

On 9 May 1950, French Foreign Minister Robert Schuman read a statement drafted by Jean Monnet which would come to define both their careers. Framing the project as a means of ensuring that 'war

[39]This idea was advanced by Monnet to de Gaulle as early as October 1943; see 'Conversation du dimanche 17 octobre 1943', 17 October 1943, AME 33 1 18, FJME. For France's attempts to pursue such policies after the war, see William Hitchcock, *France Restored: Cold War Diplomacy and the Quest for Leadership in Europe, 1944–1954* (Chapel Hill: University of North Carolina Press, 1998); Alan Milward, *The Reconstruction of Western Europe, 1945–1951* (London: Routledge, 1984); and Raymond Poidevin, 'Frankreich und die Ruhrfrage 1945–1951', *Historische Zeitschrift*, 228:2, April 1979, 101–119.

[40]At the Québec Conference of September 1944, Roosevelt and Churchill agreed upon the Morganthau Plan for the 'pastoralisation' of Germany, involving the dismantling of the majority of post-war Germany's heavy industry and of internationalising (or annexing to Germany's neighbours) the most industrialised regions of Germany, including the Ruhr. Churchill criticised the plan as 'unnatural, unchristian, and unnecessary', but seems to have endorsed it in exchange for the post-war continuation of Lend-Lease aid. The plan was never fully implemented by the Allies, and from 1946 the United States gradually overturned the policy. See Mark A. Stoler, *Allies in War: Britain and America against the Axis Powers, 1940–1945* (London: Hodder, 2005), 170 and Hans-Peter Schwarz, 'The Division of Germany, 1945–1949' in Melvyn P. Leffler and Odd Arne Westad (eds), *The Cambridge History of the Cold War* (Cambridge: Cambridge University Press, 2010).

[41]Alan Milward has famously argued that 'the Schuman Plan was invented to safeguard the Monnet Plan'. See Milward, *The Reconstruction of Western Europe*, 395.

between France and Germany becomes not only unthinkable but materially impossible', Schuman proposed the pooling of the two countries' coal and steel industries and the creation of a supranational body to oversee the industries.[42] The dramatic declaration read by Schuman of a scheme to pool French and German industries had been kept as secret as possible, catching the public – in France and abroad – by surprise.

Internationally, the British were among the most upset – a reaction accurately predicted by Monnet beforehand.[43] The announcement came on the eve of the London Conference where American, British, and French foreign ministers were meant to discuss the existing occupation system for Germany, including issues such as the limitations then in place on German industry.[44] The Schuman Declaration presented the French Foreign Minister's opposite numbers in London and Washington with a *fait accompli*; while this was welcomed by the Americans, who had long encouraged some form of European cooperation, it infuriated the British Labour government and particularly the Foreign Secretary, Ernest Bevin.[45] Meeting with Schuman and US Secretary of State Dean Acheson on 11 March in the context of the now-disrupted London Conference, Bevin did not mask his anger at Schuman. Bevin protested, telling Schuman and Acheson that 'all three governments were administering Germany and [Bevin] thought that

[42]Déclaration de Robert Schuman, 9 May 1950

[43]As early as 1943 Jean Monnet had predicted that the British reaction to a French initative for European integration would 'probably be hostile', although he added that 'Great Britain might not be able to avoid joining the union itself'. See 'Quelques éléments pour l'élaboration d'une thèse française de la reconstruction économique', 3 August 1943, AME 33 2, FJME.

[44]On the international political context of the Schuman Declaration, and for the Foreign Minister's motivations for announcing the plan when he did, see William Hitchcock, 'France, the Western Alliance, and the Origins of the Schuman Plan, 1948–1950', *Diplomatic History*, 21:4, 1997, 603–630.

[45]On American support for European integration, the most thorough account is Gérard Bossuat, *La France, l'aide américaine et la construction européenne, 1944–1954* (Paris: Comité pour l'Histoire Economique et Financière de la France, 1997). See also Gillingham, *Coal, Steel and the Rebirth of Europe, 1945–1955*. Bevin, whose health was failing, had been in hospital for nearly a month and had only learned of the initative after it had been pronounced publicly. Note de Guillaume à van Zeeland, 16 June 1950, 12 284, MAEB.

the principle of consultation had been established' In a thinly veiled threat, 'he wondered whether this was intended to set a new precedent, and what deductions he should draw'.[46] Acheson, keen to support the French initative, defended Schuman, pointing out that 'there were also occasions, such as the devaluation of sterling [in 1947], when other governments had caused similar embarrassment'.[47] Raising this disconcerting parallel quieted Bevin somewhat, although the British government led by Clement Attlee would soon decide not to take part in Schuman's initiative.[48]

Bevin was hardly alone in being caught off-guard by Schuman's intervention. A number of Schuman's own colleagues in Cabinet were blindsided by the announcement, in some cases entrenching pre-existing grudges against the Foreign Minister. Neither the Minister for Finance and Economic Affairs, Maurice Petsche, nor the Secretary of State for Economic Affairs, Robert Buron, had been fully briefed let alone consulted before Schuman's public announcement.[49] Petsche complained that 'the thought of a High Authority not under control by Ministers was *franchement inconcevable*',[50] while President of the National Assembly Edouard Herriot was deeply critical of the lack of consultation between Monnet and other governments, particularly in London, grumbling 'this is not how we

[46]'Record of conversation between Mr Bevin, Mr Acheson and M Schuman, 11 May 1950', 11 May 1950, PREM 8 1428, TNA.

[47]Ibid. As noted above, the devaluation of sterling in August 1947 severely disrupted France's fragile economy and posed further obstacles for the Monnet Plan. See also Margairaz, 'La réconstruction matérielle'.

[48]On the British response to the Schuman Declaration and the negotiations leading to the creation of the ECSC, see Edmund Dell, *The Schuman Plan and the British Abdication of Leadership in Europe* (Oxford: Oxford University Press, 1995) and Christopher Lord, *Absent at the Creation: Britain and the Formation of the European Community, 1950–1952* (Dartmouth: Aldershot, 1996). Sir Edwin Plowden, a high-level civil servant, later recalled that 'it took all Acheson's diplomatic skills to stop Bevin from immediately issuing a statement condemning Schuman's announcement'. See Plowden, *An Industrialist in the Treasury: The Postwar Years* (London: André Deutsch, 1989), 86.

[49]Note du Comte de Meeus d'Argenteuil à van Zeeland, 23 May 1950, 12 284, MAEB. Petsche, a member of the *Républicains d'action paysanne et sociale*, had a long-standing rivalry with Schuman, while Buron belonged to Schuman's party, the MRP.

[50]'Discussion between Sir E. Hall-Patch and M. Putsch [sic] on the Schuman Plan', 19 June 1950, FO 371 85853, TNA. The last two words appear in French in the original British document.

treat our friends'.[51] Particularly interesting is the reaction of Georges Bidault. As Prime Minister,[52] he had been approached by Monnet with the plan to pool French and German coal and steel industries in late April 1950.[53] Bidault's indifference to the plan prompted Monnet to try the next most influential minister in government, Robert Schuman, who endorsed the plan enthusiastically and announced it to the world on 9 May. Following the declaration, Bidault fumed that 'the idea had been launched by M Schuman without previous adequate consultation with [Bidault] and the other French ministries'.[54] Given the enthusiastic support of the German and American governments for the plan, however, there was little Bidault could do but go along with the initative he had passed over days earlier.

Beyond the French Cabinet, the CSSF was hardly pleased with Monnet's plan. While a number of foreign governments were sent a draft of the Schuman Declaration mere hours before it was announced,[55] even this slight courtesy was not extended to the CSSF. In a number of ways, this failure to consult or even inform the CSSF was not out of character for Monnet. Monnet's strategy had been to develop a bold plan in secret, secure a powerful backer, and then spring it on an unsuspecting public – an approach hardly conducive to a broad consultation with all stakeholders beforehand. Moreover, vital decisions pertaining to the steel industry had routinely been taken by French ministers without informing the relevant employers' association (or the Organisation Committee) since 1940: as we have seen, the dissolution of the *Comité des forges*, the creation of CORSID, the maintenance and reform of the Committees after the war, their ultimate abolition, and indeed the creation of the CGP and the Monnet Plan were all taken without informing

[51]Note de Guillaume à van Zeeland, 16 June 1950, 12 284, MAEB.

[52]*Président du Conseil* was the title of the Head of Government in the Fourth Republic; this is generally translated as 'Prime Minister'.

[53]Lettre de Jean Monnet à Georges Bidault, 28 April 1950, AMG 1, FJME. According to Monnet's memoirs, the reason Bidault did not respond favourably to the proposal was because he hadn't bothered to read it. See Monnet, *Mémoires* (Paris: Fayard, 1976) and Georges-Henri Soutou, 'Georges Bidault et la construction européenne 1944–1954', *Revue d'histoire diplomatique* 3:4, 1991.

[54]Telegram from Canadian Ambassador in Paris (Vanier) for the Secretary of State for External Affairs, 2 June 1950, RG 25 6529 10094–40, LAC.

[55]See, for example, 'Télégramme de Guillaume à van Zeeland', 9 May 1950, 12 284, MAEB.

industrialists beforehand. The fact that the CSSF was similarly left in the dark in 1950 is by no means exceptional; rather, it reminds us – beyond Monnet's proclivity for secretive strategy – of the lack of political influence held by the employers' association for steel since the end of the Third Republic.[56] Moreover, given the surprising and controversial nature of the Schuman Plan, Monnet opted to announce the key aspects of the scheme publicly precisely to thwart individual groups – whether the CSSF or the British government – from insisting on changes to the plan in its early stages.[57]

Caught by surprise and not entirely sure what to make of the audacious if still woolly proposal, the CSSF's initial response was cautious. In June 1950, Aubrun set out the position of the CSSF:

> The programme which has been mapped out, and of which we only know the general outline at this stage, seems to respond in principle to valid concerns, but the specifics of their implementation will need to be studied closely. The day that the government calls on us, we will not hesitate to bring to this initiative all the fruits of the experience we have acquired.[58]

The tactfully worded tone of support voiced for the Schuman Plan was tempered with Aubrun's allusion to the fact that the CSSF had not been consulted; he also made clear that the CSSF expected to be called upon to take part in shaping the final arrangement. Aubrun reiterated this position in a letter to Schuman and Monnet in July, stating that 'in response to the intentions expressed in the declaration of 9 May, the French steel industry could only... respond favourably'.[59] This expectation that the CSSF would be closely involved in the negotiations, however, proved to be misplaced.

[56]Some historians have suggested that this political influence enjoyed by the *Comité des forges* under the Third Republic continued until 1950–1952, with the creation of the ECSC being a turning point in this respect. This study, however, contends that such influence ended in 1940. For the case of the continuation of the *Comité des forges*, see Baumier, *La fin des maîtres de forges* and Gerbet, *La construction de l'Europe*.

[57]Monnet, *Mémoires*.

[58]Note de Guillaume à van Zeeland, 10 June 1950, 12 284, MAEB.

[59]Lettre d'Aubrun à Schuman (with a copy also sent to Monnet), 12 July 1950, 81 AJ 135, AN.

Negotiating Europe

On 20 June 1950, the first meeting of the delegations of the 'Six' took place in Paris. Two weeks earlier, the British government had announced that it would not take part in the negotiations but would be kept informed of their progress by the French.[60] Monnet urged the members to 'preserve the momentum created by the French proposal' by ensuring that 'the negotiations take place quickly and that they lead immediately to concrete results', proposing that 'the treaty negotiations be completed by the end of July and that the High Authority be set up as soon as the treaty has been ratified'.[61]

The initial structure of the High Authority proposed by Monnet, and which he hoped would be approved hastily by the delegations of the other five countries, drew heavily on the model that had been put in place at the CGP. Indeed, Robert Marjolin, Monnet's deputy at the CGP and later a Vice President of the European Commission, claimed that 'the functional model of the Monnet Plan was transposed to the European level' with the creation of the ECSC.[62] As the executive, the High Authority would be placed above national governments just as the executive of the CGP had been placed above the ministries. Crucially, Monnet also proposed the creation of two Modernisation Commissions – for coal and steel, respectively – based on those at the heart of the CGP. These Commissions would 'undertake the necessary studies for the entirety of the industries for which the High Authority is responsible [and] liaise with the existing bodies for technical research in the participating countries'.[63] In this proposal we see the extent to which the CGP acted as a model in the early stages of the negotiations, and the importance attributed by Monnet attributed to the Modernisation Commissions, themselves the successors to Vichy's Organisation Committees, in the smooth functioning of the CGP. He further posited the creation of 'consultative committees, made up of professionals and representatives from workers' organisations', reflecting the tripartite structure of the Modernisation Commissions. Monnet also proposed the addition of a 'committee of 50 members elected annually by

[60]'Communiqué released by French government', 3 June 1950, FO 371 85846, TNA.

[61]'Note pour le comité interministériel', 12 June 1950, AMG 2 2, FJME.

[62]Robert Marjolin, *Le travail d'une vie. Mémoires 1911–1986* (Paris: Robert Laffont, 1986).

[63]Note sur les missions de la Haute Autorité, 7 June 1950, 81 AJ 152, AN.

the parliaments of each country and chosen from among them', anticipating an eventual European assembly.[64]

In the event, the negotiations took much longer than Monnet had hoped. While Schuman was able to declare on 12 July that 'no insurmountable obstacles remain and we must therefore finish' the negotiations to establish the ECSC quickly, the talks dragged well beyond the late July deadline initially set by Monnet, with the text of the treaty only being agreed upon in April 1951. Over the course of the negotiations, the shape of what would become the ECSC shifted significantly from Monnet's original sketch. The leader of the Dutch delegation, Dirk Spierenburg, proposed the addition of the Council of Ministers made up of representatives of the national governments, fearing 'it would be dangerous to hand over exorbitant powers to a council of technicians'.[65] Max Suetens, the lead Belgian delegate, objected to the idea of sending national parliamentarians to be members of the European Assembly, on the grounds that 'parliament only holds power as a whole and parliamentarians in isolation hold no power'.[66] Given that authority could best be exercised by national ministers, Suetens backed the Dutch call for an intergovernmental Council while calling for reforms to the assembly.[67] The proposed Modernisation Commissions, meanwhile, evolved into Directorates for Coal and Steel, respectively. While their functions remained similar to those of the Modernisation Commissions, they were comprised chiefly of technicians and thus departed from the tripartite structure of the Modernisation Commissions and their predecessors. As for the Consultative Committee, it

[64]'Note pour le comité interministériel', 12 June 1950, AMG 2 2, FJME.

[65]Compte-rendu de la séance restreinte, 3 July 1950, AMG 3 3. This was resisted by the German delegation, led by Walter Hallstein, which argued that an intergovernmental Council would undermine the supranational character of the Schuman Plan.

[66]Compte-rendu de la séance du lundi 3 juillet 1950, 3 July 1950, 12 284, MAEB. The term 'democratic deficit' was coined in the 1970s to reflect the fact that the members of the European Assembly were not directly elected; see David Marquand, *Parliament for Europe* (London: Jonathan Cape, 1979).

[67]A thorough account of these wide-ranging negotiations is beyond the scope of this study. The best description of the negotiations is provided by Dirk Spierenburg and Raymond Poidevin, *Histoire de la Haute Autorité de la Communauté européenne du Charbon et de l'Acier. Une expérience supranationale* (Bruxelles: Bruylant, 1993). See also Klaus Schwabe (ed.), *Die Anfänge des Schuman-Plans* and Berthold Rittberger, 'Which Institutions for Post-war Europe? Explaining the Institutional Design of Europe's First Community', *Journal of European Public Policy* 8:5, 2001, 673–708.

was agreed that its powers should be constrained. Early drafts had given industrialists the power to appeal any decision made by the High Authority,[68] but by the end of June 1950 this right was restricted to national governments only, limiting industrialists to a strictly consultative role within the Consulative Committee.[69] The idea of creating a European Court of Justice was also introduced and made its way into the treaty.[70] Through months of negotiations among the Six, the shape of the emerging ECSC differed importantly from the blueprint first advanced by Monnet.

While negotiations among the six delegations continued apace, the CSSF found itself excluded from virtually every meeting. From the beginning of August, Aubrun wrote to Monnet requesting that a representative of the CSSF, namely Alexis Aron, be present at preparatory meetings to discuss the common market, given that the questions bound to be discussed 'demand a deep knowledge of a great number of technical details, which obviously only the Profession could possess'.[71] Monnet responded negatively to Aubrun's request, on the grounds that the meetings being held would be 'limited to one representative per delegation' and that Aron's presence would 'remove the intended spirit from these restricted meetings'. Monnet reassured Aubrun that 'Aron will continue to be invited to all meetings which experts from other delegations will attend'.[72] An examination of the records of the meetings, however, shows that Monnet's explanation was far from accurate. While a number of restricted meetings – at which only the head of each delegation was present – did indeed take place,[73] there was a busy schedule of larger meetings involving the delegations of each country, including representatives from the steel

[68]'Recours', 7 June 1950, 81 AJ 152, AN. This note, prepared by Pierre Uri, would have allowed industrialists to appeal any decision that was supported by less than two-thirds of the members of the High Authority.

[69]'Résumé du projet de traité', 19 June 1950, 81 AJ 152, AN. According to this note, a member state could call on the High Authority to put together an ad hoc Court of Appeal with five members to appeal a particular decision taken by the High Authority.

[70]See Anne Boerger, 'La Cour de Justice dans les négociations du Traité de Paris instituant la CECA', *Journal of European Integration History*, 18:2, 2008, 7–33.

[71]Lettre d'Aubrun à Monnet, 5 August 1950, AMG 18 4, FJME.

[72]Lettre de Monnet à Aubrun, 7 August 1950, AMG 18 4, FJME.

[73]These meetings were held throughout the summer and it was at these meetings that many of the broader important questions, such as the creation of an intergovernmental Council, were discussed.

and coal industries of the other five countries. Indeed, France was exceptional in being the only country whose delegation did not include a representative from its coal or steel industries, preferring instead to rely on the expertise of members of the CGP and relevant ministries.[74] Monnet was in fact critical of the other countries having 'more delegates than I would have wanted' and being 'overloaded with experts', unlike the French delegation he had assembled.[75] The Working Group on Production and Prices, for instance, chaired by Etienne Hirsch, first met on 4 July and included representatives from the coal and steel industries from five countries, France being the only country to exclude its own industrialists.[76] Only after repeated requests from Aubrun was a representative from the CSSF finally able to attend, but by this point the majority of the work had been concluded and the Working Group was dissolved a fortnight later.[77] It was clear that Monnet and Schuman preferred to keep the French delegation firmly in the hands of the CGP and the relevant ministries even at the risk of further upsetting Aubrun and his colleagues.

If Aubrun's initial position had been cautious and offered conditional support for the Schuman Plan, provided the CSSF would have the opportunity to examine and influence the details of the final arrangement, the realities of the negotiations process prompted Aubrun to adopt a much harder line. By September, Aubrun castigated Monnet for breaking his word and continuing to exclude representatives from the CSSF: 'the foreign delegations were given, by the French delegation, proposals which had not been preceded by a consultation with French experts, nor even an unofficial

[74]See 'Liste des délégations', June 1950, AMG 2 2, FJME. Despite the exclusion of representatives from employers' associations, one civil servant in the French delegation did have experience in industry: Jacques Desrousseaux, the Director for Mines and Steel in the Ministry for Industry and Commerce. In this capacity, however, he represented his ministry and by extension the State, just as the ministry's representative who sat in on CORSID's meetings represented the State rather than industrialists. Moreover, while Desrousseaux had been Director of Mines in French Indochina from 1938 until 1947 and was an expert in the coal industry, he never worked in the steel industry. He therefore did not possess the 'deep knowledge of a great number of technical details' for the steel industry which Aubrun or Aron clearly did, nor did he advocate the CSSF's position during the negotiations.

[75]Monnet, *Mémoires* (Paris: Fayard, 1976), 465.

[76]Compte-rendu de la réunion du Groupe du Travail 'Production-Prix', 4 July 1950, 12 284, MAEB.

[77]Lettre d'Aubrun à Pleven, 13 November 1950, 81 AJ 135, AN.

exchange of views between experts and members of various delegations'.[78] Monnet ignored the letter and let a month pass before writing to Aubrun – and even then did not address Aubrun's criticisms directly.[79] Setting out the CSSF's position that October, Aubrun urged that 'the elimination of customs barriers must not be realised – this is our conclusion and our demand – until a rational organisation of production, overseen by the High Authority, *has been set up and duly proven itself*'.[80] He pleaded that the High Authority be established in the first instance and, 'after a year or two, we can examine the option of proceeding – with cool heads – with the gradual loosening of customs barriers'.[81] While his letter was not explicitly hostile to the content of the plan, Aubrun clearly sought to slow things down considerably and hoped to reopen discussion on a number of points. His request was flatly ignored by Monnet.

In November, an exasperated Aubrun wrote directly to the Prime Minister, René Pleven,[82] describing the CSSF's 'intolerable, humiliating' situation. He set out how the CSSF had been excluded from crucial meetings that their counterparts from the other five delegations were able to attend, and how Monnet refused to share documents such as early drafts of the treaty with the CSSF, even while 'they were in the hands of all the foreign experts' from the other delegations. 'We continue to be systematically excluded' from the negotiations, Aubrun bewailed, '*the object of which is to decide the fate of our firms*'. Aubrun admitted that 'if we are occasionally called in and consulted, this is done only intermittently and in such a summary and incidental way that we can legitimately believe that they only wanted to avoid being blamed for ignoring us entirely'.[83] While

[78]Lettre d'Aubrun à Monnet, 6 September 1950, AMG 18 4, FJME.

[79]Lettre de Monnet à Aubrun, 2 October 1950, AMG 18 4, FJME.

[80]Note de la CSSF: Bilan du plan Schuman pour l'industrie, 12 octobre 1950, AMG 18 2, FJME. Text underlined in the original.

[81]Ibid.

[82]René Pleven succeeded Bidault as Prime Minister in July 1950. Pleven had been Monnet's deputy in the Franco-British Coordination Committee in 1940 and joined the Free French that year, later holding the portfolios for foreign affairs and finance in the CFLN. In October 1950 he gave his name to the ill-fated Pleven Plan, proposing a European Army and the European Defence Community.

[83]Lettre d'Aubrun à Pleven, 13 November 1950, 81 AJ 135, AN. A copy was also sent to Monnet. Text underlined in the original.

Monnet protested that Aubrun's depiction of the negotiations 'strangely distorts the facts', his insistence that the CSSF had been invited to all the meetings that their counterparts from the other five countries had attended is not supported by the documents, which instead reveal that the French delegation was routinely the only one that did not include a representative from its steel industry.[84]

It is understandable why Monnet chose to minimise the CSSF's influence as much as possible. Given the CGP's assessment of the CSSF, it is clear that Monnet and Aubrun represented two strikingly different conceptions of industrial organisation. Furthermore, as Monnet pointed out to Aubrun, the French steel industry had received a greater share of CGP funds than any other industry, and its successful modernisation was largely thanks to the Monnet Plan.[85] In this context, it is understandable why Monnet felt no obligation to make concessions to the CSSF. Most importantly, Monnet was in the midst of an ambitious and unprecedented task: negotiating the pooling of two vital industries of six countries and 'realising the first concrete foundations of a European Federation'.[86] Monnet later admitted that 'the truth is we were not ready to negotiate such a vast undertaking for the common good with vested interests' like the CSSF.[87] Negotiating an agreement among the six delegations was a formidable enough challenge, and Monnet succeeded admirably. This was made easier by having the French delegation speak with one voice, which meant limiting the extent to which the CSSF or other 'vested interests' could influence the proceedings with their own particular demands. This greater objective was better served by Monnet relying on the services of the CGP like the Modernisation Commission for Steel rather than the CSSF.[88] As Robert

[84]Lettre de Monnet à Aubrun, 17 November 1950, 81 AJ 135, AN.

[85]Lettre de Monnet à Aubrun, 17 November 1950, AMG 18 4, FJME. Aubrun objected that his 'intention is not... as you seem to imply, to misunderstand the services rendered by the Monnet Plan to the French steel industry'. Lettre d'Aubrun à Monnet, 22 November 1950, AMG 18 4, FJME.

[86]This phrase is from Monnet's 'Note pour le comité interministériel', 12 June 1950, AMG 2 2, FJME.

[87]Monnet, *Mémoires*, 460.

[88]Monnet admitted that 'the entirety of the necessary technical studies' were drawn up by the CGP rather than the CSSF, adding that this done 'for the benefit of the [steel] industry'. Lettre de Monnet à Aubrun, 17 November 1950, 81 AJ 135, AN.

Schuman would later tell Aubrun in response to the latter's complaints of the CSSF's exclusion, 'this is the cost of the unity of Europe'.[89]

Competing for Credibility

As the CSSF found itself on the margins of the negotiations, it attempted to influence the views of French decision-makers. The CGP countered this strategy with its own efforts to discredit the CSSF's positions. The inevitable result was a steady worsening of an already poor relationship between the two organisations. From the autumn of 1950, the CSSF and the CGP released a series of studies predicting the effects of the Schuman Plan on the French steel industry. The CSSF's were invariably grim: a common market would open France's vast internal markets to Belgian and Luxembourgish industry, 'a considerable advantage [to those countries] to the detriment of France alone'. Meanwhile, with the removal of interallied restrictions on the German economy and 'guaranteed access to Italy of the primary materials which it is so sorely lacking', the CSSF argued, 'one can only conclude that *in the final assessment, regarding the relative cost price and the opening of the common market, France appears as the only losing party*'.[90] From the CSSF's perspective, the Schuman Plan would be a disaster for French industry.[91]

In a report prepared only four days earlier, the CGP, drawing upon studies done by the Modernisation Commission for Steel, presented a far more optimistic assessment of the effects of the Schuman Plan on the French steel industry. It concluded that 'we see numerous advantages that France can draw, in the steel sector, from the realisation of the Schuman Plan', adding that 'it is up to the efforts of French producers to ensure that

[89]Lettre de Schuman à Aubrun, 19 June 1951, 81 AJ 135, AN.

[90]'Note sur le plan Schuman', 13 December 1950, AMG 18 2, FJME. Text underlined in the original.

[91]Industrialists from other countries expressed similar apprehensions soon after the Schuman Declaration, fearing that their national industry would lose out while others thrived in the common market. Their reservations were overcome in part through the involvement of industrialists in the negotiations of the Treaty of Paris. On the reservations of Luxembourg's industrialists, see 'Note du Vicomte Berryer, Ministre de Belgique à Luxembourg, à van Zeeland. Objet: Plan Schumann [*sic*]', 1 June 1950, 12 284, MAEB; for the position of Belgian industrialists, see 'Note du Colonel Mampuys à Monsieur le Ministre de la Défense Nationale. Objet: Les répercussions de la proposition Schuman de pool franco-allemand de l'industrie sidérurgique', 24 May 1950, 12 284, MAEB.

this competition [with the other members of the ECSC] will, in the long term, ensure a favourable expansion of our industry in an enlarged market'.[92] In other words, the Schuman Plan would present positive opportunities for the French steel industry, provided it could be competitive enough to seize them. If French industrialists could not and the Schuman Plan instead allowed the French market to be overrun by their neighbours' industry, the CGP suggested, this would be their own fault. By December 1950, the terms of the debate between the CGP and the CSSF had been clearly drawn.

In an apparent attempt to reconcile such contradictory reports, the CGP created a Committee, led by Etienne Hirsch and Paul Gardent, to 'complete the studies done so far on the repercussions of the Schuman Plan on the situation of the French steel industry in relation to those of other European countries'.[93] The first session saw three representatives from the CSSF – Jules Aubrun, Alexis Aron, and Louis Charvet[94] – appear before the Committee. The meeting was a disaster. Aubrun began by 'reiterat[ing] that the Schuman Plan offers no advantage to the French steel industry'. When Hirsch pressed the three men to divulge 'which factories would ultimately be unable to survive competition' from the other members of the ECSC, Aron refused to share any information, saying that 'there will be a bitter fight, but ultimately every single factory will survive and none shall be closed', demanding to know 'why [Hirsch and Gardent, and by extension the French delegation in favour of the Schuman Plan] want to close factories'. Hirsch tried to reassure the CSSF representatives that 'the High Authority will have neither the power nor the purpose to close factories', suggesting there had been a misunderstanding. Aron replied that 'the preoccupation of the Plan seems to be to open borders and close factories'; Aubrun added that those putting together the treaty 'seem to be inspired by a hatred of industry and a

[92]'Note relative aux effets du Plan Schuman sur les industries de l'Acier en France', 9 December 1950, AMG 18 2, FJME.

[93]Procès-verbal de la réunion tenue le 2 janvier 1951, Comité Hirsch-Gardent, 2 January 1951, AMG 18 3, FJME. A copy is also preserved in 81 AJ 135, AN. Etienne Hirsch was a collaborator of Monnet's in the CGP and succeeded him as Commissioner for the Plan in 1952. Paul Gardent was a member of Jean-Marie Louvel's cabinet in the Ministry for Industry and Commerce.

[94]Louis Charvet was Deputy Director General of Air France from 1934 until 1945, after which he became Delegate General of the CSSF.

desire to reduce its power'. Hirsch and Gardent, seemingly flabbergasted by the CSSF's responses, tried in vain to get additional information regarding the least efficient steel firms. Aubrun maintained his refusal, absurdly adding that 'it is impossible for me to respond to any of these questions unless they are first submitted in writing'. He then dismissed the Committee's work as 'entirely secondary', adding that he 'would like to know where the important issues are discussed', before concluding that he had 'the impression that there is no proper French delegation where the French position can be defended'.[95] It was clear that relations between Monnet and his collaborators, on the one hand, and the CSSF, on the other hand, were a shambles.

Interestingly, in the final report of the Committee, Hirsch and Gardent chose to ignore the CSSF's interventions altogether. The report, submitted to Monnet in February, painted a surprisingly rosy picture of the French steel industry and the support of its industrialists for the Schuman Plan.[96] The report included a list of all the industrialists who had appeared before the Committee, described as 'representatives from ten groups or steel firms whose combined capacity represents roughly 80% of total French steel production'. Based on the evidence provided by such an important group of industrialists, the Committee reached a clear conclusion: 'the French steel industry is well placed...to face the competition from the steel industries of neighbouring countries in the context of the Schuman Plan'.[97] By associating the CSSF with the Committee's work and then presenting conclusions utterly at odds with those presented by Aubrun and Aron, the CGP further marginalised Aubrun and his attempts to influence ministers. Perversely, by appearing before the Committee, Aubrun and Aron had unwittingly lent their names to a document advancing a position very much the opposite of the one they held.

The CSSF's concerns that the High Authority would seek to close the least efficient firms were not without foundation. In many respects this was a continuation of the drive towards concentration pursued by the

[95]Ibid.

[96]'Rapport sur les travaux du comité chargé d'examiner les effets du plan Schuman sur la sidérurgie française', 21 February 1951, AMG 18 3, FJME.

[97]Note à l'attention de Monsieur le Ministre des affaires étrangères (unsigned letter from the CGP), 11 April 1951, 81 AJ 135, AN.

CGP and staunchly opposed by the CSSF under the Monnet Plan. In the first draft of what would become the Schuman Declaration, Monnet explictly foresaw the closing of the least efficient factories. 'The rationalisation of production and the harmonisation of economic policies' of the member states, he wrote, 'will progressively lead to the disappearance of firms that are far too disadvantaged in terms of productivity'. To address the inevitable weeding out of the weakest factories, Monnet suggested the creation of a fund to compensate the firms that would be forced to close.[98] This candid assessment, likely deemed too controversial, was deleted from the final version of the declaration. Monnet later publicly condemned 'cartels' – a term he habitually used to describe the CSSF. In a note prepared for the French press the same day as the Schuman Declaration, Monnet attacked cartels for 'being concerned only with a single industry and with profits [. . .] to the detriment of the common good'. He explicitly contrasted the CSSF's position with that of the CGP and the emerging ECSC:

> The objective of a cartel is to maintain high and stable profits, and the conservation of the status quo. From there, fixing prices so as to ensure the survival of marginal companies and to allow better placed firms to make a differential income. The objective of the proposed organisation [under the Schuman Plan] is to increase production and productivity through the improvement of techniques, opening up larger markets, and rationalising production.[99]

With such statements published in the French press at the time when Monnet was consciously excluding the CSSF from the treaty

[98]Premier projet (de la proposition française), corrigé par J[ean] M[onnet], undated but written in late April 1950, AMG 1 2, FJME. Monnet also suggested to the other delegations that their national steel industries should be rationalised, with guidance from the High Authority, by cutting the least efficient firms – a proposal that caused alarm amongst the Italian steel industrialists, among others. See Ruggero Ranieri, 'The Italian Steel Industry and the Schuman Plan Negotiations' in Schwabe, *Die Anfänge des Schuman-Plans* (Brussels: Bruylant, 1988).

[99]Note destinée à la presse, 9 May 1950, AMG 1 3, FJME. The purpose of this note was largely to reassure the public that the eventual ECSC would not be a cartel itself, but the text is also clearly critical of the CSSF. There was a general preference among French and German industrialists for simply recreating a steel cartel as had existed in the interwar period, as this would allow the industry to decide upon rules rather than politicians; see Françoise Berger, *La France, l'Allemagne et l'acier (1932–1952)* (Thèse de doctoral, Université de Paris I, 2000), 924–925.

negotiations, it is easy to understand how Aubrun's opposition became ever firmer.[100]

Further efforts were made by Monnet and his collaborators to discredit the increasingly hostile CSSF. At the end of January 1951, Monnet circulated a document that attacked the CSSF for holding 'exorbitant powers held by no other professional organisations'. The document concluded that the CSSF was 'a rigid system, meant to last for the period of shortages following the war, which has transformed itself into a cartel, without the official approval of the State'. It added that since the CPS guaranteed each factory its percentage of the total production of the steel industry, 'factories no longer have the slightest reason to be active or innovative, nor to be concerned with the quality of their products'.[101] The CSSF's opposition to the Schuman Plan was thus presented as a self-interested attempt to defend the CSSF's unjustifiable fiefdom. The CSSF was also accused of deliberately under-producing in 1950 to maximise profits, a charge angrily denied by Aubrun.[102]

More damaging still, the CGP launched its own studies to challenge the figures provided by the CSSF that supported the latter's argument that the Schuman Plan would be singularly disadvantageous to the French steel industry. In addition to the Modernisation Commission for Steel, which was well placed to analyse the figures provided by the CSSF, Monnet consulted the Belgian economist Philippe de Sellier de Moranville, a firm supporter of the Schuman Plan then based at the United Nations in Geneva. De Sellier argued that the CSSF's 'study

[100]According to Gérard Bossuat, the CSSF's opposition to the Schuman Plan was due entirely to the fact that steel industrialists 'understood immediately that Monnet would oppose the cartelisation that they were used to'. See Bossuat, 'Jean Monnet. La mesure d'une influence', *Vingtième siècle* 15:1, 1996, 68–84, 77.

[101]'Note sur les pouvoirs de la Chambre syndicale et du CPS, 21 January 1951, AMG 18 1, FJME. An earlier version of this document, dated 11 December 1950, was prepared for Monnet by Jean Ripert.

[102]Aubrun felt obliged to 'formally reject any accusation of under-production [*freinage*]' by the French steel industry. See 'Note sur l'évolution de la production sidérurgique française' by Aubrun, 25 October 1950, AMG 8 5, FJME. Many industrialists claimed that they deliberately underproduced under Vichy as a patriotic means of cutting off supplies to the German war economy. In 1950, that same accusation was levelled against industrialists who were now accused of being anti-patriotic by placing their own profits ahead of the needs of the country.

seems to have been written with a certain bias and a certain lack of objectivity', and that Aubrun's colleagues ultimately 'arrived at conclusions which are utterly false'.[103] He endeavoured to study the question further with his colleagues, but underlined to Monnet that 'it is essential that nobody learn that we are busying ourselves with refuting the arguments of the Chambre syndicale'.[104] Within two weeks, however, Aubrun had heard from several sources that Monnet was questioning the figures provided by the CSSF. A clearly irritated Aubrun demanded that Monnet 'inform [Aubrun] of the precise points with which you take issue', adding that 'we had cross-checked and discussed these figures with your staff [and understood] that they had been accepted'.[105]

By the first week of 1951, Monnet was writing to ministers informing them that the CSSF's opposition to aspects of the Schuman Plan was unfounded and based on false figures. Writing to Pleven, Monnet claimed that the CSSF's documents from December 1950 'in no way constitute a serious basis for appreciating the effects the Schuman Plan will have on the French steel industry', adding that Aubrun's objections 'were clearly formed *a priori* and without any justification from the figures', which were themselves 'extremely contestable'.[106] Monnet was right to highlight that the CSSF's opposition to the Schuman Plan seemed to stem more from an objection in principle than from the figures in the document prepared by the CSSF in December. Yet even after the detailed study of cost price commissioned by Monnet and completed by the Modernisation Commission for Steel in collaboration with the Steel Section of the Ministry for Industry and Commerce, the differences in the supposedly 'false' figures were minimal. In calculating their cost price, for example, the CSSF chose to base its figures on the first months of 1950 on the grounds that this represented a typical

[103]'Commentaire sur la 'Note sur le Plan Schuman' daté du 13 décembre' prepared by de Sellier, 21 December 1950, 81 AJ 155, AN.

[104]Lettre de Sellier à Monnet, 21 December 1950, 81 AJ 155, AN.

[105]Lettre d'Aubrun à Monnet, 6 January 1951, AMG 4, FJME. Aubrun names Georges Villiers, President of the CNPF, as the one who told him of Monnet's comments, but adds that 'this is not the first time that your opinion on this matter has been shared with me'.

[106]Schéma pour la lettre au Président du Conseil de Jean Monnet, 4 January 1951, AMG 11 4, FJME.

production period. The study commissioned by Monnet, meanwhile, based its figures on the production data for the month of June 1950, when production costs were slightly lower. The difference, however, was strikingly small: instead of the CSSF's figure of 20,400 francs for the base cost price, the CGP study advanced the figure of 19,900 francs, revising the figure down by less than 2.5 per cent.[107] Given the subjective nature of projecting future production costs, the difference between the two sets of figures was negligible.[108] If Monnet was dismising the CSSF's criticisms as 'formed in advance and bearing no justification from the figures', the gap between Monnet's vociferous denunciation of the CSSF's position and the paltry difference between their respective estimates suggest that Monnet was guilty of the same transgression. Monnet's decision to use the figures from June 1950, which featured the lowest cost price of any month for which data was available, similarly suggests that he highlighted figures that supported his position while ignoring others that weakened it, precisely as he accused Aubrun of doing.[109] Aubrun was certainly trying to obstruct the negotiations and the CSSF's decision to base their figures on production costs from earlier in 1950 was not without bias. It was clear,

[107]'Remise au point des éléments retenus par la Chambre syndicale dans ses notes sur la comparaison des prix de revient et incidence du Plan Schuman sur ces prix', 11 January 1951, AMG 11 4, FJME.

[108]Philippe Mioche has observed that neither set of figures 'was terribly reliable – not due to any insincerity on either side, but because so many factors remained unknown'; see Mioche, 'Le patronat de la sidérurgie française et le Plan Schuman en 1950–1952' in Klaus Schwabe (ed.), *Die Anfänge des Schuman-Plans,* 310. Alan Milward has similarly stated that the French government, including the CGP, was in no position 'to forecast with any reasonable accuracy the likely impact of their policies on the steel industry'; see Milward, *The Reconstruction of Western Europe*, 374. In a note to Etienne Hirsch, the Deputy Director for Mines and Steel at the Ministry for Industry warned that 'it would be fanciful to base estimates on the figures provided' by his ministry. See Lettre de Herbin à Hirsch, 5 September 1950, PU 22, HAEU.

[109]In a letter to the French Cabinet, Monnet rejected the CSSF's figures entirely on the grounds that Aubrun and his colleagues 'systematically ignored certain elements that are favourable to the French steel industry and deliberately failed to take into account elements that are unfavourable to the steel industries' of the other countries. While Monnet's characterisation is legitimate, the figures produced by the CGP are similarly biased. See 'Remise au point des éléments retenus par la Chambre Syndicale dans ses notes sur la comparaison des prix de revient et incidence du Plan Schuman sur ces prix', 20 January 1951, AMG 18 2, FJME.

however, that the disagreement between the CGP and the CSSF went beyond objective figures but hinged instead on their pre-existing convictions.

In the early months of 1951, Aubrun's position had been successfully undermined by Monnet. It was widely circulated that the CSSF had falsified its figures in an effort to defend an inefficient and closed system amounting to a cartel, despite the relatively minor differences between the projections of the CSSF and those of the CGP. The recommendations of the Hirsch–Gardent Committee, meanwhile, further weakened the CSSF's position, even if this was achieved precisely by ignoring the concerns raised by Aubrun and Aron before the Committee. As the negotiations entered their final stages the CSSF's influence remained marginal.[110]

As the treaty negotiations concluded, a desperate Aubrun sent off a final round of pleas to the members of Cabinet. He warned Robert Schuman that the implementation of the treaty in its current form would lead to 'the decline or the collapse of the French steel industry, [with] severe social and economic consequences for the country as a whole'.[111] By April 1951, however, it was clear that the most relevant ministers – particularly Schuman at Foreign Affairs and Jean-Marie Louvel at Industry[112] – were no longer entertaining Aubrun's objections. Indeed, when one industrialist wrote to Maurice Schumann, Secretary of State for Foreign Affairs, to set out his opposition to the treaty, Schumann sent a copy to Monnet and asked him to draft a reply on his behalf.[113] This example demonstrates the influence Monnet held over ministers and the trust they accorded him, which helped ensure that his arguments succeeded against those of

[110]Another notable critic of the treaty was the French Communist Party, which argued that the Schuman Plan was a ploy to unite Europe's industrial capacity under American leadership in preparation for an attack on the Soviet bloc. According to the Communist daily *L'Humanité*, the ECSC 'is not supranational, as they would have us believe: it is American'. See 'Le plan Schuman, un pas de plus vers la guerre, a été signé hier à Paris', *L'Humanité*, 19 April 1951.

[111]Lettre d'Aubrun à Schuman, 5 April 1951, AMG 15 5, FJME.

[112]Louvel (MRP) replaced Robert Lacoste as Minister for Industry in February 1950.

[113]Lettre de Maurice Schumann à Jean Monnet, 3 December 1951, 81 AJ 155, AN. Schumann addresses Monnet as 'Mon cher ami' and begins by stating 'I consider the opposition of a *trust* like USINOR as a complement and even, to a certain extent, as useful'. For the letter from USINOR's Director General, see Lettre de René Damien à Maurice Schumann, 28 November 1950, 81 AJ 155, AN.

industrialists who opposed the creation of the ECSC. The contrast between the degree of influence exerted upon ministers by Monnet and Aubrun could hardly be more marked.

In a last-ditch effort two days before the Treaty of Paris was due to be signed, Aubrun wrote to Paul Bacon, the Minister for Labour and Social Security, trying to convince him to oppose the treaty on the grounds that 'the hundreds of thousands of workers whose fate, directly or indirectly, is linked to' that of the French steel industry were in peril.[114] Bacon, like his colleagues in Cabinet, refused to support Aubrun. Robert Schuman finally responded to Aubrun's letter in June, two months after the treaty had been signed, justifying the way in which the treaty had been negotiated. 'It was the responsibility of the Government alone' to negotiate the treaty, he wrote, adding that 'the Government has done its duty, careful to serve not only the common good, but also the interests of producers, users, and workers'. In Schuman's eyes, building Europe was far more important than assuaging every concern voiced by 'particular interests' like the CSSF. He then reiterated Monnet's assurance that 'the representative of the Chambre syndicale took part in the discussions of the technical commissions in the same way and to the same extent as their counterparts from the other countries', a claim that could only draw renewed protestations from Aubrun.[115] In his 14-page response to Schuman, Aubrun poured out his grievances, fuming that the barring of the CSSF from the vast majority of the negotiations 'can only be understood as proof of a deliberate desire to exclude' the CSSF.[116] Aubrun concluded that the product of the negotiations had fallen short of the promise of the Schuman Declaration and that the CSSF 'regretfully [cannot] support' the treaty.[117]

Aubrun's obvious failure to successfully oppose the treaty or even to gain meaningful concessions signalled the end of his career as the main

[114]Lettre d'Aubrun à Paul Bacon, 16 April 1951, AMG 16 4, FJME. Bacon is considered to be the father of the SMIG (the first guaranteed minimum wage in France), which he introduced in 1950. Interestingly, a national minimum wage had first been proposed by René Belin in the 1941 Labour Charter but was never implemented.

[115]Lettre de Schuman à Aubrun, 9 June 1951, 81 AJ 135, AN.

[116]Lettre d'Aubrun à Schuman, 19 June 1951, 81 AJ 135, AN.

[117]Ibid.

representative of the French steel industry, a position he had held since 1940. He remained President of the CSSF until the following year, but in practice more and more of his functions were handed over to its first Vice President, Pierre Ricard. Speaking in July 1952, the same month the Treaty of Paris entered into force, Ricard recanted the CSSF's long-standing opposition to the Schuman Plan and the bitter words Aubrun had written to Schuman a year earlier. Noting that French steel production in May 1952 'broke all records', he offered a rosy version of the development of the ECSC, claiming that 'the French steel industry always showed itself to support the aims of' the Schuman Plan. He added that 'all French steel industrialists are resolute in their desire to do all that is necessary for the treaty to succeed', concluding that the CSSF 'gives its wholehearted support to the policies being pursued by the government'.[118] The dramatic about-face of the CSSF confirmed the victory of Monnet's vision of industrial organisation in France.[119]

[118]'La sidérurgie française et le plan Schuman. Une conférence de M Pierre Ricard', 4 July 1952, 81 AJ 135, AN. The industry did ultimately gain some concessions, most notably the commitment to canalise the Moselle River, which would make heavy industry in Lorraine more competitive.

[119]It is worth remembering that many of the same concerns voiced by the CSSF were shared by their counterparts in the other five countries. Fears that the High Authority would have too much power, and that it would try to close down inefficient mines and forges, were voiced at various times by Belgian, Luxembourgish, and Italian industrialists. Again, the governments' desire to 'build Europe' tended to override these concerns, but in all these cases the industrialists' views affected the delegations' positions during the negotiations. Ultimately, the steel industrialists of the other five countries were able to gain concessions that were not extended to the French industry, particularly favourable transition periods. The Belgian steel industry, for its part, was finally won over by the prospect of using coking coal from the Ruhr that would be cheaper than Belgian coal. In the case of Luxembourg, where steel represented over 80 per cent of the country's industrial production, the government generally supported the industry's position, and the Italian government was similarly supportive overall of the Italian steel industry's position. This contrasts markedly with the French case, where the steel industry's representatives were uniquely and consciously marginalised by the French delegation. Useful national case studies are provided in Klaus Schwabe (ed.), *Die Anfänge des Schuman-Plans.* For the Italian case, the most thorough study is Ruggero Ranieri's doctoral thesis, *L'espansione alla prova del negoziato. L'industria italiana e la CECA 1945–1955* (Florence: EUI, 1988); for Belgium, see René Leboutte, 'L'industrie sidérurgique belge et ses réseaux dans les années 1950'in Michel Dumoulin (ed.), *Réseaux économiques et construction européenne* (Brussels: Peter Lang, 2004), 163–188.

Good Europeans: the French Members of the ECSC

Following the signature of the Treaty of Paris, the task became finding suitable candidates to appoint to the High Authority. Of the nine members of the High Authority, as least one would come from each member state, with France and Germany each guaranteed two. It was quickly agreed that Jean Monnet should be named not only as one of the two French members, but as President of the High Authority, a post he gladly accepted. In choosing the remaining eight members, it was agreed that one representative should come from a trade union; Paul Finet was thus chosen as the Belgian member.[120]

One of the least controversial appointments was that of the second French member. With a new-found diplomatic tone, the CSSF, particularly Pierre Ricard, insisted that a French steel industrialist be named to the High Authority. This suggestion was welcomed by both Monnet and the French government, as this would reinforce the CSSF's belated endorsement of the project. Along with the presence of Finet, the inclusion of a single industrialist would also suggest a measure of tripartism within the High Authority. One name quickly emerged that seemed to please all sides: Léon Daum. Alongside Aubrun, Roy, and Jean Dupuis, Daum had spent the war running the Organisation Committee for Steel. In 1948 he was named President of SOLLAC, a firm established under the Monnet Plan that ran one of two massive wide-band continuous-strip mills.[121] Moreover, he had enthusiastically backed the merging of the steel firms of La Marine, of which he was Director General, and Saint-Etienne under the Monnet Plan. While his support was largely due to the advantage this had for his firm, it fitted nicely with the CGP's strategy of concentration in the steel industry.[122] His cooperation with Monnet in this context

[120]'Message de M Monnet à MM Etzel et Pothof (sic)', 28 July 1952, AMH 1 3, FJME. Paul Finet was Secretary General of the *Fédération générale du travail de Belgique*, one of the two main trade union federations in Belgium. The junior German member, Heinz Potthoff, was a politician from the Social Democratic Party (SPD) who also had a background with the trade union the *Deutsche Gewerkschaftsbund*.

[121]SOLLAC, in Lorraine, and USINOR, in Nord, were the sites of these two giant steel mills, which at the time were the largest in Europe. The new American equipment for these two firms consumed the majority of the funds available under the Monnet Plan.

[122]'Rapport sur la modernisation de la sidérurgie de la Loire et les problèmes qu'elle se pose', October 1951, 80 AJ 11, AN.

reassured the incoming President of the High Authority that Daum would be a collaborative member of the High Authority. Aubrun, meanwhile, had worked closely with Daum in the Organisation Committee for Steel throughout the war, and eagerly endorsed the candidacy, believing that Daum would act as 'one of our own' within the ECSC.[123] Despite Monnet and Aubrun agreeing on the candidate, it was then Prime Minister Antoine Pinay who proved to be Daum's most enthusiastic backer.[124] The French Premier also knew Daum well from the war: Pinay had spent the Vichy years as President of the Organisation Committee for Leather and sat alongside Daum in the regime's *Conseil national*, a non-democratic assembly set up under Pétain to replace the Republic's parliament. Indeed, Pinay had been banned from running for elected office in 1944 as a result of his involvement with Vichy; upon appeal this prohibition was lifted after Pinay claimed that he had engaged in some limited forms of resistance to the regime.[125] Not surprisingly, Daum's page-long biography circulated among the national delegations omitted any reference to the important positions he held under Vichy.[126] In some circles, it was Jean Monnet who was the more controversial French member, as some German industrialists protested that he was not sufficiently sensitive to particular issues facing the Saarland.[127] Meanwhile Daum, who had eagerly accepted a cabinet position at Vichy 12 years earlier, was approved unanimously as a member of the

[123]Spierenburg and Poidevin, *Histoire de la Haute Autorité de la Communauté européenne du Charbon et de l'Acier*, 70–71. In the estimation of Philippe Mioche, Daum's nomination amounted to 'compensation offered to the steel industrialists'; see Mioche, 'Le patronat de la sidérurgie française et le Plan Schuman', 314.

[124]Jean Monnet, *Mémoires* (Fayard: Paris, 1976), 546. This is confirmed in Spierenburg and Poidevin, *Histoire de la Haute Autorité* and Mioche, 'Le patronat de la sidérurgie française'.

[125]Sylvie Guillaume, *Antoine Pinay, ou, La confiance en politique* (Paris: FNSP, 1984). Guillaume argues that Pinay's exclusion from holding an elected office was due to the machinations of his enemies in the French Communist Party. The debate over the *patron résistant* under Vichy is discussed in Chapter 4.

[126]'Biographie de M Léon Daum', undated but from July 1952, AMH 1 4, FJME. Chief among Daum's credentials highlighted were his time, since 1927, as (Deputy) Director General of Marine et Homécourt and his role as President, from 1950, of the French delegation to the Steel Committee at the OECE.

[127]'Lettre de Filliol', 18 June 1952, P 6353, MAE.

first High Authority and was praised by Monnet for his '*rayonnement moral*'.[128]

Beyond Daum's inclusion in the High Authority, industrialists were also guaranteed representation, if only in a consultative role, in the ECSC's Consultative Committee. Two members were named from among the French steel industry: Pierre Ricard and Robert Baboin.[129] Ricard had by this point emerged as Aubrun's de facto successor, although he would only formally assume the presidency of the CSSF after Aubrun's retirement the following year. Like Aubrun and Pinay, Ricard had spent the war as President of an Organisation Committee, in this case for Foundry, and was therefore intimately involved in Vichy's New Industrial Order. Baboin, for his part, had been Director for Steel in Vichy's Ministry for Industrial Production, where he worked closely with Jean Bichelonne in particular.[130] Indeed, it was Baboin who attended CORSID's meetings as the representative of his ministry during the war and put pressure on the industrialists to comply with the government's schemes to deport French workers to Germany, especially the STO.[131] Clearly, involvement with the Vichy regime was no drawback for the industrialists appointed to the ECSC. Indeed, given the wartime experience of Daum, Ricard, and Baboin, it is Monnet who stands out for his involvement with the Resistance as opposed to Vichy's Organisation Committees during the war.

[128]Jean Monnet, *Mémoires*, 546. Daum had been offered the Industrial Production portfolio by Pierre Laval in Vichy's government, and Daum accepted. At the eleventh hour the offer was withdrawn and Laval instead appointed trade unionist René Belin. See René Belin, *Du Secrétariat de la CGT au gouvernement de Vichy* (Paris: Albatross, 1978), 127–128.

[129]A third member of the CSSF, representing the Saar, was also named. The Saarland's steel industries were administered as part of France until 1955, when the territory was restored to the Federal Republic of Germany.

[130]After the war Baboin was named Director General of the mines in Saarland which were administered by France.

[131]These schemes were generally opposed by Organisation Committees but supported by the Vichy government. For Baboin's presence at CORSID's meetings, and his demands that they comply with the STO, see 'Comité d'organisation de la sidérurgie. Région du Centre et de l'Ouest. Réunion du 16 février 1943', 16 February 1943, 139 AQ 82, AN.

Conclusion

By the time the Treaty of Paris entered into force in 1952, France's economy had changed dramatically from the period in which the Organisation Committees were established. Over the course of the 1940s, the wide-ranging network for allocating and sub-allocating raw materials and production orders by sector had evolved into a much more liberal system that now involved six countries. With the French and the broader Western European economic recoveries of the 1950s, the central purpose of the Organisation Committees – that of managing scarce resources – subsided, and the focus instead turned to increasing production and lowering production costs. While ministers like Robert Lacoste and André Philip continued to regret the abolition of the Committees well beyond 1946, the economic situation of the 1950s affirmed that the tightly State-managed institutions of Vichy were no longer necessary to ensure economic growth in France.

In the early stages of the negotiations for the Schuman Plan, the CGP's Modernisation Commissions served as a blueprint for what soon became the Directorates for Coal and for Steel. Although the Modernisation Commissions were themselves the successors to the Organisation Committees, the Directorates of the ECSC ultimately bore little resemblance to the Committees. While the Committees had been run by industrialists under Vichy and later became tripartite following the Liberation (as did their successors, the Modernisation Commissions), the Directorates were composed almost entirely of technicians and bureaucrats. This evolution itself reflects the broader evolution of France's economic statecraft in the mid-twentieth century: while industrialists held significant power until 1944, even under Vichy, this gave way to the tripartism of the 'post-war moment', which then turned into the management by technicians and bureaucrats – or 'technocracy' – associated with France's *Trente glorieuses.*[132] Moreover, the lengthy negotiations preceding the Treaty of Paris altered the initial sketches for the ECSC's architecture considerably, such that the line from Vichy's institutions to the Directorates is only one of many influences on the final shape of the ECSC.

[132]On the evolution of French capitalism during this period, see Richard Kuisel, *Capitalism and the State in Modern France: Renovation and Economic Management in the Twentieth Century* (Cambridge: Cambridge University Press, 1981) and Michel Margairaz, *L'Etat, les finances et l'économie*. On technocracy in post-war France, see Delphine Dulong, *Moderniser la politique: aux origines de la Ve République* (Paris: L'Harmattan, 1997).

More interesting is the struggle between CORSID's successors, the CMSID and the CSSF, over how French industry should be run in the post-war era. For the CMSID and the CGP of which it was one of the keystones, the rationalisation of production and the concentration of factories were essential to allow it to thrive on the world market. The CSSF, for its part, remained preoccupied with protecting each individual firm. With the unveiling of the Schuman Plan, this clash became both more urgent and more virulent. The CGP unsurprisingly argued that the best opportunities for the French steel industry would come through European projects like the ECSC; the CSSF steadfastly opposed this perceived strategy of 'open[ing] borders and clos[ing] factories', fearing that such a European project would threaten not only individual firms but the national industry as a whole. While the CSSF resorted to alarmist protestations and the preparation of seemingly biased figures to defend their position, it was the CGP that proved far more resourceful by orchestrating a campaign to undermine the credibility of the CSSF and its arguments. Using similarly biased figures and occasionally questionable methods – and bolstered by the broad desire among the French Cabinet for the political project of the Schuman Plan to succeed – Monnet and his collaborators successfully marginalised the CSSF. In Monnet's and Schuman's eyes, these machinations to exclude the obstructionist CSSF were justified as the expedient path to the ambitious goal of uniting Europe.

One of Monnet's biographers has described how, 'where Monnet sensed basic opposition, he sought almost military means to contain, outflank, or overrun it'.[133] Monnet certainly resorted to such tactics when facing the CSSF and emerged triumphant: by 1952 the ECSC was operational, Aubrun had been marginalised even within the industry, and his successor, Pierre Ricard, was pledging his support for the ECSC. Indeed, the approach was so successful that Monnet opted to use it for another ambitious project launched in 1950: the European Defence Community (EDC).[134] As with the Schuman Plan, Monnet drafted this

[133]François Duchêne, *Jean Monnet: The First Statesman of Interdependence* (London: Norton, 1994), 358.

[134]The EDC, proposed by René Pleven in what was known as the Pleven Plan in October 1950, would have seen the creation of a European Army, made up of soldiers from the Six. It was presented as a means to prevent the recreation of a German Army, an option being pushed by the United States in response to the perceived threat of the Soviet Union, particularly after the outbreak of the Korean War in June 1950. The most thorough account of the EDC remains Edward Fursdon, *The European Defence Community: A History* (London: Macmillan, 1980); for

determined scheme with just a small handful of close collaborators, Etienne Hirsch chief amongst them. Again, experts and representatives from the relevant field were consciously excluded. In Monnet's words, 'once again, we left out the specialists, who make things more complicated and resist change. We had no need for military experts, just as we had no need for steel industrialists to make steel European.'[135] While Monnet had successfully excluded the *patronat* from the Schuman Plan negotiations and created the ECSC despite their objections, he met with palpable defeat over the EDC. The French Army proved to be a more formidable opponent than the CSSF had been, and the broad political support enjoyed by the Schuman Plan contrasted with the attacks against the EDC from members of every political party.[136] Ultimately, the National Assembly voted against the EDC in August 1954, effectively killing the initiative. This marked a severe setback for the European project and for Jean Monnet personally; in response to the vote, he announced that he would resign as President of the High Authority of the ECSC. Following his resignation, meant to take effect in February 1955, it was initially agreed that until a permanent replacement could be found, 'the interim president of the High Authority will be, not the first Vice President Etzel (German), but the doyen, the second French member Léon Daum'.[137] As with his near-appointment as Minister for Industrial Production in July 1940,

Jean Monnet's role in the EDC, see Renata Dwan, 'Jean Monnet and the European Defence Community, 1950–1954', *Cold War History*, 1:3, 2001, 141–160.

[135]Monnet, *Mémoires*, 501.

[136]De Gaulle, now the driving force behind the right-wing party the *Rassemblement du peuple français* (RPF), warned that the EDC would cause France to 'disappear', while PCF stalwart François Billoux asserted that 'Europe is an idea of Hitler's'; see Eric Roussel, *Jean Monnet* (Paris: Fayard, 1996), 588 and, for the opposition of the French Army, 654. Although the Socialist Prime Minister at the time, Pierre Mendès France, supported the plan, the SFIO and Radical deputies were divided over the issue, while most, but not all MRP deputies supported the EDC. Philippe Vial has pointed out that while most of the army opposed the EDC, this position was not unanimously held within the army; see Vial, 'Le militaire et la politique: le maréchal Juin et le général Ely face à la CED' in Michel Dumoulin (ed.), *La Communauté européenne de défense, leçons pour demain?* (Brussels: Peter Lang, 2000), 135–160.

[137]See 'Lettre de démission de Jean Monnet', 10 November 1954 and 'Note pour messieurs les ministres des affaires étrangères et du commerce extérieur. Objet: succession de M Monnet à la présidence de la Haute Autorité de la CECA', 4 February 1955, 17 771 20 6, MAEB.

however, Daum was denied the role of President of the High Authority when Monnet opted to remain in place until his successor could be chosen; this was the reason for organising the Messina Conference in June 1955, after which Monnet officially stepped down from the High Authority he had been so instrumental in creating.[138] Following his departure, he opted to focus his energies on civilian nuclear energy in Europe, culminating in the creation of Euratom in 1958. Having successfully outdone the *maîtres de forges* but been bested by the supporters of the French military establishment, Monnet was attracted to nuclear power in part because it lacked the long-standing 'vested interests' he had confronted in recent years. In nuclear energy, he found another sector where 'the method from the Schuman Plan could be fully and successfully applied'.[139]

[138]Monnet was succeeded by René Mayer, while Daum remained the second French member. At the Messina Conference, a ground-breaking agreement was reached to work towards the creation of a European Common Market as well as Euratom; this led to the Treaty of Rome of 1957 and the establishment of the European Economic Community the following year.

[139]In his memoirs, Monnet describes how he found the 'native state' of the sector appealling, adding that, 'if there were one sector where the method from the Schuman Plan could be fully and successfully applied, it was' nuclear energy. See Monnet, *Mémoires*, 470. Monnet encountered resistance from the military establishment yet again when he tried, unsuccessfully, to insist that signatories of the Euratom treaty renounce the use of nuclear weapons, which a number of French generals saw as 'necessary to [French] security'. See Pierre Guillen, 'La France et la négociation du Traité d'Euratom' in Michel Dumoulin, Pierre Guillen and Maurice Vaïsse (eds), *L'Energie nucléaire en Europe. Des origines à Euratom* (Brussels: Peter Lang, 1994), 111–130.

CHAPTER 9

Conclusions

The year 1940 has memorably been called the 'fulcrum of the twentieth century', given the far-reaching consequences of the Fall of France on the international order.[1] By examining French industrial organisation between the Fall of France and the creation of the ECSC, this book reassesses the legacy of Vichy's industrial policies of 1940, revealing them to be a turning point with a multifaceted legacy for post-war France and Europe. In addition to identifying previously overlooked yet striking continuities of institutions and individuals, this study allows us to reappraise issues ranging from the influence of industrialists on French and European policy to Jean Monnet's famous *méthode* and the delicate question of links from Vichy to the ECSC.

During the first months of the Vichy regime, the establishment of a New Industrial Order saw the creation of novel institutions and a decisive change in the leadership of French industry. While myriad alternatives to the liberal economic order of the Third Republic had been circulating amongst intellectuals in the 1930s,[2] the most influential model for the

[1]David Reynolds, '1940: Fulcrum of the Twentieth Century?', *International Affairs*, 66:2, 1990.

[2]See Olivier Dard, *Le rendez-vous manqué des relèves des années trente* (Paris: Presses universitaires de France, 2002) and Jackie Clarke, *France in the Age of Organization: Factory, Home and Nation from the 1920s to Vichy* (Oxford: Berghahn, 2011).

© The Author(s) 2017

L.-A. Brunet, *Forging Europe: Industrial Organisation in France, 1940–1952*, Security, Conflict and Cooperation in the Contemporary World, DOI 10.1057/978-1-349-95198-7_9

Organisation Committees in the summer of 1940 was the analogous system of the Third Reich – which certainly seemed worthy of emulation in the aftermath of the Wehrmacht's victories across Europe. The creation of such centralised institutions with sweeping powers to coordinate production across the nation was unprecedented in France and consciously adapted elements of the Reich's industrial model – and was looked upon approvingly by the Nazi authorities. Similarly, while the idea of ousting the pre-war elites of the *grand patronat* can be traced to the interwar years – notably to Jacques Barnaud's writings[3] – it was only in 1940, as a direct result of the Fall of France, that policies were put in place that realised these objectives. Consequently, the owner-presidents with significant political influence under the Third Republic personified by figures like François de Wendel were replaced with managerial technicians from the private sector, typically equipped with credentials from the Ecole Polytechnique and the Ecole des Mines and managerial experience at large, but not the largest, firms in the sector. In the case of the steel industry, this turnaround elevated individuals such as Jules Aubrun, Eugène Roy, and Léon Daum to the most influential positions in the nation's industry – a rank they maintained until the end of their careers in the post-war era.

The hasty establishment of the Organisation Committees and the appointment of their members in 1940 proved to be an enduring change to the organisation of French industry. Well before the Liberation of France, the CFLN had decided that Vichy's Committees should be maintained and subjected to a number of reforms. These reforms proved to be strikingly consistent with the Vichy legislation of August 1940, however; as one CFLN member noted at the time, the proposed reforms such as the inclusion of labour representation, the reduction of the overall number of Committees, and even the removal of sitting members could all be realised 'simply by applying the text of the Vichy law'.[4] Correspondingly, the re-establishment of employers' associations after the end of the Vichy regime by no means amounted to the simple restoration of the pre-war *Comité des forges*. The exclusion of the pre-war leadership of the employers' associations proved to be permanent, as did the promotion of individuals like

[3]Jacques Barnaud, 'L'Industriel', *Nouveaux cahiers*, no. 2, 1 April 1937.

[4]'Maintien éventuel du CO du bâtiment et des travaux publics', 26 January 1944, CFLN 686, MAE. This observation was made by Leprince.

Jules Aubrun, who was named President of the resurrected employers' association for steel, the CSSF. While there were a number of pre-war antecedents for this change in industrial leadership – Henri de Peyerimhoff, the President of the *Comité des houillères* until 1940, has been described as a *fonctionnaire patronal*[5] – 1940 saw the torch pass from one group of industrialists to another.

These new leaders of French industry, however, struggled to influence French policy-making concerning industry. The CSSF never matched the political influence of the pre-war *Comité des forges*, when its president was not only the owner-president of one of France's largest firms but also a prominent member of the National Assembly and an owner of the leading newspaper of record, *Le Temps*. The dissolution of employers' associations and the creation of the Organisation Committees in 1940 were decided by Vichy's Minister for Industrial Production and handful of his collaborators. Later, the fate of the Committees in post-war France was determined by the CFLN, their reform in liberated France was dictated by the post-war Minister for Industrial Production, and their ultimate dissolution in 1946 was the result of a vote in the National Assembly. The creation of the Monnet Plan and later of the ECSC were realised by a small group of government insiders. Despite the obvious ramifications for French industrialists, in none of these cases were they consulted or even informed until after the ink on the legislation was already dry. Claims that the CSSF was essentially a continuation of the pre-war *Comité des forges* with its widespread political influence are at odds with the reality of industrialists' inability to shape policy following 1940.[6] Indeed, the CSSF was forced

[5]Alain Chatriot, 'Henri de Peyerimhoff (1871–1953), le gentleman du charbon' in Olivier Dard and Gilles Richard (eds), *Les permanents patronaux: éléments pour l'histoire du patronat en France dans la première moitié du XXème siècle* (Metz: Université Paul Verlaine de Metz, 2005), 45–73. Despite having a similar background to many of the Vichy-era industrial leaders, de Peyerimhoff was sacked in 1940 and never regained an influential role within the industry.

[6]See, for example, Jean Baumier, *La fin des maîtres de forges* (Paris: Plon, 1981); Pierre Gerbet, *La construction de l'Europe* (Paris: Imprimerie nationale, 1983); Philippe Mioche, 'Les comités d'organisation de la sidérurgie: un lieu d'affrontement entre modernisateurs de la sidérurgie et gardiens de la profession?' in Hervé Joly (ed.), *Le comités d'organisation et l'économie dirigée du régime de Vichy* (Caen: CRHQ, 2004); Annie Lacroiz-Riz, 'Les comités d'organisation et l'Allemagne: tentative d'évaluation' in ibid.; Matthias Kipping, *La France et les origines de l'Union européenne. Intégration économique et compétitivité internationale* (Paris: CHEF, 2002).

to watch passively as decisions such as the establishment of the Monnet Plan and the dissolution of the Organisation Committees were made by the French government. Given this lack of influence on French industrial and ultimately European policies, this book also questions the importance that some studies attribute to transnational networks of industrialists during this period. It has been argued that between the interwar years and the 1950s, a European identity emerged among Western European industrialists, which positively influenced the early steps of European integration.[7] Given the opposition of the French steel industry to the Schuman Plan, however, and Monnet's predilection for sidelining industrialists as mere 'vested interests',[8] the impact of such transnational networks on French policy is far from apparent. Indeed, the only benefit Aubrun seems to have derived from such cross-border networks amongst steel industrialists was the occasional shred of information about the ongoing ECSC negotiations which Monnet had refused to give him. Yet this merely underlines the impotence of the CSSF and its inability to shape policy, no matter how crucial it was to the French steel industry. Despite claims that the *maîtres de forges* enjoyed far-reaching political influence until the creation of the ECSC in 1950, in reality this influence ended decisively in 1940 and was never regained.

As the Organisation Committees are situated at the crossroads of private and public interests, involving both employers and the Ministry of Industrial Production, they provide an invaluable perspective on the debates between different French actors in the decade preceding the Schuman Declaration and on the contested nature of 'national interests'. Alan Milward has famously argued that the early stages of European integration were driven by the national interests of the respective member states, and that the European project thus 'rescued' the nation state.[9] Milward's account has sometimes been caricatured as depicting nation

[7]Eric Bussière, 'Les milieux économiques face à l'Europe au XXe siècle', *Journal of European Integration History*, 3:2, 1997, 5–21; Robert Frank (ed.), *Les identités européennes au XXe siècle* (Paris: Publications de la Sorbonne, 2004); Françoise Berger, *La France, l'Allemagne et l'acier (1932–1952): de la stratégie des cartels à l'élaboration de la CECA*, PhD thesis, Université de Paris I, 2000.

[8]Jean Monnet, *Mémoires* (Paris: Fayard, 1976), 460.

[9]Alan Milward, *The European Rescue of the Nation State* (London: Routledge, 1992).

states as 'allegedly coherent actors'.[10] While this study maintains the importance of the French state, it has also demonstrated that the State was by no means a coherent actor with a single voice between 1940 and 1952. Aside from the number of regime changes this period witnessed, at each stage there were competing interests among various state and non-state actors. The dilemma of the STO, for example, reveals divisions not only within the Vichy Cabinet (and indeed between Speer and Sauckel in the Nazi government), but also between the Ministry for Industrial Production and the industrialists charged with running the Organisation Committees. Differing opinions over national interests led to clashes between Monnet, on the one hand, and Robert Lacoste and André Philip, on the other, who opposed what they saw as the concentration of industrial and economic powers in the CGP; the dispute between Monnet and the CSSF over the Schuman Plan is yet another example of two competing conceptions of national interests. The fact that Monnet's definition of national interests tended to carry the day is largely explained by his ability to influence decision-makers, notably de Gaulle and Schuman.

The creation of Vichy's Organisation Committees also had a significant influence on the Monnet Plan. While historians have focused on the question of economic planning – entertained intermittently by Vichy before being taken up with determination by the Provisional Government of the French Republic[11] – the legacy of the Committees on the French institutions responsible for economic planning in the post-war period, particularly the CGP, has been ignored. Indeed, such continuities have been obscured by the tendency to associate the Committees solely with the Vichy regime, and accordingly to overlook the reformed Committees as they existed under the Provisional Government of the French Republic. In light of the analysis of the reformed Committees provided in Chapter 6, this book reveals the

[10]See Wolfram Kaiser, Brigitte Leucht and Morten Rasmussen, *The History of the European Union: Origins of a Trans- and Supranational polity, 1950–1972* (London: Routledge, 2009), 2–4. The authors are generally critical of the 'nation-focus of modern historians', which they deride as 'an endemic intellectual disease' that can only be remedied by a genuinely transnational approach to history. Milward's study in fact focuses on governments negotiating and forging coalitions of different interests, both public and private, for the sake of democratic consensus for particular policies. See Milward, *The European Rescue of the Nation State.*

[11]Richard Kuisel, 'Vichy et les origines de la planification économique, 1940–1946', *Mouvement social* 98, 1977, 77–101; Philippe Mioche, *Le Plan Monnet. Genèse et élaboration, 1941–1947* (Paris: Publications de la Sorbonne, 1987).

direct influence of the Organisation Committees on the so-called 'keystones' of the Monnet Plan, the Modernisation Commissions. By 1946, the Organisation Committees were industry-specific, tripartite institutions responsible for the coordination of production across France. In creating his Modernisation Commissions, Jean Monnet effectively replicated the existing Organisation Committees, imitating their tripartite composition, drawing extensively on the documentation produced by the Committees during the war, and even appointing figures from the Vichy Committees to the new Modernisation Commissions. Moreover, as soon as the Commissions had been created, Monnet began lobbying for the existing Committees to be abolished and for their powers to be transferred to the parallel bodies he had established under the CGP – a demand that was largely met following the dissolution of the Organisation Committees in 1946.

Likewise, this book questions and complicates the often laudatory portrait of Jean Monnet presented by many historians. The inclusion in the Modernisation Commissions of employers, workers, and civil servants is widely identified as 'the originality and indeed the foundation of French planning'.[12] Yet despite the prevalent claim that 'Vichy's [Organisation Committees] seem to have had little or no influence on the CGP in creating the commissions',[13] Monnet was well aware that this supposed innovation was already the *modus operandi* of the existing Organisation Committees. Just as he had argued in 1943 that Vichy's Committees should be maintained in post-war France for their pragmatic utility, he similarly recognised the usefulness of insisting upon the originality of the Commissions rather than the debt they owed to their Vichyste predecessors. Monnet's insistence that the Commissions and the CGP 'occupied a territory that had until that time been with neither name nor master' reflects his shrewd political acumen more than the reality of the origins of the Modernisation Commissions.[14]

Furthermore, this study sheds light on Monnet's celebrated *méthode* of bringing people together and reaching a consensus. His closest

[12]Etienne Hirsch, *Ainsi va la vie* (Lausanne: Fondation Jean Monnet pour l'Europe, 1988), 89. Cf. Richard Kuisel, *Capitalism and the State in Modern France* (Cambridge: Cambridge University Press, 1981), Philippe Mioche, *Le Plan Monnet* (Paris: Publications de la Sorbonne, 1987), Eric Roussel, *Jean Monnet* (Paris: Fayard, 1996).

[13]Kuisel, *Capitalism and the State*, 227.

[14]Monnet, *Mémoires* (Paris: Fayard, 1976), 347.

collaborators within the CGP described Monnet's approach as 'a true team effort'; historians have similarly emphasised that Monnet 'treated most colleagues and politicians openly and honestly, and did not connive behind their backs'. Monnet himself wrote that his task in gaining support for the Plan and the ECSC was 'to persuade, not compel, private enterprise to act in accordance with public needs'.[15] Yet this portrait of Monnet is confounded by his dealings with Jules Aubrun during the ECSC negotiations. This study reveals the range of tactics used by Monnet to exclude, misrepresent, and ultimately discredit the CSSF's often legitimate objections to the Schuman Plan. As such, Monnet's method did indeed involve conniving behind Aubrun's back to compel rather than persuade the CSSF to abide by the Treaty of Paris. While Monnet's motivations may have been essentially noble throughout this period – his priorities were the revival of the French economy and later the creation of 'Europe' – his occasionally unscrupulous methods sit uneasily alongside the usual depiction of Monnet as the open and honest consensus builder.[16]

The question of continuities from Vichy to the ECSC is admittedly a sensitive although by no means a new one. In a note sent to Jean Monnet in July 1944, Lambert Blum-Picard raised some stimulating questions concerning the legacy of the New Economic Order in Europe established under the Nazis:

> Is the violent unification of Europe under German dominance a lasting phenomenon or one that will leave deep traces? Does it provide a model for future [European] construction? Lessons may certainly be learned from the organisation put in place for [economic] planning for a vast region. But nothing lasting in terms of the economic realities themselves seems likely to persist.[17]

[15]Sherrill Brown Wells, *Jean Monnet: Unconventional Statesman* (London: Lynne Rienner, 2011), 100 and 247. A similar portrait emerges in the other principal biographies of Monnet; cf. Pascal Fontaine, *Jean Monnet l'inspirateur* (Paris: Jacques Grancher, 1988), François Duchêne, *Jean Monnet. The First Statesman of Interdependence* (London: Norton, 1994), and Roussel, *Jean Monnet.*

[16]As discussed in Chapter 8, a number of other individuals, from Georges Bidault to René Massigli to Ernest Bevin, felt marginalised by Monnet when he and Schuman launched the Schuman Plan.

[17]Note 'sur l'organisation de l'Europe d'après-guerre' and Lettre de Blum-Picard à Monnet, 12 July 1944, AME 56 2, FJME.

Despite Blum-Picard's assessment, both he and Monnet were early supporters of maintaining the Organisation Committees which had been set up precisely to incorporate French industry into the New Economic Order in Europe outlined by the Reich's Economics Minister. As Secretary General for Industrial Production in liberated France, Blum-Picard helped oversee the reform of the Committees, ensuring they became genuinely tripartite bodies as had been foreseen in the Vichy law. Monnet, for his part, replicated these reformed Committees as the Modernisation Commissions of the Monnet Plan, which in turn influenced his proposal for the institutional structures of the ECSC. Does this mean, then, that Vichy 'provide[d] a model for future [European] construction'?

In his provocative study of ideas from Vichy to the ECSC, Antonin Cohen argues that the National Revolution did indeed provide a conceptual model for central aspects of the ECSC. Cohen focuses on the wartime writings of Monnet's collaborators such as Pierre Uri and Paul Reuter, both of whom were based at the Ecole d'Uriage, a kind of Vichy think tank. He argues not only that the idea of 'community' they espoused under Vichy was anti-democratic, but also that they maintained this conception in the post-war era as they cooperated with Monnet on developing the Schuman Plan for a European 'community'.[18] The fact that no European Assembly was initially proposed in the Schuman Declaration is thus explained by Cohen by the desire of Monnet and his team to 'circumvent parliamentarism'.[19] In focusing on institutional history, this study has not attempted to analyse the ideas of 'Europe' or 'community' held by various actors, or how these evolved over time. It nonetheless complements Cohen's recent study by demonstrating how Monnet adapted institutions created by Pétain's regime for his post-war initiatives. Cohen highlights the juxtaposition by Monnet and his collaborators between technocratic, apolitical efficiency, on the one hand, and the chaotic instability of parliamentary democracy, on the other.[20] Monnet's criticisms of the obstructionist tendencies of party politics and his insistence that the CGP bypass parliament and be accountable directly to the

[18]Pierre Uri was a student of François Perroux at the Ecole d'Uriage, where Reuter was also a lecturer. See also Bernard Bruneteau, *Les «collabos» de l'Europe nouvelle* (Paris: CNRS, 2016).

[19]Antonin Cohen, *De Vichy à la Communauté européenne* (Paris: Presses Universitaires de France, 2012), 4.

[20]Ibid., 401–413.

Prime Minister are well-known. His attitude towards the Organisation Committees, however, has been overlooked, but is particularly instructive. The purportedly apolitical and 'technocratic' Committees developed in the early months of the Vichy regime and based on the Nazis' analogous offices were justified at the time on the grounds of their practicality, even if they fell far short of the ideal of 'industrial democracy'. Within the CFLN, Monnet and others called for the maintenance of these bodies, again placing pragmatism above democracy. The CFLN explicitly recognised that the Committees were 'anti-democratic [and] the creations most characteristic of the Vichy administration'.[21] Monnet nevertheless insisted on 'using [Vichy's] existing administrative apparatus in its entirety' in post-war France, without demanding that they undergo any significant changes.[22] In 1946, Monnet created parallel institutions to the reformed Committees in the form of the Modernisation Commissions, and only then did he call for the former's abolition – provided their duties be transferred to his Commissions. Following the Schuman Declaration, Monnet proposed the creation of Modernisation Commissions at the European level.

Despite the strong continuities from Vichy's New Industrial Order to the Monnet Plan, it is difficult to detect any significant institutional legacy from Vichy's Organisation Committees on the ECSC. The key institutions of the ECSC – from the High Authority to the Assembly or the Court of Justice – have no institutional precedents from the Vichy regime. Furthermore, the Council, in which the representative of the democratic government of each member state has an equal voice, is the antithesis of the Berlin-centred schemes for any form of a 'New European Order' developed under the Reich. The strongest continuity may be seen in the Directorates for Coal and for Steel of the ECSC, two technical offices intended to provide relevant studies to the High Authority which were modelled on the Modernisation Commissions; indeed, Jean Monnet initially proposed the term 'Modernisation Commissions' for these ECSC offices. Yet the role of these Directorates was decidedly marginal and they were far from being the 'central pillars' or the 'keystones' of the ECSC, as the Organisation Committees and the Modernisation Commissions had been for their

[21]Rapport Leprince, 26 January 1944, CFLN 686, MAE.

[22]'Note sur la première étape de la reconstruction en France', 22 September 1943, AME 33 1, FJME.

respective institutional structures. Moreover, the composition of these Directorates differed markedly from that of its predecessors. While the Organisation Committees under Vichy had been de facto run by employers, and the reformed Committees and the Modernisation Commissions were tripartite, the Directorates of the ECSC were staffed almost entirely by technicians – among the first European civil servants. The tripartism of the Committees and the Commissions were instead manifested by the ECSC's Consultative Committee, where quotas of industrialists and trade unionists were allocated to each member state.[23] Vichy's law of 16 August 1940 had foreseen workers, employers, and civil servants working together to coordinate industrial production, an ambition ultimately realised under the GPRF with the reformed Organisation Committees and the CGP's Modernisation Commissions. By the early 1950s, however, this emphasis on tripartism was being overshadowed by the preference for apolitical 'technocrats', a tendency that would reach its apogee in France in the 1950s and 1960s and, at the European level, give rise to the figure of the 'Eurocrat'.[24]

The motivations of Jean Monnet and Robert Schuman for proposing the pooling of the French and German coal and steel industries similarly owe little to Vichy. For Monnet, the Schuman Plan represented an effective means of shoring up the Monnet Plan at the national level and furthering the development of France's steel industry and its economic revival more broadly.[25] For Schuman, the decision to spring the proposal on the eve of the London Conference, where German economic issues were to be discussed, gave France the diplomatic initative and undercut Anglo-American plans to remove constraints on German industrial production without adequate guarantees for France.[26] Both men were similarly moved by the desire to prevent the re-emergence of Germany as a

[23]'Note sur la répartition des sièges (producteurs et utilisateurs) au Comité consultatif', 7 June 1952, PU 43, HAEU.

[24]This shift towards supposedly apolitical 'technocrats' can also be traced to the Vichy regime, with its renunciation of party politics and the emergence of managerial experts in influential positions. See Delphine Dulong, *Moderniser la politique. Aux origines de la Ve République* (Paris: L'Harmattan, 1997).

[25]Alan Milward, *The Reconstruction of Western Europe* (London: Routledge, 1984) and Frances Lynch, *France and the International Economy* (London: Routledge, 1997).

[26]William Hitchcock, 'France, the Western Alliance, and the Origins of the Schuman Plan, 1948–1950', *Diplomatic History*, 21:4, 1997, 603–630.

military threat to France. Despite their markedly different trajectories during the war, neither individual had embraced the vision of 'Europe' held out by Walther Funk in July 1940 or by Vichy intellectuals.[27] The 'Europe' launched by the Schuman Declaration in May 1950 was driven by more pragmatic and immediate concerns of French national interests, not by any affinity with failed Nazi projects. Despite this lack of direct Vichy influence on Monnet's initiative in 1950, however, this book has demonstrated that Monnet and his colleagues in the CFLN and post-war French administrations had no reservations with appropriating aspects of Vichy's New Industrial Order that could be reoriented towards projects such as the modernisation of French industry. Consequently, Monnet found himself drawing on Committees which had themselves been modelled on Nazi institutions and geared towards facilitating Vichy's contribution to the Reich's war economy. Stripped of their association with Vichy, and replicated and rechristened as Modernisation Commissions, these institutions provided Monnet with the tools to effect the revival of French industry and to contribute, if only in a limited fashion, to the creation of the ECSC. While Cohen has stressed Monnet's 'anti-parliamentarism', this study rather shows Monnet's indifference to the origins of institutions that he deemed useful. Others have noted that Monnet tended to accept an idea on its own merits, regardless of how senior or junior the person who proposed it.[28] Likewise, as has been shown here, he had no qualms with maintaining or adapting Vichy's institutions if he believed this to be pragmatic and advantageous.

While the direct institutional continuities from Vichy to the ECSC may not be very extensive, the continuities in personnel are especially striking. The second French member of the High Authority, Léon Daum, had been deeply implicated in the Vichy regime, from accepting an ill-fated Cabinet appointment from Pierre Laval and being one of CORSID's four members during the war to sitting on Vichy's own anti-democratic consultative assembly, the *Conseil national*. The

[27]See Bernard Bruneteau, *«L'Europe nouvelle de Hitler»: une illusion des intellectuels de Vichy* (Monaco: Rocher, 2003).

[28]See François Duchêne, 'Jean Monnet's Methods' in Douglas Brinkley and Clifford Hackett, *Jean Monnet: The Path to European Unity* (Basingstoke: Macmillan, 1991), 184–209.

industrialists named to the ECSC's Consultative Committee, Pierre Ricard and Robert Baboin, had similarly been important figures in the Organisation Committees under Vichy.[29] In this respect, France's appointments to the ECSC stood out from those made by the other member states. Despite the well-documented continuities in the Italian national administration from the fascist to the post-war regimes, Italy consistently appointed members of the High Authority with impeccable Resistance credentials.[30] For their part, German members of the High Authority tended to have unremarkable wartime records, although several had been conscripted for military service under the Reich.[31] Just as France was the only member of the Six to exclude representatives of its own heavy industries during the negotiations for the ECSC, France was exceptional for appointing almost exclusively individuals who had played key roles in Vichy's New Industrial Order.

The most common associations of Hitler's New Order with today's EU tend to rest primarily on the power and influence of Germany, infamously prompting Margaret Thatcher's Secretary for Trade,

[29]Pierre Ricard was President of the Organisation Committee for Foundry while Robert Baboin was Director for Steel in the Ministry for Industrial Production under Jean Bichelonne. As such, Baboin took part in the meetings of relevant Organisation Committees.

[30]On administrative continuities in Italy, see Roy P. Domenico, *Italian Fascists on Trial, 1943–1948* (Chapel Hill: University of North Carolina Press, 1991), Claudio Pavone, *Alle origini della repubblica: scritti su fascismo, antifascismo e continuità dello Stato* (Turin: Bollati Boringhieri, 1995) and Sabino Cassese, *L'Italie, le fascisme et l'Etat. Continuités et paradoxes* (Paris: Rue d'Ulm, 2014). Italy's first member of the High Authority, Enzo Giacchero, was a member of the *maquis* in northern Italy from 1943. His successor, Piero Malvestiti, was a long-standing opponent of Mussolini's regime and was convicted for 'antifascist activities' in 1934. See Mauve Carbonell, *Des hommes à l'origines de l'Europe: biographies des membres de la Haute Autorité de la CECA* (Aix-en-Provence: Publications de l'Université de Provence, 2008).

[31]Ibid. The notable exception on the German side is Karl-Maria Hettlage, appointed to the High Authority in 1962. During the Second World War he was an advisor to Albert Speer in the Ministry for Armaments and War Production. See Carbonell, 'Karl-Maria Hettlage (1902–1995): un expert au service de l'Europe et des Allemagnes', *Journal of European Integration History*, 23:1, 2006. On the evolution of West Germany's policies towards individuals with past ties to Nazism, see Norbert Frei, *Vergangenheitspolitik: Die Anfänge der Bundesrepublik und die NS-Vergangenheit* (Munich: Beck, 1996) and, specifically on German industrialists, S. Jonathan Wiesen, *West German Industry and the Challenge of the Nazi Past, 1945–1955* (Chapel Hill: University of North Carolina Press, 2001).

Nicholas Ridley, to dismiss the Economic and Monetary Union (EMU) as 'a German racket designed to take over the whole of Europe'.[32] By focusing on institutions for specific industries at the national level for the full decade preceding the Schuman Declaration, rather than the history of ideas or transnational networks, this book has instead revealed important continuities in French industrial policies and individuals that force us to re-evaluate the origins of the Monnet Plan and the ECSC as well as the complex legacy of Vichy. Additional studies adopting a similar approach, for example analyses of national institutions in the other founding member states of the ECSC stretching back to 1940, would further improve our understanding of the multifarious links between the New European Order and the early stages of European integration.

In the French case, the prevalent selection of individuals who had held important positions under Vichy to contribute to the ECSC can in part be explained by their expertise. Just as the Organisation Committees were maintained in 1944 due to their practical value, the men who had managed them for four years had built up invaluable expertise that could be used in other contexts, as their post-war careers demonstrate. Yet the trajectory of these individuals can only be appreciated by considering the extent to which French industrialists participated in the 'new European economic order' floated by the Reich. The Organisation Committees themselves were modelled upon Nazi institutions, and from the very beginning Vichy intended the Committees to contribute to the German war economy. Even those disinclined to assist the Nazi war effort in 1940 recognised the immediate exigencies of filling orders for Germany, given that this was the only realistic means of keeping French factories running. Based on previously unexploited archival sources, this book has shown that the Organisation Committees had no misgivings about producing for the Reich and welcomed the opportunity to take on the production of more goods for Germany, even though this allowed the Reich to increase its armaments production. Yet if this business reasoning or 'managerial logic'[33] of the Committees required producing for the

[32]'Saying the Unsayable about the Germans', *The Spectator*, 14 July 1990. Ridley was forced to resign over these comments.

[33]See Renaud de Rochebrune and Jean-Claude Hazera, *Les Patrons sous l'Occupation* (Paris: Odile Jacob, 1995).

Reich, it also demanded that they staunchly oppose the deportation of their workers to Germany, even if this put the Committees at odds with the Vichy government and the Nazi authorities. The Committees accordingly went to great lengths to undermine schemes like the STO in a bid to preserve the work force of French industry. In this context, labels such as 'resistance' and 'collaboration' are not terribly helpful, given that neither accurately describes the actions or the motivations of the Organisation Committees during the war.

Under Vichy, the members of the Organisation Committees supported cooperation with Germany only when they considered it to be beneficial to their industry – hence the acceptance of more production orders for the Reich yet the refusal to deplete the industry's labour force through deportations to Germany. As head of the CSSF, Jules Aubrun based his response to the Schuman Plan in 1950 on the same criteria: new initiatives involving Franco-German cooperation were worthy of endorsement only if they clearly benefitted the French steel industry. While the political, economic, and ideological context of 1950 was dramatically different from that of a decade before, this central question with which Aubrun and Daum had wrestled under Vichy again informed their positions towards the Schuman Plan. This debate over whether a country's interests are best served through some form of 'European' cooperation or instead by a strictly national strategy influenced the decisions of industrialists and politicians between 1940 and 1952, as indeed it continues to do today.

Bibliography

Archival Sources

Archives Nationales, Paris and Pierrefitte-sur-Seine, France

2 AG, *Papiers des chefs de l'Etat, Etat français*
3 AG, *Papiers des chefs de l'Etat, Charles de Gaulle*
AJ 40, *Archives allemandes de l'occupation*
AJ 41, *Organismes issus de l'armistice de 1940*
68 AJ, *Comités d'organisation et de récupération*
72 AJ, *Papiers du Comité d'histoire de la Deuxième Guerre mondiale et fonds privés relatifs à la période 1939–1945*
80 AJ, *Commissariat Général du Plan, 1946–1965*
81 AJ, *Activités du Commissariat Général du Plan, 1945–1976*
83 AJ, *Main-d'œuvre française en Allemagne, 1942–1945*
139 AQ, *Compagnie des forges et aciéries de la Marine-Homécourt*
C I, *Archives des assemblées nationales*
F 12, *Commerce et industrie*
F 14, *Travaux publics*
F 37, *Commissions financières*
F 60, *Secrétariat général du gouvernement et services du Premier ministre*

Institut d'Histoire du Temps Présent, Paris, France

72 AJ, *Papiers Maisonneuve*

© The Author(s) 2017

L.-A. Brunet, *Forging Europe: Industrial Organisation in France, 1940–1952*, Security, Conflict and Cooperation in the Contemporary World, DOI 10.1057/978-1-349-95198-7

Archives Diplomatiques, La Courneuve, France

Guerre 1939–1940 Vichy
Papiers 1940
CFLN

Centre des Archives Economiques et Financières, Savigny-le-Temple, France

Ministère de l'économie nationale et des finances

Institut d'Histoire Sociale, Nanterre, France

98 J, *Fonds Belin*

Centre des Archives du Monde du Travail, Roubaix, France

AJ 40, *Comité des houillères*
104 AQ, *Fonds Zeiss-Ikonta*
106 AQ, *Fonds Otto Wolff*
123 AQ, *Fonds SA Forges et aciéries Firminy*
139 AQ, *Fonds de Marine et d'Homécourt*
175 AQ, *Fonds Compagnie des forges de Châtillon-Commentry et Neuves-Maisons*
208 AQ, *Fonds Marine-Wendel*
AS 40, *Comité d'organisation des combustibles minéraux solides*
AS 72, *Conseil national du patronat français (CNPF)*

Fondation Jean Monnet Pour l'Europe, Lausanne, Switzerland

Archives Jean Monnet
AME, *La Seconde Guerre mondiale (1938–1946)*
AMF, *Le plan de modernisation et d'équipement de la France (1946–1952)*
AMG, *Le Plan Schuman (1950–1952)*
AMH, *La Communauté européenne du charbon et de l'acier (1952–1955)*
AMM, *Notes manuscrites*

Historical Archives of the European Union, Florence, Italy

CEAB, *Haute Autorité de la CECA*
EH, *Fonds Etienne Hirsch*
PU, *Fonds Pierre Uri*

Bundesarchiv-Militärarchiv, Freiburg im Breisgau, Germany

RW 19, *Oberkommando der Wehrmacht*
RW 24, *Rüstungsdienstellen (Frankreich)*
RW 25, *Rüstungsdienstellen (Belgien und Nordfrankreich)*
RW 34, *Deutsche Waffenstillstandskommission*
RW 35, *Der Militärbefehlshaber in Frankreich*

National Archives, London, United Kingdom

ADM, *Records of the Admiralty, Naval Forces, Royal Marines, Coastguard and Related Bodies*
FO, *Foreign Office*
GFM, *Copies of Captured Records of the German, Italian and Japanese Governments*
MT, *Ministry of Transport*
PREM, *Prime Minister's Office*
SOE, *Special Operations Executive*
T, *Treasury*
WO, *War Office*

Archives diplomatiques, Bruxelles, Belgium

Plan Schuman
Présidence de la Haute Autorité

Library and Archives Canada, Ottawa, Canada

Schuman Plan

Published sources

L'Humanité
Journal officiel
Nouveaux cahiers
Le Temps

Online sources

'Bulletins de notes d'élèves-ingénieurs du corps des mines. Promotions entrées à l'Ecole de 1853 à 1960', Les Annales des Mines, annales.org/archives/images/n1, last accessed 26 July 2014.

Memoirs

Abetz, Otto. *Histoire d'une politique franco-allemande 1930–1950: mémoires d'un ambassadeur*. Paris: Stock, 1953.

Baudouin, Paul. *The Private Diaries (March 1940 to January 1941) of Paul Baudouin. Under-Secretary of State and Secretary of the War Cabinet in M. Paul Reynaud's Administration, April 1940 to May 1940; Foreign Minister under Marshal Pétain, June 1940 to January 1941*. Tr. Charles Petrie. London: Eyre and Spottiswoode, 1948.

Belin, René. *De la C.G.T. au Gouvernement de Vichy (1933–1942)*. Paris: Editions Albatros, 1978.

Benoist-Méchin, Jacques. *A l'épreuve du temps*. Paris: Perrin, 1989.

Blocq-Mascart, Maxime. *Chroniques de la Résistance*. Paris: Corréa, 1945.

Boris, Georges. *Servir la République*. Paris: Julliard, 1963.

Bouthillier, Yves. *Le drame de Vichy*. Paris: Plon, 1951

Cathala, Pierre. *Face aux réalités. La direction des finances françaises sous l'occupation*. Paris: Triolet, 1948.

De Gaulle, Charles. *Discours et messages, 1940–1946*. Paris: Berger-Levrault, 1946.

De Gaulle, Charles. *Mémoires de guerre. L'appel, 1940–1942*. Paris: Plon, 1954.

De Gaulle, Charles. *Mémoires de guerre. L'unité, 1942–1944*. Paris: Plon, 1956.

De Gaulle, Charles. *Mémoires de guerre. Le salut, 1944–1946*. Paris: Plon, 1959.

Hirsch, Etienne. *Ainsi va la vie*. Lausanne: Fondation Jean Monnet pour l'Europe, 1988.

Joxe, Louis. *Victoires sur la nuit. Mémoires 1940–1946*. Paris: Flammarion, 1981.

Laval, Pierre. *Laval parle: notes et mémoires*. Geneva: Editions du cheval ailé, 1947.

Lehideux, François. *De Renault à Pétain. Mémoires*. Paris: Pygmalion, 2001.

Kehrl, Hans. *Krisenmanager im Dritten Reich*. Düsseldorf: Droste Verlag., 1973.

Marjolin, Robert. *Le travail d'une vie. Mémoires 1911–1986*. Paris: Robert Laffont, 1986.

Martin, Roger. *Patron du droit divin*. Paris: Gallimard, 1984.

Monnet, Jean. *Mémoires*. Paris: Fayard, 1976.

Mornet, André. *Quatre ans à rayer de notre histoire*. Paris: SELF, 1949.

Nicolle, Pierre. *Cinquante mois d'armistice: Vichy 2 juillet 1940–26 août* 1944. *Journal d'un témoin*. Paris: A. Bonne, 1947.

Pétain, Philippe. *Discours aux Français*. Jean-Claude Barbas, ed. Paris: Albin Michel, 1989.

Pétain, Philippe. *Quatre années au pouvoir*. Paris: Couronne littéraire, 1949.

Peyrouton, Marcel. *Du service public à la prison commune. Souvenirs.* Paris: Plon, 1950.
Plowden, Edwin. *An Industrialist in the Treasury: The Postwar Years.* London: André Deutsch, 1989.
Pucheu, Pierre. *Ma vie.* Paris: Amiot-Dumont, 1948.
Speer, Albert. *Inside the Third Reich.* Tr. Richard and Clara Winston. New York: Macmillan, 1970.

Secondary Works (Books and articles)

Adelman, Jonathan, ed. *Hitler and His Allies in World War II.* London: Routledge, 2007.
Alary, Eric. *La ligne de démarcation.* Paris: Perrin, 2003.
Alary, Eric. *Les Français au quotidien, 1939–1949.* Paris: Perrin, 2006.
Allen, Robert C. *Farm to Factory: A Reinterpretation of the Soviet Industrial Revolution.* Princeton: Princeton University Press, 2003.
Altwegg, Jürg. *Die langen Schatten von Vichy.* Munich: Carl Hanser Verlag, 1998.
Aly, Götz. *Hitlers Volksstaat: Raub, Rassenkrieg und nationaler Sozialismus.* Frankfurt: S. Fischer, 2005.
Andrieu, Claire. *Le programme commun de la Résistance. Des idées dans la guerre.* Paris: Editions de l'Erudit, 1984.
Andrieu, Claire. *La Banque sous l'Occupation. Paradoxes de l'histoire d'une profession.* Paris: Presses de la Fondation nationale des sciences politiques, 1990.
Andrieu, Claire, ed. *La spoliation financière. Mission d'étude sur la spoliation des Juifs en France.* Paris: Documentation française, 2000.
Andrieu, Claire, Philippe Braud and Guillaume Piketty. *Dictionnaire de Gaulle.* Paris: Robert Laffont, 2006.
Andrieu, Claire, Lucette Le Van and Antoine Prost, eds. *Les nationalisations de la Libération. De l'utopie au compromis.* Paris: Presses de la Fondation nationale des sciences politiques, 1987.
Arnaud, Patrice. *Les STO. Histoire des Français requis en Allemagne nazie 1942–1945.* Paris: CNRS, 2010.
Arnoult, Pierre. *Les finances de la France et l'Occupation allemande.* Paris: Presses universitaires de France, 1951.
Aron, Robert. *Histoire de Vichy.* Paris: Fayard, 1954.
Aron, Robert. *Histoire de l'épuration.* Paris: Fayard, 1974.
Azéma, Jean-Pierre. *De Munich à la Libération 1938–1944.* Paris: Seuil, 1979.
Azéma, Jean-Pierre et François Bédarida, eds. *La France des années noires.* Paris: Seuil, 2000.
Azéma, Jean-Pierre et Olivier Wieviorka. *Vichy, 1940–1944.* Paris: Perrin, 2004.
Bähr, Johannes and Ralf Banken. 'L'organisation de l'économie allemande sous le national-socialisme 1933–1945. Synthèse et bilan critique des recherches' in

Hervé Joly, ed. *Les Comités d'organisation et l'économie dirigée du régime de Vichy*. Caen: Centre de recherche d'histoire quantitative, 2004, 21–38.

Bähr, Johannes and Ralf Banken, eds. *Das Europa des 'Dritten Reichs': Recht, Wirtschaft, Besatzung*. Frankfurt: Klostermann, 2005.

Barasz, Johanna. 'Un vichyste en Résistance, le général de la Laurencie', *Vingitème siècle*, 2007/2, no. 94, 167–181.

Barjot, Dominique, ed. *Stratégies industrielles sous l'Occupation*. Special issue of *Histoire, économie et société*, 11:3, 1992.

Barkaï, Avraham. *Das Wirtschaftssystem des Nationalsozialismus*. Frankfurt: Fischer, 1988.

Baruch, Marc Olivier. *Servir l'Etat français. L'administration en France de 1940 à 1944*. Paris: Fayard, 1997.

Bauchard, Philippe. *Les technocrates et le pouvoir*. Paris: Arthaud, 1966.

Bauer, Michel and Bénédicte Bertin-Mourot. *Les 200: Comment devient-on un grand patron?* Paris: Seuil, 1987.

Baumier, Jean. *La fin des maîtres de forges*. Paris: Plon, 1981.

Beauvois, Yves. *Léon Noël: de Laval à de Gaulle via Pétain (1888–1987)*. Villeneuve-d'Ascq: Presses universitaires du Septentrion, 2001

Belot, Robert. *La Résistance sans de Gaulle*. Paris: Fayard, 2006.

Beltran, Alain. 'Les entreprises d'électricité (production thermique)', *Histoire, économie et société*. 1992, 11:3, 437–443.

Beltran, Alain, Robert Frank and Henry Rousso, eds. *La vie des entreprises sous l'Occupation*. Paris: Belin, 1994.

Berger, Françoise. 'Les sidérurgistes français et allemands face à l'Europe', *Journal of European Integration History*, 3:2, 1997, 35–52.

Berger, Françoise. 'Die Beziehung zwischen der französischen und der deutschen Eisen- und Stahlindustrie', *Zeitschrift für Unternehmensgeschichte*, C.H. Beck, 2006, 159–180.

Berger, Françoise. 'Alexis Aron, ingénieur sidérurgiste', *Archives juives*, 1:44, 2011, 136–139.

Bergère, Marc, ed. *L'épuration économique en France à la Libération*. Rennes: Presses universitaires de Rennes, 2008.

Berle, Adolf and Gardiner Means. *The Modern Corporation and Private Property*. New York: Macmillan, 1932.

Berstein, Serge. *Histoire du gaullisme*. Paris: Perrin, 2001.

Berstein, Serge and Pierre Milza. *L'Année 1947*. Paris: Presses de Sciences Po, 2000.

Biard, Jean-François. *Le socialisme devant ses choix: la naissance de l'idée de plan*. Paris: Publications de la Sorbonne, 1985.

Bloch, Marc. *L'Etrange défaite*. Paris: Armand Colin, 1957.

Bloch-Lainé, François and Jean Bouvier. *La France restaurée*. Paris: Fayard, 1986.

Bloch-Lainé, François and Claude Gruson. *Hauts fonctionnaires sous l'Occupation*. Paris: Editions Odile Jacob, 1996.

Boerger, Anne. 'La Cour de Justice dans les négociations du Traité de Paris instituant la CECA', *Journal of European Integration History*, 18:2, 2008, 7–33.

Bonin, Hubert. 'Peut-on imaginer des banquiers patriotes et résistants (1940–1944)?' in *Guerres mondiales et conflits contemporains* no. 243, vol. 3, 2011, 45–58.

Bossuat, Gérard, ed. *D'Alger à Rome, 1943–1957*. Louvain: Ciaco, 1989.

Bossuat, Gérard. *L'Europe occidentale à l'heure américaine, 1944–1952*. Brussels: Complexe, 1992.

Bossuat, Gérard. *L'Europe des Français, 1943–1959: La IVe République aux sources de l'Europe communautaire*. Paris: Publications de la Sorbonne, 1996.

Bossuat, Gérard. 'Jean Monnet. La mesure d'une influence', *Vingtième siècle* 51:1, 1996, 68–84.

Bossuat, Gérard. *La France, l'aide américaine et la construction européenne, 1944–1954*. Paris: Comité pour l'Histoire Economique et Financière de la France, 1997.

Bourdieu, Pierre. *La nobless d'Etat*. Paris: Editions de Minuit, 1989.

Bourdrel, Philippe. *L'épuration sauvage, 1944–1945*. Paris: Perrin, 2002.

Brana, Pierre et Joëlle Duseau. *Robert Lacoste (1898–1989). De la Dordogne à l'Algérie, un socialiste devant l'histoire*. Paris: L'Harmattan, 2010.

Broch, Ludivine. *Ordinary Workers, Vichy and the Holocaust: French Railwaymen and the Second World War*. Cambridge: Cambridge University Press, 2016.

Broszat, Martin. *Der Staat Hitlers: Grundlegung und Entwicklung seiner inneren Verfassung*. Munich: Deutscher Taschenbuch Verlag, 1969.

Brun, Gérard. *Technocrates et technocratie en France*. Paris: Albatros, 1985.

Bruneteau, Bernard. *L'Europe Nouvelle» de Hitler, une illusion des intellectuels de Vichy*. Monaco: Editions Du Rocher, 2003.

Bruneteau, Bernard. *Les collabos de l'Europe nouvelle*. Paris: CNRS, 2016.

Bruttmann, Tal, ed. *Persécutions et spoliations des Juifs pendant la Seconde Guerre mondiale*. Grenoble: Presses Universitaires de Grenoble, 2004.

Buchheim, Christophe and Marcel Boldorf, eds. *Europäische Volkwirtschaften unter deutscher Hegemonie 1938–1945*. Munich: Oldenbourg Akademie Verlag, 2012.

Burnham, James. *The Managerial Revolution*. New York: John Day, 1941.

Burrin, Philippe. *La France à l'heure allemande*. Paris: Seuil, 1995.

Bussière, Eric. 'Les milieux économiques face à l'Europe au XXe siècle', *Journal of European Integration History* 3:2, 1997, 5–21.

Bussière, Eric, Michel Dumoulin and Silvain Schirmann, eds. *Milieux économiques et intégration européenne au 20e siècle. La crise des années 1970*. Brussels: Peter Lang, 2006.

Bussière, Eric, Michel Dumoulin and Gilbert Trausch, eds. *Europa: L'idée et l'identité européenne, de l'antiquité au XXIe siècle*. Brussels: Mercator, 2001.

Buton, Philippe. *Les lendemains qui déchantent. Le Parti communiste français à la Libération*. Paris: Presses de la Fondation nationale des sciences politique, 1993.

Cahigne-Oudin, Anne-Lucie, *La France dans les jeux d'influences en Syrie et au Liban*. Paris: Harmattan, 2009.

Cantier, Jacques. *L'Algérie sous le régime de Vichy*. Paris: Odile Jacob, 2002.

Capuano, Christophe. 'Travailler chez Schneider sous l'Occupation. Le cas des usines du Creusot' in Christian Chevandier and Jean-Claude Daumas, eds. *Travailler dans les entreprises sous l'Occupation*. Besançon: Presses universitaires de Franche-Comté, 2007, 187–207.

Carbonell, Mauve. 'Karl-Maria Hettlage (1902–1995): un expert au service de l'Europe et des Allemagnes', *Journal of European Integration History* 23:1, 2006, 67–85.

Carbonell, Mauve. *Les Hommes à l'origine de l'Europe*. Aix-en-Provence: Publications de l'Université de Provence, 2008.

Cassese, Sabino. *L'Italie, le fascisme et l'Etat. Continuités et paradoxes*. Paris: Rue d'Ulm, 2014.

Cazes, Bernard and Philippe Mioche, eds. *Modernisation ou décadence. Etudes, témoignages et documents sur la planification française*. Aix-en-Provence: Publications de l'Université de Provence, 1990.

Céline. *D'un château l'autre*. Paris: Gallimard, 1957.

Chapsal, Jacques. *La vie politique en France de 1940 à 1958*. Paris: Presses Universitaires de France, 1984.

Chardonnet, Jean. *Le charbon. Sa production, son rôle économique et social*. Paris: Arthaud, 1948.

Clarke, Jackie. *France in the Age of Organization: Factory, Home and Nation from the 1920s to Vichy*. Oxford: Berghahn, 2011.

Cohen, Antonin. *De Vichy à la Communauté européenne*. Paris: Presses Universitaires de France, 2012.

Cointet, Jean-Paul. *Pierre Laval*. Paris: Fayard, 1993.

Cointet, Jean-Paul. *Expier Vichy: l'épuration en France 1943–1958*. Paris: Perrin, 2008.

Cointet, Michèle. *Le Conseil National de Vichy*. Paris: Amateurs de Livres, 1989.

Colas, Dominique, ed. *L'Etat et les corporatismes*. Paris: Presses Universitaires de France, 1988.

Conan, Eric and Henry Rousso. *Vichy, un passé qui ne passe pas*. Paris: Fayard, 1994.

Coulon, Eric. *Les Forges d'Audincourt*. Strasbourg: Coprur, 2006.

Courtois, Stéphane and Marc Lazar. *Histoire du Parti communiste français*. Paris: Presses Universitaires de France, 1995.

Coutau-Bégarie, Hervé and Claude Huan. *Darlan*. Paris: Fayard, 1989.

Crémieux-Brilhac, Jean-Louis. *La France libre: De l'appel du 18 juin à la Libération*. Paris: Gallimard, 1996.

Daley, Anthony. *Steel, State, and Labor*. Pittsburgh: University of Pittsburgh Press, 1996.

Dard, Olivier. *La synarchie, le mythe du complot permanent*. Paris: Perrin, 1998.

Dard, Olivier. 'Les technocrates: archéologie d'un concept, généalogie d'un groupe social' in Olivier Dard, Jean-Claude Daumas et François Marcot, eds. *L'Occupation, l'Etat français et les entreprises*. Paris: Association pour le développement de l'histoire économique, 2000, 213–228.

Dard, Olivier. *Le rendez-vous manqué des relèves des années trente*. Paris: Presses universitaires de France, 2002.

Dard, Olivier, Jean-Claude Daumas et François Marcot, eds. *L'Occupation, l'Etat français et les entreprises*. Paris: Association pour le développement de l'histoire économique, 2000.

Dard, Olivier and Gilles Richard, eds. *Les permanents patronaux: éléments pour l'histoire du patronat en France dans la première moitié du XXème siècle*. Metz: Université Paul Verlaine de Metz, 2005.

Daumas, Jean-Claude, Alain Chatriot, Danièle Fraboulet, Patrick Fridenson and Hervé Joly, eds. *Dictionnaire des patrons français*. Paris: Flammarion, 2010.

Dejonghe, Etienne, ed. *L'Occupation en France et en Belgique, 1940–1944*. Lille: Revue du Nord, 1987.

Dell, Edmund. *The Schuman Plan and the British Abdication of Leadership in Europe*. Oxford: Oxford University Press, 1995.

Desquesnes, Rémy. 'L'Organisation Todt en France (1940–1944)', *Histoire, économie et société*, 11:3, 1992, 535–550.

Domenico, Roy P. *Italian Fascists on Trial, 1943–1948*. Chapel Hill: University of North Carolina Press, 1991.

Dougherty, James. *The Politics of Wartime Aid: American Economic Assistance to France and French Northwest Africa, 1940–1946*. Westport: Greenwood, 1978.

Douzou, Laurent. *La Résistance française: une histoire périlleuse*. Paris: Seuil, 2005.

Dreyfus, Jean-Marc. *Pilages sur ordonnances: aryanisation et restitution en banques en France, 1940–1953*. Paris: Fayard, 2003.

Dreyfus, Michel. *Histoire de la CGT: cent ans de syndicalisme en France*. Brussels: Editions Complexe, 1995.

Duchêne, François. 'Jean Monnet's Methods' in Douglas Brinkley and Clifford Hackett, eds. *Jean Monnet: The Path to European Unity*. Basingstoke: Macmillan, 1991, 184–209.

Duchêne, François. *Jean Monnet: The First Statesman of Interdependence*. New York: Norton, 1994.

Dulong, Delphine. *Moderniser la politique. Aux origines de la Ve République*. Paris: L'Harmattan, 1997.

Dumoulin, Michel, ed. *Plans des temps de guerre pour l'Europe d'après-guerre, 1940–1947*. Brussels: Bruylant, 1995.

Dumoulin, Michel, ed. *La Communauté européenne de défense, leçons pour demain?* Brussels: Peter Land, 2000.

Durand, Yves. *Le nouvel ordre européen nazi. La collaboration dans L'Europe allemande 1938–1945*. Paris: Editions Complèxe, 1990.

Du Réau, Elisabeth. *L'idée européenne au XXe siècle*. Brussels: Complexe, 1996.

Duroselle, Jean-Baptiste. *L'Abîme*. Paris: Imprimerie nationale, 1982.

Dwan, Renata. 'Jean Monnet and the European Defence Community, 1950–1954', *Cold War History* 1:3, 2001, 141–160.

Eck, Jean-François. *Histoire de l'économie française depuis 1945*. Paris: Armand Colin, 2004.

Ehrmann, Henry W. *Organized Business in France*. Princeton: Princeton University Press, 1957.

Evrard, Jacques. *La deportation des travailleurs français dans le IIIe Reich*. Paris: Fayard, 1972.

Ferro, Marc. *Pétain*. Paris: Hachette, 1993.

Fishman, Sarah, Robert Zaretsky, Ioannis Sinanoglou, Leonard V. Smith and Laura Lee Downs, eds. *France at War: Vichy and the Historians*. Oxford: Berg, 2000.

Fleming, D.F. *The Cold War and Its Origins, 1917–1960*. London: Allen and Unwin, 1961.

Fogg, Shannon. *The Politics of Everyday Life in Vichy*. Cambridge: Cambridge University Press, 2009.

Fondation Charles de Gaulle. *Le rétablissement de la légalité républicaine (1944)*. Paris: Editions Complexe, 1996.

Fontaine, André. *Histoire de la Guerre froide, vol. I, De la révolution d'octobre à la guerre de Corée*. Paris: Fayard, 1967.

Fontaine, Pascal. *Jean Monnet l'inspirateur*. Paris: Jacques Grancher, 1988.

Foot, M.R.D. *The SOE in France: An Account of the Work of the British Special Operations Executive in France 1940–1944*. London: British Broadcasting Corporation, 1966.

Fourquet, François. *Les Comptes de la puissance*. Paris: Recherches, 1980.

Fraboulet, Danièle. *Les Entreprises sous l'Occupation. Le monde de la métallurgie à Saint-Denis*. Paris: CNRS, 1998.

Frank, Robert, ed. *Les identités européennes au Xxe siècle*. Paris: Publications de la Sorbonne, 2004.

Frei, Norbert. *Vergangenheitspolitik: Die Anfänge der Bundesrepublik und die NS-Vergangenheit*. Munich: Beck, 1996.

Freymond, Jean. *Le IIIe Reich et la réorganisation économique de l'Europe 1940–1942*. Paris: Leiden, 1974.

Fursdon, Edward. *The European Defence Community*. London: Macmillan, 1980.

Garnier, Bernard and Jean Quellien, eds. *La main-d'œuvre française exploitée par le IIIe Reich.* Caen: Centre de Recherche d'Histoire Quantitative, 2003.
Gerbet, Pierre. *La construction de l'Europe.* Paris: Imprimerie nationale, 1983.
Gildea, Robert. *Marianne in Chains: Daily Life in the Heart of France during the German Occupation.* New York: Picador, 2004.
Gildea, Robert. *Fighters in the Shadows: A New History of the French Resistance.* London: Faber & Faber, 2015.
Gillingham, John. *Coal, Steel and the Rebirth of Europe, 1945–1955.* Cambridge: Cambridge UP, 1991.
Gillingham, John. 'De la coopération à l'intégration: la Ruhr et l'industrie lourde française pendant la guerre', *Histoire, économie et socciété* 11: 3, 1992, 369–395.
Golsan, Richard J. *Vichy's Afterlife: History and Counterhistory in Postwar France.* Lincoln: University of Nebraska Press, 2000.
Gordon, Bertram M. *Collaborationism in France During the Second World War.* Ithaca, NY: Cornell University Press, 1980.
Grenard, Fabrice. *La France du marché noir (1940–1949).* Paris: Payot & Rivages, 2008.
Groux, Guy and René Mouriaux. '1944. Les syndicats, la légalité républicaine et le pluralisme' in Fondation Charles de Gaulle, *Le rétablissement de la légalité républicaine.* Paris: Editions Complexe, 1996, 755–765.
Gruson, Claude. *Les Origines de la planification française.* Paris: Dunod, 1968.
Guillaume, Sylvie. *Antoine Pinay, ou, La confiance en politique.* Paris: FNSP, 1984.
Guillen, Pierre. 'La France et la négociation du Traité d'Euratom' in Michel Dumoulin, Pierre Guillen and Maurice Vaïsse, eds. *L'Energie nucléaire en Europe. Des origines à Euratom.* Brussels: Peter Lang, 1994.
Haslam, Jonathan. *Russia's Cold War: From the October Revolution to the Fall of the Wall.* New Haven: Yale University Press, 2011.
Hayes, Peter. 'La stratégie industrielle de l'IG Farben en France occupée' in *Histoire, économie et société,* 11:3, 1992, 493–514.
Hills, John, John Ditch, and Howard Glennerster. *Beveridge and Social Security: An International Retrospective.* Oxford: Calrendon, 1994.
Hitchcock, William. 'France, the Western Alliance, and the Origins of the Schuman Plan, 1948–1950', *Diplomatic History* 21:4, 1997, 603–630.
Hitchcock, William I. *France Restored: Cold War Diplomacy and the Quest for Leadership in Europe, 1944–1954.* Chapel Hill: University of North Carolina Press, 1998.
Hoffmann, Stanley, ed. *In Search of France.* Cambridge, MA: Harvard University Press, 1963.
Holter, Darryl. *The Battle for Coal: Miners and the Politics of Nationalization in France, 1940–1950.* DeKalb, IL: Northern Illinois University Press, 1992.
Imlay, Talbot. *Facing the Second World War: Strategy, Politics, and Economics in Britain and France, 1938–1940.* Oxford: Oxford University Press, 2003.

Imlay, Talbot and Martin Horn. *The Politics of Industrial Collaboration During World War II: Ford France, Vichy and Nazi Germany.* Cambridge: Cambridge University Press, 2014.

Jabbari, Eric. *Pierre Laroque and the Welfare State in Postwar France.* Oxford: Oxford University Press, 2012.

Jäckel, Eberhard. *Frankreich in Hitlers Europa.* Stuttgart: Deutsche Verlag, 1966.

Jackson, Julian. *The Popular Front in France: Defending Democracy, 1934–38.* Cambridge: Cambridge University Press, 1988.

Jackson, Julian. *France: The Dark Years.* Oxford: Oxford University Press, 2001.

Jackson, Julian. *The Fall of France: The Nazi Invasion of 1940.* Oxford: Oxford University Press, 2003.

Jackson, Julian. *De Gaulle.* London: Haus, 2003.

Jeanneney, Jean Noël. *François de Wendel en République: l'argent et le pouvoir, 1914–1940.* Paris: Seuil, 1976.

Johnson, D.W.J. 'Britain and France in 1940', *Transactions of the Royal Historical Society* 5:22, 1972, 141–157.

Joly, Hervé. 'Prosopographie des dirigeants des Comités d'organisation' in Olivier Dard, Jean-Claude Daumas and François Marcot, eds. *L'Occupation, l'Etat français et les entreprises.* Paris: Association pour le développement de l'histoire économique, 2000, 245–260.

Joly, Hervé, ed. *Faire l'histoire des entreprises sous l'occupation. Les acteurs économiques et leurs archives.* Paris: Comité des travaux historiques et scientifiques, 2004.

Joly, Hervé, ed. *Les Comités d'organisation et l'économie dirigée du régime de Vichy.* Caen: Centre de recherche d'histoire quantitative, 2004.

Joly, Hervé. 'Les comités d'organisation: un ensemble vaste et disparate' in Hervé Joly, ed. *Les Comités d'organisation et l'économie dirigée du régime de Vichy.* Caen: Centre de recherche d'histoire quantitative, 2004, 83–94.

Joly, Hervé, ed. *L'Economie de la zone non occupée 1940–1942.* Paris: Editions du Comité des travaux historiques et scientifiques, 2007.

Joly, Hervé. 'Mobilités patronales dans l'après-guerre et impact de l'épuration' in Marc Bergère, ed. *L'épuration économique en France à la Libération.* Rennes: Presses universitaires de Rennes, 2008, 83–100.

Jones, Adrian. 'Illusions of Sovereignty: Business and the Organization of Committees of Vichy France', *Social History* 11:1, January 1986, 1–31.

Jörnmark, Jan. *Coal and Steel in Western Europe: Innovative Change and Institutional Adaptation.* Göteborg: Göteborg University Press, 1993.

Julliard, Jacques. 'La Charte du travail' in René Rémond, ed., *Le gouvernement de Vichy, 1940–1942.* Paris: Presses de la Fondation nationale des sciences politiques, 1972.

Kahn, Daniela. *Die Steuerung der Wirtschaft durch Recht im nazionalsozialistischen Deutschland. Das Beispiel der Reichsgruppe Industrie.* Frankfurt: Klostermann, 2006.

Kahn, Sylvain. *Histoire de la construction de l'Europe depuis 1945.* Paris: Presses Universitaires de France, 2011.

Kaiser, Wolfram. *Christian Democracy and the Origins of European Union.* Cambridge: Cambridge University Press, 2007.

Kaiser, Wolfram, Brigitte Leucht and Michael Gehler, eds. *Transnational Networks in Regional Integration: Governing Europe 1945–1983.* Basingstoke: Palgrave Macmillan, 2010.

Kaiser, Wolfram, Brigitte Leucht and Morten Rasmussen, eds. *The History of the European Union: Origins of a Trans- and Supranational Polity, 1950–1972.* London: Routledge, 2009.

Kaiser, Wolfram and Antonio Varsori, eds. *European Union History: Themes and Debates.* Basingstoke: Palgrave Macmillan, 2010.

Kedward, H.R. *In Search of the Maquis: Rural Resistance in Southern France.* Oxford: Oxford University Press, 1993.

Kipping, Matthias. *La France et les origines de l'Union européenne. Intégration économique et compétitivité internationale.* Paris: CHEF, 2002.

Klemann, Hein and Sergei Kudryashov. *Occupied Economies: An Economic History of Nazi-Occupied Europe, 1939–1945.* London: Berg, 2012.

Knapp, Andrew, ed. *The Uncertain Foundation: France at the Liberation, 1944–1947.* Basingstoke: Palgrave Macmillan, 2007.

Kuisel, Richard. 'The Legend of the Vichy Synarchy', *French Historical Studies* 6:3, 1970, 365–398.

Kuisel, Richard. 'Vichy et les origines de la planification économique (1940–1946)', *Le mouvement social* 98, January–March 1977, 77–101.

Kuisel, Richard. *Capitalism and the State in Modern France: Renovation and Economic Management in the Twentieth Century.* Cambridge: Cambridge University Press, 1981.

Kupferman, Fred. *Laval: 1883–1945.* Paris: Balland, 1987.

Laborie, Pierre. *L'opinion publique sous Vichy.* Paris: Seuil, 1990.

Lackerstein, Debbie. *National Regeneration in Vichy France: Ideas and Policies, 1930–1944.* Farnham: Ashgate, 2012.

Lacouture, Jean. *De Gaulle. Le rebelle, 1890–1944.* Paris: Seuil, 1984.

Lacouture, Jean. *De Gaulle. Le politique, 1944–1959.* Paris: Seuil, 1985.

Lacroix-Riz, Annie. *Industriels et banquiers sous l'Occupation. La collaboration économique avec le Reich et Vichy.* Paris: Armand Colin, 1999.

Lacroix-Riz, Annie. 'Les comités d'organisation et l'Allemagne: tentative d'évaluation' in Hervé Joly, ed. *Les Comités d'organisation et l'économie dirigée du régime de Vichy.* Caen: Centre de recherche d'histoire quantitative, 2004, 47–62.

Lambert, Pierre-Philippe et Gérard Le Marec. *Vichy 1940–1944. Organisations et mouvements.* Paris: Grancher, 2009.

Laroque, Pierre. *Les rapports entre patrons et ouvriers.* Paris: Aubier, 1938.

Laub, Thomas J. *After the Fall: German Policy in Occupied France, 1940–1944.* Oxford: Oxford University Press, 2010.

Laughland, John. *The Tainted Source: The Undemocratic Origins of the European Idea.* London: Little, Brown and Company, 1997.

Le Bot, Florent. 'La naissance du Centre des jeunes patrons (1938–1944). Entre réaction et relève', *Vingtième siècle* 2012/2, numéro 114, 99–116.

Leboutte, René. 'L'industrie sidérurgique belge et ses réseaux dans les années 1950' in Michel Dumoulin, ed. *Réseaux économiques et construction européenne.* Brussels: Peter Lang, 2004.

Le Crom, Jean-Pierre. *Syndicats nous voilà! Vichy et le corporatisme.* Paris: Editions de l'Atelier, 1995.

Lefeuvre, Daniel. 'Vichy et la modernisation de l'Algérie: Intention ou réalité ?', *Vingtième siècle*, vol. 42, no. 1, 1994, 7–16.

Lefèvre, Sylvie. *Les relations économiques franco-allemandes de 1945 à 1955. De l'occupation à la coopération.* Paris: Comité pour l'histoire économique et financière de la France, 1998.

Leffler, Melvyn P. *The Specter of Communism: The United States and the Origins of the Cold War, 1917–1953.* New York: Hill and Wang, 1994.

Lemmes, Fabian. 'Collaboration in wartime France, 1940–1944', *European Review of History: Revue européenne d'histoire*, 15:2, April 2008, 157–177.

Leucht, Brigitte. *The Transatlantic Origins of European Competition Policy.* Forthcoming.

Lipgens, Walter. *Documents on the History of European Integration.* 3 vols. Berlin: Walter de Gruyter, 1984.

Lord, Christopher. *Absent at the Creation: Britain and the Formation of the European Community, 1950–52.* Dartmouth: Aldershot, 1996.

Lottman, Herbert R. *The People's Anger: Justice and Revenge in Post-liberation France.* London: Hutchinson, 1986.

Loubet, Jean-Louis. 'Le travail dans quelques entreprises automobiles françaises sous l'Occupation' in Christian Chevandier and Jean-Claude Daumas, eds. *Travailler dans les entreprises sous l'Occupation.* Besançon: Presses universitaires de Franche-Comté, 2007, 177–186.

Loubet del Bayle, Jean-Louis. *Les non-conformistes des années 30: une tentative de renouvellement de la pensée politique française.* Paris: Seuil, 1969.

Lynch, Frances. 'Resolving the Paradox of the Monnet Plan: National and International Planning in French Reconstruction', *Economic History Review* 37:2, 1984, 229–243.

Lynch, Frances M.B. *France and the International Economy: From Vichy to the Treaty of Rome.* London: Routledge, 1997.

Marcot, François. 'La direction de Peugeot sous l'Occupation: pétainisme, réticence, opposition et résistance', *Mouvement social* 189, October–December 1999, 27–46.

Marcot, François. 'Qu'est-ce qu'un patron resistant?' in Olivier Dard, Jean-Claude Daumas and François Marcot, eds. *L'Occupation, l'Etat français et les entreprises.* Paris: Association pour le développement de l'histoire économique, 2000, 277–292.

Margairaz, Michel. *L'Etat, les finances et l'économie. Histoire d'une conversion 1932–1952.* 2 vols. Paris: Comité pour l'histoire économique et financière de la France, 1991.

Marquand, David. *Parliament for Europe.* London: Jonathan Cape, 1979.

Marrus, Michael. 'Vichy avant Vichy', *Histoire* 3, November 1979, 72–92.

Mazower, Mark. *Hitler's Empire: How the Nazis Ruled Europe.* New York: Penguin, 2008.

Mazower, Mark. *No Enchanted Palace: The End of Empire and the Ideological Origins of the United Nations.* Princeton: Princeton University Press, 2009.

McIvor, Arthur. *A History of Work in Britain 1880–1950.* Basingstoke: Palgrave, 2001.

Mérigot, Jean-Guy. *Les Comités d'organisation.* Bordeaux: Université de Bordeaux, 1943.

Michel, Henry. *Vichy Année 40.* Paris: Robert Lafont, 1966.

Milward, Alan. *The German Economy at War.* London: Athlone Press, 1965.

Milward, Alan. *The New Order and the French Economy.* Oxford: Oxford University Press, 1970.

Milward, Alan. *War, Economy and Society, 1939–1945.* Berkeley: University of California Press, 1977.

Milward, Alan. *The Reconstruction of Western Europe, 1945–1951.* London: Routledge, 1984.

Milward, Alan. *The European Rescue of the Nation State.* London: Routledge, 1992.

Mioche, Philippe. *Le plan Monnet. Genèse et élaboration 1941–1947.* Paris: Publications de la Sorbonne, 1987.

Mioche, Philippe. 'Les « maitres de forges » en quête de transparence. Archives de la sidérurgie et histoire économique' in *Vingtième siècle. Revue d'histoire*, vol. 20, no. 1, 1988, 103–112.

Mioche, Philippe. 'Un tournant dans l'histoire technique de la sidérurgie: la création de l'Irsid', *Histoire, économie et société* 8:1, 1989, 119–140.

Mioche, Philippe. 'Les entreprises sidérurgiques sous l'Occupation', *Histoire, économie et société* 11:3, 1992, 397–414.

Mioche, Philippe. 'Une vision conciliante du futur de l'Europe: le plan d'Alexis Aron en 1943' in Michel Dumoulin, ed. *Plans des temps de guerre pour l'Europe d'après-guerre, 1940–1947.* Brussels: Bruylant, 1995.

Mioche, Philippe. 'Les comités d'organisation de la sidérurgie: un lieu d'affrontement entre modernisateurs de la sidérurgie et gardiens de la profession?' in Hervé Joly, ed. *Les comités d'organisation.* Caen: Centre de recherche d'histoire quantitative, 2004, 95–108.

Mioche, Philippe. 'Jean Monnet, businessman avant l'Europe', *Journal of European Integration History* 36:2, 2012, 143–158.

Mouré, Kenneth. 'Economic Choice in Dark Times: The Vichy Economy', *French Politics, Culture & Society* 25:1, Spring 2007, 108–130.

Moyn, Samuel. *The Last Utopia: Human Rights in History*. Cambirdge, MA: Harvard University Press, 2012.

Naasner, Walter. *Neue Machtzentren in der deutschen Kriegswirtschaft*. Boppard am Rhein: H. Boldt, 1994.

Noiriel, Gérard. *Les origines républicaines de Vichy*. Paris: Hachette, 1999.

Nord, Philip. *France's New Deal*. Princeton, NJ: Princeton University Press, 2010.

Novick, Peter. *The Resistance Versus Vichy: The Purge of Collaborators in Liberated France*. London: Chatto & Windus, 1968.

Osokina, Elena. *Our Daily Bread: Socialist Distribution and the Art of Survival in Stalin's Russia, 1927–1941*. London: M.E. Sharpe, 2001.

Overy, Richard. *The Morbid Age: Britain between the Wars*. London: Penguin, 2009.

Ory, Pascal. *Les collaborateurs*. Paris: Seuil, 1976.

Passmore, Kevin. *The Right in France from the Third Republic to Vichy*. Oxford: Oxford University Press, 2013.

Pasture, Patrick. *Imagining European Unity since 1000 AD*. Basingstoke: Palgrave Macmillan, 2015.

Patel, Kiran Klaus. 'Provincialising European Union: Co-operation and Integration in Europe in a Historical Perspective', *Contemporary European History* 22:4, 2013, 649–673.

Patel, Kiran Klaus. *The New Deal: A Global History*. Princeton: Princeton University Press, 2016.

Paxton, Robert O. *Vichy France: Old Guard and New Order*. New York: Alfred A. Knopf, 1972.

Paxton, Robert O. and Michael Marrus. *Vichy France and the Jews*. New York: Basic Books, 1981.

Pavone, Claudio. *Alle origini della repubblica: scritti su fascismo, antifascismo e continuità dello Stato*. Turin: Bollati Boringhieri, 1995.

Péan, Pierre. *Une jeunesse française: François Mitterrand, 1934–1947*. Paris: Fayard, 1994.

Perrin, Régine. *Le marché du charbon, un enjeu entre l'Europe et les Etats-Unis de 1945 à 1958*. Paris: Publications de la Sorbonne, 1996.

Peschanski, Denis and Jean-Louis Robert, eds. *Les Ouvriers en France pendant la Seconde Guerre mondiale*. Paris: CNRS, 1992.

Poidevin, Raymond. 'Frankreich und die Ruhrfrage 1945–1951', *Historische Zeitschrift* 228:2, April 1979, 101–119.

Poidevin, Raymond and Jacques Bariéty. *Les relations franco-allemandes, 1815–1975*. Paris: A. Colin, 1977.

Prévotaux, Julien. *Une européisme nazi. Le Groupe Collaboration et l'idéologie européenne dans la Seconde Guerre mondiale.* Paris: François-Xavier de Guibert, 2010.

Radtke-Delacor, Arne. 'Produire pour le Reich. Les commandes allemandes à l'industrie française (1940–1944)', *Vingtième siècle. Revue d'histoire* 70, avril–juin 2001, 99–115.

Radtke-Delacor, Arne. 'La position des comités d'organisation face aux autorités allemands: la pomme de discorde des commandes allemandes en 1940–1941' in Hervé Joly, ed. *Les comités d'organisation*, Caen: Centre de recherche d'histoire quantitative, 2004, 63–71.

Rasmussen, Morten. 'European Rescue of the Nation State? Tracing the Role of Economics and Business' in Wolfram Kaiser and Antonio Varsori, eds, *European Union History: Themes and Debates.* Basingstoke: Palgrave Macmillan, 2010.

Reiter, Julius. *Entstehung und staatsrechtliche Theorie der italiensichen Carta del Lavoro.* Frankfurt: Peter Lang, 2005.

Reynolds, David. '1940: Fulcrum of the Twentieth Century?', *International Affairs*, 66:2, 1990, 325–250.

Rioux, Jean-Pierre. *La France de Quatrième République, L'ardeur et la nécessité 1944–1952.* Paris: Seuil, 1980.

Ritschel, Daniel. *The Politics of Planning: The Debate on Economic Planning in Britain in the 1930s.* Oxford: Clarendon Press, 1997.

Berthold Rittberger. 'Which Institutions for Post-war Europe? Explaining the Institutional Design of Europe's First Community', *Journal of European Public Policy* 8:5, 2001, 673–708.

Rizzi, Bruno. *La Bureaucratisation du monde.* Paris: Presses modernes, 1939.

Rochebrune, Renaud de and Jean-Claude Hazera. *Les patrons sous l'Occupation.* Paris: Odile Jacob, 1995.

Rouquet, François. *L'épuration dans l'administration française. Agents de l'Etat et collaboration ordinaire.* Paris: CNRS, 1993.

Roussel, Eric. *Jean Monnet.* Paris: Fayard, 1996.

Rousso, Henry. *Le syndrôme de Vichy.* Paris: Seuil, 1987.

Rousso, Henry. *Vichy. L'événement, la mémoire, l'histoire.* Paris: Gallimard, 2001.

Rousso, Henry, ed. *De Monnet à Massé. Enjeux politiques et objectifs économiques dans le cadre des quatre premiers Plan (1946–1965).* Paris: CNRS, 1986.

Rousso, Henry. 'L'organisation industrielle de Vichy', reprinted in Henry Rousso, *Vichy. L'Événement, la mémoire, l'histoire.* Paris: Gallimard, 1992, 79–109.

Rousso, Henry. 'L'épuration en France: une histoire inachevée', reprinted in Henry Rousso, *Vichy. L'Événement, la mémoire, l'histoire.* Paris: Gallimard, 1992, 489–552.

Rousso, Henry. 'Les élites économiques dans les années 1940: épuration et transition', reprinted in Henry Rousso, *Vichy. L'Événement, la mémoire, l'histoire.* Paris: Gallimard, 1992, 553–593.

Rousso, Henry and Michael Margairaz. 'Vichy, la guerre et les entreprises', reprinted in Henry Rousso, *Vichy. L'événement, la mémoire, l'histoire*. Paris: Gallimard, 1992, 174–231.

Sabin, Guy. *Jean Bichelonne. Ministre sous l'Occupation 1942–1944*. Paris: France-Empire, 1991.

Sanders, Paul. *Histoire du marché noir, 1940–1946*. Paris: Perrin, 2001.

Sauvy, Alfred. *La vie économique des Français de 1939 à 1945*. Paris: Flammarion, 1978.

Schwabe, Klaus, ed. *Die Anfänge des Schuman-Plans 1950–51*. Brussels: Bruylant, 1988.

Schwarz, Hans-Peter. 'The Division of Germany, 1945–1949' in Melvyn P. Leffler and Odd Arne Westad, eds. *The Cambridge History of the Cold War*. Cambridge: Cambridge University Press, 2010.

Shennan, Andrew. *Rethinking France. Plans for Renewal 1940–1946*. Oxford: Clarendon Press, 1989.

Shennan, Andrew. *De Gaulle*. London: Longman, 1993.

Soutou, Georges-Henri. 'Georges Bidault et la construction européenne 1944–1954', *Revue d'histoire diplomatique*, 3:4, 1991, 267–306.

Spierenburg, Dirk and Raymond Poidevin. *The History of the High Authority of the European Coal and Steel Community: Supranationality in Motion*. London: Weidenfeld and Nicolson, 1994.

Stoler, Mark A. *Allies in War: Britain and America against the Axis Powers, 1940–1945*. London: Hodder, 2005.

Stone, Dan, ed. *The Oxford Handbook of Postwar European History*. Oxford: Oxford University Press, 2012.

Sutton, Michael. *France and the Construction of Europe, 1944–2007. The Geopolitical Imperative*. New York: Berghahn Books, 2007.

Sweets, John F. *Choices in Vichy France: The French under Nazi Occupation*. New York: Oxford University Press, 1986.

Telò, Mario. *Dallo Stato all'Europa. Idee politiche e istituzioni*. Rome: Carocci, 2004.

Temin, Peter. 'Soviet and Nazi Economic Planning in the 1930s', *Economic History Review*, 44:4, 1991, 573–593.

Tewes, Ludger. *Frankreich in der Besatzungszeit 1940–1943. Die Sicht deutscher Augenzeugen*. Bonn: Bouvier Verlag, 1998.

Tooze, Adam. *Wages of Destruction: The Making and Breaking of the Nazi Economy*. London: Penguin, 2007.

Turpin, Frédéric. *André Diethelm, 1896–1954. De Georges Mandel à Charles de Gaulle*. Paris: Les Indes savants, 2004.

Umbreit, Hans. *Der Militärbefehlshaber in Frankreich 1940–1944*. Boppard am Rhein: Harald Boldt Verlag, 1968.

Verheyde, Philippe. *Les mauvais comptes de Vichy. L'aryanisation des entreprises juives*. Paris: Perrin, 1999.

Vial, Philippe. 'Le militaire et la politique: le maréchal Juin et le général Ely face à la CED' in Michel Dumoulin, ed. *La Communauté européenne de défense, leçons pour demain?* Brussels: Peter Lang, 2000.

Vigna, Xavier. *Histoire des ouvriers en France au XXe siècle*. Paris: Perrin, 2012.

Vinen, Richard. 'The French Coal Industry During the Occupation', *The Historical Journal* 33:1, 1990, 105–130.

Vinen, Richard. *The Politics of French Business 1936–1945*. Cambridge: Cambridge University Press, 1991.

Vinen, Richard. *Bourgeois Politics in France 1945–1951*. Cambridge: Cambridge University Press, 1995.

Vinen, Richard. *The Unfree French. Life Under Occupation*. London: Penguin, 2007.

Virgili, Fabrice. *La France 'virile'. Des femmes tondues à la Libération*. Paris: Payot, 2000.

Waddington, Lorna. *Hitler's Crusade. Bolshevism and the Myth of the International Jewish Conspiracy*. London: Tauris, 2007.

Wall, Irwin M. *The United States and the Making of Postwar France*. Cambridge: Cambridge University Press, 1991.

Wells, Sherrill Brown. *Jean Monnet: Unconventional Statesman*. London: Lynne Rienner, 2011.

Wiesen, S. Jonathan. *West German Industry and the Challenge of the Nazi Past, 1945–1955*. Chapel Hill: University of North Carolina Press, 2001.

Wieviorka, Olivier. *Une certaine idée de la Résistance. Défense de la France 1940–1949*. Paris: Seuil, 1995.

Woloch, Isser. 'Left, Right and Centre: The MRP and the Post-War Moment' in *French History*, 21:1, 2007, 85–106.

Woloch, Isser. *The Postwar Moment: The Allied Democracies in the Aftermath of World War II*. Forthcoming.

Wylie, Neville, ed. *The Politics and Strategy of Clandestine War: SOE, 1940–1946*. London: Routledge, 2007.

Yagil, Limore. *«L'Homme nouveau» et la Révolution nationale de Vichy (1940–1944)*. Paris: Presses universitaires de Septentrion, 1997.

Young, John W. *France, the Cold War, and the Western Alliance 1944–1949: French Foreign Policy and post-war Europe*. Leicester: Leicester University Press, 1990.

Unpublished Theses

Berger, Françoise. *La France, l'Allemagne et l'acier* (1932–1952). *De la stratégie des cartels à l'élaboration de la CECA*. PhD thesis. Paris: Université de Paris I, 2000.

Lemmes, Fabian. *Arbeiten für das Reich: die Organisation Todt in Frankreich und Italien, 1940–1945*. PhD thesis. Florence: European University Institute, 2009.

Mioche, Philippe. *La sidérurgie et l'Etat en France des années quarante aux années soixante*. Doctorat d'Etat. Paris: Université de Paris IV, 1992.

Ranieri, Ruggero. *L'espansione alla prova del negoziato, L'industria italiana e la CECA 1945–1955*. PhD thesis. Florence: European University Institute, 1988.

Rhodes, M.J. *Steel and the State in France, 1945–1981*. PhD thesis. Oxford: Oxford University, 1985.

Rousso, Henry. *Les Comités d'organisation, aspects structurels et économiques (1940–1944)*. Master's thesis. Paris: Unversité de Paris I, 1976.

Spina, Raphaël. *La France et les Français devant le service du travail obligatoire (1942–1945)*. PhD thesis. Cachan, Val-de-Marne: Ecole normale supérieure, 2012.

Index

A
Algeria, 58, 80, 92, 99n83, 118, 119n11, 121n21, 124–125, 131, 132, 136n67, 140, 141n85
Anti-Semitism, 83n19, 124, 125, 152, 57n39, 159, 175
Archives, 13–14, 16, 35n62, 54, 70n53, 79, 128, 179, 194n66
Armaments production, 22, 38, 92, 103, 111, 265
Armistice, 19–24, 26, 37, 42, 43, 53, 80, 86, 117, 127, 168
Aron, Alexis
  and CSSF, 156, 159n47, 160, 187, 188, 198, 211, 213, 214–221, 224, 225, 228, 229, 232–246, 248, 250, 255–257, 259, 266
  and OPSID, 149, 152, 153, 159–160, 182, 187, 197–197, 219n20
Aryanisation, 9
Attlee, Clement, 227
Aubrun, Jules
  and CORSID, 54, 56, 57, 62, 64–68, 71–76, 79, 80, 82, 83, 88–90, 93–100, 102, 106, 107–113, 130, 151–156, 158, 159–160, 167, 169, 171, 175, 181–182, 187, 188, 197, 198, 206, 207
  and CSSF, 156, 159n47, 160, 180, 182, 187–188, 198, 206, 215, 216, 219n20, 220, 224, 225–230, 257, 259, 266
  opposition to Schuman Plan, 240, 240, 241, 245
Automotive industry, 71

B
Baboin, Robert, 98, 99, 248, 264
Barnaud, Jacques, 31, 39, 40, 41–45, 47, 51, 54, 69–70, 76, 80, 215n6, 254
Baudouin, Paul, 24n18, 24n20, 64n36, 84
Belgium
  ECSC negotiations, 256, 259
  industry during war, 24–25
  reaction to Schuman Plan, 72
Belin, René, 13, 19, 28, 30, 31, 33–34, 35–43, 45, 50, 54, 57–63, 65, 66, 6, 83n19, 86, 88n42, 120n18, 128n42, 134, 163, 170, 216

© The Author(s) 2017

L.-A. Brunet, *Forging Europe: Industrial Organisation in France, 1940–1952*, Security, Conflict and Cooperation in the Contemporary World, DOI 10.1057/978-1-349-95198-7

Beveridge, William, 173
Bevin, Ernest, 226, 227
Bichelonne, Jean, 13, 30, 31, 42, 76, 80, 91, 100–106, 109–112, 121, 137n70, 154, 155n34, 248
Bidault, Georges, 196, 228, 234n82
Billoux, François, 2, 137n71, 141, 180, 195, 196, 251n136
Blum, Léon
  and Monnet Plan, 3, 4, 11–13, 17, 122n23, 166n72, 174, 177, 189–192, 194, 195, 199, 205, 207, 209, 210
  and Popular Front, 31, 59, 61, 177, 183n26, 186
Blum-Picard, Lambert
  and creation of Organisation Committees, 45, 53
  and Monnet Plan, 194, 195
  and post-war influence of Nazi New Order, 257, 261
  and reform of Organisation Committees, 16
Bolshevism, *see* Communism
Bossuat, Gérard, 6n12, 7n16, 226n45, 240n100
Bouthillier, Yves, 42, 64, 84, 128n42
Bureau, Albert, 197, 206, 216
Bureau de normalisation de la sidérurgie (BNS), 108–110, 153

C

Cartels, 239
Chambre syndicale de la sidérurgie française (CSSF)
  creation of, 155
  and the Monnet Plan, 239
  and the Schuman Plan, 240, 245
Charte du travail, *see* Labour Charter
Churchill, Winston, 138, 225n40
Class struggle, 58, 79, 84
CNR Programme, 116, 129, 137n71, 139, 141–142, 146, 179
Coal
  imports from Germany, 200
  imports from Great Britain, 22
  imports from United States, 218n16
  Modernisation Commission for Coal, 200
  Organisation Committee for Coal, 57, 60, 67, 100, 157, 182n23
  from the Ruhr, 165n70
  shortages, 200
Cohen, Antonin, 8, 260, 263
COH, *see* Organisation Committee for Coal
Cold War, 5, 5n11, 84n22, 162n54, 190n50, 225n39, 225n40, 251n134
Collaboration
  definitions of, 119
  economic collaboration, 16, 44, 50, 52, 64, 103n98, 116, 119, 157n41, 158
Comité d'action socialiste (CAS), 118, 119, 196n74
Comité des forges, 3, 16, 26n29, 55, 55n8, 56, 57, 61, 61n30, 65, 67, 68, 71–75, 74n68, 155–156, 198, 214, 215, 215n6, 216, 216n7, 217, 228, 229n56, 254, 255
Comité français de Libération nationale (CFLN)
  creation of, 131n48
  and debates of industrial policy, 144
Commissariat général du Plan, *see* Monnet Plan
Commissions de modernisation, *see* Modernisation Committees
Communism, 82, 84, 225

Communist Party (PCF), 139n77, 141, 142, 144, 159, 162, 177, 178, 181, 182, 183, 184, 188, 194n69, 197n81, 202, 251n136
Comptoir des produits sidérurgiques (CPS), 72, 75, 108–110, 187, 213, 216, 240
Concentration (in steel industry)
  and Albert Speer, 80
  and ECSC, 2, 4, 7, 8, 11, 15
  and Monnet Plan, 3–4, 11, 13, 190
Confédération générale du patronat français (CGPF), 26n29, 55, 145n97, 155, 156n35
Confédération générale du travail (CGP), 13, 122n23, 174n101, 189, 191–197, 199, 202–203, 205–207, 211, 213, 214, 217–224, 228, 230, 233, 235, 236–240, 242, 243, 250, 257, 258, 259, 260
Conseil national de la Résistance (CNR), *see* CNR Programme
Conseil national du patronat français (CNPF), 156, 180, 183, 187–188, 241n105
Conseil national (Vichy), 66, 76, 88, 88n42, 116, 117, 156n35, 263
Coquegnot, Henri, 62, 98
CORSID, *see* Organisation Committee for Steel
Courtin Report, 121, 122, 122n23
Couve de Murville, Maurice, 123, 124, 126, 128, 129, 130

D

Daum, Léon
  and Conseil national, 66, 76, 88, 247
  and CORSID, 56, 68, 71, 76, 83n16, 88, 88n39, 89, 90, 95, 96, 98, 99, 112, 159
  and ECSC, 246–251
  and labour deportations, 97, 97n70, 112
  and National Revolution, 76n72, 82n13, 87n35, 89, 112
  offer to join Vichy government, 2, 58, 80, 113
De Gaulle, Charles
  and CFLN, 89n45, 116, 117, 122, 124, 129, 133, 137, 138
  and economic policy, 46
  and foreign policy, 178
  and Free France, 20n4
  and GPRF, 89, 142, 145, 174, 175, 181
  Monnet Plan, 11, 13, 177, 189, 190, 191, 194, 195, 199
  opposition to EDC, 250–251
  resignation, 144, 151, 171, 194, 197
Délégation générale à l'Equipement national (DGEN), *see* Economic planning
Diethelm, André, 135–145, 194, 194n69
Dupuis, Jean, 57, 65, 216, 246
Dupuy, Eugène, 108, 153

E

Ecole des Mines, 69n45, 70, 71, 87n32, 108, 254
Ecole Polytechnique, 69–70, 76, 254
Economic planning
  interwar ideas on, 22, 30, 31, 54, 69, 70
  post-war conceptions of, 11, 17, 30, 46, 47, 51, 64, 77, 90
  under Vichy, 15, 17, 30, 63, 75

Employers
  and Modernisation Commissions, 16–17
  and Organisation Committees, 14, 16, 17, 19, 26, 27, 28–37, 41, 43, 49, 51, 53
Epuration
  evolution of, 15, 17
  and Organisation Committees, 16, 152, 159
  and steel industry, 15, 89, 152
Euratom, 193n62, 252, 252n139
European Coal and Steel Community (ECSC)
  creation, 4, 8, 214, 227n48, 229n56, 230, 244, 253, 256, 263
  negotiations, 227n48, 231, 232, 259, 264
European Defence Community (EDC), 250, 250n134, 251n134
European integration, 2, 4–9, 11, 17, 46n92, 226n45, 256, 265
European Union (EU), 1, 2, 13, 17, 264

F

Families (of related Organisation Committees), 86, 87, 99
Fanton d'Anton, André, 62
Fourth Republic, 3, 7, 126n36, 138n72, 192n60, 212, 216, 221
Freinage, *see* Underproduction
Führerprinzip, 64
Funk, Walther, 46, 102, 263

G

Gazier, Albert, 141, 141n85, 221
German Military Administration in France, 14, 170
Germany
  and coal, 5, 21–23, 53–54
  economic policies, 10
  France's policy towards, 46, 49
  French workers going to, 16, 80, 90, 91, 101, 113, 248
  and Organisation Committees, 163, 164, 166, 171, 175, 206
  and the Schuman Plan, 5, 9, 213, 225, 229, 236, 237
Giacobbi, Paul, 137, 140, 141, 142, 145
Giraud, Henri, 124, 131–135, 161
Gouin, Félix, 196, 209, 210n135
Gouvernement provisoire de la République française (GPRF)
  and épuration, 89n45, 145n97, 151–152
  and industrial policy, 136
  and Liberation, 146, 148
Great Britain
  coal exports, 166n71
  diplomatic relations, 6, 138, 227n48, 246, 262
  influence on Modernisation Commissions, 17, 222, 223
  response to Schuman Declaration, 226
Grenier, Fernand, 137n71, 141
Guizot Report, *see* Laffon Report

H

Harmonisation of French steel products, 110
High Authority of the ECSC, 251
Hirsch, Etienne, 193, 193n62, 193n64, 204, 205, 205n118, 206, 207, 209, 233, 237, 237n93, 238, 242n108, 243, 251
Hirsch-Gardent Committee, 243
Hitchcock, William, 143

Hitler, Adolf, 1, 1n3, 2, 6, 17, 64, 84n25, 103, 106n113, 264

I
Imlay, Talbot, 28n37, 93n54, 105n109
Industrialists
change in leadership, 153
and épuration, 152, 154, 156–161, 187
representation on Modernisation Commissions, 198, 204, 231–232, 262
representation on Organisation Committees, 3, 12, 28, 38, 40, 47, 49, 51, 54, 61–64, 71, 121, 130, 145, 157, 187, 265
and Schuman Plan, 245, 245n119, 249, 251, 266
Italy
and ECSC, 264
and occupation of France, 20–21
in Second World War, 117–118
and steel indsutry, 236

J
Joly, Hervé, 10, 35n61, 158–159
Joxe, Louis, 136, 136n67, 137, 138, 141n87, 150

K
Kehrl, Hans, 105, 105n110, 106, 112, 219
Kuisel, Richard, 11n29, 12, 59n20, 165, 173, 174n100, 189, 205, 205n118, 206

L
Labour Charter, 33, 62, 79, 80–84, 88–90, 112, 134, 135, 170
Labour deportations
and opposition of Organisation Committees, 102
and Vichy policy, 99–100, 112
Lacoste, Robert, 177–179, 184, 186, 189, 208, 209, 222, 223, 224, 249, 257
and Monnet Plan, 177, 189, 209, 223, 257
and opposition to Vichy, 188
and reform of Committees, 178
and support for maintaining Organisation Committees, 143–144
Lacroix-Riz, Annie, 56, 73n66, 74
Laffon Report, 119, 120, 122, 123, 134
Lafond, Henri, 80n3, 87, 87n32, 167
Laroque, Pierre, 30, 31, 83, 83n19, 164n62
Latourte, Jean, 153, 153n27, 197, 206, 216
Laval, Pierre, 66, 80n4, 83n19, 90–93, 98n80, 106, 106n113, 124, 248n128, 263
Lehideux, François, 36, 57n12, 67–68, 71, 81–82, 91, 128n42, 129n43, 155n34, 175, 189
Lepercq, Aimé, 57, 67n45, 68, 70, 76, 100, 100n45, 112, 130, 131n47, 157, 182n23
Leprince, 135, 146, 169, 169n83, 170, 254n4
Liaison Office, 39, 40n79, 41–45, 47, 49, 51, 53, 62
Liberation, 3, 5, 11, 19, 28, 36, 109, 116, 119, 121, 122, 126, 127, 138, 146, 157–158, 166, 168, 172, 174, 175, 194, 198, 201, 222

Liberté syndicale, *see* Union rights
Louvel, Jean-Marie, 237n93, 243
Luxembourg, and ECSC, 62, 236

M
Managerial logic, 77n73, 113, 265
Manifeste des douze, 57, 121n21, 141n85
Marine et Homécourt, 247n126
Marjolin, Robert, 193, 193n61, 209, 230
Marshall Plan, 166, 166n72, 199n90, 224, 224n37
Marty, André, 142, 181, 181n14
Mendès France, Pierre, 137n41, 142, 143, 144
Michel, Elmar, 35, 38, 40, 44, 47, 50, 85, 118n9, 122, 149n9, 163, 190
Militärbefehlshaber in Frankreich, *see* German Military Administration in France
Milward, Alan, 101n86, 103, 103n103, 166n72, 225n41, 242n108, 256
Minimum wage, 85, 85n28, 244n114
Mioche, Philippe, 12, 56, 73n65, 74, 74n68, 160n49, 190
Monnet, Jean
  and abolition of Organisation Committees, 121, 177, 185, 203n111, 213, 222, 249
  and anti-parliamentarism, 263
  and CFLN, 11, 126n36, 131n48, 132, 156, 174, 194, 208, 234n82, 254, 261, 263
  and CGP, 13, 122n23, 174n101, 189, 191, 192, 192n60, 193, 193n61, 194, 194, 194n69, 195, 196, 197, 199, 202, 203, 203n111, 205, 206, 207, 211, 213, 214, 217, 218, 220, 221, 222, 224, 224n35, 228, 230, 233, 235, 236, 237, 238, 238n93, 239, 240, 242, 242n109, 243, 246, 249, 257, 258, 260, 262
  and EDC, 251
  and EURATOM, 193n62, 252, 252n138, 252n139
  and French steel industry, 5, 198–199, 221, 223, 229, 235, 238, 240, 241, 243, 242n109, 243, 244, 245, 248, 250, 256
  and his method, 203, 204n116, 224n35
  and public opinion, 146, 208, 210n136
  and support for Organisation Committees, 144, 209
  See also Monnet Plan
Monnet Plan
  difficulties of, 221
  establishment of, 177, 256
  and Modernisation Commissions, 17, 174n101, 177, 194, 195, 196, 199, 204, 207, 209, 210, 211, 212, 222, 223, 230, 260, 261, 263
  and Organisation Committees, 4, 12, 13, 17, 175, 189, 190, 191, 192, 194, 204, 207, 209, 210, 211, 213, 222, 228, 230, 246, 247, 248, 249, 254, 258, 260, 261
  and Schuman Plan, 5, 17, 213, 225, 229, 245, 260, 262, 266
  support for, 195, 209
Morgenthau Plan, 225
Mouvement républicain populaire (MRP), 162, 178, 183, 184, 196, 202, 251n136

N

Nationalisations, 118, 119, 139n77, 144, 144n95, 179, 179n8, 180, 180n9, 181, 181n16, 182, 183, 184, 186
National Revolution
  and creation of Organisation Committees, 16, 30, 53, 63, 68, 85, 90, 130, 155
  failure of, 32, 55
  and industrial policy, 33
Netherlands
  and the ECSC, 231
New Deal, 29, 29n38
New Economic Order in Europe, 46, 102, 110, 116, 259–260
Noël, Léon, 38–40
Non-conformists, 8n20, 29–31, 43, 70
Nord, Philip, 12n33, 21, 30, 66, 72, 110, 179, 182, 205, 207
North Africa
  Organisation Committees in, 123, 202n107, 211
  workers from, 99
Nouveaux cahiers, 70, 169, 169n81

O

Office central de répartition des produits industriels (OCRPI)
  creation of, 83
  dissolution of, 136–137
  under Fourth Republic, 126n36, 141n85
  German influence on, 50
  reform of, 163, 166
Office professionnel, *see* Professional Office
Organisation civile et militaire (OCM), 100, 130
Organisation Committee for Coal (COH)
  creation of, 15, 16, 28, 30, 33–34
  members of, 65, 66, 68, 69, 77, 111, 113, 216
Organisation Committees
  abolition of, 177, 185, 186, 203n111, 213, 222, 249
  and contributions to German war economy, 5, 16, 91, 101, 106, 109, 265
  creation of, 15
  German influence on, 50
  and Modernisation Commissions, 177, 191n54, 192–196, 198–212
  opposition to, 188
  and opposition to labour deportations, 97, 99, 102, 112
  reforms of, 16, 168, 206
  Resistance views of, 207, 247, 248
  staffing of, 60, 71
  and tripartism, 16, 54, 57, 60, 61, 62, 246, 249, 262
Organisation Committee for Steel (CORSID)
  abolition of, 74
  contributions to German war economy, 91
  creation of, 228
  and labour deportations, 97
  members of, 73, 75, 83n14, 88, 100, 112, 151, 169, 175
  and National Revolution, 63
  post-war reform of, 148
  successors of, 221, 250
Organisation Todt, 94n59

P

Parti républicain de la liberté (PRL), 184

Pétain, Philippe
  influence on creation of Organisation Committees, 34
  and reform of Organisation Committees, 33
Peyerimhoff, Henri de, 55n8, 68, 70, 70n55, 158n46, 182n23, 198, 255, 255n5
Philip, André, 174, 188, 189n46, 196, 197, 203n111, 204n116, 205n118, 212, 223n31
Pinay, Antoine, 68, 68n49, 247, 247n125, 248
Pleven, René, 2, 210n136, 234, 234n82, 241, 250n134
Popular Front, 31, 59, 61, 177, 183n26, 186
Prisoners of war (POWs), 93, 97
Professional Office
  abolition of, 177
  and creation of Organisation Committees, 45, 53
  and Modernisation Commissions, 177–210, 208, 222
  as new name for Organisation Committees, 148–149, 150
  reforms of, 150
Professional Office for Steel (OPSID)
  abolition of, 147
  and CMSID, 208
  leadership of, 71, 197–198, 216
  naming of, 148–149
  reform of, 148–151, 160–163, 164, 165, 177–210
Pucheu, Pierre
  attempt to join Resistance, 80n4
  trial of, 125, 125n31, 154–155
  views of industrial organisation, 137

R

Radtke-Delacor, Arne, 14n39, 35n61, 48n101, 91n49, 103–104
Rassemblement du peuple français (RPF), 184n31, 251n136
Raty, Jean, 159
Renault, 25, 67, 71, 81n5, 144n95, 179n8
Resistance
  among employers, 155n33, 107
  interior Resistance, 117, 119, 162, 78n4
  and Organisation Committees, 15, 16, 39, 43, 76, 93, 100, 116–123, 125, 127, 128, 129, 130, 131, 133, 135, 138, 139, 140, 142, 158, 162, 166, 184, 190, 207, 248, 263, 265
  overseas Resistance, 11n31
Reuter, Paul, 260
Révolution nationale, *see* National Revolution
Ricard, Pierre, 68, 68n49, 70, 159n47, 245, 245n118, 246, 248, 250, 264, 264n29
Roosevelt, Franklin Delano, 29, 124n30, 125n33, 131n48, 138, 172, 225n40
Rousso, Henry, 9, 9n23, 13n35, 34n57, 79n1, 87n35, 116n4, 125n32, 158, 205, 206, 215n3, 224n35
Roy, Eugène, 57, 65, 72, 97, 156, 197, 198, 206, 216, 246, 254
Ruhr, 5, 65, 165n70, 200, 217, 218n16, 224, 225n40, 245n119

S

Sauckel, Fritz, 91, 91n50, 99, 102, 103, 257

Schneider, 61n30, 62, 65, 67, 67n44, 73, 96n68, 103n100, 106n112, 181, 181n14
Schuman Declaration, *see* Schuman Plan
Schumann, Maurice, 243, 243n113
Schuman Plan
  and French steel industry, 5, 229, 236, 237, 238, 240, 241, 245, 256, 266
  international response to, 226, 226n44
  motivations for, 226n44, 259, 262–263, 266
  negotiations, 231n67, 233, 234, 239, 245n119, 256, 259
  ratification, 142
Schuman, Robert
  and ECSC, 4, 8, 9, 17, 227n48, 231, 237, 245
  and Vichy, 4, 5, 8, 9, 14, 17, 139, 213, 249, 257, 258, 261, 262, 263, 264, 265, 266
Service du travail obligatoire (STO)
  development of policy, 97n70, 98, 100, 103, 106, 112
  response of Organisation Committees, 13, 91, 111
  See also Labour deportations
Shortages
  during war, 101, 105, 106, 200, 210, 225, 240
  following Liberation, 148–149, 163
SIDENOR, 72, 110
Small and Medium-sized Enterprises (SMEs), 59, 60, 66, 89, 116, 136, 160, 160n49, 187
Socialist Party (SFIO), 162n54, 178
Soviet Union, 48, 90, 225, 250n134
Speer, Albert, 80, 101, 102, 103, 113n136, 219, 264n31
Speer-Bichelonne agreement, 109, 110, 112

T

Technocracy, 69n52, 108n122
Thorez, Maurice, 148n4, 188
Tooze, Adam, 10n38, 48n101, 92, 101n89, 103
Trade unions
  involvement in post-war Organisation Committees, 120
  and Modernisation Commissions, 177, 261
  opposition to Vichy, 122, 188
  under Vichy, 66, 161, 163, 170, 175, 188, 205, 262
  See also Tripartism; Union rights
Treaty of Paris, 236n91, 244, 245, 246, 259
Tripartism
  and ECSC, 246, 261
  and Monnet Plan, 246, 262–263
  and Organisation Committees, 16, 54, 57, 59, 61, 246, 261
  and post-war reforms, 222n28
Trusts, 33, 34n56, 54, 59, 60, 61, 81, 84, 89, 118, 119, 120, 172, 180n8, 181, 188

U

Underproduction, 92n54, 216n9, 240n102
Union rights
  re-establishment in metropolitan France, 115, 117
  re-establishment in North Africa, 132
  removal of, 145n97
United Kingdom, *see* Great Britain

United States
imports from, 218n16
and Schuman Plan, 224–226
and Second World War, 7
Uri, Pierre, 13, 260n18

V
Vichy
continuities from, 9, 12, 13, 31, 191, 259, 261, 263
economic policy, 33
foreign policy, 2n5, 5, 119
Vinen, Richard, 73n65, 87n35, 93, 97, 97n70, 100n85, 156n37, 179n8

W
Wendel, François de, 55n30, 66, 67, 61, 74, 75, 76, 156, 198, 254
Wirtschaftsgruppen, 25–26, 36, 49, 51
as model for CO, 36
Workers
and deportations, 96, 97, 99, 103n103, 106, 110, 112, 266
and strikes, 85, 89
and trade unions, 43, 85, 171, 177, 189
See also Trade unions; Tripartism

CPSIA information can be obtained
at www.ICGtesting.com
Printed in the USA
LVOW13*2112030418
572144LV00016B/221/P

9 781349 951970